MILITANT MINERS

John McArthur, aged 70.

MILITANT MINERS

Recollections of John McArthur, Buckhaven;
and letters, 1924-26, of David Proudfoot, Methil,
to G. Allen Hutt

Edited by
IAN MacDOUGALL
Honorary Secretary, Scottish Labour History Society

POLYGON BOOKS

First published 1981

ISBN 0 904919 50 1

Typeset 11/12 point Times by
Edinburgh University Student Publications Board,
1 Buccleuch Place,
Edinburgh,
EH8 9 LW.

Printed and bound in Great Britain by
The Scolar Press,
59/61 East Parade,
Ilkley,
Yorkshire,
LS29 8JP.

FOREWORD

A RECORD of a lifetime like John McArthur's has a double importance, for
history and for the labour movement of which it was part and parcel, and
by which it ought not to be forgotten. He is one of those many men and women
of our troubled century, scattered about the world, who have spent themselves
in trying to change the world's face; and he has had his share in changing the
face of Britain, even if not all his hopes have been fulfilled. A lifelong
champion of his social and political creed, he stands out also in this chronicle
as a character — a man, and a Scotsman, whom his countrymen should want
to know of. He belonged to a generation of the British labour movement which
produced a striking number of remarkable figures, and in these pages we meet
with many of them, as well as with individuals of various other species.

The book is again twofold in being built on a double foundation. It makes
use of written materials, either in print, like newspaper files, or unpublished,
like the collection of letters which it includes of another left-wing stalwart,
David Proudfoot of Methil; it draws also on oral sources, primarily the
recollections of John McArthur himself.

Oral history, of which we are given here a fine example, has only in recent
years come to have a recognised standing. It can be invaluable in rescuing from
oblivion a great deal that would otherwise vanish without trace. It is not an
easy method, for everything depending on memory, our own or anyone else's,
has to be painstakingly checked. For Ian MacDougall the task, a very long
drawn-out one, has been a labour of love, but of science as well. He is a
historian by training, with an unequalled knowledge of labour history in
Scotland and its records. Nobody could have performed the work more
worthily.

MICHAEL McGAHEY,
President, Scottish Area, National Union of Mineworkers.
VICTOR KIERNAN,
Emeritus Professor of Modern History,
University of Edinburgh.

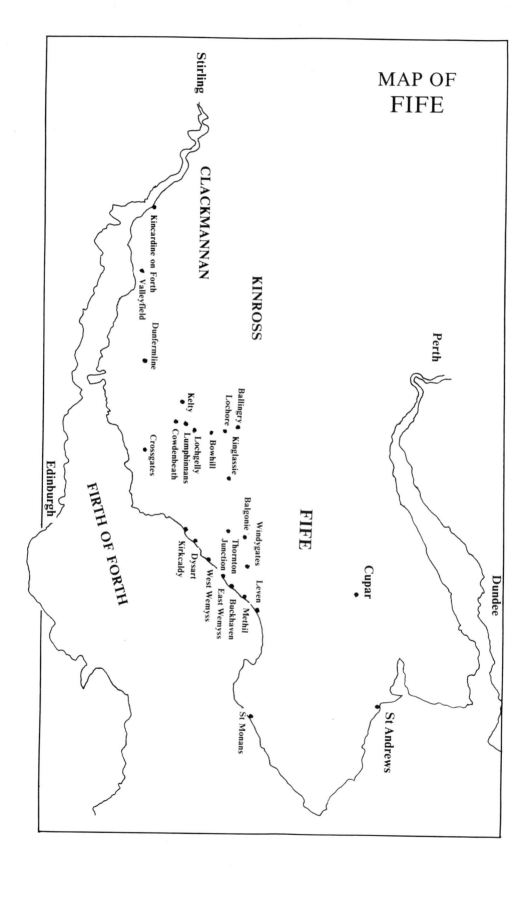

MAP OF
FIFE

TABLE OF CONTENTS

TABLE OF CONTENTS

THE LETTERS OF DAVID PROUDFOOT

INTRODUCTION

FIFE miners, by means of a stay-down strike, were the first in Europe more than a century ago to win the eight-hours day.[1] A similar spirit of dedication and determination, escorted by humour, marches through the industrial and political testimony here of two militant Fife miners of the inter-war years: John McArthur of Buckhaven, now in his eighty-second year, and the late David Proudfoot of Methil, who died in 1958.

Both the tape-recorded recollections of John McArthur, who retired in 1964 as Fife District Secretary of the National Union of Mineworkers, and the letters of David Proudfoot, who for a time in the early 1930s was General Secretary of the United Mineworkers of Scotland, add to existing knowledge of the industrial and political struggles in the Fife coalfield in the 1920s and 1930s. In those struggles, which to a considerable extent were local reflections of national issues or crises, John McArthur and David Proudfoot were leading participants. Both were centrally involved in the splits, in 1922-23 and again in 1928-29, in the Fife miners' union. Both describe from their personal involvement the remarkable organisation of the miners and other workers in East Fife during the 1926 General Strike, where the Workers' Defence Force with its 750 men under the leadership of ex-army warrant officers and n.c.o.s appears to have been the strongest in Britain. Both men were local leaders in the prolonged six months' lock-out of the miners in '26, both suffered from the subsequent victimisation of militants by the coal companies. Both were witnesses to the strong antipathy between Philip Hodge, General Secretary of the Mineworkers' Reform Union of Fife, Kinross and Clackmannan, and William Adamson, General Secretary of the "old" Fife miners' county union, who was also Secretary of State for Scotland in the Labour Governments of 1924 and 1929-31. John McArthur, as a full-time student at the Scottish Labour College, records his impression of its leading tutor, the Clydeside revolutionary John Maclean, in what proved to be one of the last years of Maclean's life; while David Proudfoot provides in his letters to the left-wing London journalist George Allen Hutt a detailed almost day-by-day account of the intensive effort made to build up in Fife the membership and effectiveness of the recently formed Communist Party of Great Britain, of which both he and John McArthur were leading local members.

I first met John McArthur more than ten years ago. One of the few

---

1 R. Page Arnot, *A History of the Scottish Miners* (London, 1955), 51.

surviving militant leaders of the inter-war years in the East Fife coalfield, John seemed unlikely ever to write up his half century of experience in working-class movements — but at our meeting he agreed to tape-record his recollections. Our first recording was made in October 1969, our last in December 1971; and even then it seemed certain that his well of relevant recollection was far from dry. The total typed transcript of the recording ran to 468 foolscap pages.

The method we followed in tape-recording was for John to prepare in advance of each of our four- or five-hour sessions (which were at weekly, fortnightly, monthly or occasionally longer intervals) his recollections of a particular aspect or phase of his experience. As a practised speaker he recorded fluently and uninterruptedly for an hour or so at a time. His recollections were checked so far as was possible against trade union and other records, press reports, and books and pamphlets such as *Barriers of the Bureaucrats: Fife Breaks Through*, which he and David Proudfoot had jointly written in 1929-30. The great bulk of the Proudfoot papers were not deposited in Buckhaven and Methil Public Library until after most of John's recordings were completed, so he did not consult those papers at all while preparing his own material. The reader may therefore compare John's recollection with the contemporary comments on some of the same events and personalities made by David Proudfoot. My opinion, formed during our tape-recording sessions and since then, is that John McArthur has an unusually clear and reliable, though of course not infallible, memory and that what he has to say here is a notable contribution to the oral history of Scottish working people.

An attempt has been made, allowing for necessary editing, to preserve and present John McArthur's recollections exactly as he recorded them on the tapes. Alterations made to the transcript for the purposes of publication were all submitted for his approval, and he also patiently answered the hundreds of supplementary questions with which I plied him by post concerning points of detail.

For reasons of space, John's recollections extend here only as far as the 1939-45 war. The interested reader may consult the full transcript of the recordings in the custody of the Oral History Unit of the Department of History at Edinburgh University.

During one of our early recording sessions John McArthur mentioned that David Proudfoot had for many years between the wars corresponded with the left-wing London journalist, G. Allen Hutt. Hutt, who had retired in 1966 as chief sub-editor of the *Daily Worker*, confirmed that he had indeed an "immense Proudfoot archive", and agreed to deposit it in the Buckhaven and Methil Public Library.[2] The library already held some Proudfoot papers deposited by his widow in 1962. Hutt, a graduate in history from Cambridge University, author of several books on trade unionism and labour history, an outstanding authority on newspaper typography, editor for twenty-five years of *The Journalist* and President in 1967-68 of the National Union of Journalists, described Proudfoot as "a tireless and extremely lucid letter-

2 For a list of the contents of this collection see I. MacDougall, ed., *A Catalogue of some Labour Records in Scotland* (Edinburgh, 1978), 511-13.

writer" whose letters gave "an extraordinarily vivid picture of the struggle in the Fife coalfields of those days, including the General Strike". He agreed that, with his help, I should edit the letters for publication; unfortunately, because of pressure of work, I was unable even to make a start on editing the letters for several years and, in the meantime, in 1973, at the age of seventy-one, Allen Hutt died.

Proudfoot appears indeed from these letters as a "tireless" correspondent. May 1924 is the date of the earliest surviving letter; it was probably also one of the first, if not indeed the first, he wrote to Hutt, to whom he had been introduced that month at Methil by the labour historian and Communist Party leader, Robin Page Arnot. Between that date and February 1942, when the correspondence appears to have ceased, Proudfoot had written some 300 letters to Hutt. All except a score were written between May 1924 and September 1931, when Proudfoot resigned both from his position as full-time General Secretary of the United Mineworkers of Scotland and from membership of the Communist Party. The height of the correspondence was reached between 1925 and 1929, during which years Proudfoot wrote to Hutt on average once a week. Only a few of the letters were typed, the overwhelming majority being written in Proudfoot's neat and legible handwriting. The average length of the letters, 1924-42, is five pages of quarto; but eleven ran to more than seventeen pages each, and the longest of all, in May 1929, to twenty-eight pages. Altogether the letters written between 1924-42 total about 400,000 words. Consequently only a part of the whole collection — the first three years — could be published in the present volume.

Proudfoot's letters to Hutt constitute a unique surviving source within Scotland of detailed comment by a militant worker — an intelligent, articulate and energetic activist — on contemporary industrial and political struggles, above all those of the Fife miners. Unfortunately, of Hutt's replies to Proudfoot only half-a-dozen have survived. Like John McArthur, Proudfoot at his best has a gift with words. His sardonic humour, as in his description of the Rt. Hon. William Adamson falling foul of irate women at a miners' meeting, is accompanied by a pungency and bluntness that he himself ascribes to the typical miner: "no poetical effusions, no frills, but straight from the shoulder in Coal Jock's own".

Proudfoot's dedication and energy in carrying out his trade union and political activities is the more remarkable given his recurrent attacks of "dingy" — apparently a relic of the malaria which John McArthur tells us Proudfoot had contracted during his years as an infantryman in the 1914-18 war. It is hardly surprising that, sometimes encompassing a double shift of sixteen hours in his job as a checkweigher at Wellesley Colliery, Methil, in addition to his manifold political and trade union activities — even his phenomenal energy at times burns low: "At times I feel absolutely fed up and feel like chucking it".

In editing the letters for publication I have amended or inserted paragraphing and punctuation where necessary, corrected Proudfoot's few misspellings, written out in full his abbreviations (except in obvious commonplace cases), put titles of publications he mentions into italics, and placed in square brackets the very occasional unintentional omission of a word or words. Proudfoot's own use of italics, of quotation marks and capitals, as well as his very occasional slips of syntax or grammar, have been preserved. The half-dozen letters written by others than Proudfoot have been foot-noted. Proudfoot's address in Methil has been retained at the top of the first letter only: unless otherwise indicated all the letters were written from that address. Throughout 1924, Proudfoot addressed his letters to Hutt as "Dear Comrade", but from January 1925, after visiting him in London, as "Dear George". To save space, the form of greeting has been omitted after the first letter in 1924. Similarly, Proudfoot's signature and almost invariable expression of "best wishes" to Hutt and, from 29 June 1926, to "Comrade Mrs Hutt, baby, and yourself", have been omitted. The form in which the dates of the letters is given has been standardised. Otherwise, the letters are as Proudfoot wrote them.

In some cases information about Fife activists and others has been so difficult to obtain that it has been necessary to settle for estimates of their ages by John McArthur, and these have been given as, e.g., "about ten years older than J.McA.". To all those — trade unionists, librarians, historians, relatives of deceased activists, and others — who provided information or photographs, or otherwise gave encouragement and help in the making of this book I am very grateful. They include R. Page Arnot, Jack Ashton, Andrew Beattie, Mrs J. Bird, Mrs D. Black, Mrs Kath. L. Black, John Bryson, Mrs Evelyn Cameron, William K. Campbell, George Canning, Nicholas Clarke, John B. Cook, Lawrence Daly, D. K. Davidson, Mrs Jenny Davidson, Don Duff, Councillor D. Duffy, Mrs Jean Dunbar, Alex Eadie, M.P., Mrs Ella Egan, William Finnie, Mrs M. C. Fraser, John Grant, Finlay Hart, Mr Henderson of Wemyss, Mrs Avis Hutt, James Jack, David Johnston, Jack Keddie, Professor V. G. Kiernan, F. Kitchener, Ron Knowles, W. Lamb, my brother George C. MacDougall, Ronald McLaren, A.L.A., J. Miller, James Milne, Mrs Milne of Dunfermline, Mrs Nan Milton, J. C. Murray, Mrs Susan Ord, Miss Barbara Proudfoot, Betty Reid, Miss Elizabeth Ross, Daniel M. Sim, D. Spalding, S. Scott, Murdoch Taylor, Mrs Doris Thomson, P. C. Walters, A. A. Wilson, Andrew Wilson, and Bruce Young, as well as the editors of the Fife local newspapers, and, not least, my wife Sandra and our children. I need hardly add that none of those mentioned is responsible for any shortcomings in the book, responsibility for which is mine alone.

For donations towards meeting the cost of publication I wish warmly to thank Michael McGahey, President, and the Executive Committee of the Scottish Area, National Union of Mineworkers, and also all other unions and trades councils affiliated to the Scottish Trades Union Congress that responded to the appeal issued by its General Council. Fife Regional Co-operative Society Ltd. also made a donation.

Finally, I am very grateful to John and Mrs Helen McArthur for all their friendship, hospitality, and patience.

Edinburgh, May 1980.   IAN MacDOUGALL

SOME PRINCIPAL
EVENTS

1904-05   Revolution in Russia: the "Great Rehearsal".
1911   British Socialist Party formed from Social Democratic Federation
           (S.D.F.) and some branches of Independent Labour Party (I.L.P.).
1912   *The Miners' Next Step* published by the South Wales Miners'
           Reform Committee.
1914   Great War begins.
1915   Shop Stewards' Movement emerges on the Clyde. Glasgow Rent
           Strike.
1916   Easter Rising in Dublin. John Maclean first imprisoned in Scotland.
1917   Mutinies in French army (May/June). Revolution in Russia — Tsar
           overthrown (March); Bolshevik Revolution (November).
1918   John Maclean again imprisoned but released to fight General
           Election in Gorbals. Great War ends.
1918-21   "The Troubles" in Ireland. Civil War and Wars of Intervention in
           Russia.
1919   Forty Hours Strike in Scotland. Sankey Commission on Coal
           Industry. Miners granted a Seven Hours Day. Abortive Communist
           (Spartakist) uprising in Germany. Shortlived Communist
           Government in Hungary (Bela Kun). Formation of Communist
           (Third) International.
1920   "Tramp Trust" formed by John Maclean. Bowhill, Fife, miners'
           strike. National Datum Line strike by miners (October). Beginning
           of inter-war recession.
1920/21   Formation of Communist Party of Great Britain. First full-time
           students attend Scottish Labour College.
1921   National lock-out of miners (March to July). Collapse of Triple
           Industrial Alliance on Black Friday (15 April). Formation of Red
           International of Labour Unions in Moscow. Formation of National
           Unemployed Workers' Movement.
1922   First national Hunger March on London.
1922/23   Formation of Mineworkers' Reform Union of Fife, Kinross and
           Clackmannan as a left-wing breakaway from the miners' county
           union.
1923   Occupation of the Ruhr by France and Belgium. Death of John
           Maclean (November).

1924   First Labour Government (January to October). The J. R. Campbell case. The Zinoviev, or "Red", Letter scare. A. J. Cook becomes General Secretary of the Miners' Federation of Great Britain. The National Minority Movement formed. Dawes Plan to regulate German reparations. Death of Lenin.

1925   Britain returns to the Gold Standard. "Red Friday" (31 July). Samuel Commission on coal industry appointed. Formation of Organisation for the Maintenance of Supplies (O.M.S.). Labour Party annual conference urges unions not to elect Communists as delegates to Labour conferences and debars Communists from individual membership of the Labour Party. Communist Party leaders arrested and imprisoned.

1926   National lock-out of miners (May to November). General Strike (4-12 May). Miners' hours increased to eight per day.

1927   Reunion of Mineworkers' Reform Union with Fife miners' county union.

1928/29   Formation of right-wing breakaway miners' union in Fife by William Adamson and its recognition by National Union of Scottish Mine Workers and Miners' Federation of Great Britain.

1929   Formation (April) of militant United Mineworkers of Scotland as rival to National Union of Scottish Mine Workers and to miners' county unions. Wall Street Crash (October) — world slump begins.

1929/31   Second Labour Government led by Ramsay MacDonald.

1930   Coal Mines Act gives miners a seven-and-a-half hours day.

1931   Formation of "National" Government by Ramsay MacDonald.

1933   Hitler and the Nazis get into power in Germany.

1935   William Gallacher elected Communist M.P. for West Fife.

1936   Spanish Civil War begins (July). United Mineworkers of Scotland dissolved.

1938   The Munich Agreement.

1939   The Nazi-Soviet Non-Aggression Pact (21 August). Second World War begins (1 September).

1944   National Union of Mineworkers formed from Miners' Federation of Great Britain.

1947   Nationalisation of coal industry.

THE RECOLLECTIONS OF
JOHN McARTHUR

1

SHOES ALL THE
YEAR ROUND

I WAS born on February 18, 1899, at Buckhaven in East Fife, where my father was a miner. I have lived all my life at Buckhaven, except for a year during the 1914-18 War when I worked in the Cumberland iron ore mines, and a year during 1920-21 when I was a full-time student under John Maclean, the Clydeside revolutionary, at the Scottish Labour College in Glasgow.[1]

My parents belonged to Kincardine-on-Forth, a village in West Fife. My mother had worked there in the Kilbagie paper mills. My father's family were all miners. My father and his three brothers had worked with my grandfather in the pits in Clackmannanshire, just over the county border from Kincardine-on-Forth. When the pits there fell on hard times around 1890 my father and his brothers came further east in Fife. One brother moved to Fordell, another to Methil, a third to Cowdenbeath where later he became manager of Kirkford Colliery, and my father and mother with my eldest brother Peter came to Buckhaven.

I was the fourth child in a family of five. Peter was ten years older than me, George eight, and Betsy four; Margaret was four years younger than me. Betsy when she grew up became a dressmaker; Margaret, after many years at home helping my mother while the rest of us were out working, became a hospital worker. Like our father and his father before him, my brothers Peter and George and I became miners. Peter and George as a matter of fact died as miners. Peter died in hospital as a result of an accident in Muiredge Colliery in August 1925. George died in 1946, at the age of fifty-five, from dust in the lungs or pneumoconiosis.

My father was a great physical culture enthusiast. He had skipping ropes, Indian clubs, and fencing equipment. He was also quite renowned for fisticuffs, but as he got older and some of the local lads wanted to test their ability with him the family gradually persuaded him to give it up.

My mother was very active in all social questions at Buckhaven. She had trained herself in first-aid and home nursing. So she was an unpaid midwife. If anyone died she was called on to dress the corpse. If any youngster was taken ill — "Run for Mrs McArthur." We complained in the family that we hardly saw her. If the church ran a bazaar she took an active part. She was also active

1

in the co-operative educational and parliamentary committee. She took part in the formation of the first Co-operative Women's Guild in Buckhaven and served for twenty-five years as president.

My grandmother, my mother's mother, also lived with us. She was a widow. She worked as a farm labourer in the fields around Buckhaven until my brothers left school and began to work. Then she gave up field labouring and more or less ran our house so that my mother could attend to her "public" duties. Grandmother died when she was eighty-four. She had never learned to read or write.

We also had a lodger in the house, Bob Cuthbert. Bob had come to live with us at the age of fourteen, shortly before I was born. He had run away from his home in the north-east of England because of unsatisfactory conditions. My parents told me the story. Herring fishing boats from Buckhaven would do six, seven or eight weeks' seasonal fishing at South Shields. Their return at the end of the season was always an attraction and there was a turn-out by most of the local people to welcome the fishermen home. My father was on the pier on one of these occasions when some of the fishermen asked him, "Are you needing a drawer?" A drawer was a miner's assistant who generally started work about age fourteen. The fishermen explained they had a boy aboard who had run away from home and had wanted to come up to Scotland. But they had no work for him. My father agreed to take the boy and let him stay with us and find him work as a drawer. So Bob Cuthbert was regarded as almost one of our family.

I was lucky to have been born the fourth of my parents' five children. The grinding poverty that prevailed at that time did not fall so harshly on me as it had done on my two brothers and elder sister. They were at work while I was still at school, so their wages helped to increase the family's income and made things easier for me than it had been for themselves. The cycle of poverty and "affluence" among miners in those days began when a miner got married and started to rear a family. The family were usually in straitened circumstances until the youngsters left school and began to work. The best period in the miner's life lasted from then until the youngsters got married and started their own families. My boyhood came within that more "affluent" period, when my father, grandmother, my two brothers and older sister, and Bob Cuthbert were all employed and earning money for the joint family income. Other children at my school had to go without shoes in summer because their parents could not afford them; I was lucky enough to have shoes all the year round. But on warm sunny days I used to discard my shoes and run around the beach or harbour, clambering on the rocks or playing football in the sands, as barefoot as my pals were forced to be by their parents' poverty.

At the time I was born Buckhaven was still mainly a fishing village, not deep sea but line fishing, with seasonal fishing for herring at South Shields, Yarmouth, the north of Scotland and occasionally across on the west coast. It was quite a treat to get Loch Fyne herring at that time. But collieries had opened up on the fringe of the village, and because the population was mainly engaged in fishing, imported labour was needed to work the collieries. There was obviously a conflict of ideas, background and outlook between the mining and fishing communities. Miners went in for football, cycling, quoits, and running, tended their gardens and kept dogs. The fishermen did none of these things. Their sports were mainly water sports — boat racing, swimming, and fishing competitions, though they did also have tug o' war. Their only pets were cats. The fishermen were very religious, regular churchgoers, and their choir singing was excellent. They kept Sundays strictly, and their dinner was put on to simmer all Saturday, for no cooking was allowed on the sabbath. After morning church they would take a walk along to the cemetery, and in the evening attend another church service. We youngsters in the mining community passed our Sundays playing football on the beach or bird-nesting. We jeered at our fisher schoolmates as they promenaded to the church or cemetery. As young lads it was as much as our lives were worth to be seen going out with a girl from a fishing family. We could always be sure of a scrap if that happened. The fisher people were very clannish. They were mostly closely related, almost inter-bred. They all wore black or blue jerseys and scarves, and we used to say that was because any of them who died were related to all the rest.

Old Buckhaven was built on the lower ground lying next to the sea. The land to the rear and north of the village was rising ground and was only built on in later years. Very few houses in Buckhaven had a piped water supply. Water was obtained from a well outside in the street and carried in pails into the houses. None of the older houses had toilets. In later years, when there was an agitation for improved facilities, we used to complain that the people in Buckhaven had to regulate their bowels by the ebb and flow of the tide, because the rocks, when the tide was back, were used as a toilet.

The house my family stayed in provided better facilities than most of the others. Most of them were single or two-apartment houses. Many of them, because of the rising ground at the back, had the ground floor built into the embankment, with no rear windows and open only to the sea side. The house we were in was a three-apartment. It was close to the harbour and the garden led on to the beach. One of my earliest recollections is of a piped water supply being brought into our house and a toilet being built outside. This was as big a boon to us then as later on pithead baths were to the miners.

Our house, unlike those in the mining rows, had a big garden. We had berry bushes, grew most of our own vegetables, and kept hens. My brothers and Bob Cuthbert kept racing pigeons, as many miners in Fife did. My early interests centred on these racing pigeons, as well as on football and sport generally.

I was always good at football at school. I attended the school in Buckhaven later known as Braehead School. It was one of the very early schools at which there was a free issue of books and school materials. I remember the controversy that arose whether children would be capable of looking after books they had not paid for directly. It was to the credit of the early Social Democratic Federation socialists who controlled the local Wemyss School Board that these progressive steps were taken at that time.[2]

I took school as something that had to be done. I never did the work enthusiastically. The only important thing seemed to be to get school over and get out to work earning pocket-money. I was an atrocious handwriter and no good at woodwork. But I took arithmetic and maths in my stride. That was a benefit because some of the teachers let us out early if we completed the day's work in maths satisfactorily.

At that time there was a higher grade for those who wanted to stay on at school after the age of fourteen. For those who did not, then the supplementary, as it was termed, was available. I had no desire to stay on at school and opted for the supplementary, much to the disappointment of some of the teachers and to the annoyance of my parents. There was quite a row in the family about that because they were anxious that I should remain on at school. But I thought I knew better than them. I remember my teacher, Mr Kelso, who was a socialist, visiting our house and speaking to my father to try to get me to stay on at school. But I left school and got started to work so that I could get pocket-money on a Saturday like my chums.

2

'LIFT YOUR PUGS'

I STARTED work in August 1913 at Muiredge Colliery, Buckhaven. The colliery belonged to the Wemyss Coal Company. I had been anxious to get work as an electrician at the pit. But I was always getting pushed off. So I started work as a filler and drawer with a miner who was friendly with my parents.

Miners at that time usually worked in pairs, a man and a youth. The man, called the face man or hand-got man, won the coal, secured the roof, built the wooden pillars to form the roadway, and laid rails along which were moved the wooden hutches or tubs, each holding nine, ten or eleven hundredweights of coal. The youth, called the filler and drawer, filled, or shovelled, the coal won by the face man into the hutch or tub. After pushing or "drawing" the hutch to the "lie" or wheel-brae, the youth, by means of a detachable steel chain wound round a pulley, sent the full hutch down the incline toward the pit shaft, and by gravitation the movement of the full hutch pulled up an empty one for filling. This process went on throughout the shift. The filler and drawer had to make sure that each hutch he despatched carried his face man's token or pin-number, so that a record could be kept at the pithead of the payment due per ton. He also helped the face man with the work at the face, and gradually served his "apprenticeship" in this way. The filler and drawer was usually paid a day-wage, whereas the face man was normally a piece-worker. I worked for three years as a filler and drawer before becoming a face man at the age of seventeen.

As a boy of fourteen I thought I was lucky to get the princely sum of 2s. 9d. (about fourteen pence) a shift. That was the standard rate for a boy of my age. The hours of work were eight a day, plus winding time. That is, the miners began to be lowered down the pit half-an-hour before the shift actually began, so that they would be at their place of work underground a full eight hours. This was in contrast to the eight hours "bank to bank" system, where miners were lowered down, completed their shift, and were raised again to the surface, all within eight hours.

We had a six-day working week on day shift, five-day on back shift. Day shift was from six o'clock in the morning down the pit till two, back shift from two in the afternoon till ten. We worked back shift alternate weeks. The day shift included Saturday up to two o'clock. Saturday afternoon was the day when everybody went to the football match. It was generally a terrific scramble to get home, wash, get something to eat, and be in time for the football match.

One of the things that my family was anxious to do was to get working on their own, without working to a contractor. A contractor worked under the employer and himself employed men. He was paid either so much per ton his men produced, or so much per person he employed — so much the lamp, as the miners said. The contractor system was a vicious one, for the contractor was used by the employer to chase on the men, speed up their rate of working, carry tales back to the employer, and act as a buffer between him and the men. The miners' unions in all the coalfields of Britain were constantly campaigning for an end to the contractor system. It was gradually overcome but was not finally abolished until the establishment of the National Union of Mineworkers and the advent of nationalisation at the end of World War II.

My father was friendly with another miner who had a big family, and the two families combined together to take a contract at Wellsgreen Colliery, about a mile-and-a-half from where we lived in Buckhaven. This was early in 1914, about six months after I had begun work at Muiredge Colliery. The contract was to be worked solely by the two families, without anybody else being brought in who would be exploited by the contractor. We worked at Wellsgreen Colliery, which belonged to the Fife Coal Company, developing a new section of the pit until shortly after the war broke out in August 1914.

My father was one of the old school of mining, a highly skilled picksman. It was a treat to watch him working. As a result of training he was ambidexterous, could shovel with either hand, and use the pick lying first on one shoulder then on the other. The steady beat-beat of that hand-got pick was a work of art. Old miners like my father were carefully trained men that performed the complete operation of a miner. They undercut the coal, kept enlarging the cutting until they would get four or five feet undercut. Then they would use a hand-boring machine, bore holes, make up their own explosives and blow the coal down, then form the roadway, help fill off the coal, and secure the roof. Every part of the process of mining was performed by the picksman who was a face man.

For a face man, my father used a wide variety of tools. He used light holding picks, some long in the grain, other shorter. He had heavier picks for cutting the coal and breaking it up, heavier picks still to deal with stone work. For coal that was easy to bore he had a fast borer, for difficult or hard coal a slower borer. He also had a cleaner for cleaning borings out of a hole, a stemmer for stemming the shot hole, a heavy hammer or mash, a mash-axe, wedges, splinters, and so on. He had almost a hutchful of tools. In contrast, all that a stripper — a miner working on a machine-cut face — needed was a shovel, a pick, sometimes a pick with a mash end, and a mash. Unlike the picksmen-miners like my father, the strippers were careless about the condition in which they left the coal face since it was not their sole responsibility.

The outbreak of the 1914 war brought a change in our place of work down Wellsgreen pit. The section we were in was still in the process of development, so it did not then have a high productivity. Many young miners were joining the armed forces and there was a shortage of miners. So the coal companies tried to concentrate on their highest production sections down the pit and closed the others. My father and I were therefore sent to a section in the pit that was undercut by a coal-cutting machine. This section was only about three feet high, in contrast to the section we had always worked in, which was four-and-a-half to five feet high and where the coal was hand-got by the pick.

The coal-cutting machine was a revolving disc with picks attached that did the undercutting. The holes had to be bored by a hole-borer, the roadway was made by brushers on the opposite shift. The job of the miner was to blow down this coal with explosives and fill it off. Because the section was so low we had to work on our knees.

My father was unaccustomed to this form of work. The section was under a contractor, Big Bob Muir. Muir was a big, bulky man who did no work of his own but just supervised the work of all the others.

On the first day I was filling and drawing my father's hutches, with about ten hundredweight in each hutch, transporting it fifty to sixty yards down to the main transport junction, when Muir said to me: "See and tell your father to lift his pugs."

I did not know what that meant but I duly repeated what the contractor had said. "Dad, you've got to lift your pugs."

"What's that?" my father said. "What the hell's pugs?"

"I don't know," I said, "but you've got to lift them."

"Son," he said, "that's the best thing you've said the day. Here ye are, lift them and put them in the tub."

"Pugs" in fact meant coal the machine had failed to cut, but it was a new word to my father, who had never worked in a machine-cut section before. He was fed up working in unfamiliar conditions, so when I had reported that he was to "lift them" he thought it meant he had to lift his graith, or tools — that is, to pack up and leave the pit altogether. The contractor had not meant that at all, but my father had no regrets at leaving.

This complete change in methods of work had a serious effect upon picksmen-miners like my father and brothers. They had to look for work away from machine-mining if possible. So, in December 1914, we left Wellsgreen Colliery and came back again to Muiredge Colliery and the Wemyss Coal Company.

3

TRADE UNIONIST
AND SOCIALIST

IN my early days down the pit I found the work very hard. In addition to filling the coal into tenhundredweight hutches, or tubs as the Fife miners called them, we young lads had to draw the hutches out of a level road on to a wheel-brae. The full tub running down the incline brought up the empty tub. We repeated the process during the whole of the shift. In most cases, due to pressure of the roof, the road got lower and lower and if a drawer was pushing a full tub, his back would invariably come in contact with the roof. The young miner generally had scratches and abrasions and healing sores on his back from the shoulder to the hip. Always the miner felt he had a sore back. I remember going out for a walk one night and asking one young lad who had just begun work down the pit, "How's your back?"

"Oh," he said, "I've an awfy sair back. I can hardly sleep at night, my back's that sore. But it's not so bad. They tell me you get used to it."

"No, no," his older brother said, "that's not what happens — you just get used to having a sore back."

On this job we started at Muiredge, one incident sticks out in my mind. This part of the colliery was ventilated by a connecting road with a neighbouring colliery, the Rosie. Intake air came down Rosie Colliery and passed through a level road into the section of Muiredge that we were working in. The Rosie Colliery was notorious for underground fires. A datal, or day-wage, oncost worker, a middle-aged man, weak in intelligence, was employed at the junction where one road from Rosie met the road from the section we were working in at Muiredge. Each day at the commencement of the shift he had to call at the surface and get a canary in a cage, take it down, and leave it hanging above his head. This was to detect whether there were any obnoxious gases or fire-damp coming from Rosie Colliery into the workings at Muiredge. One day we came out, all complaining of not feeling too well, some complaining of headaches, and some had been sick. The oncost worker said to us when we came round to the junction, "Do any of you know what's wrong with this canary? It's lying on its back with its feet in the air."

He had not known the purpose of the canary. It just showed how precarious was our existence at that time. I think that was probably the nearest of the narrow escapes I had.

There was one improvement that was beginning to take place about the period when I first entered the pits at Buckhaven. The conflict between the fishing and mining communities was beginning to die down. With the decline of the fishing industry young fisher lads increasingly had to find permanent work down the pits. That removed one of the earlier reasons for sharp divisions and conflicts between the two communities. Since fishing had been in the main a seasonal occupation, it had not been uncommon for fishermen to seek temporary employment in mining during their off-season. Fighting for trade union wages and working conditions that was so essential to the permanent miner did not seem so essential to the fishermen. They had been prepared to take temporary work underground without regard to the established practices fought for by the miners. This was a very serious bone of contention.

There had been a running fight between the miners and employers about the filling or shovelling of small coal. This was known as the struggle for Billy Fairplay. The employers tried to insist that the miners had to fill large not small coal. If they did fill small coal, a deduction was made from their wages. The employers had insisted that the miners should work not with shovels but with graips, or forks, so that the small coal would fall through the tines. The miners resisted. One aspect of the conflict had been that the fishermen, when they came underground on temporary employment, brought fishing baskets, herring baskets, and filled the coal into them. That met the owners' wishes but was opposed to the miners'. But as the fishermen's sons became employed full time in the pits and not in fishing, the conflict between fishermen and miners gradually broke down. We considered it a matter of extreme importance and a very progressive step when we as young miners from the mining community made special pals with the young miners from the fishing community. Building this common front of unity was very important for the development of trade unionism and political activity and organisation in our area.

By the time my father, my brothers Peter and George, and Bob Cuthbert and I returned from Wellsgreen to Muiredge Colliery at the end of 1914, I was beginning to take an interest in trade unionism. I soon became an active member of the Fife miners' union. Consequently I ran foul of the management at Muiredge Colliery. I refused to work overtime on the bing. Binging the coal meant stacking it on the surface during the period of slack trade. When demand did increase, miners were expected by the coal company just to go on to work overtime on the bing at a fixed rate per hutch or tub. I said, "I am doing enough when I am working a recognised shift and I am not working overtime." The management said, "The war's on, we need coal. You are a young lad, you will have to work extra time or we'll have to consider your future." I told them that was up to them but I was sticking to a recognised trade union principle. So I was put under pressure all the time by the management at Muiredge. They kept this up till the 1921 lock-out; after it was over they excluded from the colliery not only me but also my family.

At the time I was becoming active in trade unionism my interest in politics was increasing. There had been a very active branch of the Social Democratic Federation at Buckhaven and the adjoining burgh of Methil for some years before the war. It apparently had played an active role in trying to help the revolutionaries in Russia in 1905. I remember some of the older hands explaining to me how they had tried to ship arms to the revolutionaries from Methil docks but how, when searches were made, they had to dump the arms over the side of the ship into the docks.[1]

The S.D.F. branch in the pre-war days had issued a monthly bulletin,[2] and had managed to secure some representatives on the Buckhaven town council, which was quite an advance. One of these town councillors, and a leading local figure in the S.D.F., was John Cormie. He had once been a miner, and proved an exceptionally capable leader of the socialist and labour group on the town council, where he became a bailie. The Wemyss Coal Company had given Cormie the monopoly of supplying explosives to all their pits and this contract had enabled him to give up his job as a miner. The miners therefore regarded Cormie as bought over by the employers. His standing declined among local working men, he took badly to drink, and after the war he went out of politics altogether.

But before the war, Cormie and my father were quite friendly, and he often came to our house when my parents were having a get-together on a Saturday night. My mother was famed for making scones, and Cormie and others were invited to come for their supper. There was generally political discussion and as a youngster I was all ears and would not go to bed so long as the discussion lasted. And as my mother was active in the co-operative movement, I became familiar with town council affairs and local political activity.

When the war came in 1914, the local S.D.F. organisation — or British Socialist Party, as it had become from 1911 — split from top to bottom.[3] It went out of existence as an organised active body. All the members who remained active supported the pro-war attitude of H. M. Hyndman, the Party leader.[4]

As a young miner of fifteen or sixteen, I used most evenings to meet with my pals at Bank Corner in Buckhaven, where older miners also congregated. Mining villages at that time customarily had a main centre where, in the evenings after work, people would gather together and argue out the events of the day. Bank Corner was one of four corners at a street junction. Each of these corners had become the meeting place of a particular group. The lads who went to the Masonic Order congregated on one corner, the fitba' experts on another, and to Bank Corner gravitated those of us interested in political questions. There were regular nightly arguments which centred in the main on working-class economics and politics and the fight against the war.

We were not conscious socialists but we believed the war was creating terrible misery and hardship. Reports were coming in that pals we had had at school were casualties. There was also a feeling that the shortage of food was worse in the mining areas than in more favoured areas. The purpose of the war, and what would arise from it, was occupying our thoughts more and more. In the main our opposition to the war took a semi-pacifist line: we would refuse to go into the army on the ground that it was an imperialist war.

My increasing interest in politics led me in 1915 to fill up a membership form of the Independent Labour Party.[5] But there was no branch of the I.L.P. at Buckhaven or Methil so I remained a member on paper only.

On Saturday evenings the young lads used to take a 4½d. ride into Kirkcaldy on the single-deck tramcar, or "mustard box" as we called it because of its colour. Kirkcaldy was a larger town six miles away. We attended the dancing there, and if we were chasing after young girls we would be in Kirkcaldy again on Sunday nights.

But I very soon began to develop more serious interests at Kirkcaldy. There was no real branch of the I.L.P. there, but there was an active branch of the British Socialist Party, which had a fairly well-appointed hall in Rose Street. During the winter they had Saturday night and Sunday meetings there; in the summer they held regular propaganda meetings outdoors at the entrance to Beveridge Park or at the Port Brae on the sea front. I joined the branch and began to attend it regularly in the winter of 1915-16 with two of my pals from Buckhaven, Johnny O'Neill and Bobby Venters.[6]

The meetings were old style, with a piano. We were given socialist hymn books when we went into the meeting, which generally began or finished up with a socialist song. It was there, too, that we managed to get copies of the Industrial Workers of the World songbook.[7] There appeared to be more meat in these songs than in the socialist hymn book, and we became more susceptible to the stuff contained in the I.W.W. book.

Kirkcaldy branch of the B.S.P. was opposed to the war and followed the line then pursued by, among others in the party nationally, John Maclean and William Gallacher on Clydeside.[8] Shortly after I joined the branch, John Maclean, the Clydeside revolutionary schoolteacher, who was the leading figure in the British Socialist Party in the West of Scotland, was coming round the Fife coalfield addressing propaganda meetings and trying to organise socialist educational classes as part of the Scottish Labour College.[9] Some of us young lads in Buckhaven persuaded Maclean to open a class for us on Marxian economics and industrial history. I had already heard Maclean giving a lecture on economics shortly after the war began, when I had been on a visit to Glasgow, and had been highly impressed by him. But he gave us only one lecture at Buckhaven when he was arrested for his anti-war speeches and, in April 1916, sentenced to three years' penal servitude.

The B.S.P. branch in Kirkcaldy suggested we should continue the class with the help of one of their older members, William Dunbar.[10] Dunbar was the manager of an insurance business. I asked old Bob Lamb, who was chairman of the B.S.P. branch, how Dunbar would compare with Maclean as a teacher. Bob Lamb's answer was characteristic. "With Maclean," he said, "you sit with your mouth open, you swallow everything, and when he finishes you close your mouth and have the revolution. But Mr Dunbar will try to convince you of the correctness of the arguments he is putting forward, he will

11

hold your attention, and he will hope you will make a good socialist afterward."[11]

We therefore continued classes in Buckhaven on Marxian economics and industrial history under the tutorship of Willie Dunbar. He was a rather cynical and caustic speaker. He certainly held our attention and started to open our eyes to a whole field of thoughts and ideas completely new to us. The history and outline of Britain's position we had been given at school was very soundly shattered by Mr Dunbar. He said, for instance, that the reason the sun never set on Britain's empire was because God could not trust the imperialists in the dark. His lectures had the effect of shattering any idea of patriotism and opened up approaches new to us. He argued that coal fires would become a thing of the past in the new system of society which would do away with all that wasteful use of resources, and that coal would be used only for its many by-products. He also said that the sea was not being properly exploited and should be farmed as the land was. These were all ideas out of the blue to a bunch of young miners. They obviously had a very profound effect on us and developed our desire to study more.

The B.S.P. branch at Kirkcaldy had a wide range of books and pamphlets for sale: the writings of Marx, the pamphlets of Engels, and many others of a Marxist nature. When we were in funds we certainly bought and read books such as Marx's *Capital*, Morgan's *Ancient Society*,[12] and (we were flying high) Joseph Dietzgen's *Positive Outcome of Philosophy*.[13] I had the greatest difficulty in trying to understand them. But I gradually acquired an understanding of Marx and of history. Other books I read at that time included *Our Noble Families*, by Tom Johnston,[14] and Blatchford's *Merrie England* and *Britain for the British*.[15] I also bought regularly *The Socialist*, organ of the Socialist Labour Party,[16] the *Labour Leader*[17] and the Glasgow *Forward*,[18] which were I.L.P. papers, and *The Call*,[19] the B.S.P.'s paper. Johnny O'Neill, Bobby Venters and I were avid readers, and our reading was the general subject of argument among ourselves and the lads who drifted to Bank Corner in Buckhaven.

Willie Dunbar became to all of us a very revered father figure. He had a tremendous impact on the young people of Buckhaven who were attending his class. That impact continued so far as I personally was concerned until the General Strike in 1926 when he shocked me by his attitude and I went hell for leather for him, as I tell below.[20]

John Maclean came back and lectured occasionally to us in the class at Buckhaven during 1917-18, as he was released from jail after serving only a year of his three-year sentence. But in the summer of 1918 he was again arrested and jailed, this time five years' penal servitude for sedition.

Of the people who strongly influenced me in the political and social ideas of my youth, John Maclean and Willie Dunbar were the two most prominent.

4

IN THE CUMBERLAND
IRON-ORE MINES

IN the later part of 1916, going on to 1917, work in some of the pits in Fife was very irregular because the export of steam-coal that they produced was hampered by the success of the German U-boat campaign. We were only getting employed three or four days a week. The U-boat campaign had also affected the import of iron-ore from Spain and Sweden. The Government therefore wanted to expand home production of iron-ore, and asked miners who were not working a full week to volunteer for work in the iron-ore mines. In Fife we were not sure if this was a genuine effort or whether there was some manoeuvring by the Government against the iron-ore workers. So those of us who were militant young miners associated with William Dunbar's class at Buckhaven sent John O'Neill as our representative down to the Cumberland iron-ore mines to check on the situation. He reported that the scheme was a genuine attempt to increase production and was not being opposed by the trade union covering iron-ore miners. A number of us from Fife therefore volunteered through the branches of the Fife miners' union. I was one of those accepted and went down to work at Millom on the Cumberland coast in September 1917.

My period in the iron-ore mines, which lasted a year, had quite an influence on me. Those of us who had volunteered were housed at a small village called Haverigg, about a mile from Millom, in army-type camps that had been specially built for us. Among the differences we immediately found in the iron-ore mines compared with what we were used to in the coal mines in East Fife was that at Millom they used wax candles underground for lighting. The candles were stuck on to the miners' helmets with a handful of sticky clay. In those pits in Fife where naked lights were permitted we had shortly before progressed from the use of tallow or oil lamps to the American type of carbide headlights.

The coal miners in Scotland had been agitating for years for pithead baths, but without much success. It was quite a surprise to us to find the Cumberland iron-ore miners, whom we regarded as much more primitive in their productive methods than we were in Fife, had a form of pithead baths in use. They certainly needed them: the iron-ore grime was extraordinarily difficult to remove. It seemed to get inside the pores of the skin, and even after a thorough wash, it still came oozing out. Our underclothes were always stained with the stuff.

Another outstanding difference was in the method and organisation of the work. In Scotland we had been accustomed to the individual acting under contract with the employer or manager, and working in conflict with his neighbours, each man for himself. But in the iron-ore mines at Millom they were working a system known as stoop and room, or pillar and stoop. The seam of iron-ore was about eighty feet thick. The miners worked the top leaf first, the top nine or ten feet of the seam, leaving two or three feet below that untouched, and then they began to dig out another nine or ten feet under that. In this way they worked down to the bottom of the seam. They transported the iron-ore from the working place in a small tip-up bogie, and tipped the ore from the bogie down a man-made shaft or hopper at the bottom of which was a trapdoor operated by a lever. The trapdoor was then opened and the ore dropped on to ten-hundredweight bogies waiting below on the main transport road.

They worked nine men to a working place, with three shifts, twenty-seven men in all. There was a twenty-eighth man, usually the oldest and most experienced, working with each group. He was the woodman. His job was to go up to the pithead and select the timber and heavy wood needed, and arrange its transport down to the working place for his men. The team of twenty-eight shared equally in the earnings. This was a completely co-operative venture, and was in sharp contrast to what we had in Fife, where every face man on piece-work worked for himself alone.

In addition, these Cumberland men entered into what they called a monthly bargain with the colliery official. If the men were not offered a contract to their satisfaction they took it easy till the following month. If, then, they got a contract to their satisfaction, they would enter into competitive work. But while they were taking it easy, they had a fall-back wage. That again was an advance on anything that we had in Fife.

Another new feature to me (though I knew it was in operation in the Welsh coalfield) was the recompense for working on afternoon shift or night shift. The policy was six working days on day shift, five on the back shift, and five on the night shift, by not working Sunday night. That was different from what we were accustomed to. On the back shift and night shift, where you worked five shifts, you were paid a bonus shift. If you worked four shifts you were paid for five, but if you worked three or less, you were paid for the actual shifts worked. This was another improvement on anything we had in the Scottish coalfield, where there was always grousing about working on back shift and night shift, loss of social amenities and so on. Compensation had always been demanded for it, but we had never succeeded in establishing what the lads in the iron-ore mines had. These things showed us we had a long way to go even to come in line with the improvements in facilities that other miners had secured.

The system of employment of boys was also different from ours in Fife.

Our boys went straight to the coal face at the age of fourteen without any preliminary training and learned the work of the adult miner while filling and drawing. A boy working with his father or elder brothers, as I had been, was lucky, for they made sure he received a thorough training in all aspects of the miner's work. In the iron-ore mines in Cumberland a boy began work on the surface, greasing bogies, and gradually moved from job to job, still on the surface, until he was sixteen, and only then did he go underground. He worked at the pit-bottom, handling bogies, before proceeding on a fixed cycle of jobs on the transport roads. At that stage he was still on a fixed day wage. Any spare time a boy had at work he spent learning how to use a hammer and jumper — a long steel rod for boring holes for explosives. This was highly skilled but extremely laborious and exhausting work. Then, at the age of nineteen, the boy was automatically transferred to a face production job, where he was accepted as a full member of the twenty-eight-man team and paid exactly the same wage as each of the others.

Living in the camp was a very fruitful period for some of us young people from Fife. It drew together all those who had socialist leanings and we formed socialist groups. We read and distributed the *Labour Leader*, the Glasgow *Forward*, and *The Socialist*, the organ of the Socialist Labour Party. We complained about the kind of food we were being dished up and staged a strike on the issue. Some of the lads got a few drinks, threatened to wreck the camp, and beat up the police when they came. So the camp officials sent for Mr Adamson, general secretary of the Fife miners' union, to come down from Scotland.[1] Mr Adamson spent an hour in the camp and tried to tell us that he had had kippers with his tea there and that the food was better than he could get at home. He had to leave the camp in rather a hurry. We also conducted anti-war activity and sought to develop that agitation by bringing into the camp pacifist speakers that were on the run from call-up to address meetings of the miners. Our camp became a haven for a number of lads of that character who were on the run.

Following the German offensive in 1918 there was need for more soldiers. But we were anti-war and thought we were doing the right thing by not joining the armed forces. We did not realise there was a role for us to play inside the armed forces in those times. We were not going to join the forces and take part in an imperialist war if we could avoid it. Our objective at that time was to escape to Ireland, where there was no conscription. When we were going to be subject to a ballot for the call-up, some of us young lads arranged to get a boat from Millom to Ireland. It was all nicely arranged, the time for departure was fixed. But the lad who was to get the boat for us failed at the last moment to appear with it. Later we discovered that he had been flirting with the wife of the owner of the boat and when the owner found out he cancelled the loan of his boat, just as we were waiting with our bundles to leave camp. So our plan fell through, or I might have landed in Ireland.

Instead, I was sent back from Millom to Fife in August 1918 to take my chance in the ballot at Muiredge Colliery for call-up to the army. I was quite pleased when my name was not drawn. But the authorities told me to go back to work again at Muiredge and I never returned to Cumberland. My experiences there left a very profound impression on me as to what we should be agitating for in the mining industry.

5

POST-WAR FERMENT

THE Great War and the first year or two after it was a period of trade union and political ferment for me just as it was for so many other workers in Britain. There was our local activity in Fife. There was the Clydeside shop stewards' agitation and the rent strike, the Irish revolt, the impact of the Russian Revolution, the crushing of the Spartakist revolt in Germany and the killing of Karl Liebknecht[1] and Rosa Luxemburg,[2] the returning soldiers, the serious discussions as to whether workers could achieve their emancipation by parliamentary or anti-parliamentary means. These things led to tremendous fervour among the militants with whom I was associated but also among the workers as a whole.

It was around the end of the war that, in addition to John Maclean and Willie Dunbar, a third socialist agitator, William Gallacher of the Clyde shop stewards' movement, began to have a great influence on me and in later years became my closest personal friend. I had first heard Gallacher speak early in the war at the B.S.P. branch at Kirkcaldy. At that time the differences were coming out between the section of the B.S.P. supporting Hyndman, who were for the war, and the section supporting John Maclean, with whom Gallacher was closely associated, who were opposed to the war. After that, I knew Gallacher mostly by repute, by reading, by getting to know the work of the Clyde Workers' Committee movement,[3] the strikes that took place on Clydeside, the rent strike which he was closely associated with,[4] and the fight against conscription. We young ones in Fife were very concerned when Gallacher was arrested in 1916 for an article in the shop stewards' paper, *The Worker*.[5] He was the editor of the paper but we learned subsequently he had nothing to do with the article, which had actually been written by a very prominent Glasgow I.L.P.er who posed as a pacifist at the beginning of the war and then, when he was too old for call-up, became, like some others, quite a good patriot. It was in this atmosphere that Gallacher became a very well-known personality in the advanced movement.

Those of us who were militant trade unionists and socialists in Fife had contact with the Clyde shop stewards' movement during the later stages of the war. At that period we acquired copies of *The Worker* and sold them in Fife. Johnny O'Neill, one of our group of militants in East Fife, a Lanarkshire man who had worked in the United States for a time then came from the

Lanarkshire pits to work at Buckhaven, had known Gallacher and John Maclean before the war — like them, he was a member of the British Socialist Party. Johnny kept us informed about the shop stewards' movement on the Clyde. He was also closely linked with Irish militants and had a large print of Wolfe Tone in the living-room of his house.[6]

We took a close interest in the Irish struggle. There were quite a number of Irish militants in Fife with whom we had the closest association because in those days Irishmen were expected to be "agin the Government" and for the trade union and labour movement. Without exception all of them that I knew were militant left trade unionists and politicians. Just after the war these Irish militants brought through Countess Markiewicz, who had fought in the Easter Rising, to speak at the Co-operative Hall in Methil.[7] The meeting was packed to the door — tremendous support — and she got a tremendous reception. We were also influenced by James Connolly, the Irish socialist leader who had close associations with Scotland,[8] and by Jim Larkin, leader of the Irish Transport and General Workers' Union.[9] We had read Connolly's pamphlets, and I heard him address a meeting at Kirkcaldy not long after the war began and before I had joined the British Socialist Party. So I had taken a close interest in the 1916 Rising at Dublin.

The Russian Revolution, and in particular the Bolshevik Revolution, had a profound effect upon us. In spite of everything the Press tried to work up against the revolution, the one thing we clung to was that the Bolsheviks had made John Maclean their consul in Scotland. Maclean was by that time a hero amongst us young miners. We felt instinctively that if the Bolshevik government could appoint Maclean its consul then it must be a good government. So right from the start, without at first knowing much about the political events or theory attached to the revolution, we were instinctively for the Bolsheviks. The old socialists, and some who were Marxists, used to argue that it was not possible to have a successful revolution in a backward country like Russia. It was necessary to have an advanced, industrially developed country before you could pass over to the next stage of social development. But we argued that if it were possible for the Russians to carry through a revolution how much easier it would be for us with out industrial background and knowledge to make a revolution successfully if we managed to get rid of the employing capitalist class.

Meantime there had been developing among some of the more militant trade unionists in Britain a movement to reform the unions in the interests of their members. A very strong reform movement of that character had developed before the war among the miners in South Wales. The Unofficial Reform Committee of the South Wales miners had published in 1912 the influential pamphlet, *The Miners' Next Step*. Copies of this pamphlet circulated amongst us young lads in the Fife miners' union who had contact with the British Socialist Party, and it was at the Party rooms in Kirkcaldy that I got a copy early in 1917 before I went off to work in Cumberland. A miners' Reform Committee already existed in Fife by the time I became an active trade unionist. It was a fairly loose organisation, without properly formed branches, membership or rules. It mainly centred round the leading activists in the mining villages and small towns. Among these activists, who were mainly drawn from politically active groups, were Bob Lamb and John Boyd of Gallatown, David Proudfoot of Methil, Gardner of Leven, Peter Hastie of Windygates, Tom Smith of Methilhill, William Kirker, Jimmy Galloway and John Bird of Bowhill, Tom Smith of Lumphinnans, Andrew Jarvie of Valleyfield, the brothers Peter and William Swain and the Thomson brothers of Coaltown of Balgonie.[10] The Reform Committee in Fife met monthly and organised support in the branches for carrying out militant policies in the miners' union. We issued leaflets as and when necessary and occasionally sent reports of our activities to *The Worker* in Glasgow.

Some of the things that interested me in *The Miners' Next Step*, or in the subsequent discussions to which the pamphlet contributed, were first of all the idea that we should have a five-day working week as against the eleven-day fortnight that we had in Fife, and that we should have a six-hours' working day — in Fife we had eight hours, plus winding time, that is, eight-and-a-half hours.

Then there was the question of periodic elections of full-time officials in the union. This was a new idea to us as we had accepted that an agent — that is, a full-time officer of the union — was appointed for life.

The idea of greater democracy within the union appealed to us. It meant that those who represented the Fife miners' union on the executive committee of the Scottish federal union — the National Union of Scottish Mine Workers — should be elected by branch financial vote instead of by the county Delegate Board.[11] It meant that the two N.U.S.M.W. representatives who sat on the executive committee of the Miners' Federation of Great Britain should also be elected by branch financial vote, instead of by a rota system that could lead to a couple of duds being appointed.[12] And it meant that the agents should be appointed by individual ballot vote of all the miners in the county union.

The difference between a branch financial vote and a Delegate Board vote was very important in Fife. The organisation of the Fife miners' union was different from that of most other county miners' unions in Scotland, such as Lanarkshire, Stirlingshire, and West Lothian. In those counties, the branches were based on the pits where the miners worked. But in Fife, as in Ayrshire, the branches were based on the village or town where the miners lived, regardless of where they worked. This meant that some of the bigger villages in Fife had over 1,000 members in their branch, while the small villages would have only forty or fifty members. But at the central Delegate Board, or county executive committee, which met at the head office in Dunfermline, the small branch carried exactly the same voting power as the biggest branch. The bigger branches held most of the young militant miners. Naturally, those of us who were militant wanted the big branches to have a proportionately larger say in the union.

Our plea that votes should represent roughly the actual paying membership seemed soundly based in democratic procedure. If it were granted it would transform the policy decisions of the delegate conferences: militants would have considerably more influence in the union. The fight for the financial vote was therefore an all-important issue on the successful outcome of which depended real democratic control of the union and its policies by the members.

Provision for the financial vote was already in the rules of the Fife miners' union. Once a question had been discussed at a monthly meeting of the Delegate Board, and again at the following meeting of a branch, the branch delegate to the Board could call for a financial vote to be taken. The financial vote was recorded according to the amount of members' subscriptions drawn in by the branch, remitted to the county office at Dunfermline, and shown in the financial returns published each month. In such a vote a big branch could cast, say, £50 or £60 for or against a resolution, while a small branch could cast, say, £4 or £5.

We therefore considered that, short of a ballot vote, the financial vote was the most democratic method. But as the fight between the militants and William Adamson, general secretary of the union, and his supporters, became keener, Adamson bluntly refused to allow the financial vote. This led, as I shall explain below, to the first split in the Fife miners' union in 1922-23.[13]

Two other ideas closely interested militant miners in Fife around the end of the Great War. One was holidays with pay. This was an immense attraction to us, as we had never had paid holidays. My father worked in the pits until he was seventy, but I do not remember him ever having a paid holiday. The other suggestion was that there should be full compensation paid to the lads coming back from the forces until they obtained work.

These were the ideas round which we campaigned inside the miners' union. We were able to set up contacts with the South Wales miners in particular. They had similar ideas. My recollection is that John Maclean helped make some contacts between us in Fife and South Wales miners, among whom he had also worked. It was John Maclean who arranged for John Bird, a young militant miner from Bowhill, to go down to work in the South Wales coalfield during the war, to keep him from being drafted into the army. Maclean arranged with A. J. Cook that Bird should be given employment at the colliery where Cook was a checkweigher, and that he should reside in Cook's own home.[14] The first occasion I met A. J. Cook, who subsequently became general secretary of the Miners' Federation of Great Britain, was in 1919 at a miners' Reform Committee meeting at the Socialist Labour Party bookshop in Renfrew Street, Glasgow.

So there was a lot of development in the later part of the war. Our miners' unofficial reform movement in Fife had led us into contact with similar groups of miners elsewhere, and also contributed to our contacts with the shop stewards' movement. We could get tremendously interested meetings in Fife. One of the speakers we used at that time was James MacDougall, who also had some association with the shop stewards.[15] He was imprisoned in 1916 along with Maclean for an anti-war speech he had made in Glasgow. Unfortunately, he had not got sufficient strength of character to withstand his experience in prison. It broke this lad and he became a nervous wreck. He was released from jail and militants at one of the pits at Blantyre in Lanarkshire invited him to be checkweigher. He quickly associated himself with the militant miners, and was a powerful speaker. MacDougall was John Maclean's right-hand assistant.

Maclean himself was nominated at the general election of December 1918 as Labour candidate for Gorbals in Glasgow. But as he was still in jail, William Gallacher ran his campaign as shadow candidate. Groups of us from Buckhaven and Methil who could spare the fare went through by train to Glasgow to take part in the election campaign, and to attend the big rallies demanding Maclean's release from prison. We usually travelled through on Sundays when we were not on back shift till the following day. This was the first time I saw Gallacher at a big meeting. It was in the St Andrew's Hall, an overflow meeting. The second time we went to Glasgow was when Maclean was released from Peterhead prison, ten days before the election. I remember us lining up outside the St Andrew's Hall and marching to George Square. It gave us a great feeling of taking part in a big movement; the whole agitation was on a much bigger scale than anything we had experienced in the mining villages and small towns of Fife.

So when the First World War ended in 1918, there was this tremendous ferment amongst the active elements in the mining industry in Fife. Politically, there was an attempt to try to get some common understanding of what was necessary. At that time, towards the end of the war and immediately after it, there was no unified political organisation in East Fife, but simply loose attachments. We felt the need for carrying out systematic propaganda. Leven shorehead, a couple of miles from Buckhaven, was our favourite stamping ground for Saturday night and Sunday night meetings. The regular feature in the summertime was that everybody interested in politics made tracks for the speakers' forum there. We dished up a real old mixture. Each week we would be putting forward propaganda that had no relationship at all to what had been said the week before. We had, for example, from the Independent Labour Party, Jimmy Maxton and Campbell Stephen from Glasgow and Stewart from Edinburgh.[16] They would tell us that the only hope for the salvation of the working class was through Parliament. Then we had Willie Gallacher, J. R. Campbell, Tommy Clark, and one or two others from Glasgow and Edinburgh, who said that parliamentary action was dissipating the energy of the workers and what was required was industrial action by the organised working class along the lines of the shop stewards' movement.[17] We had Foulis,[18] a leader of the engineering and shipbuilding workers from Edinburgh, who told us that the only road was one big industrial union and that we should go for the development here of the Industrial Workers of the World as was in operation in America, Canada and Australia. Then we would have speakers who were influenced by the Sinn Fein organisation — like Captain White, son of General White of Ladysmith fame.[19] He used to tell us that the only road open to us was the developing of something similar to the Irish Citizen Army.[20] Then we had Socialist Labour Party speakers, like Tom Bell and Arthur McManus of Glasgow, and Jimmy Clunie of Dunfermline, who sold *The Socialist* and the pamphlets of the American socialist Daniel De

Leon.[21] Clunie and other S.L.P.ers used to tell us it was no good participating in industrial action, that strikes were hopeless: the only thing was to continue with our propaganda until everybody was a convinced socialist and then we would end capitalism overnight and we would waken up under the new socialist order. So that speakers with all sorts of views were given the opportunity to speak at Leven shorehead. The crowds used to turn up, and we could sell tremendous amounts of literature — pamphlets, and so on — at these meetings, and take a big collection. We were able from these collections to bring speakers for a week's propaganda tour in the district, pay for their board and lodging and pay them a wage. This showed the tremendous interest in the discussions that were going on at that time.

Among the fiercest discussions amongst us young people who were interested in politics were those on parliamentarism and anti-parliamentarism. There was serious disappointment following the success in the pre-war elections in increasing the number of Labour M.P.s. Most of them were elderly trade union officials, like William Adamson, general secretary of the Fife miners' union. Not many of them were avowed socialists but were more sympathetic to Liberal-Labour working together. The support given the Liberal Government, then the war coming on, the turning down of international promises made before the war about opposing wars and of taking strike action if need be to prevent them, the betrayal of the German Social Democrats, the French Socialists and of Labour in Britain by their leaders, who all went pro-war, created a feeling of opposition to those people who were in Parliament. There was this idea that to go into Parliament was to weaken the whole struggle of the organised militant workers, that it was betraying the advanced movement. There was therefore a very, very strong feeling amongst the militants with whom I associated, of the need for powerful industrial organisation, and of hostility to anyone who participated in parliamentary activity. This feeling was aggravated by further wartime and immediate post-war events: the mutinies in the British army and the French army;[22] the murder of Karl Liebknecht and Rosa Luxemburg at the hands of the Social Democrats and German officer class; the setting up of the Bela Kun government in Hungary;[23] the whole fight of the Russian workers. All of us younger people were in a hurry — we could not see big changes coming through parliamentary or local government action, and we talked contemptuously of what people wanted to do on the local town council. So this was the sort of atmosphere in which we were developing our knowledge of politics, an atmosphere for an entirely new political alignment. What form this was to take was a matter of continual discussion amongst us. All of us were agreed that there should be a linking up with the revolutionary elements of the various countries. We were able to get considerable contact with the new elements coming in at Methil Docks and we learned also from these sailors of the ferment that was going on on the continent.

One of the outstanding propagandists for anti-parliamentarism was a lad from Glasgow, Jack Leckie. Leckie was of Irish extraction. I was not always sure whether he was arguing for Sinn Fein or for the communist organisation in this country, but he was a most fiery, robust speaker. At the time Leckie was touring East Fife, the local Labour Party organisation was trying to popularise Tom Kennedy, who had been the organiser for the Social Democratic Federation, as a possible parliamentary candidate for Kirkcaldy Burghs. We arranged a debate between Leckie and Kennedy in the biggest hall in Buckhaven.[24] The subject was "Parliamentarism or Anti-Parliamentarism". The S.D.F. supported Kennedy, and our nondescript group that was arguing for something more militant supported Leckie. The provost of the burgh acted as chairman and the hall was packed. This was a remarkable meeting. Kennedy was the staid, respectable parliamentarian, dressed in a black suit, stiff collar, his shirt cuffs sticking out, so very precise and polite, just wagging his finger to emphasise his points — very respectable, the greatest decorum. Leckie, on the other hand, found that the hall was too hot and asked permission of the audience to take his jacket off. Then he was getting still hotter and he rolled up his shirt sleeves. Then he took off his tie, rolled back his shirt collar and pranced up and down the whole length of the platform, shouting what had Kennedy's pals in Germany done to his pals Rosa Luxemburg and Karl Liebknecht? He said he knew what *he* would like to do — and put his fist under Kennedy's nose. It was real rousing stuff. The most remarkable thing was that when the vote was taken it was overwhelmingly in favour of Leckie. That showed how strong the general feeling among us was that to go into Parliament or local authority was to betray the revolutionary attitude of the socialists and the early pioneers we were associated with.

Leckie was a powerful orator. When he spoke at our meetings in Fife he tried to link up the Sinn Fein development in Ireland with the situation in Britain. And he would tell the miners that they had to practice marching and drill. It was not unusual for him to have a big meeting and to finish up with a march of two or three miles to Leven and back to Buckhaven, telling the lads to keep demonstrating. Leckie made his mark in Fife but he did not develop any real organisation: he was more the agitator. He was always on the fringe of illegality and I sometimes wondered if the police deliberately allowed him to move freely so that they could check on those with whom he made contact. Gradually the mining comrades began to realise that this was not the best road to travel that Leckie was urging. The last time I saw Leckie was in 1920-21, when I was at the Scottish Labour College. By that time he had become a very successful businessman as central European traveller for a tobacco firm.

Out of this welter of confusion that existed, this hotch-potch of ideas, with no clear central agreement amongst the speakers, though all were agitating for a change, protesting against the existing order of things, one common thing that bound all of us was support for the Russian Revolution and the Bolsheviks and opposition to the intervention in Russia and the continued war there. We were conscious that some organisation was needed to unify all these elements. Thus we formed the Fife Communist League. It included the S.L.P. elements, which were led mainly by Jimmy Clunie and Jimmy Birrell, another Marxian lecturer, both from Dunfermline;[25] and the I.L.P. elements, who were drawn mainly from East Wemyss, Cowdenbeath, Kelty and Dunfermline, and those of us that were in the B.S.P. but mainly in the Reform Committee movement. The League was the beginning of a unified political party. It had no national connections but we wished to get affiliation to the new Communist or Third International.[26] The League had a committee that met every fortnight; to start with, Jimmy Clunie was generally in the chair, and a Kirkcaldy B.S.P. comrade was the secretary. We set up branches, and sought to conduct agitation and propaganda through the League. We were most anxious that there should be a political party that would represent our ideas. We were disillusioned with the work of the Parliamentary Labour M.P.s, who all of them had identified themselves with the war, and the trade union officials who had also shown themselves to be closely associated with war activity and not anxious to lead a fight for substantially improved conditions for the workers.

6

SANKEY AND DATUM LINE

AT the time of the Forty Hours Strike in Glasgow in January 1919, we had a surface workers' strike over hours in the Fife coalfield. The surface workers were to have a forty-nine hours week and the dispute was over the question when they should begin and end their shift. It was an unofficial strike and was led by an I.L.P. member, Bob Beattie of Lumphinnans. Beattie was a very fine agitator, a respected leader of his tradesmen's group.[1] In East Fife those of us in the Miners' Reform Committee took steps to associate ourselves with the surface workers' strike and asked miners in the area to support it. But the official leadership of the Fife miners' union conducted a campaign against the strike and this campaign culminated in a big meeting on one of the local football fields at Bayview, Methil, now the ground of the Scottish Football League club East Fife. That was the only occasion I can remember when the use of the ground was granted for a miners' meeting.

The principal speaker for the official leadership of the union against us was Joe Westwood. Later on Joe became a Labour M.P. and, after the 1939-45 war, Secretary of State for Scotland. But in 1919 he was a full-time collector and organiser for the union in the Crosshill-Lochore-Glencraig area.[2]

At this Bayview meeting all the war stuff was trotted out: we were pro-German, we had been getting German gold. The men who had returned from the trenches were incited by Westwood and other official speakers against the lads "that were stabbing them in the back". Eventually the miners whose feelings had been worked up against the strike made a rush against its leaders as they stood on the platform beside the official union speakers and threatened to throw them into the Methil Docks. A semi-riot developed. That broke the unofficial strike in East Fife.

At this time the struggle for voting control of the Fife miners' union was proceeding apace. There was activity going on simultaneously in Methil, East Wemyss, Bowhill, Glencraig, Lochore, Kelty — the major pits and villages of importance. In East Fife our effort was concentrated on winning the position of branch delegate, as the delegate attended the monthly conference of the union, where policy was decided. This struggle provided me with my first experience of an attempt by right-wing official union leaders to overcome the election of a member who favoured a left militant policy. In Buckhaven branch at our A.G.M. in December 1918 we had elected John O'Neill, who was a member of the Reform Committee, as delegate. O'Neill had defeated an older man, James Neilson, who although a socialist was anti-Reform Committee and a one hundred per cent supporter of William Adamson, the right-wing general secretary.[3] Many of the elderly socialists resented us youngsters — it was the old tale: "I was doing this when you were in nappies." The war and the Bolshevik Revolution had created a schism and we young ones were told we had "no patience". When Neilson reported his defeat to Adamson — the Rt. Hon. Adamson, as he was at that time the leader of the Parliamentary Labour Party at Westminster — Adamson arranged for a meeting in the biggest hall in the town to have the election overturned. It was in keeping with Adamson's line that anything was good enough to spite us. Buckhaven had previously been one of "his" branches till we had started an organised opposition. We first got the branch meetings held on Sunday mornings, then we had a whip round our supporters so that we could muster a majority at the meetings.

The special meeting that Adamson called was a crowded-out affair. There must have been between 800 and 1,000 miners present. But the suggestion that a branch vote appointing delegates should be overturned was so unthinkable to the democratically minded miners that Adamson was not allowed to finish his speech and had to withdraw from the platform. The miners then unanimously reaffirmed the decision taken at the annual general meeting. This was my first experience of effort being made to overcome decisions arrived at democratically at a constitutionally run meeting. Unfortunately, we were to have many more experiences of this sort in both the Fife and Scottish coalfield from then on. Adamson was merely a forerunner in trying to whip up "the silent majority" to correct "the militant usurpers" — he has had many followers since.

Following the end of the war, there was an agitation by the Miners' Federation of Great Britain for a reduction of hours, improved wages and working conditions, and nationalisation of the mines. Because of this agitation and the demand by the miners for a strike, the Lloyd George Coalition Government resorted to a favourite tactic to buy time — they set up a Royal Commission — the Sankey Commission. The representatives of the M.F.G.B. on the Commission did quite a remarkable job. Robert Smillie, Herbert Smith, and Frank Hodges, and the economist Sir Leo Chiozza Money, were assisted by R. H. Tawney and Sidney Webb, two other nominees jointly agreed between the union and the Government.[4] We were treated to long screeds in the Press on what Smillie in particular was saying to the coalowners. The exposure of the coalowners and of the landowners — the Duke of Northumberland and his kind — was extraordinarily telling.[5] The Sankey Commission brought out the mess the owners were making of the coal industry, and the need for nationalising it; the rotten housing conditions that miners were living under in miners' rows were particularly sharply brought out by the evidence of the Scottish miners' representatives.

All this was of great interest to us miners. We would rush home from work and pick up our papers to see what our fellows were saying to the coalowners, landowners and houseowners. The Sankey Commission condemned the system of ownership in the industry and said it was necessary to consider nationalisation. On the question of hours, it said there should be an immediate reduction from eight to seven, with one winding time, and if the economic circumstances of the industry justified it, a further reduction to six hours per day from 1921. The miners, because of their militancy, were able to force the Government and the private employers to give us a seven-hours day. Fifty years later, in spite of all the modern technological advance and the tremendous increase of productivity, the miners were still working not seven but seven-and-a-quarter hours per day. That was the rate of progress on the question of hours in the mining industry in those fifty years — we had gone backwards. The six-hours day was the carrot in front of the donkey's nose: it never materialised. The questions of nationalisation and of wages were referred to the Government. On wages, the proposal was that we should accept the recommendations of the Sankey Commission as something for immediate acceptance and development. Those of us who were active in the union smelt a rat, that it did not give us what we wanted. We felt strong enough to take it. Therefore we urged that we should reject these recommendations and resort to industrial action to secure what we were after. We were defeated within the M.F.G.B., however, and I think the main reason for our defeat was that there was a very powerful suggestion made that if the terms were immediately accepted there would be a payment of two shillings per shift, backdated for approximately four months. We were told we were asking that the miner should give up £7, £8, £9 or £10 of back money, and that if they accepted our line they would be landed in a struggle without that back money. That, I think, swayed the vote and the miners therefore accepted the recommendations. But it was not long before the Government said they were not going to proceed with the recommendation for nationalisation. They never intended to proceed with the recommendation on the six-hours day. They did operate the penny per ton welfare levy recommended, which certainly laid a basis for a number of improved facilities being provided in the mining areas. But the nationalisation of the distribution of coal, which was recommended, has never yet been put into operation.

If the distribution of coal had been kept out of private hands, a very substantial means of public income would have been provided. The private distribution system meant that coal was being sold to the consumer at a price that the producer did not control. It was one of the weakening factors in the whole struggle of the miners because they had always been told that while they might have a legitimate claim for more wages, there was nothing in the kitty. So we had another sharp lesson on the astute policy of Lloyd George and his colleagues. Because the circumstances were favourable to the miners at that time it was necessary for the Government to buy time, to make promises, give hidden assurances, and as circumstances changed to break these assurances. That was what happened on that occasion, because the moment the economics of the industry altered — as they did by 1921 — we were met with a demand for a return to the eight-hours day, for the reduction of wages, and for competition with the Polish and other low-wage industries on the continent.

Before that happened, however, we were told by the Lloyd George Government and the coalowners late in the summer of 1920 that the country desperately needed an increased output of coal. We were told in the mining industry that if we would agree to our wages being related to the national output, then the Government and the coalowners would be favourably inclined to look at an increase in wages, for which we had been agitating. The proposal was that they would take the actual national weekly output at the time and if output increased by a certain ratio we would be given a shilling a day. At the time they made this proposition we were entitled to an increase of two shillings. So, if we accepted, this Datum Line — as it was called — would be the basis on which wages would be determined in the future. If national output went above that figure, we would get an increase; but if it came below it, we would suffer a reduction.

The Miners' Federation took a ballot over the question of a strike for increased wages. The ballot resulted in a big majority for strike action. The so-called Datum Line strike then followed in the middle of October. The strike lasted for a fortnight and eventually the terms offered by the Government were accepted as a temporary settlement that was to expire on 31 March 1921. The Datum Line settlement gave the miners an increase in wages but the increase was related to an increase in output. To start with, the miners got a couple of bob of an increase. We viewed that as simply a bribe to get the proposals accepted and to prevent any further strike action.

But the demand for British coal started to decline from the autumn of 1920. The decline in demand gradually depressed the Datum Line and the miners lost the increased wages they had received, and actually suffered reductions. So that this attempt to base miners' wages on national productivity ultimately meant a reduction for the miner. This was a further demonstration of how, when conditions became favourable for the miners, the owners changed the basis of payment. In the old days miners' wages had been determined by the selling price of coal. That was allowed to operate so long as it was not substantially to the advantage of the miners. During the war, when there was a drastic shortage of coal, the British coalowners had been able to sell any old rubbish so long as it was black, and get fantastic prices for it. Because prices had shot up in consequence of the war, the miners would have had very substantial increases in wages if the old form of ascertainment of wages had been continued. But in order to get out of that, the employers ended that form of agreement, the Government was brought in to assist the employers and, "in the national interest", fixed wages on a sliding scale based on the cost of living. This was a further illustration of how the Government could come to the assistance of the coalowners as circumstances warranted. That should be kept in mind when the argument is used that trade unionists ought to separate industrial action from political action — one of the arguments generally used by right-wing Labour people that we should not resort to industrial action to secure political objectives. The employers have used political action whenever the circumstances warranted.

The Datum Line strike more or less coincided with the beginning of a new stage in my own life, for in the early autumn of 1920 I left Buckhaven and the pits for a year, in order to study full time at the Scottish Labour College in Glasgow.

7

FROM COAL EDGE
TO COLLEGE

THE Scottish Labour College had been formed in 1916. It was a movement of workers' educational groups in Glasgow, Lanarkshire, Fife, and elsewhere, not a building. The formation of the College was due largely to the educational work carried on by John Maclean. Maclean, who was a graduate of Glasgow University and a schoolteacher by profession, had begun around 1906 to organise and teach workers' study classes, especially in Marxian economics. I had heard Maclean giving a lecture on economics shortly after the war had begun and had been highly impressed by him, and as I have already mentioned, some of us young lads in Buckhaven had persuaded him to open a class for us on Marxian economics and industrial history early in 1916, but he had given us only one lecture when he was arrested for his anti-war speeches and sent to jail. So there had been some difficulty during the war in building up the Scottish Labour College because of Maclean being sent to prison in 1916 and again in 1918, but also because of the need to secure financial support from the trade unions.

But by 1919-20 workers' educational classes associated with John Maclean and the Scottish Labour College were well established in the Fife-Clackmannan coalfield, as well as in many other areas. I remember in the spring of 1919 attending a conference organised in Kirkcaldy by the national committee of the College to develop the classes on a wider scale and if possible develop full-time classes. An agitation was conducted in the Fife miners' union to get the union tied up with the development of full-time classes. Maclean himself put up a proposition that the miners and others that could be induced should finance some full-time students who would come under him at the College. This was following the example of South Wales, which very definitely influenced Maclean's attitude on workers' education. The Central Labour College, which had been formed in 1909 after the revolt by worker-students against the kind of teaching they had got at Ruskin College, Oxford, was being financed during the war by the South Wales Miners' Federation and the National Union of Railwaymen. Most of the leading South Wales miners, including Frank Hodges, general secretary of the M.F.G.B., had come through the Central Labour College. Another Welsh lad, D. J. Williams, became a full-time Scottish Labour College tutor in Fife, and was up here till 1926, when he went back and became a miners' M.P. for one of the Welsh constituencies.[1]

The Fife miners' union had supported previous efforts to develop working-class education. Long before the war, when Ruskin College was being publicised, the union had decided to send a member there as a full-time student. There was a ballot of the branches and the man sent was W. M. Watson. The miners decided to extend his year at Ruskin and gave him a second year. So he was there in 1906 and 1907. He was given an allowance of £52 a year. When Watson came back from Ruskin College he became a full-time union collector, then political organiser for the Scottish miners, and ended up as Labour M.P. for Dunfermline Burghs.[2] After Watson's return from Ruskin, the Fife miners decided to send another member there. It was a lad from Buckhaven, John Thomson, who got this second place. I did not know him but I knew his brothers and other members of his family. They were militants and supporters of ours in the miners' union at Buckhaven. I believe John Thomson had been active as a young lad in the S.D.F. But after he had completed two years at Ruskin, financed by the miners' union, he had decided to go abroad, and emigrated to Australia.

By 1919 there was a Fife Committee of the Scottish Labour College. The leading figures on it were Jimmy Clunie of Dunfermline, a painter by trade and a member of the S.L.P., and Jimmy Birrell, a joiner turned shopkeeper and insurance agent, who was also from Dunfermline and in the S.L.P. The Fife Committee was active in trying to get trade union and Co-operative connections and affiliation fees so that full-time classes by the Scottish Labour College could get away to a good start. Eventually, it was decided that there should be a full-time class started in 1920 in Glasgow. Those of us in the Reform Committee were successful in carrying a decision in the Fife miners' union that the union should grant a donation to the College and finance three students from the union. We were aware that in other parts the same kind of agitation was going on. Lanarkshire miners' union carried a similar decision; Ayrshire agreed to finance one student. The toolmakers' union also decided to finance a full-time student.

In the Fife miners' union the branches were asked to submit nominations for the three places the union had decided to finance. There were something like fifty-six nominations altogether from the branches and it was decided to hold an eliminating exam.

I was keen to go to the College. When I had left school and was unable to secure work as a colliery electrician, I must have harboured ideas that some time I would get a job as an electrician because I elected to go to night school. But in doing that I had come up against the barrier or dividing line between those who were miners and those who were officials in the colliery. If one studied the theoretical subjects of mining at night school, which a number did, it meant that eventually one intended to cross the line between being an ordinary miner and using the position to exploit the miners. So even at that early stage I had opted not to study the theoretical side of mining, but to study electrical engineering. It was quite all right to start with, but that was the period of the war when teachers were volunteering for service or being called up, and there were changes of teachers, shortages of teachers. We had no continuity of study and the whole atmosphere tended to repel one instead of attracting to continued study at night school. That was the finish of what one might call my routine schooling.

I had not been particularly keen on study while at school and cannot recollect ever doing any homework. But I had developed a thirst for knowledge after I left school. I remember buying up expensive Marxian classics and trying to acquire the meaning of these books in the late night. But this presented a difficulty because my father and brothers and myself worked together in the pit as a team, which meant we worked in the same working places but on opposite shifts — the old man and I on one shift, the two older brothers on the other. If I was on back shift, and came into the house after ten o'clock at night, by the time I got washed up, got a meal, and so on, my brothers would be going to bed for the early five o'clock rise in the morning. We slept in the same room and I would want to keep the light on to read, while they would want the light out to sleep. So there had been that difficulty of trying to study after working hours. We had never really overcome that difficulty, although my brothers were very sympathetic to my desire to acquire more knowledge. There were only occasional outbursts in this connection.

So I was keen to become a full-time student at the Scottish Labour College. But in my branch of the Fife miners' union the secretary belonged to the anti-Reform Committee side and he claimed he had never received notification about nominations for the College. So here again were the beginnings of new developments inside the union, with my branch being denied the opportunity to submit a nomination. But a neighbouring branch, Wellsgreen, whose secretary over many years, John Briggs, was an old-style socialist and staunch trade unionist who knew my father and family well and had known me from childhood, nominated me.[3] So I went along with the other fifty-six or so nominees to sit the eliminating exam at the miners' union boardroom in Victoria Street, Dunfermline. The exam was arranged by the Fife Labour College and we were supervised by Jimmy Clunie to make sure there was nothing improper being done.

Afterwards I was informed that I was one of the three successful candidates. The other two were John Welch of Cowdenbeath[4] and John Bird of the Reform Committee at Bowhill.

8

AT THE SCOTTISH
LABOUR COLLEGE

BIRD, Welch and I took up our duties at the Scottish Labour College in September 1920, shortly before the Datum Line strike by the miners began. Most of our classes were held in rooms in the offices of the Scottish Trades Union Congress in St Vincent Street, Glasgow.

The three of us had financial difficulties to begin with. The decision by the Fife miners' union to finance three full-time students had been obtained against the opposition of the leaders of the union, Willie Adamson, general secretary, and company. In consequence of that there were long delays in providing us with our grants. The union had decided to pay £150 to single men for the year, and £200 to married men. Welch and I were single, Bird was married. Bird's wife was expecting a kiddie soon after he started at the College, so he was to get another £50 when his kiddie was born.

Even after we had arrived at the College and had bought books and paper and so on, weeks and weeks went past and no attempt was made to pay us our allowances. We were certain the delay was due to deliberate maliciousness on Adamson's part. The financial secretary of the union was James Cook and he was a very efficient office worker, regardless of his weakness as a trade union official.[1]

So Bird, Welch and I walked up to Queen Street station in Glasgow every time we knew there was to be a meeting of the executive of the Scottish miners' union, in order to buttonhole the executive members from Fife as they came off the train, and point out to them that we were still without an allowance. But it required another fight in the branches of the union in Fife before any payment was made to us. Thus the three of us certainly found things rather tight in our first few weeks at the College, and I had to depend for support on my brothers.

The tutors at the College were John Maclean himself and Willie McLaine. McLaine was a B.S.P. propagandist, came, I think, from the Manchester area, and finished up subsequently as a research worker for the Amalgamated Engineering Union.[2] McLaine took the classes in Industrial History and Trade Union Law; John Maclean took the classes in economics, public speaking,

33

arithmetic and algebra. All these classes were held in the mornings. We got quite a shock when Maclean told us we were to go in the afternoons to classes specially arranged for us at a business training college in Bath Street, to study shorthand, bookkeeping, English and Esperanto. We had deputation after deputation at John Maclean, saying that we could not see the value and the purpose of going for shorthand, bookkeeping, business training and methods, or Esperanto. We said we were at various stages in development and some of us were finding it extremely difficult to take on these subjects. But you could not budge Maclean when he was set on anything. His reply was that we would be amazed at how little business knowledge trade union officials had and that very often when we were in negotiations with the employers the knowledge of shorthand to take notes of what was being said would be invaluable. He said trade union officials were often tricked because something was said to have been decided in negotiations that had not been decided at all. So if we were to be trained as trade union officials of the future we must have business knowledge, bookkeeping experience, and be able to take shorthand notes. We had difficulty in accepting this, and said: "If we are going to become trade union officials we will have secretaries who will do this work for us." However, Maclean was adamant on it.

My opinion was that Maclean was asking too much of us. We were a bunch of lads who had all left school at fourteen or younger, we had had no real training in study, and to give us a crash course on such a wide variety of subjects was asking too much. I think we would have got better results out of our period as full-time students at the Scottish Labour College if the subjects had been fewer in number. However, that was the curriculum that was laid down.

Some of the subjects presented us with difficulties. For example, some of the lads had not the foggiest idea about arithmetic or algebra. That meant that some of us who had been lucky enough to have studied them before had to act as coaches or tutors for the lads who had not. This naturally slowed down the whole course.

In addition, it was not easy to take lads who had done hard manual labour and put them in a classroom and expect them to do that for hour after hour, and then to study at night as well. Having said all that, however, I certainly found my year at the Scottish Labour College was a most valuable experience. It meant coming in close contact with John Maclean and knowing his method of teaching economics. It also meant generally getting a broader insight into the labour movement, not merely the mining industry.

Maclean struck us as a tremendous personality. His method was the old-fashioned style of lecture, explanations on the blackboard while we sat taking notes, and then questions and discussions afterwards. And then sometimes he would tell one of us: "You'll have to come out next day and give your impressions of this lecture." I can remember that we would be studying much of the night to make sure we knew the subject, but next day John would come in and apparently he had forgotten what he had asked us to do and we would be quite relieved. He would forget for a day or two and then he would suddenly come back and say, "Right, come out and give us your lecture now." This method kept us on our toes the whole of the time.

There were only nine full-time day students at the Labour College: three of us from the Fife miners' union, three from the Lanarkshire miners' union — Andrew Fagan, William Allan, and William Crawford — and James Hunter from the Ayrshire miners' union. Robert Spence, who was much older than the rest of us, was sent by the Glasgow toolmakers' union. Later on he became Labour M.P. for Berwick and East Lothian.[3] Then there was a lad from Canada, whose name I cannot now remember, who had been a lumberjack and who was interested in Marxism. He had seen something about the College in a Canadian journal and came across as a private student without being sponsored by any trade union.

One or two of the lads were real characters. Andrew Fagan of Blantyre, from the Lanarkshire miners' union, was certainly one. Fagan had come across from Ireland at the age of seventeen. He had had little or no schooling and arithmetic and algebra were completely foreign to him. But in the most difficult subjects, such as trying to get an understanding of Dietzgen's *Science of Understanding* and *Philosophy*, on which John Maclean lectured and which were part of the reading we had to do, Fagan curiously enough was the outstanding pupil in the College.[4]

Fagan sat beside me in the classes and I got quite friendly with him. Even those intimate with him would not have known that he was actively associated with Sinn Fein. One day Fagan said to me:

"Do you stay out Kelvin Hall district?"

"Aye."

"I'm going out that way today," he said. "Do you know a wee sweetie shop out there in ————— Street?"

"No, I don't," I said, "but we'll find it."

So when the College finished that day Fagan and I walked toward the Kelvin Hall area, where I stayed in the local school house with the janitor, Wullie Currie, and his family, who were relatives of John Bird. Fagan had a parcel under his arm. We were not sure where the street was that Fagan was looking for so he said he would ask the policeman who was on point duty at a street junction. He just marched up to the policeman and asked where the street was, and was directed. He found the street and handed the parcel in at the sweetie shop.

Next day he said to me, "You wouldn't know what was in the parcel?"

"No."

"Oh," he said, "that was some revolvers and ammunition. I just drop it in there at the shop and the sailor picks it up and takes it in his kit bag."

I did not know who the sailor was and I did not ask. I did not ask either where the sailor took the parcel, though I could have made a good guess. The remarkable thing was that Fagan had the parcel under his arm when he had marched up to the policeman on point duty.

This was the one and only occasion Fagan and I quarrelled. I objected to him having the parcel at the College. It could have incriminated all of us, especially John Maclean and of course the whole Labour College movement.

That same afternoon — it was in May 1921 — there was a raid in Glasgow by the I.R.A., a police black maria was ambushed, a police superintendent shot, and an I.R.A. prisoner in the van rescued. Paddy Lavin, an Irish lad who was secretary of the Scottish Labour College, was arrested that night and so was Fagan. There had in fact already been raids almost weekly on Paddy Lavin's office by the police, who were regularly visiting people suspected of being associated with the I.R.A. Paddy had offered to give them the key of his office so that they could come in whenever they felt like it.[5]

Fagan was kept in jail for six months without a trial and then released. When some of us from the College visited him in jail, he said: "Those stupid so-and-so's that act as detectives were hunting all over the house. I said, 'What are you hunting for?' 'Ah,' they said, 'we're hunting for ammunition.' I said, 'What the hell are you looking up the chimney for? Do you think I keep ammunition behind the fire?'."

That was the kind of lad he was. But they got nothing from him. It was a good job that Fagan had got rid of his parcel the day before his arrest or all of us at the College would probably have been arrested too for activities that we were not actually engaged in.

I had no more contact with Fagan after I left the College in the summer of 1921. Years afterward I learned he had eventually got work on the roads with Lanark County Council and by then was a foreman.

The leading lad of the three from the Lanarkshire miners' union was Willie Allan. He was younger than me. Like Andrew Fagan, he lived at Blantyre. Willie was of Polish extraction and had been reared as a Catholic. He had a continual fight on his hands at home because his people were still staunch Catholics but he refused to have any connection with the Church. I remember he used to joke that every time his mother paid over a shift to the Church he took another shift off to compensate.

Willie was a very brilliant young lad, a very capable, powerful speaker. He was also a wonderful mimic. He could mimic all the Lanarkshire and Scottish miners' union officials and often he had us in stitches at his performance.

He made a tremendous impact on the Lanarkshire coalfield. Later on, after leaving the College, he continued his work in Lanarkshire in the Minority Movement and the Communist Party.[6] He became an executive member of the Lanarkshire miners' union, then in 1927 he was appointed its general secretary. He was also one of the panel run shortly after that for office in the National Union of Scottish Mine Workers, and as he had Lanarkshire and Fife behind him he should have become automatically elected to the secretaryship. However, in the struggle that developed, as I will explain below, he was denied the appointment.[7] In the subsequent struggle, during which the United Mineworkers of Scotland was inaugurated, he was automatically asked to be its general secretary.

John Welch, one my two fellow miner students from Fife, came from Cowdenbeath. He was very friendly with William Watson, M.P. for Dunfermline Burghs, and was his protege. Watson and his wife actually financed Welch for a second year of study at the Central Labour College in London when he finished his year at the Scottish College.

Welch was a member of the Labour Party, without any Left leanings at all. He was good at many of the subjects some of the rest at the College found difficult: English, arithmetic, algebra, bookkeeping, shorthand, and writing essays. But in grasping the essence of Marxism, the need for working towards a Marxist organisation and the political issues, he was not so hot. When Welch came back from London in 1922 he became interested in full-time Labour Party organisational work and became a paid organiser in the Edinburgh area. He was a member of Edinburgh Town Council from 1938 to 1948 and became a bailie, but died quite young in 1948. He was a nice, friendly, pleasant fellow.

The other Fife student was John Bird, a prominent Reform Committee man in Bowhill. He was a propagandist when I knew him first — one of the youngest but an exceedingly fluent speaker, with a good grasp of language. Bird was always very presentable, well dressed, and therefore had a very good platform manner. He was a force to be reckoned with in the working-class movement. As a less experienced youngster I was surprised that, when it came to the examination at the Fife miners' office at Dunfermline for entry to the College, Bird took less marks than I did to qualify. But because we were friendly before the examination we arranged to "dig" together while at the College with some relatives of Bird in Glasgow, the Curries, at Kelvin Hall school house. We were thus in close association for all the time Bird was there.

Bird had early come under the wing of John Maclean. Maclean had close associations with the Left group at Bowhill and on his earlier visits there he had been impressed by the ability of Bird. That was during the war, and at that time Maclean was most anxious to keep the young likely lads from being drafted into the army. As there was unemployment and part-time employment developing in Fife, and the coal from South Wales was much more important to the war effort, Maclean got in touch with the South Wales comrades and arranged with A. J. Cook that Bird should be given employment at the colliery where Cook worked and that he should reside in Cook's own home. Bird had therefore left Fife for a period, worked in Wales, and stayed with A. J. Cook. When he came back he was even more active in the Miners' Reform Committee in Fife leading up to the 1921 lock-out.

There is no doubt that Bird was a remarkable man in many ways. While not given to sound, solid organisational detailed work, he had a flamboyancy, an effervescence, an ability to attract attention, to think schemes up which would bring about publicity. Like Willie Allan, Bird had a rather lighthearted approach to most problems. But he had an exceedingly facile mind. He was inclined to stunt displays in order to bring out the point, and liked to show off. We used to call him a stunt merchant. He was always thinking out new ideas of that sort.

He also had this same thing concerning his appearance. In those days most of us miners dressed in solemn dark-coloured clothes — a blue serge suit, white shirt, and black knitted tie, when you were dressed up. Wages were very tight. You could maybe afford shoes at 7s. 6d. to 10s. (37½ to 50 pence) a pair.

If so, you could consider yourself lucky. But Bird did not believe in dark-coloured clothes. He had got to get light-coloured, well-cut clothes: no tie, but rather bows or fancy shirts. He would always have some glittering badge in his buttonhole. One morning when we were travelling back to College after a weekend in Fife he was wearing a beautiful pair of brown shoes.

"Hallo," I said, "there's surely somebody been treating you?"

"Oh, aye," he says, "my mother, my mother gave me that pair of shoes."

"Where did you get them?"

"In Bowhill."

"Oh, by Jesus!"

"They should be good," he says, "they were three guineas."

That was typical of Bird and showed how foppish, or exhibitionist, he was. His parents spoiled him, in contrast to his rather uncouth brother George. But Bird could use this talent, if I could call it that, for good purposes as well.

9

THE BOWHILL STRIKE
AND PAPER MONEY

BIRD was an active member of a very big influential group of militants in Bowhill. Bowhill was without doubt the hub of the Left movement amongst the miners in Fife at the time.

In August 1920, the month before we began at the Scottish Labour College, Bird took an active part in a local strike at Bowhill pit. This was a local issue affecting wages and working conditions in the pit. The Bowhill Committee were unable to resolve the dispute with the management and decided to call a strike. But the Fife miners' union central officials in Dunfermline, under the leadership of William Adamson, the general secretary, refused to recognise the strike. The decision of these officials could not be overturned till the next Delegate Board meeting, which was some four weeks away. In the interval there would be no strike pay available for the Bowhill men.

At this time the miners in general were showing an increased degree of militancy. There was also a keen fight within the Fife union as to whether or not democratic control and the wish of the majority should prevail, or whether official control from Dunfermline should be maintained. So this was the background to the Bowhill strike, the question of majority rule, greater democratic control, or officialdom.

The Reform Committee lads who were active in the union were confident that they could get adequate branch support for making the Bowhill strike official. So there was a feeling that in the course of time strike pay would be paid. But the Bowhill branch committee, under the influence of John Bird particularly, decided on an adventure that had never been tried so far as I know anywhere else in the British trade union movement.

Bowhill had been a centre of militant political and trade union activity for many years. It was one of the centres regularly attended by John Maclean. He had lectured classes there on Marxian economics, industrial history, and so on. And the question of what was money, what was the value of money, was one that was being regularly discussed both by the older comrades and by the younger ones with whom Bird was associated. The idea that money was merely a paper form of exchange and had of itself no real value but only had the value for which it could be exchanged, brought the Bowhill lads to the decision that they would print their own money. Probably their idea arose partly because certain Co-operative societies in Fife issued special tokens for co-operators to use in place of money. So the Bowhill committee, wanting to extend this and do something dramatic, even if it was a stunt — for that was one of Bird's favourite lines of approach — had a meeting with all the traders. They told them they were going to issue money and guaranteed they would make this good eventually. This, however, was a gamble; it was taking a great risk.

But the Bowhill committee went ahead and printed paper notes, with the designation of a pound value, ten shillings, five shillings, half-a-crown, two shillings, and so on. The notes were signed by the four branch officials, including Bird as delegate, and Jimmy Galloway, the secretary.

I remember attending the first meeting when the Bowhill branch paid out strike pay with their own paper money. Most of the strikers were incredulous and thought it was a game. But the young lads said, "All right, we'll test this. We'll go and buy a packet of Woodbine." They tendered a branch paper note for a small purchase of Woodbine and got back coins of the realm in change. Then there was whoopee. They said, "This is good."

So the branch continued each week issuing these paper money notes. When the delegate conference of the Fife miners' union did take place, the decision — as Bowhill had hoped and anticipated — was to recognise and make the strike official. Thus union funds had to be paid retrospectively to the day that the strike had broken out. When this money was eventually paid to the Bowhill branch committee they went round the shopkeepers, took in their own branch paper notes and redeemed them with the strike pay from Dunfermline.

Word got round, however, that enquiries were being made by H.M. Treasury about "forging" of money. The branch were not too sure of their legal position. So they burned all of their paper money they could get their hands on, though I believe one or two of these notes are still in existence.

It was the first time that I know of that a branch committee had issued its own money and that shopkeepers readily accepted it. And it was a novel way of proving John Maclean's Marxian economics points that he had been making to his classes at Bowhill and elsewhere.

But the Bowhill strike was significant in another way, too. It was allowed by William Adamson to drag on and on. My view is that the delay in settling it was part of a deliberate policy on the part of Adamson, in collaboration with the Fife Coal Company. Once it had been decided to give strike pay to the strikers in Bowhill, Adamson wanted to drag out that strike so that eventually it would almost drain the union of its financial resources. Then he used the fact that there were not funds left to pay any other strikers because the Bowhill men, under their Red influence, had usurped all the strike money — money that should have been available to the whole of the men when the 1921 lock-out came along. This was used as a powerful lever and argument against the militants in the Fife miners' union. The Bowhill dispute could quite well have been settled if the officials at Dunfermline had come in to support the Bowhill men instead of allowing the strike to drag on and on.

Many of the eventual difficulties in the union — lack of funds, inability to pay affiliation fees to the National Union of Scottish Mine Workers, going into arrears, and so on — probably could be ascribed to the Bowhill dispute. But instead of all this being the responsibility of the Reds who supported the Bowhill strike, it was, in my view, the responsibility of Adamson and his colleagues, who used it deliberately to try and discredit the whole of the movement that was gaining strength in the Fife coalfield at the time.

10

JOHN MACLEAN

JOHN Bird, as I have mentioned, had early come under the wing of John Maclean. When we were at the Labour College, Maclean made a special point of always taking Bird along with him to his meetings and showing copies of the Bowhill paper money. Maclean used to deliver lectures and put arguments all over the West of Scotland on this question of the Bowhill strike committee issuing their own money.

During our period at the Labour College, Maclean was very active in outside agitational work, particularly agitation amongst the unemployed, as well as organising the College classes. He always used to bring out the value of a knowledge of Marxian economics as a guide to action, and he always opposed the idea of acquiring knowledge for its own sake at his classes. He also tried to make us aware of the tremendous efforts being put up to subvert the trade union and labour movement. For example, he held the view that Omar Khayyam, widely quoted in the movement at that time by people who wanted to show their knowledge, was deliberately being pushed in the trade union movement in order to develop the idea that there was no need to be active in agitational work — the idea of "have a good time, drink up, boys, and be merry, for tomorrow, why, tomorrow we are with the days that are gone".[1] Maclean argued that this was poison for the labour movement and that we should fight against it wherever it was raised.

In addition to that, according to Maclean, a wide section of the active lads were being misled by a damaging little book that had been planted in the socialist movement here. It was one of the publications by Charles Kerr & Co. of Chicago — *The Collapse of Capitalism*, by Herman Cahn.[2] Cahn's book was an alleged Marxian exposition of the situation and had been written towards the end of the war. Maclean argued that this type of publication was deliberately infiltrated into the movement to convince militants that they did not require to take any action, that things would by the very development of economics sort themselves out; that there was no need for day-to-day agitation, no need to fight because, basing ourselves on the knowledge of Marx, the changes would come around and the people would automatically overthrow capitalism and usher in the new system of society. That kind of argument was certainly fairly prevalent at the time on the basis of Cahn's book.

There were also the arguments trotted around at that time by Daniel De Leon, published in America, that it was wrong to participate in day-to-day agitation for improved wages or hours or for better allowances to the unemployed, and so on — the job was to carry out a continual agitation until we had converted everybody to become socialists and then to make a fight only for socialism. These kinds of arguments were combated fiercely by Maclean.

He himself had an argument that was similar to part of the argument used by Cahn on the question of money — if money came to be seriously inflated it would bring about the collapse of capitalism. Maclean in these arguments with us tried to describe the use of money, the basis of gold and its reflection in paper notes. He said that one of the ways to upset capitalism and reduce the cost of living would be for the trade unions to argue for the destruction of Bradburys, as he called the £1 and ten shilling notes.[3] This was a big argument used by John Maclean in the class work. I have long held the view that it was the agitation of John Maclean on the need to destroy paper money to demonstrate that paper money only had value provided people had faith in it, that led to the experiment in Bowhill when John Bird and his fellow militant there, Willie Kirker, who were definitely under the influence of Maclean, issued the paper money in the local strike in August 1920. There was no question that it came out of the air. It was a matter being peddled in the classes run by Maclean at the time.

When Maclean was doing his agitational work he used John Bird and myself from the College at his evening meetings whenever he could. We helped to sell pamphlets, distribute leaflets, and so on. As part of our training in public speaking, we would be put up to chair the meetings. It was at this time that Maclean was conducting a wide agitation and he had formed, a few months before we began at the College, his "Tramp Trust Unlimited". These were his lieutenants. One was Harry McShane. Harry was very hard working and sincere and worshipped Maclean. No job was too menial or difficult for McShane.[4] But the other members of the Tramp Trust were a bunch of hangers-on, spongers living on Maclean's popularity and exploiting him. There was Jimmy MacDougall, whom I have already mentioned. Then there was a big ex-policeman, Sandy Ross. He was a big lad, powerfully built, with big feet. He used to describe to his audiences how he joined the socialist movement. He said he was listening to a socialist speaker, very intently listening to him, when he felt a terrific pain in his feet. He felt the pain passing from his feet right up his legs and then up into his brain. He said that was his brains leaving his feet and going to his head.[5] The other member of the Tramp Trust was Peter Marshall.[6]

We were very bitter about what we considered was the use made of Maclean by MacDougall, Ross and Marshall. Maclean could get well-attended meetings and big collections. He lived on the barest expenses for himself and at all times used that money to develop the movement as he understood it.

I remember as a green propagandist going out with Maclean to Motherwell. Maclean had advertised this meeting as the "Second Battle of Motherwell'. I was not aware at that time of the first "battle" but found out later that it had taken place some months earlier, in June 1920.

When the meeting I attended took place there was a colossal crowd. Motherwell was a strong centre of the Orangemen. The Orange leader at that time was Sir Edward Carson.[7] Maclean got up at the meeting and attacked Carson, and the whole line of the British in Ireland — the scandalous use of the Black and Tans, the whole concept of Britain's interference and savagery, the use of Scottish troops.[8] He made special reference to Northern Ireland, Carson, and the Orangemen. The audience was getting more and more out of hand. The shout got up, "Up Derry!" The crowd rushed in. The platform went over. We had visions of an awful lot worse happening. But while there had been a concentration of supporters of Carson to have a go at Maclean, his open advocacy of support for the struggle in Southern Ireland and for the Sinn Fein led to a counter shout of "Up Dublin! Up Dublin!" It was the first time I had heard it. Irishmen and Irish connections from all over Lanarkshire had come in to protect Maclean in this Orange stronghold. There was a rally by the "Up Dublin!" boys that pushed the "Up Derry!" boys back and they put a solid phalanx round the platform and said to Maclean, "Go on, John, we'll see that you get leave to speak."

It finished up as an extraordinarily successful meeting. But what I was concerned about was that Maclean had made no attempt to get support prior to that meeting. It was a support got without his effort and apparently without his knowing. But he went into the lion's den, flung challenges right and left, and finally came out of it very well.

In May 1921, towards the end of my year at the Labour College, Maclean was again sent to prison for three months for sedition. I visited him regularly in prison in Glasgow, along with Harry McShane. Even in prison Maclean was a remarkable man. He wore a lounge suit, not prison clothes, because he was a political prisoner. We asked him, "How are you feeling, John?" But he had not time to tell us how he was feeling. All he wanted to know was how were the classes going, how was the College going, how were the meetings going, what was planned for the future. He was just a hive of energy. He would tell Harry McShane where he was to have the next meetings and what he was to do. He had a pamphlet drafted out — McShane was to get it filled in. All the time we were there all he could talk about was the movement, the developments, nothing personal. It was the struggle outside, how he saw it, and what he wanted done before we came back to see him again. Poor old Harry McShane had just to be like a wee sponge and take it all in, take all the advice and guidance he got and make sure he reported to Maclean next time he visited him. Maclean was really a most amazing personality. It was not possible to come in contact with him without having a great respect for him.

At Maclean's trial and sentence three years earlier, in May 1918, to five years' penal servitude for sedition, one of the witnesses against him was a lad employed by the Fife Coal Company as a safety inspector, John Ford.[9] Fife miner militants never forgot that, and those of us — Abe Moffat and Alex Moffat, John Wood and myself — who had some influence in the miners' union in later years always went to town on Mr Ford if he was brought into

44

our meetings with the Fife Coal Company as an alleged expert on safety.[10] We never let a chance slip of trying to get our own back on him for his traitorous conduct in acting as a spy against Maclean in 1918.

While I was at the Labour College I noticed that Maclean's behaviour was beginning to be affected by his prison experiences. I remember on the night of the "Up Dublin!" boys and the "second battle of Motherwell", he said he was quite overjoyed by the response he had got at the meeting. He said to us, "All right, boys, I've got a steak pie in the house. Come home with me. We'll have our supper."

So we went to Maclean's house in Glasgow. There was Captain White, son of General White of Ladysmith fame, John Bird, and I think Harry McShane, as well as myself and Maclean. It was the first time I had been to Maclean's house. When we got in he looked at the dresser and exclaimed:

"There's been somebody in here. That sugar is different from what it was when I left. There's someone been in here."

I said, "Oh, I don't think so, John, there's nobody been in here."

"That's not where I left that sugar," Maclean said.

He had a big steak pie on the dresser and he grabbed that, went out to the ash bucket, and dumped the pie in it.

I remember big Captain White saying, "Hey, you silly so-and-so. I'm starving. I'll eat it."

"You can't take that, that's been tampered with," said Maclean.

"I don't care," said White, "I'll eat it."

But Maclean would not let us eat the steak pie. Instead he went out and bought fish suppers, and we had a fish supper and looked at the steak pie in the dustbin.

I remember another occasion, in the autumn of 1920, when this complex of Maclean showed itself. John Bird and I were accompanying Maclean to a meeting at Vale of Leven. We were chalking up that the meeting was to take place that evening, and because a lot of people travelled by train to the shipyards we were chalking all the pavements on the approaches from the station. Workers were coming in from their work in the early evening, and one lad came off the train, was overjoyed to see Maclean, approached us and said, "Hullo, John. Are you having a meeting here tonight?"

Maclean said, "Yes."

"Oh," said the lad, "that's good. Well you'll come up and see the wife and have your tea with us?"

But Maclean was not keen to go to the lad's house for tea. But the chap insisted — he obviously thought the world of Maclean — and we went along to his house for tea.

It was an ordinary working-class family. The wife of the house did not know we were coming but she laid the table, put what she could on it, and fried bacon and egg and sausage. When it was ready she said to John Maclean, "Here you are, John, just you sit here. The rest of you sit there."

But Maclean, instead of sitting at the seat she had asked him to sit at, went and sat at the other side of the table. And to cover it up I sat down at the seat John had been asked to sit at. I just looked at him, shook my head, and said to myself, "God Almighty, what's wrong wi' you, sir?" The incident made me feel very uncomfortable. I could not see Maclean's behaviour as reasonable or logical.

The third time something like that happened in my own experience was after I had gone back home to Fife from the Scottish Labour College. Maclean came through to speak in Cowdenbeath. Some of us of course went to the station to welcome him. When we were coming down from the station he said, "Oh, look, I've got a prescription I'd like to get made up that I'd prefer to get made up in Cowdenbeath. I don't want to go to the chemist's shop. Will one of you take it in?"

I said, "Aye, I'll take it in, I'll take it in."

Again it struck me that he was suspicious that if he went for medicine in Glasgow, where he was known, probably some alteration to the medicine would be given him.

It was while I was a student at the Labour College that Maclean refused an invitation from Lenin to go to the Soviet Union and receive care from medical specialists at a holiday resort on the Black Sea. The invitation was brought to him by William Gallacher. Gallacher had been out at the Communist International meeting in Moscow in the summer of 1920 with John S. Clarke, who was editor of *The Worker* and a regular propagandist and lecturer in Fife.[11] They came back when I was at the Labour College, and when there was a conference, which I attended, in Glasgow on 2 October to try and form a Scottish Communist Labour Party.

Various moves were being made at the time to try and get a unified Communist organisation in this country. The Communist Party of Great Britain had been formed at a unity convention at the beginning of August in London. Unity committees for Scotland organised the conference in Glasgow to discuss what steps could be taken. There had been a call from the Third International that there should be only one Communist Party in each country. Certain people were invited to Moscow to discuss this. They included Gallacher and John S. Clarke. William McLaine, one of our tutors at the Labour College, who was a member of the British Socialist Party, was a delegate to the conference in Moscow. John Maclean had been invited but was refused a passport by the British Government and had been unable to make the journey.

So when this Scottish Communist conference was held in Glasgow on 2 October I attended it as a delegate from the Fife Communist League. I remember this conference quite vividly. The same old differences of view were fiercely expressed. We had the Socialist Labour Party representatives who were against having a unified Party if the unified Party was to participate in parliamentary and local government elections and was to be affiliated to the Labour Party. Jimmy MacDougall, who was one of the speakers at the conference, was putting forward the point of view that John Maclean was trying to popularise at the time, and that was the formation of a Scottish Republican Labour Party. Maclean was considerably influenced by events in Ireland.

46

In the course of the conference, William Gallacher appeared and asked leave to address the meeting. He said he had just arrived back from the conference of the Third International in Moscow. Gallacher gave his report of that conference and urged that, as he and all the delegates there had agreed, there should be only one Communist Party in each country. He said the British representatives had agreed while in Moscow that they should come back and urge the formation of one Communist Party, a unified Party, unifying all those sections of the British movement that were in favour of affiliation to the Third (Communist) International, and that we should support this.

It was rather a stormy meeting, but finally it finished up with support for the proposal of one Party for Britain. A Provisional Committee was elected to meet the other sections of the movement in order to try and get a basis for agreement. The next we heard there was to be a conference called in Leeds early in 1921. The Leeds conference decided on one Party for Britain.

But at the Glasgow conference in October 1920 I noted particularly Gallacher's reference to his long conversations with Lenin, that Lenin had said he had a very high opinion of John Maclean. Those of us who were in close contact with Gallacher understood he was conveying privately to Maclean that Lenin had extended a special invitation for Maclean to visit the Soviet Union as their guest, and also for a period of rest and recuperation, as they were aware of what he was going through. They had had to treat many of their comrades for similar ailments.

Maclean was overjoyed at first when he was told this. But he was associating with the rump elements that were left out of the Socialist Labour Party in Glasgow, and who were using Maclean's popularity to try to keep their rump organisation going. They started a story that this was a method of getting him into a corrective camp; that the Third International were opposed to his Scottish Communist organisation; that he was not going to play the Third International role, so it wanted to make him a prisoner. Then Maclean blew his top. It was like the last one that spoke to him had the effect on him.

Subsequently I was shocked when Maclean made a bitter attack on Gallacher, along the lines that Gallacher was simply wanting him out to the Soviet Union so that he could be put in their concentration camps, and that would allow a free field for those that wanted to form one Communist Party throughout Britain. Gallacher was without doubt the closest friend, associate, and most loyal supporter that Maclean could have had.

It is a matter for regret that other people influenced Maclean in his period of illness and that the trip to the Soviet Union did not materialise due to John's refusal, and his health, due to continual overwork, gradually declined. I was very sorry about that because I thought Maclean was a remarkable man. I had the highest respect for him and it was a pity to see the effect that prison and a whole combination of circumstances had on him. His wife and family had left him by that time. He found this very difficult, and I do not think John really recovered from that.

My feeling was one of tremendous admiration and respect for a courageous fighter regardless of the odds. He maybe was not a good committee man. I could not see him, with his pugnacious attitude, becoming a good man in a Party, wherein you have got to give way with your own personal desires or wishes to conform to a line of action worked out in agreement with others. Maclean was a voracious reader, a tremendous intellect, but was essentially an individualist, at his best working in a group where he was the driving force and the others followed on. His premature death in November 1923 at the age of forty-four removed an outstanding leader from the working-class movement in Scotland.

11

THE '21 LOCK-OUT

TWO other things that happened while I was at the Scottish Labour College in 1920-21 were that I got married, and that the miners' lock-out of 1921 began.

The girl I married, in December 1920, was Helen Smith. Helen was one of a family who had originally lived in St Monance, one of the Fife fishing villages to the east of Buckhaven. Her people were employed in the fishing industry. Helen's father was a cooper to trade. Her mother before marriage had followed the fishing industry as well, as a herring gutter, travelling around during the herring seasons to the English fishing ports, and north to Fraserburgh and Peterhead.

In 1911, during a period of slackness in the fishing industry and when work was expanding in the mining industry, Helen's family had decided to come along from St Monance to the Methil district, where her father got employment in the then developing Wellesley Colliery. He was employed on the surface, but suffered a pretty severe injury and after becoming fit for work again he decided to go in for selling fish. So by the time I met Helen at Buckhaven her family had a fairly successful fish saleman's business. They rented the house at Methil in which they stayed, but in order to get facilities for fish-curing, stables, and keeping all the vans and storing boxes, they later bought a house at Buckhaven with a large back garden on which they built the outhouses that were needed.

When we got married, my wife had no personal experience of the life and conditions of the miners, although two of her older sisters had also married miners in the Methil-Buckhaven area.

At that time there was a serious housing shortage and it was exceptionally difficult to get a house when you married. Like nearly all the other young couples at that time, when we married we started in sub-letting a room from my wife's parents. This was a help in a way because when I was victimised for a lengthy period following the 1921 lock-out we were living in family, and thus the exceptionally low unemployment benefit was not just so harsh on us as it was on others.

My wife's parents, being of fisher extraction, were as was usual very religious in outlook, especially Helen's mother and her father's brother, who also lived with them at the time. Helen's father, however, did not trouble. When Helen and I got married we were married before the sheriff in Kirkcaldy by special licence. I can remember the look of incredulity on the part of my mother-in-law that we were not getting married in the church.

How often I got home from the Scottish Labour College to see Helen depended on how much money I had. But I used to try to get home about once a month.

A few months after we got married, the 1921 miners' lock-out began. That was at the end of March. I was still at the Labour College under John Maclean, but when the struggle broke out, the students decided that there was not any hope of carrying on studying in the College — their job was back in the coalfield. So at the beginning of the lock-out all of us left for home in order to participate in the struggle.

There are two aspects of the events of 1921 that I think are worth recording. First of all, the miners never accepted 1921 as a strike; they always claimed that it was a lock-out. The Government had decontrolled the mines just beforehand, and the owners issued an ultimatum that the mines would only continue provided reductions in wages were accepted by the miners. In this way they also gave notice to the safety workers who were employed in the pits. So for the first time in the knowledge of the trade union the miners and safety workers took joint action. Everyone in the pits was withdrawn — tradesmen, safety workers, pumpmen, winding enginemen joined the miners who were locked out. This created quite a furore amongst the employers, the Government, and the Press. They said we were completely damaging the industry for all time, that the pits would be flooded because pumping workmen were withdrawn. They said we were deliberately stopping the pumps and allowing water to creep up, and where ponies were still being used underground, as at Leven, they claimed that the miners were responsible for drowning the poor old ponies. We had this last question raised in the House of Commons by the recently elected Labour M.P. for Kirkcaldy Burghs, Tom Kennedy. Kennedy attacked this claim on the ground that the employers had had plenty of time to take the ponies up out of the pits into the fresh air above ground but that they had continued to allow them to remain underground, and that the employers themselves were responsible for not taking precautions to safeguard the lives of the ponies. This thing therefore eventually dropped. But meantime, in Fife as elsewhere, the coalowners tried to keep the pumps going by recruiting scab labour. They had conducted a campaign prior to the lock-out in the ranks of the students, and they were able to man a number of pits with misguided students and colliery officials and clerks. Before very long, however, the strongest opposition was evidenced amongst the miners over this. In almost every part of Fife, spontaneous mass meetings of the men almost simultaneously objected to the steam-raising and pumping being continued by the blacklegs. The mass meetings decided to march on the pits and demand the withdrawal of these men.

In East Fife about 3,000 men started at Leven Colliery. The police tried to stop them but they were brushed aside. The men gave the students ten minutes to make up their minds that they would be better to go home. Discretion was the better part of valour and they decided they wanted to go home. So did the colliery officials. The fires were then drawn, the pumps stopped, the machinery stopped.

Scenting victory at one pit, the miners marched from one pit to another right along the line, closing down every pit in our area. There were not enough police to stop this mass movement of the men. This was the first occasion we had seen big groups of men forcing their will on the employer in this way. In other parts of Fife similar things were happening. It happened at Kinglassie and up around Bowhill and in Kelty. An incident at Cowdenbeath got plenty of prominence, in which Mr Spalding, the manager at one of the collieries, was engaged in keeping the fires going.[1] He was chased out and the miners forced him to walk in front of them. There was a police baton charge and a number of arrests followed and there were lads who were eventually tried and imprisoned. The agitation for the release of a militant, William Easton, and the others arrested was a matter of tremendous importance at the time.[2]

The miners' conception of the struggle was that everyone left the pit. They were quite sure nobody would blackleg, nobody wanted to go down the pit and nobody could go without adequate knowledge and skill. So their job was to sit around and do nothing but drag out the time in the hope that all the coal in Britain would be used up, and eventually the shortage of coal would force the employers and the country to concede the terms that the miners wanted. That was the general approach and to try to get that changed and get the miners to play an active role, a positive role in the struggle always called for extreme effort. For example, because of the shortage of union funds it was necessary to make sure that the miners were not starved into submission. The cheapest and most effective way to feed masses of people with a minimum of money was to organise central kitchens, which would be run by the wives with the help of the miners themselves. The kitchens would cook on a mass basis. So these soup kitchens were opened up in each locality, controlled by the miners' strike committee. Strenuous efforts were made to obtain bulk food supplies, rather than distribute individual donations as strike pay. This meant you could prevent actual starvation from forcing a return to work.

The second aspect I would like to mention is the whole atmosphere that was built up amongst us at the time. There had been the development of the Triple Alliance at national level of the Miners' Federation, the National Union of Railwaymen, and the road Transport Workers' Federation. In all the negotiations prior to the 1921 lock-out there had been declarations of support, of strike action, by the Railwaymen, A.S.L.E.&F., and even the railway clerks. There were declarations of support also by the dockers, and other unions such as the E.T.U. London committee and the Post Office organisation. With such a wide expression of support nationally the miners were looking forward with tremendous enthusiasm to this new weapon that was being forged in order to fight in the miners' defence against the employers and the Government. There was the keenest anticipation of what was likely to eventuate from the calling into action of the Triple Alliance.

We were stunned when we came to realise that some manoeuvring was going on at London level that we had not known anything about, that Frank Hodges, general secretary of the Miners' Federation, was being involved in this along with Jimmy Thomas and C. T. Cramp of the Railwaymen, Harold Gosling of the Transport Workers, as well as others, and that there were doubts as to whether the actual sympathetic action by these other organisations was going to materialise.[3]

Our friends locally in the N.U.R. informed us that special meetings of the N.U.R. were being called to discuss whether or not they would accept postponement by the Triple Alliance of the proposed strike, or whether they would take action in support of the miners. We were informed that that night, Tuesday, 12 April, a couple of days before what became known as Black Friday, there was to be a meeting of the N.U.R. men at Thornton, about four miles from Buckhaven.

Thornton was a key railway station. It was our opinion that if we could stop Thornton we could paralyse the whole of the railway system on this side of Scotland. Accordingly, hurried meetings were arranged and it was agreed that we should have a mass demonstration from East Fife concentrating on Thornton and to get there at the time of the Railwaymen's meeting. There was also to be a simultaneous demonstration from Bowhill and district, converging on Thornton.

We were youthful and enthusiastic and understandably we made many mistakes in handling this demonstration. We had never thought out what were likely to be the consequences of taking 6,000 or 7,000 miners at ten o'clock at night into a small village. While we — David Proudfoot of Methil, Alex Gordon of Leven, and Bob Thomson and myself from Buckhaven — had personal leadership of most of our local people from East Fife, we did not understand the necessity for marshals to control the marchers and keep discipline.[4] All we were interested in was getting to Thornton with as big numbers as possible. If the railwaymen did not come out on strike with us that was too bad — we would use our power and strength to stop the railway junction anyway.

When we got to Thornton we found the Railwaymen's meeting was in the Town Hall. The hall was packed. But we walked in, we — the leaders of the miners' demonstration — marched up on to the platform and demanded that the Railwaymen come out on strike with us.

There was a furore in the place. The N.U.R. branch officials who were in charge of the meeting walked out. In consequence of that there was no official trade union branch decision. But the miners said that was all right. We had got fixed up with the militant railwaymen with whom we were associated and we decided we were going to picket the key points at the railway junction. There were locomotive sheds, the various lies where the shunting was done, and there was the station and the signal-boxes.

It was arranged that the East Fife contingent, under my leadership, was to go to the station and stop all trains coming through there. The other miners, from Bowhill and district, moved off to the other picketing points.

At the station we were having altercations with train crews as they came in. We got a number of them to put their engines into the sheds. The stationmaster was ranting and raving.

Eventually a signalman approached us and said, "Look, I want to give you boys a tip-off. We've just got it on the phone that the police force from all over Fife are converging on Thornton and there are armed marines also on the way."

We had a hurried consultation and said, "Well, we've done all we can. We'd better pull out." I suggested to our East Fife lads that instead of marching back up to Thornton village, which was about a mile-and-a-half away from the station, we would go home via the railway.

So we marched home by the railway branch line from Thornton to Buckhaven and Methil. We sent out advanced pickets to see if there was anybody trying to intercept us. But it had apparently never occurred to the police that we might be walking home along the railway. All of us East Fife lads managed to get home without any incident.

It seems, however, that incidents did develop in Thornton village. They had an innocent beginning. The lads from other parts of Fife who had marched up there felt, "Well, we want to have fish and chips and a bottle of lemonade." They crowded into the little cafe in the village. The wee Italian lad who owned it could not serve them as quickly as they wanted, and he started giving them cheek. So they stepped over the counter and served themselves. Most of it started in fun but it developed in earnest. Other elements tried to take advantage of this incident. Apparently there were some shop windows broken and some looting from them. We were also tipped off later that goods had been looted from some wagons at the railway junction.

We knew nothing about all this that night and I am convinced that no one in the East Fife contingent participated in that form of activity because we were out of the village at the time.

When the police buses turned up they by-passed Thornton in fact and went right on to Bowhill. By that time the Bowhill lads were straggling home, in twos and threes and small groups. As they approached the entrance to Bowhill, the police batoned them down and asked them, "Have you been at Thornton?" Their pockets were searched. The casualties included John Bird, my fellow student at the Labour College, and another militant leader at Bowhill, Willie Kirker.

I remember getting into bed in the early morning. My wife and I were staying with her parents in their house because we had not been able to secure a house of our own. I had just got into bed when my father-in-law came into the bedroom and said, "Is Johnny home?"

I wakened up and said, "Aye, what's wrong?"

"There's a sergeant and a picket of armed marines at the door with fixed bayonets," he said.

"Oh, aye," I said. "Is there anybody at the back door?"

"Wait till I see," he said. "No."

"Well," I said, "gie me time to get my clothes on. I'll scoot oot the back door and gie them a race for it. They're no' catchin' me as easy as that."

But, fortunately, when my father-in-law did answer the door to the marines they were asking for the hall keys to take over the big hall in the town. They had come to the wrong door — the hallkeeper lived next door to us. So it was a false alarm and I got back into bed.

12

PUBLIC SPEAKER

EVENTUALLY there were long drawn-out police cases in connection with the Thornton incident. Nobody from East Fife was involved. We were lilywhites.

Bird and Kirker were given three months' jail each and there were some twenty-three other miners who were drawn up in court cases. And this was eventually one of the things that our old friend Mr Adamson, general secretary of the Fife miners' union, used against the militant movement. He claimed that this mad action of the miners, landing in court cases, had actually involved the union in £7,000 legal costs to defend members.

The whole Thornton incident showed our inexperience, in the unofficial leadership in East Fife, in handling big groups of men. First, as I said, it was a mistake to take undisciplined, uncontrolled big groups into a small village late at night without seeing that marshals kept them disciplined, kept them entertained, and kept them doing a useful job.

Secondly, to march into a trade unionist strike meeting and demand that they take action again showed our enthusiasm but also our inexperience. If we had gone in and appealed to the Railwaymen as trade unionists to come out and take action in the common cause with us we probably would have had a better effect on the meeting. But they were loyal trade unionists—the N.U.R. had a reputation for that—and they had received a telegram from their accredited national official. They would have as loyally stood by the miners if the telegram had been different, but they had loyally carried out their trade union rules.

The final thing was that we did not think it was necessary to safeguard our railway contacts who appeared on picket with us at Thornton Junction station. But then the railway companies took action against them and dismissed them from their employment subsequently to the police action. We should have safeguarded these men. It was the flush of enthusiasm, inexperience and lack of political knowledge that I think was responsible for the mistakes we made. But the whole Thornton incident did show a real fighting spirit on the part of the miners who marched from East Fife and elsewhere and were anxious to make a real go on the question of the lock-out.

Two aspects arising from this Thornton incident had an effect on me. Bird and Kirker were advertised to speak at a mass meeting in East Wemyss and when those of us in the leadership in Buckhaven area went along there, some 700 or 800 people had gathered. We were still waiting on the arrival of the speakers when a motor cyclist arrived to tell us that Bird and Kirker would not be present. They had been arrested over the Thornton incident.

We were then in a wee bit of a difficulty. None of us present were accomplished speakers. We had spoken at trade union branch meetings. However, we all said, "All right, we'll have to go on." I said to Jimmy Hope, who was one of the local leaders from East Wemyss, "All right, Jimmy, you take the chair, speak as long as you're able, and I'll follow on." So Jimmy spoke for about twenty-five minutes and he was an outstanding success.[1]

I followed on, and I must have been successful too because we got a wonderful reception at the finish of the meeting. I remember when I came down off the soap-box, the boys said, "Very good. That was good, Johnny."

I said, "Aye, that's all right. But what did I say?"

But that was the ice broken for me, as far as public speaking was concerned. I had got over my stage-fright and was able after that to address public meetings without any trembling or butterflies in the stomach.

The second aspect arising from the Thornton incident was that when I went back to the Labour College, once the lock-out had settled down to a war of attrition, I had to go back on my own because John Bird was a guest of His Majesty. Bird did not get back to College at all before its session finished.

I mentioned Jimmy Hope of East Wemyss. Jimmy was an outstanding personality. His father had been under manager at Michael Colliery, at East Wemyss. That was before my time and I did not know him. Jimmy I knew by repute because he had been a young professional footballer, and before the war had played for Raith Rovers at Kirkcaldy before being transferred to Stoke City. Jimmy got married at Stoke and when the war interrupted football he came back into East Wemyss and started work in Michael Colliery. Unfortunately he suffered an injury there to his knee. After the war, he told Stoke he would not be fully fit; they asked him to go down and tried their best, but Jimmy could not get fully fit. After Jimmy became unemployed another football team came for him and offered to pay him wages for a year, in a gamble that they could make him fit. But Jimmy was too honest to take advantage of anybody. He said, "I don't think I could play in a manner satisfactory to myself. I don't want to let you down." So Jimmy continued working in the pit and carrying out his political and trade union activity in the village. He was a member of the I.L.P. after the war, but when his branch discussed whether they should go over to the Communist Party following its formation in 1920, Jimmy brought over the whole of his branch and formed a branch of the Communist Party in East Wemyss.

Jimmy was a very likeable and pleasant personality. But he was a curious character. I can remember how we tried in our speakers' classes when we were learning public speaking to polish Jimmy up, improve his pronunciation, his English, instead of speaking in the broad Scots Doric. We tried to mould Jimmy to the pattern of some of the leading speakers, to get him carefully to prepare his notes and to speak from notes. But if he had prepared for a meeting and had notes he would speak in a stilted fashion. He was restricted, stultified, not effective, and made a very poor impression. But if he was put up impromptu and had to speak without prior knowledge, he spoke in the broad Doric, he had a ready fund of humour which simply poured out of him, and he was one of the most attractive speakers that we developed in East Fife — provided always he had not got prior knowledge and a prepared speech.

13

'HOW THE HELL DID YOU GET IN HERE?'

THE 1921 lock-out ended in July after thirteen weeks of struggle, with the miners defeated and forced to accept big reductions in their wages. Just at that time I had finished my year at the Labour College in Glasgow and I returned to Buckhaven and looked for employment. My father and two brothers, with whom I had worked before going to the College, had taken no part in any of the activity in the coalfield at the time. But they were kept out of their jobs for three weeks after all the rest of the men had resumed work in the pit, and the only likely reason was my own activity during the lock-out.

This was the first time my father and brothers had actually been without work apart from periods when they were officially on strike. The fact that my father had to walk about the streets unable to get work had a profound repercussion on him. We had a terrible job to get him to go down to the Labour Exchange and sign on. He felt that it was a tremendous lowering of his dignity to go there and sign on to ask for charity, as he put it.

There was no work at all for me when I came back. It was a particularly difficult time in view of the fact that I had got married and now had added responsibilities. I was actually kept out of employment by the Fife and Wemyss Coal Companies for eighteen months after the lock-out ended. Then I managed to get back into Muiredge pit, which belonged to the Wemyss Coal Company, because the manager, Bob Mercer, was off ill.[1] I got started and was at work when he came back. I remember when he came round to my working place underground, he said, "Hullo, how the hell did you get in here?"

"H'm," I said, "it's a guid job that you take ill now and again. I'm in and you won't get me out without having a lot of trouble." We had an argument about it but no action was taken.

Muiredge pit was at that time exclusively got on the pick, that is, hand-got. There were eventually machine-got sections opened up. But the difficult geological conditions often prevented workmen from earning piece-rate earnings. So they had to approach the manager and ask for deficiency money to make them up to a reasonable wage.

Bob Mercer, the manager at this pit, was a real character. He seemed to enjoy having an argument, a tussle or a fight with any workman in the pit. His policy was that if a new man came into the pit and worked in deficient conditions, he made no allowance when he made up his pay. If the workman went into the colliery office to demand proper allowances he would probably get it, but only after a real battle; thereafter he would not have any further trouble.

If on the other hand the workman, having received less than the minimum wage, did not go in to make a real fight for his wages, then he never would get them made up in that pit again.

Bob Mercer used to make sure that I had more than the recognised wage. I think he hoped that that would shut my mouth. When the boys on the face would be grumbling at the wage they were getting I used to show them my pay line and say, "There, that's what you get if you shoot oot your neck. If ye are prepared to tak what comes tae ye, ye just have yersels tae blame."

Because giving me increased wages did not appear to shut my mouth, Bob Mercer resorted to another method. Any little out-of-the-way piece of coal that had to be won, I was always directed there. So that I could go ben to work and come back out the working place and very seldom see another workman. It was a question of isolation. I was so convinced that was so, that I deliberately for some weeks hardly filled any coal, just to see what the management would do. They never questioned what I was doing. This went on until a machine face-line was opened up in the section where I worked. Because I was being put into these isolated quarters, when the deputy or fireman came round we always engaged in lengthy discussions. The fireman became very friendly with me, so that as soon as Bob Mercer was on holiday, I said: "Look, I have been isolated long enough. What about giving me the next road on that machine face?"

"Oh, that's all right," the fireman said, "I've no objection." I was then promoted to the machine face, where I was beside the rest of the workmen and where the wages were better than they had been in those isolated, out-of-the-way pockets of coal that I had been asked to win out. I was there on that face-line until the lock-out or strike of 1926, following which I did not get back again.

14

UNION DEMOCRACY

IN this period after the 1921 lock-out there was developing in the coalfields in Scotland as a whole, but particularly in Fife, an intensified fight for broader control by members of the union as against the attitude of the officials. In 1922 and 1923 things were hotting up. All along, the miners in Scotland had wanted to merge all the existing county unions — in Fife, Lanarkshire, Ayrshire, and so on, which had full local autonomy and separate delegate conferences — into one union. Even before my time the Scottish miners had been fighting for this. They had actually carried the proposal by majority decision in their branches, but this was sidetracked by the officials calling themselves the National Union of Scottish Mine Workers. The officials' salaries and expenses would be met out of the county unions' affiliation fees to the N.U.S.M.W. But the officials and executive members of the N.U.S.M.W. retained autonomous power on all questions of policy within the county organisations. Thus when, in the later 1920s, David Proudfoot and I, after a series of ballots in Fife, were elected as agents, we took up office in the Fife miners' union, but the Executive of the N.U.S.M.W. refused to accept us as agents or to pay our salaries. The question of who were to be representatives on the N.U.S.M.W. from the various county unions loomed large as a very important issue.

Secondly, there was continual trouble in the Fife miners' union as to how policy should be decided. As I have already mentioned, the union in Fife was organised on a branch residential basis, that is, the miner joined the branch where he resided, not always where he worked. Sometimes the two coincided, but the basis of organisation was residential. A big town with 1,500 to 2,000 miners had one branch, just the same as the small rural village in an isolated area would be a branch. When it came to voting at a delegate conference of the union it was one delegate one vote. This meant that the small rural branches were getting a tremendous preference over the big branches who were representing the bulk of the membership. Always there was a demand for votes to be representative of the members. It was not practical that on every issue there should be a ballot vote. But there was a rough and ready remedy available that was contained in the rules: if a delegate requested it, there could be a roll-call vote according to membership, ascertained by the money sent in to head office by that branch. Thus if each branch member paid 6d. a fortnight contribution and a branch had forty members, that would register £1 a fortnight or £2 a month. If another branch had 2,000 members that would show in the increased financial returns from that branch. So it was possible to ascertain members' wishes by the branch financial vote.

The officials countered that by saying that although a delegate represented 1,500 or 2,000 men that did not necessarily mean that there had been a big turn-out at his branch on the occasion that he was elected. Thus this controversy continued.

Naturally, the progressive militant rebel elements that were opposed to official domination were in the main concentrated in the bigger residential branches. The desire to get the financial vote generally meant that the majority membership vote would carry the day and the officials would be defeated. And vice versa, the officials knew that if they could retain the one-delegate one-vote system, no matter the size of the branch or membership represented, they could always depend on the rural areas, where in many cases branch meetings were not even held.

In addition to that basis of conflict there was a feeling amongst the membership that they had been badly let down by the lack of a fighting leadership from their officials during and immediately after the 1921 lock-out. They had also been let down and disillusioned by the failure of the much publicised Triple Alliance. This reaction among the men was reflected in steadily growing anti-official attitudes.

This question was brought to a head when a financial vote was refused at a Fife delegate conference in 1922. Two years earlier the Fife miners' union had decided, under pressure from the Reform Committee, to elect their five representatives to the Executive of the N.U.S.M.W. by ballot vote of the membership instead of, as previously, appointment by the delegate board. When the first election took place in 1921, Philip Hodge, who was associated with the Reform Committee, and Adamson were at the top of the poll and got far more votes than the other nominees.[1] So Hodge and Adamson were declared elected, and a second ballot vote was held to get the other three representatives. This resulted in a complete defeat for Adamson's pals and a complete victory for the unofficial group who were opposing him. Kirker, Bird and Bob Lamb, all of the Reform Committee, were elected. But the chairman of the union, under Adamson's guidance, got the delegate board to cancel both ballots on the grounds that not enough members had voted; and the board then declared that the five sitting representatives, who were all officials, should continue on the Executive of the N.U.S.M.W. Then in 1922, when the elections fell due again, four officials and Kirker were elected. At the subsequent board meeting the usual demands were made, in terms of the constitution, for a branch financial vote. But the chairman, under Adamson's guidance, ruled the demands out of order. The reaction to this was that many of the bigger branches, anxious to bring pressure to bear on the officials, decided that if a delegate was entitled to be present at the board for a minimum payment (it was £8 a month, no matter how many members a branch had) then the branch should withhold the rest of its contributions and bank them in the name of the branch. It was felt that this would bring financial pressure on the union and would bring the question sharply to a head. This form of protest was gradually taken up by branches. But Mr Adamson, the general secretary, and his colleagues, decided to act against this pressure. They issued instructions by circular or through Press advertisements that where a branch was refusing to send in all its contributions to head office, members should not pay their contributions to the branch. Instead they should wait until a new branch committee was set up that would pledge itself to send all the money collected to the office at Dunfermline.

So that here we had the setting up of rival branch organisations. This then developed in branch after branch. In my own branch at that time, contributions were collected in the main village hall fortnightly. It was sometimes the men themselves, sometimes their womenfolk or youngsters who would go up to the hall with the union card and pay the contribution. But when this issue developed those of us who wanted to participate in the protest by withholding contributions sat in one part of the hall, while those that were anxious to support Adamson's attitude sat in another ante-room of the hall.

This division gradually came to a head. At the first delegate conference following this development, the police were brought in by Adamson and the officials, and put at the top of the stair in the union office at Dunfermline, so that any delegate from a branch that was withholding contributions would not be allowed to enter.

This was the first occasion that I know of in the Fife miners' union that the police were used to determine who would get into a union delegate meeting and who would be kept out. Quite a number of even those delegates whose branches were sending the contributions in full refused to go into a union conference under police protection.

In consequence there were meetings supporting the protest movement and the rebel Reform Committee that was conducting this struggle. Philip Hodge, who was at that time an agent of the union, spoke in support at several of these protest meetings. There were also as usual quite a number of stormy meetings at which Adamson and his colleagues at the Dunfermline office, Mick Lee, Jimmy Robertson, and others, were not allowed to speak.[2]

Eventually, under Adamson's influence, the organisation decided to suspend Hodge from office, pending the decision of a ballot vote.

When Hodge was suspended the dissident branches that had been favouring withholding contributions and had banked the balances, met in Cowdenbeath in December 1922 and decided to set up a Mineworkers' Reform Union for Fife. This came into being in January 1923. Tommy Smith of Lumphinnans was elected chairman of the Reform Union, David Proudfoot of Methil was vice-chairman, and Willie Kirker, Bowhill, a full-time official or agent. Kirker also had control of the financial side. When later on a ballot vote was taken of those miners remaining in Fife, Kinross and Clackmannan Miners' Association — which became known as the Old Union or "Adamson's

Union" — the recommendation for the dismissal of Philip Hodge was carried through. Hodge accordingly came over from the "Old Union" and became a full-time official in the Reform Union.

15

THE REFORM UNION

I HAVE often wondered on looking back on these events whether we militants always acted wisely, or if there were other means that we could have used to continue the struggle for democratic control of the union without a split in the membership and without setting up a rival organisation. Internationally and nationally the Communist International and the Communist Party were against the militant sections of the trade unions breaking away to form rival competing unions in a given industry, and always argued that the job should be to remain within the union, argue within the union, build up fractions, nuclei and groups and challenge what they called the reactionary leadership and if need be remove them and replace them with Communists or members of the Red International of Labour Unions.[1] But in 1922-23, when it became necessary to face up to the problem in Scotland, those who were members of the Communist Party in Fife acted according to their instincts and what they felt was best for the situation in Fife, without any special regard for advice from on high. Consequently, the Communist Party and the Minority Movement groups there swung in wholeheartedly behind the fight against Adamson. With the benefit of hindsight we were, in my view, out-manoeuvred to a degree and forced into forming a rival organisation. At the time, however, everyone associated with the movement was brimful of confidence and enthusiasm, was enthusiastic for this inter-union fight, and drove ahead to build up the Reform Union.

This meant a tremendous struggle for union membership. The drive for membership was so keen that door-to-door collections were resorted to, instead of the old practice of collecting union dues in a village hall or, where the pit was the only one at a village, sometimes at the pit itself. This meant that the big drive was to see whether the Reform Union or Adamson's union could win over the very large non-union element that existed following the 1921 lock-out. There were actually more non-unionists at that time among the Fife miners than there were union members. The Reform Union went all out to try to recruit the non-unionists. Before the split there had been a joining fee, an insistence that members must keep up their contributions, and arrears had to be paid off before any benefits were obtained from the union. But these things more or less went by the board from the formation of the Reform Union. No entrance fee was insisted on, and while week-by-week visitation was made to try to ensure union contributions were paid by the members, it was always very difficult to obtain payments of arrears.

The weak aspect of this system of regular door-to-door canvassing was that it was generally the wife in the house that paid the contributions and had the contact with the union collector. In many cases a man did not know if he was in the union or not. On the other hand, the system had a beneficial effect as well. Regular contact was maintained with the house, and grievances became known to the union collectors — not only union or pit grievances, but grievances and social circumstances of all kinds affecting the family. It had always been a feature in the mining villages that the miners' union dealt not only with grievances at the pit but also with housing problems, rent problems, problems of compensation in accidents, and even family difficulties. So close contact developed between the Reform Union and the miners' homes.

In addition to these activities the Reform Union decided to run a fortnightly newspaper, *The Miner*. It was under the editorship of Philip Hodge and was sold at a halfpenny a copy. A wide section of the miners contributed to the paper.[2]

In Buckhaven three of us — myself and Bob and Willie Thomson[3] from a fisher-miner family known as the "Caledonian" Thomsons or Thomsons "Caley", after the name of their fishing boat — used regularly to sell sixty dozen copies of each issue of *The Miner*. That meant we were entitled to threepence in the shilling for local branch funds for selling the paper, but so sincere were the two Thomsons — and I was persuaded to the same view — that no commission was ever taken by our branch.

I remember being asked to attend a meeting of the Executive of the Reform Union — I was a member of the Executive from 1922 to 1927 — where Philip Hodge raised the question of a lad who was a regular contributor to *The Miner* being in financial straits. This lad was not too strong physically, had been unable to continue at work, and was compelled to resort to selling needles and pins round the doors. He was making a bare existence. Hodge suggested that since this lad was a valuable contributor to *The Miner*, if he would agree to write a fortnightly contribution the Union should make him an allowance of £3 a week. That was agreed to. The lad was Joe Corrie, who went on later to be an exceedingly well-known popular playwright.[4]

So Corrie was actually saved from difficulty by the Reform Union. He wrote articles for *The Miner* under the title of "Tales of the Black Raw". They were very popular features of each issue.

The Reform Union also published Corrie's one-act plays. Round him, with all the Reform Union contacts and the contacts with the militants in Bowhill, there was set up a drama group that acted his plays under the name of The Bowhill Players. These were just ordinary workmen and housewives. They were in great demand and very popular and a real success wherever they went. There came a time when their success spread and some of the bright boys in London wanted to take them down there. They went, but it was a terrible mistake. The players were living their lives in the plays, not acting; but when they were taken down to London the bright boys there tried to polish them up and make them actors and actresses. This they could never do. The Bowhill Players were an outstanding success in the mining villages while they were acting Corrie's one-act plays which they understood and knew, but taken out of their element, dumped down in London and put on a big stage, they were lost. The venture failed.

Corrie began to get the idea that he was a second Robert Burns and that he would benefit from living where Burns had. He moved to Alloway in Ayrshire. He still managed to write plays, but the inspiration, the umbilical cord, was cut. Instead of going from success to success it was the other kind of story.

One thing I could never forgive Corrie for. I happened to read an account of his life that he had given to the popular Press, and in it he did not consider it necessary even to refer to the assistance given him by *The Miner* and the Reform Union which had paid him £3 a week when he was starving. I think that was unforgivable, for the militant movement to be ignored in that way.

The Miner newspaper had a very important propaganda value in the Fife coalfield. In addition to that, the Reform Union built up a team of speakers who, week by week, in season and out of season, spoke at the miners' rows. There was developed a very capable, fluent group of speakers.

Fife had always been a rather peculiar place in an organisational sense. In the mining villages there were local leaders who generally became known as the uncrowned kings of these villages. One man by his reputation could wield tremendous influence. And therefore building up a team of men of this kind could carry tremendous influence in a rapid fashion all over the coalfield.

One of these men was Willie Kirker of Bowhill, who had become a full-time official of the Reform Union at its formation. One of the matters that always gave me cause for regret afterwards was the failure of Willie Kirker to adapt himself to the changed circumstances.

I had always had a great respect for him. He was a solid, dependable, matter-of-fact local leader, not given to stunts or flamboyancy like his Bowhill colleague Mr Bird. I am not sure that Kirker was suited for organisational work in an office, and at the time we did not know just how difficult it was to work in an office with Mr Philip Hodge, the other full-time official of the Reform Union. Hodge was not the easiest of persons to get on with.

Kirker did not have a good business method for handling expense accounts. I would reclaim once a month my expenses for meetings attended, bus fares. He would pay you from his own pocket sometimes, because you were at a conference instead of at the office; he would take your receipt or sometimes not ask for a receipt. My own opinion is that Kirker got into financial difficulties mainly because of his lack of business knowledge and of business ability. As he got deeper into difficulties he started to drink and gamble to try to recover money, and got deeper into the mire. When the shortcomings were discovered he was suspended by the Union, then eventually dismissed, and handed over to the police. He got time for this and when he came out he went abroad to Canada. So Kirker was completely lost to the movement in Fife afterwards. I understand he subsequently returned from Canada and took up a boarding house in Aberdeen but I never met Kirker again after his Reform Union days.

When Kirker's position as full-time official became vacant, nominations were sent in by the branches, a short leet was voted on and then the men on the short leet went together round the county addressing meetings, to give members the opportunity of knowing who the candidates were, listening to their points of view, and thereafter electing one of them. The short leet was Tom Smith, who was the chairman of the Reform Union, Pat Connelly of Lochore, and myself.[5] That was the first occasion I ran for a full-time trade union job. We spoke in all of the branches throughout the coalfield. When the ballot was taken, Tom Smith was elected; I came a near second.

16

PHILIP HODGE AND DAVID PROUDFOOT

WHILE the Reform Union and Adamson's union were fighting for membership, the miners were the main sufferers. Their conditions were to a degree neglected. Adamson and his organisation had maximum support from the coalowners, so that they were anxious at all times to keep sweet with the manager at each pit.

At many pits the management were under instructions not to deal with the Reform Union delegates. Not all of them carried this instruction out. But it was an exceptionally difficult period to deal with individual, sectional or pit grievances unless one had to resort to strike action to try to remedy these affairs.

In addition to this worsening of working conditions in the pits there was also a development where personalities became more important in the fight than real policy divisions. This expressed itself, for example, in the desire to unseat Adamson as the Labour M.P. for West Fife. In the 1923 parliamentary election the Reform Union put up Mr Hodge as candidate against Adamson. Hodge at that time was a member of the I.L.P. We had a good election campaign in the coalfield. But Adamson drew 12,000 votes and Hodge 6,000. The Parliament did not sit long in 1924. Adamson was Secretary of State for Scotland in the MacDonald Labour Government. Then the J. R. Campbell issue came up, there was another election — the famous election — the Red scare or Zinoviev letter.[1] But in the 1924 election the Reform Union Executive, because of our campaign for unity and because we were not prepared to support Hodge in a personal vendetta, decided not to put up Mr Philip Hodge against Mr Adamson, though the Tories opposed Adamson on this occasion. Mr Hodge resented the fact that we were not contesting against Adamson, and on his own account wrote a circular letter urging the miners to vote for the Tory candidate in preference to Mr Adamson, and he also wrote to the local newspapers.[2] But because we believed in democratic control, the Reform Union Executive repudiated Mr Hodge and called upon the miners to vote against the Tory, defeat the Tory, and just vote for Mr Adamson. Mr Hodge was expelled from the I.L.P. for his line on this election. I mention this to show that it was not only the question of fighting for sound trade union principles that actuated some of the leadership in this struggle. There was a tendency in Philip Hodge's association with the Reform Union to over-emphasise personal dislike of Adamson, while the rest of us had a policy dislike of Adamson.

Hodge had a reputation in the miners' movement by the time I had come into it. The reputation was that he had been a mine manager, had been good to his workers, fell foul of the Fife Coal Company, left his job as a mine manager and became a collector full time in the Valleyfield area for the miners' union. His reputation spread all over the branches and there was a very favourable basis of support for him.

I found out when subsequently I became associated with Hodge that he was born and reared in Kelty as a miner. He had studied mining for his manager's certificate. Augustus Carlow, head of the Fife Coal Company, had been at the university studying to take his B.Sc. in mining but had to take his manager's certificate and sat the same exam as Philip Hodge.[3] Hodge claimed that Augustus Carlow never forgave him because, when the results were given out, Hodge had the highest marks and Augustus Carlow came only second. Curiously enough, they had one thing in common: they both had a stutter.

Hodge was a member of the I.L.P. until his expulsion after the 1924 election. He was a voracious reader. He was sort of detached from the miners. He was not a free mixer. He married late in life a lady who was a schoolteacher, and they went to live in a cottage they bought in Townhill, on the north side of Dunfermline — again, isolated from the miners. Any time that I attended his house I always felt that Philip was a very pampered individual. His wife would put his slippers on his feet for him, and attend to him. He was treated like a little kid, with his wife mothering over him. That did not go down very well with the tough miners with whom he was associated, but it had an effect, I think, on his approach to problems. Because he was not party to the real rough and tumble of the miner's life his association with progressive ideas and any rebuffs he was getting were not taken in the same spirit as we tough youngsters took it. He developed a personal animosity against those who were taking a different line from himself. This led to cleavages between us and Hodge.

A very different personality from Hodge was David Proudfoot of Methil, with whom I was very closely associated in most of our activities locally.

Proudfoot in many ways was a very remarkable man. He had been in the army during the First World War, and was a machine-gunner in an infantry battalion. He was sent out to Salonika, went up through Greece and Bulgaria, and like very many others contracted malaria while he was there and was a continual victim to it after the war. His health, with these periodic bouts of malaria, used to affect him materially. I have seen him leaving one night apparently in the best of health and when he did not appear next morning I found on going to his house that he was knocked out with malaria. It also had other effects. He was subject to fits of depression, in my view mainly arising from this illness of his.

I first came in contact with Proudfoot in rather curious circumstances. It was at the public debate in Buckhaven between Jack Leckie and Tom Kennedy that I have already mentioned, on the issue of parliamentarism versus anti-parliamentarism. I was the doorkeeper at that debate, acting for Jack Leckie's section, and Proudfoot, whose father had been in the S.D.F., was acting as doorkeeper for Tom Kennedy's side. We got conversing there, found we had a lot of things in common, and formed a friendly association. Gradually Proudfoot ceased to have any connection with the S.D.F. and lined up with the rest of us in the fight in the miners' union and so on.

Proudfoot's father was a docker employed at Methil docks. The old man was one of the quiet, solid trade union types, interested in what his son was doing but did not play an active part himself. Proudfoot's brother was a seaman. His mother was a very fine working-class type of woman, very kindly, always anxious to befriend any of the lads who went down to her house. You could always depend on hospitality when you visited her house.

Proudfoot was not a showy speaker. He was slow, steady, more of a stodgy speaker, but generally he had well-prepared material, well-thought-out arguments. I was the more fiery speaker. We made quite an ideal team, with him giving the sound solid stuff and me finishing up with the fiery agitational stuff.

He was a wonderful organiser. He did not spare himself. He worked like a Trojan when he was interested in anything that was being undertaken. His difficulty, in my view, was his inability to work harmoniously as a collective member of a team. He would work with a team provided he proposed the action that should be taken and the group were carrying out his proposal, then he would work himself to the bone and not spare any others in the doing of it.

The second difficulty I had with Proudfoot was what I might term his inability to last the course. For example, he was one of the leaders in the formation of the Reform Union. He took part in the inaugural conference and was appointed vice-chairman at the preliminary meeting of the Union. He conducted a tremendous amount of agitational work in the building up of the Reform Union. At that time he was checkweigher at the Wellesley Colliery at Methil, and he used his position as checkweigher, and the security and influence that gave him, to build up the Union.

Proudfoot also sold a tremendous amount of Communist literature at the pit and while there he accepted responsibility along with a group of us for issuing from July 1925 the first pit paper that was issued in Scotland, "The Spark". It was issued at the Wellesley Colliery and had a colossal sale. It was a four-page, typed and stencilled paper.[4]

On the other hand, Proudfoot was the first of the group associated with the formation of the Reform Union to cry that it was time for a halt. He passed out of activity for the Reform Union and associated with others who were anxious to heal the split in order to get one union in the coalfield. The Miners' Minority Movement, formed in January 1924, as the militant, largely Communist sections, and the Communist groups were arguing at that time, up to 1926, for the liquidation of the split to try to form one union. But while the rest of us were willing to take that course by working within the Reform Union to convince our colleagues and associates, Proudfoot dropped out of the Reform Union because they did not immediately accept the line he was arguing, and he concentrated on his work at the pit and on Communist Party political activity. The same tendency showed itself later in the United Mineworkers of Scotland, as I shall mention.

But Proudfoot was, in my opinion, a remarkable personality, a tremendous driving force. He had got weaknesses like many others. But he was a positive force for advance in this area.

17

UNITY AND
RED FRIDAY

FROM about 1924 or so there were continual efforts being put up, especially at pit and village level, to try to get common action between members of the Reform Union and Adamson's union. In most cases ordinary rank and file members of both unions were in favour of common pit action on grievances. But the attitude of Adamson, his Executive and their officials at all times was to oppose any form of unity or joint action, to oppose any suggestion of a healing of the split — everything was to be carried on as it was.

The Reform Union sent delegates to trades and labour councils and thus associated with the Adamson union branches there. But generally the Adamson branches dropped away from representation on the trades councils, while the Reform Union in every case maintained its membership.

But in the Reform Union there came to be serious discussion as to where its future lay. The question was whether or not in the interests of the miners there should be unity or whether we were best to carry on as a separate organisation. One had to be in Fife at the time to realise the real depth of antagonism that existed among many miners against having any association with Adamson and his officials. That point of view in the main was held by older, well-seasoned, responsible miners. The younger men could more easily be got to appreciate the need for unity and working together.

One other feature that was working very strongly in that direction was that there had been a change in the general secretaryship of the Miners' Federation of Great Britain. During the period of the first Labour Government in 1924, Mr Frank Hodges had fallen for the blandishments that he was far too bright a star to be blushing unseen in the M.F.G.B. quarters. He was a real smart boy. He should make his career in politics. He could become a Cabinet Minister. There was nothing to stop him being a Prime Minister. He fell for this and allowed his name to go up as a parliamentary candidate and was elected in 1923. He thought his influence was so strong in the miners' union, and his colleagues were so powerful, and his services so invaluable, that the miners' union would ignore the rule that a national leader could not be an M.P. or vice versa, that it had to be a full-time job for one or the other. So

Hodges was compelled to resign. And as a result of the new election there was brought into being a new type of secretary, a member of the miners' Minority Movement from South Wales, Mr A. J. Cook.

At this time the loosely federated Miners' Reform Committees that had existed in various counties became merged into the Miners' Minority Movement, or at least the miners' section of the Minority Movement. Whereas before the leadership in the main of the Reform Committees came from the old S.D.F. or I.L.P., with the formation of the Minority Movement the leadership came more under the influence of the Communist Party. The first organising general secretary of the Minority Movement was Harry Pollitt, and the miners' section had Arthur Horner as the contact man.[1] But A. J. Cook had been closely associated with the Reform Committee in Wales, and had become a very active member of the Minority Movement in Britain. The Minority Movement contacts all over the coalfield had campaigned for Cook and regarded it as a tremendous victory when he was elected in 1924 as general secretary of the M.F.G.B.

Arthur Cook was a much changed type of representative compared with what we had had in the old staid, solid, reform, half-Liberal half-Labour type of trade union official. He was a real fiery propagandist. You would think that the old chapel-going religious fervour of South Wales expressed itself in Cook's oratory. In addition to that he spent almost every weekend touring the coalfield urging unity amongst all miners and fighting for improved wages. So that he was becoming one of the most popular leaders the trade union movement in this country had seen.

Allied to Cook's propaganda of the need for the miners to fight for improved wages, and the need for the unity of the working class as a whole around these demands, the question of the role of the Reform Union in Fife became, as I say, a question for discussion. Those who were adherents of the Minority Movement, in line with the same propaganda that had been conducted by Cook, commenced the agitation in Fife for the merging as early as possible of the two miners' unions. The question of how best and how soon this unity was to be secured became very important.

Philip Hodge and some of those who were associated with him were opposed to having any truck with the organisation of Adamson, but the younger people, of whom I was one, gradually came to have a very powerful influence inside the Reform Union.

I remember being one of a delegation that went down to the M.F.G.B. conference in order to make as wide contact as possible at the conference with a view to raising the question of what the M.F.G.B. Executive and the conference could do to further the unity between the Reform Union and the Adamson organisation. In this we had a number of people who supported us. We had Horner and Cook himself, Harry Hicken of Derbyshire, Williams of the Forest of Dean.[2] That kind of contact was very valuable for us for furthering this question of getting together.

At the same time we had the defeat of the Labour Government in 1924 over the J. R. Campbell article and prosecution. J. R. Campbell was well known in the Fife coalfield as a protege and young lieutenant of Willie Gallacher. Campbell had toured the Fife coalfield on many occasions and had actively participated in the strike activity there.

Baldwin became the Prime Minister,[3] and an old friend of the miners in the person of Winston Churchill became Chancellor of the Exchequer. The Bank of England and Churchill decided that Britain should return to the Gold Standard in 1925. This of course had an immediate effect of making goods dearer that were going out of the country. Coal, which we depended on mainly for exports, was immediately affected. In Fife, as elsewhere, orders were lost to Spain and Italy. We used to say that Churchill was probably the best friend that British big business and financiers had. At the same time, because Britain's economy could not actually afford to be on the Gold Standard, it meant that tremendous sacrifices were being called for by the workers. So that in order to compete in the foreign markets Britain had to reduce its costs. The only way that the employers in Britain knew how to reduce costs was the old-established way: cut wages. That was why one of the best known statements at the time was the saying of Baldwin that the wages of all the workers must come down.

So it was in this atmosphere that the coalowners demended in the summer of 1925 from the miners' organisations that there should be a return to the eight hours day, that there should be an alteration in the wages agreement so that wages could be slashed. The miners had been compelled to accept an agreement following the lock-out in 1921 which decided that our wages in the future were to be determined by the auditor's report, actuarial findings of the industry, based on the employers' figures, and once all costs other than wages were met. The costs included directors' fees. Then the balance was to be divided eighty-seven per cent to wages, thirteen per cent to profits. And only if the balance increased would the miners get any increase. We did have at that time, however, a safeguarding minimum, and a guaranteed make-up payment for the lowest paid men. But in this new proposal of the employers in 1925 we were told that they had been losing substantially in the operation of their mines. As a matter of fact we used to say that the owners lived fat on their losses. And it was possible that they could show at every audit a loss in terms of that agreement while they were still realising substantial profits. We had other kinds of objections to this proposed agreement. For example, the best paying aspects of the coal industry were not included in the returns for these ascertainments. We did not get the by-products plants' returns being shown, and we did not get, for example, the brickworks, or private railways, private docks. There was also our claim that there were double-barrelled companies. So that the coal companies sold coal cheap to associated steel firms and bought steel from these firms at high prices for use in the pits. The books of such coal companies showed a loss at the ascertainments. But the owners and the shareholders recouped themselves from the increased value of the allied concerns. This was a sore point and was one that was being regularly explained to the miners by us in the Reform Union. So that employers came forward with a demand for an alteration in the ratio that a bigger share would go to profits, a lesser share to wages, that the minimum make-up guarantee provided in the ascertainments would be abolished, and we would have to take the figures that the employers produced in their books to the accountants for ascertainment purposes. At all times we were at the mercy of the employers' bookkeeping without us as miners having any say or control as to how coal should be sold, the price it should be sold at, and so on. That is why the miners bitterly opposed the new proposals of the coalowners when they were submitted in 1925.

The employers again had the complete backing of the Government, and the miners then started campaigning for support from the other trade unions. It was one of the strong propaganda points made by us at the time that whenever the Government and the employers in this country decided to attack working conditions or wages they started first with the miners. The miners were regarded as being the best militant fighting organisation in the ranks of the working class and if the miners could be taken on and defeated the other unions would be toffee, easy meat, for the employers. It was very important therefore from the entire working-class point of view and for the miners that the attack being launched by the Government and the coalowners should be met and be defeated.

This was the situation leading up to the events of 1925, with the gathering strength of the trade unions, the declarations of support, the real fighting spirit being shown by the miners themselves; so that a head-on clash was almost inevitable. This was the famous occasion, Red Friday, 31 July 1925, when the Government decided to buy time. They decided to give a subsidy to the employers, in order to allow a longer period for negotiations. This calling-off of the lock-out of the miners was hailed as a victory, the day on which the Government climbed down along with the coalowners from the proposed new attack on the miners. However, the Government — and Churchill especially, with his usual swashbuckling style — made it clear that the Government of the country could not knuckle under to the demands of irresponsible trade unionists, that the Government must impose its will; it was there to govern.

It seems strange to recall these words now, because they are used today by politicians, that the Government's job is to govern. And in order to meet the challenge, as Churchill put it, from the trade unions, the Government must set up its own form of organisation, an official blackleg organisation under Government supervision, payment and control, the Organisation for the Maintenance of Supplies (O.M.S.). And they used the whole period of the nine-months' gap that had been secured by the subsidy after Red Friday to actively prepare to defeat the miners and the trade union movement.

The complaint we militants had was that the T.U.C. and the unions did not also at the same time prepare to meet the ending of the subsidised period of nine months, which would be May 1926. It was again the militants in the trade union movement who kept arguing for preparations being made to meet the next round of assault by the Government and the mineowners.

18

SOME FIFE MILITANTS

AT that time the Reform Union and the Minority Movement in Fife could field a team of speakers who went out almost every weekend, explaining these things to the miners in their villages. This had a very stiffening effect in the Fife coalfield.

Lads who could either chair a meeting or speak included David Proudfoot from Methil, William "Mosie" Murray from Leven, James Cation from Crossgates, Peter Hastie from Windygates, myself and Bob Thomson from Buckhaven, Jimmy Hope, a particularly good propagandist, from East Wemyss. From West Wemyss there were two, Reddie Henderson and a Welsh immigrant, Bert True. There was a very solid lad, William Swain from Balgonie. And in the Dysart area there was our old friend Bob Lamb, and a young lad who was coming into prominence at that time, Jimmy Ord. There were in the Dunnikier area of Kirkcaldy Davie Martin and a very solid, reliable socialist, Johnny Moir. Then further west there was the group of people in the Bowhill area who could all speak — Bird, Jimmy Galloway, and some others. In Lochgelly there was Jimmy Stewart, who was chairman of the Reform Union, and a very able branch secretary, Jim Gourdie. There was another lad who could do propaganda work, Bill Crooks, who was in the I.L.P. In the Lumphinnans area there was also a group of fellows who could speak — Tom Smith, Bruce Wallace, who became the first Communist councillor for Lumphinnans area, and a young lad coming into prominence at the time — he was in the Young Communist League and the Minority Movement — Alex Moffat. Alex subsequently became very well known, along with his brother Abe, in the Fife coalfield. There was another lad, Peter Venters, from Cowdenbeath, and a group of speakers from Kelty, the home town of Philip Hodge, included John Gordon and D. J. Williams. Williams was a very prominent speaker who was a Welsh Labour College product and who was then working for the Labour College in Fife as a full-time tutor. Then there was another outstanding comrade from Valleyfield, Andrew Jarvie, who was one of the first to be removed from the position of being a checkweigher for participating in strike activity. He was the father of Jimmy Jarvie, who subsequently became well known in the Blacksmiths' union. Further west, into

Clackmannanshire, there was a team of young lads who were very active. The leading propagandist of that group was a young lad, Tommy Miller. Miller was known to me personally first of all as a racing pigeon fancier. But he was also a good organiser in the Clackmannan area. It was one of the areas in which the Reform Union was relatively weak organisationally. We built around Miller in the Sauchie area. He subsequently became a very prominent politician in Clackmannan and convener of the County Council.[1]

As I have already said, the local branches of the Reform Union were affiliated to the trades councils in Fife. In point of fact the Reform Union were the miners' representatives because in the main the Adamson union sought not to bother with that form of contact. I was appointed chairman of Methil and District Trades and Labour Council in 1925. Up to then there had not been a bar against Communists participating in Labour organisations. But at the Labour Party annual conference that year, the right-wing leadership got a decision to bar members of the Communist Party, and part of that decision was to change trades and labour councils into trade union organisations, with Labour political organisation to be separate. In the Wemyss Parish Council election in 1925, John O'Neill and myself were elected as Communist members of the Labour and Trades Council panel of candidates.[2] Out of the Parish Council of fifteen, thirteen came off this panel and the other two were agents of the Wemyss Coal Company. This election was a very important one, particularly with regard to what developed in 1926.

These were preliminary organisational steps that were taken, but they showed the wide support that the militant section, the Minority Movement section, and the Communist representatives were gaining in the Fife coalfield at that time. They also had a very considerable bearing on the very successful organisational work that was put in when the General Strike actually did take place.

I can remember well the militants that I mentioned who were in the Reform Union and Minority Movement. William "Mosie" Murray was leader of a group in the Leven area. He did a lot of work in Leven and after 1926 became a specialist in the organisation of the unemployed round the Labour Exchange there. The unemployed organisation that we militants in the area built up had Murray as a principal contact who dealt with appeals to tribunals and all kinds of detailed organisational questions that arose at the Labour Exchange. He also did propaganda work, collecting for the National Unemployed Workers' Movement, and he was reckoned to be the Labour Exchange poor man's lawyer.[3] He had the bar put up against him following '26 and, after a period of organisational work for the N.U.W.M. and the unemployed in Leven, he subsequently found a job with the Leven Town Council in their scavenging department and continued working there up till he retired. But even after that he closely maintained his association with David Proudfoot of Methil, particularly in the Co-operative movement. He became chairman of Methil and Leven Co-operative Society after Proudfoot died.

James Cation of Crossgates, whose father was a district councillor, took a much more progressive line than his father. James played an active part in the

Kirkland area, and was one of the men who later on was at the formation of the United Mineworkers of Scotland.

We had another real local stalwart in the more rural area of Windygates, in the person of Peter Hastie. Peter Hastie was one of the old type, a sound, reliable, dependable lad, and he had a very strong influence in his village. He was also associated with the Co-operative movement, Markinch Co-op. Like others he did not get back in 1926 and became a very successful insurance agent under the agency of Mr William Dunbar, our old tutor.

There was associated with myself in Buckhaven a group of young lads who were keen and energetic. There was Johnny O'Neill, whom I have already mentioned several times. Johnny did not get back either after 1921. He dabbled between organisational work for the Communist Party and becoming a shilling-a-week packman to try and get a livelihood. There was also in Buckhaven the Thomson family, the "Thomson Caledonian" or "Caley Thomson" family I have also already referred to. This really was a very remarkable family. There were six sons, only one of them married at the time we are discussing, and two sisters, neither of whom were married. The father, old Robert Thomson, was one of the leaders of the fishing community in Buckhaven.[4] He was coxswain of the lifeboat, and three of his sons were members of its crew. He was on the fishermen's Harbour Committee and well known and respected among the fishermen. But as fishing was in decline, he had gone into the mining industry and was only a part-time fisherman by this time. The family had all gone into the mining industry as well, although they sailed boats in the evenings and weekends.

The old father was a most remarkable man, not tall, but strongly built, with a straight back, thick brown hair and beard, and even though he lived till well over ninety, he was active, and never showed a grey or white hair in his head or beard. He had a most remarkable memory for local events. It had been a family tradition to pass down information about fishing events — how the harbour was built, who built it, what the cost was, the day it was opened, the boats that went to sea, when the church was built, the first minister — and many an hour I found very interesting in getting the old man to relate the history of the village of Buckhaven, and particularly many of the fishing stories.

The family at that time worked in Michael Colliery, which was about a mile-and-a-half from where they stayed. While the sons would take the tramcar to go to their work, old Robert walked along the beach to his work and walked back, regardless of the state of the weather. Even when he was getting over the age of eighty and towards ninety, you could always find him walking around, apparently a very fit man.

This family got the name of being tight-fisted, mean and tight-fisted. But anyone who knew them, knew differently. Not one of them smoked or took a drink, which was quite a remarkable thing at the time. They lived on the seashore and used to gather sea-coal from the seashore and always kept the house well supplied in that way.

The family became interested in politics and became close associates of mine and the others who were in the movement at the time. I remember, following the end of the First War, when things were rather difficult in Russia, there was a campaign conducted in this country of aid to Russia. First of all there was a collection of working tools to send out. This Thomson family organised and led that activity. In spite of the accusation that they were tight-fisted, the unmarried sons voluntarily levied themselves five shillings a week, and paid that every week while this committee for aid to Russia was active.

Two of the brothers, Bob and Billy, who were most closely associated with me, used to sell the Reform Union's paper *The Miner* each fortnight with me, as I have said, and although we had a big sale no commission was ever taken by them for that work. Bob was active in the Reform Union, the Communist Party, the Co-op and, later on, in the United Mineworkers of Scotland. He sat on the board of the Buckhaven Co-operative Society along with me, but he had to retire from the board because his son got a job in the dairy. He then became a member of the Co-operative Education Committee and continued on that until his death. He was also associated with youth activity in Buckhaven, was secretary of the swimming club, spent much of his spare time at training the youngsters to swim and in life-saving. He did all this voluntarily till those of us who were on the education committee decided that if he was to do that he should be employed by the schools and paid a fee.

In addition, if there was to be a flag day then every organisation felt it advisable to get in touch with Bob Thomson: lifeboat, seamen, and what have you, he would be the active spirit, organising it, collecting, banking the money and handing over the cheque — all of it done voluntarily. In subsequent times he became the organiser and chairman of the Old Age Pensioners' Association, and again nearly all of the detailed organising work was done by him.

I remember I had to persuade Bob in later years to stand as a delegate of the National Union of Mineworkers. He was persuaded eventually, was elected, and later on was lucky enough to come out of the ballot as a delegate on a miners' fraternal trip to Czechoslovakia.

The Thomson family were very meticulous in everything that they attempted to do. You could always depend upon it that if arrangements were made, that we had to do a meeting, street chalking, or any detailed work, every one of the "Caley" family could be relied on to be there at the time mentioned. In all my experience there was no family for whom I had more respect and more liking and more actual admiration. The whole lot of them were of the Jimmy Higgins type: they did not want to get the prominence, they did the work.

With the exception of the oldest brother, Tom, who was married and off the house, the Thomson brothers were very close to one another.[5] Unfortunately, Walker Thomson, the youngest son, was killed in the Michael Colliery in a fall from the roof.[6] Willie Thomson, the second oldest brother, a very reliable active comrade, was also killed in the pit at Wellsgreen by a collapse of the face line. The remaining brothers went on till they retired, but three of them, Tom, Bob and Peter,[7] died within a year of one another, while John, who could hardly get round unaided because of the effect of injuries received in the pit, died in 1978. Only one sister, unmarried, is still alive.

19

BEFORE THE BATTLE

THE two lads I mentioned from West Wemyss, Reddie Henderson and Bert True, were a rather curious mixture. Reddie was extremely well liked, but not so reliable in handling cash. But no matter what scrape he got into, what local village organisation cash he handled — and some of it had not always been accounted for — he was always elected to every other committee that came along. So he was active in the Reform Union in West Wemyss. We never had any occasion when there was any shortage of cash that he had handled in the Reform Union.

The other West Wemyss lad, Bert True, who had come in from Wales, was an entirely unusual type for us in the Fife coalfield. He was always immaculately dressed, and while a cap was the usual head adornment at that time, Bert always had a soft hat, tie, and coloured hand gloves. But nonetheless he was a very able and fluent speaker and was used quite a lot in the East Fife area. Following '26 he did not get back, but, as I will mention later on, he was not made of the same material as the rest of us.

Another village that was a purely mining village and where there were local stalwarts was Coaltown of Balgonie. There was a Thomson family there who subsequently emigrated to Australia who were really first-class material. And there was a Swain family — William Swain and his brother Pete. They were miners who had a smallholding and were pigeon fliers and so on, but they were the local kingpins in the village, sound, solid, dependable lads, particularly William Swain.

Then in the Gallatown area there was my old friend and teacher, old Bob Lamb. Old Bob Lamb was a character. He would be tall, six feet at least, strongly built. I never yet saw him with a collar and tie. He was always adorned in a black muffler. He generally acted as chairman at Minority Movement or Communist Party propaganda meetings. They used to be held every Saturday and Sunday in the busy thoroughfares in Kirkcaldy — the prom or at the park gates. Bob had one of the loudest voices that I have heard. He used to say he was the foghorn because the Party could not afford any other method of advertising, and he was used as the advertiser to draw the crowd and then the intellectuals would get busy with their stuff.

Bob, along with Willie Dunbar, our subsequent Labour College tutor, had been two of the early socialists in Kirkcaldy who opposed the compulsory vaccination of children, and fought for the right of parents to say whether or not they would agree to vaccination. They themselves refused at the time that it was compulsory, and actually had a short term in prison before vaccination was made optional. Lamb was a very influential, active lad at that time. He was also associated with a younger lad, Jimmy Ord.

Jimmy Ord was an entirely different type. He was very artistic and had very good talent as a singer, a comedian; he was given to recitations, monologues. He could easily have made a good livelihood for himself had he gone on the stage. He did a lot of amateur work, a lot of concerts for Party branches, and always was very, very popular. He was in constant demand by Burns Clubs, particularly for "The Immortal Memory".

Jimmy also had the bar put up after '26 and had to find a livelihood whichever way he could best do it after that. Both he and his wife Susie were active in the Communist Party and particularly in the Co-operative movement. He later became chairman of the Pathhead and Sinclairtown Co-op, which subsequently became Kirkcaldy District Co-op, and was chairman up to the time that he died.

A third lad who played an active part in the Gallatown area was a miner by the name of Johnny Boyd. He was a delegate for the Gallatown branch of the Union up to the '21 lock-out. Thereafter he was prevented from getting back into work.

He had gone out poaching for rabbits one night after the lock-out was over, was caught, and got fourteen days in jail. He had a brother-in-law who tinkered around as a spare-time bookie. He worked in the pit but bookied in addition for himself. He persuaded Johnny Boyd to start up bookieing in the Gallatown. Boyd was a very capable man, and when he made up his mind to try and make a livelihood out of that he succeeded tremendously. He had never gambled or bookied or bet before but he made a success as a bookie with his popularity base, following his activity in the miners' union. I remember a short time after he had become a bookie I went down to do a meeting at Denbeath Bridge at Methil and was surprised to see Johnny Boyd standing at the bridge. This was just opposite a big hotel, known as the White Swan.

I said, "Hullo, Johnny, what are you doing here?"

"Oh, well," he said, "I am thinking about buying a hotel. I understand the White Swan is up for sale so I just had a look at it. But they are asking £3,000 for it and that's just too much at the moment."

So here he was within a short time of being out of jail for poaching, without having a penny, starts as a bookie, and was seriously contemplating buying a hotel.

However, Boyd kept his relationship and his contact with the progressive movement all his life. When we in the Communist Party were stuck for special donations the lads would call on Boyd. And I remember him, although he was then not so very well, coming out and trying to play a supporting role for me years later when I stood as a parliamentary candidate in Kirkcaldy Burghs in the election of 1945. But he passed away shortly after. He was active in his time, a very capable lad and also very popular.

One of the areas where a big group of capable lads was in existence was Bowhill. There was a regular team of people there capable when called on to do propaganda work in the coalfield. By that time of course the younger lads were taking possession: Bird, Kirker and Jimmy Galloway. The younger crowd coming up included John Sutherland, who years later defeated Bird in the County Council election after Bird had left the Communist Party.[1]

In Lochgelly there was also a team of comrades capable of leading the district and speaking at meetings. We had as delegate for the Reform Union branch there our old friend and close colleague in the struggle, Jimmy Stewart.

Jimmy Stewart was a very fine person indeed. He had been reared in Lanarkshire, reared as a Catholic, came into Fife, and became active in the miners' movement in the Lochgelly area. There was no polish or pretence about Jimmy. But he was a sound, solid, dependable, no-nonsense, reliable comrade. He represented Lochgelly as a delegate of the Reform Union and had been delegate previously for the Old Union. He was also put up as our representative for the chair in the Old Union before the Reform Union was formed, and again after it had merged back into Adamson's union. He became an official of the Reform Union and chairman, and also was very active later on in the United Mineworkers of Scotland as well.

Jimmy had a very strict moral code and lived up to it. I remember him saying to me, "Johnny, you are a young lad, but my advice is, if you can't be clean in your private life, you can't be clean in public life." And Jimmy tried to live up to that.

On one occasion in 1930, when we were trying to get the whole of Central Fife involved in strike action against the Fife Coal Company's attacks, we had managed to get the pits out at Kelty, we had got the Lumphinnans pit, and the key pit that we wanted out was the Mary Colliery at Lochore. The Mary had a local lad, Davie Martin, a Lochore county councillor, who was quite a good trade union official, very friendly with the Minority Movement boys but stuck to the policy of Adamson.[2] There was mutual respect between Martin and our people. But Martin was telling the miners that morning to go to work. There was a whole team of our speakers there: Proudfoot, Abe Moffat, Alex Moffat, Bob Eadie, and myself, one speaker after the other urging these men to come back down the road.[3]

There was a line of police all drawn up to try to prevent us from getting too close to the men. Realising that the men would not come down the road when we asked them, but also would not go down the pit when the other officials asked them — they were standing with their checks in their hands and did not know whether to go to work or go home — in desperation Stewart said, "I know, I'll get it now."

So he walked up to the line of police, walked up and down that line of police, lambasting them, ridiculing them and, unusual for him, using all the kinds of names that he could lay his tongue to, that would provoke them to hitting him with the baton. He was certain that if one policeman hit him, the men would walk down the road. It was a foolhardy action. Nobody could deny his bravery and his purpose. But the police were wired off too, and instead of losing the head they just grinned and laughed at Jimmy and kidded him on. Not one of them laid hands on him. So that effort, courageous as it was, actually failed, but not for the want of trying as far as Jimmy was concerned.

On another occasion, we had trouble at one of the Fife Coal Company pits, Kinglassie, which was not one of our strongest bases. It was under the control of the Ness family. Peter Ness was a full-time official for Adamson's union.[4] There was an issue that we wanted to raise with the men, and Abe Moffat and I went to Kinglassie late one day and slept the night on the rug in the single-end of the couple that put us up. We went down to Kinglassie pit first thing in the morning.

Moffat had finished speaking and I had started to speak when the police arrived, and also the other union officials, for whom the management had sent. A rumpus started. A lad was aiming a blow at me; Moffat stepped in and got his face smashed. But the miners then stepped in and stopped that from developing.

But we decided to go back to Kinglassie on the following Sunday in strength. We mobilised the whole of our speaking team, marched people over from Bowhill, Lochgelly and the surrounding districts into Kinglassie. Almost everybody in Kinglassie was turned out to this meeting, wondering whether it was going to be a donnybrook or not.

We had a lorry, a Co-operative lorry, which we used as a platform. Jimmy Stewart was chairman. I always remember his opening remarks. He said he understood that when Moffat and McArthur were across there during the week there was an attempt to prevent them speaking by actual physical force, resorting to fisticuffs. Well, we wanted to demonstrate to them today that here we are back again. And he said, "You can either have it on the platform, or you can have it down on the green. It'll be a' the same to us, either way'll do." There was a policeman present at the meeting by the name of Motion. Stewart says, "Motion, that gangs for you tae." This was typical of the man.

Stewart and his colleagues led the struggle to take over control of the new Lochgelly Miners' Institute when the Adamson union tried to shut out the people of Lochgelly. Stewart and the others marched in, took possession and shared out amongst the women of Lochgelly the good things that were being set for the opening dinner for the coalowners and their friends.

Jimmy Stewart became a Communist councillor and was the first I know of to become a magistrate in Lochgelly. The cases that came before him are a matter of Fife history. Jimmy showed how a militant worker could use the bench, not against the workers, as normally happens, but in order to get across propaganda and a militant attitude to life, to wife-beating, to people who were stealing coal, and so on. In that respect, Jimmy was an outstanding, courageous leader and he was much appreciated by us and was a warm comrade. It is a matter of regret to me that in his last days, when Jimmy took ill, his wife had become a convert back to the Catholic Church. Although we had been his closest colleagues she was persuaded that the Church should take the whole responsibility for the funeral arrangements. So his close colleagues were not allowed in the house, nor did they have any part in the funeral, although all of us made it our business to be in attendance. Jimmy was a real working-class comrade and was liked by almost everyone with whom he worked.

There was another very efficient comrade in Lochgelly, Jimmy Gourdie. Gourdie was not the type to do propaganda meetings, but he was the most efficient branch secretary that we had, I think, in our organisation. He was used by the Reform Union in our committee work, in branch reorganisation, branch guidance, how officials and secretaries should work. Gourdie was a really dependable branch official of the union.

In addition to him there was a group of local lads in Lochgelly who were able to make a considerable contribution to the struggle in those days. Some of them were in the I.L.P. One of them was Bill Crooks, who remained a member of the I.L.P. but worked closely along with Stewart and our people in the Reform Union and Minority Movement in Lochgelly and also became a councillor. And when he got squeezed out after the 1926 lock-out, he went through to Glasgow. I can remember meeting him when he was a member of the board of the St Rollox Co-operative Society.

Then there was an active group of lads in the Lumphinnans area. The leader of the Lumphinnans miners at that time was Tom Smith. Smith was active in the Reform Union and in the Old Union before it. He became the Reform Union chairman, and then when Kirker was sacked from his position as a full-time official, Smith was elected in his place. That was the occasion when I came second in the ballot vote and Pat Connelly of Lochore third.

Tom Smith's brother Bob was also quite active in the Reform Union at that time.[5] Another comrade at Lumphinnans, Bruce Wallace, played an active part and actually became the first county councillor in Fife for the Communist Party, and represented the Lumphinnans-Glencraig constituency for a number of years. Bruce Wallace also was crowded out from the pit after the 1926 lock-out, and finally accepted a job as reservoir keeper at Glenfarg reservoir in Perthshire and resigned as a county councillor. His seat on the County Council was eventually, in 1928, filled by one of our young comrades, Alex Moffat.

Alex Moffat was coming into activity in Lumphinnans before the General Strike. He was an active member of the Young Communist League along with Alice Brady, whom he married.[6] Alex Moffat's oldest brother, Jimmy, was chairman of the Lumphinnans branch of the Reform Union.[7] The whole Moffat family were more or less branch officials, branch delegates or branch committeemen, and were coming into activity in the village of Lumphinnans at that time. The younger brothers were Abe, Alex and Dave.[8] Abe was elected a parish councillor for Ballingry in 1925 as a Communist, while Alex, as I have said, became the second Communist to be elected to Fife County Council in 1928.

In Cowdenbeath there were a number of very active lads. There was the well-known comrade, Bob Selkirk. He was active in the political field in the area but had an anarchist background that made it difficult for him to fit into

85

organised trade union activity at that time.[9] There was a big I.L.P. militant group. There was also a Y.C.L. group, a Proletarian Sunday School group.[10] All forms of activity were being engaged in in the Cowdenbeath area. One of the leading trade unionists there was Peter Venters. Peter was delegate for the Reform Union and played an active role. He continued his trade union connection in Cowdenbeath right up until he retired from the Cowdenbeath National Coal Board workshops at the age of sixty-five.

In Kelty there was also a very active team of comrades who drew their inspiration more from association with Philip Hodge. In addition there were lads from other parts of Fife who were then coming into the Labour College side of the movement: Jimmy Birrell and Jimmy Clunie, both of Dunfermline, and a young lad who had come up from Wales for Labour College tutoring work, D. J. Williams. He was also quite a good propagandist and did a lot of propaganda work for the progressive side of the movement. He was actually arrested in 1926 but he went back eventually to Wales and after the 1939-45 war, became an M.P. in one of the Welsh constituencies and died there.

There was also a number of comrades in the Dunfermline area who carried out a lot of propaganda activity.

In the Lochore area the Connelly family had been always active in the trade union. Jim, the oldest brother, had been a full-time collector for the Old Union in the Valleyfield area, and then went to Stirlingshire.[11] Pat Connelly, whom I have mentioned once or twice already, was at that time a big, powerful, heavily built man. He had a ready fund of language. He used to make play with words to try to get his point across. Instead of talking about a manager, he used to talk about a man*ay*-ger. He had a whole series of phrases like that. One that stuck in my mind was when he was describing a strike by miners at Lochore at Mary pit, and the attempts made by Adamson to get them back to work. Connelly said the men at Lochore would stay on strike until Benarty Hill "becomes a gumbile". But the men went back next morning, so he was well out of touch on that occasion with the sentiments of the men.

So that covering the whole Fife coalfield there was this regular propaganda drive amongst the comrades mentioned. These were the main local propagandists. We had got to get them allied with a whole series of people who were coming into Fife from the outside. We had regular visits from Willie Gallacher, Johnny Campbell, Aitken Ferguson, and Shapurji Saklatvala, M.P.[12] Saklatvala was a member of the Communist Party when he was first elected as Labour M.P. for Battersea in 1922. He was defeated in 1923, but re-elected in 1924 as a Communist M.P. We had visits of course from Jimmy MacDougall and other members of the Tramp Trust, supporters of Maclean and his Scottish Republican organisation.

Others who paid regular visits to the Fife coalfield were Bob Stewart of Dundee and Willie Joss of Glasgow.[13] There were also one or two very powerful and influential women speakers, particularly Mrs Helen Crawfurd, who made a powerful impact on the Fife villages. Helen Crawfurd, before my time, had been an active suffragette. She was the widow of a Church of Scotland minister and was a most likeable personality. She did propaganda work in Fife and other areas prior to the General Strike, and during the General Strike and the whole of the miners' lock-out she was very prominent in the Workers' International Relief organisation, which collected relief for the miners from all over Europe.[14] She was the organising secretary here in Britain and paid regular visits to the Fife coalfield, distributing whatever relief material was available to her.[15]

Another woman who made a deep impression was Mrs Isabel Brown, wife of E. H. Brown of the Communist Party.[16] She was a very powerful, effective speaker and made her mark also with women's propaganda.

So that all of that agitational, educational, preparatory work was being carried out in the Fife coalfield prior to the coming of Red Friday in July 1925 and during the nine months of the coal subsidy leading up to the General Strike in May 1926.

20

EYES LEFT

THE General Strike was an event of staggering importance to all of us who had been active in the workers' movement. We had dreamt of the day when all workers would stand solid one with the other. We had had disappointments before, particularly with the let-down by the Triple Alliance and the desertion of the miners in '21.

I can remember that in trying to work out what 1926 would mean we felt we, the militants in Buckhaven and Methil, would have to have a series of meetings in order to get our message across. I don't think many people because of bitter disappointments in the past actually felt that the General Strike would take place. The main place for us holding meetings in the Buckhaven-Methil area was at Denbeath Bridge, and a number of us decided to hold a meeting on the Sunday a week prior to the General Strike. We had to cancel the meeting for lack of attendance. But we had a meeting the next Sunday, 2nd May, the day before the General Strike began, and one could hardly see the back of the crowd.

The strike in the Buckhaven-Methil area was a hundred per cent solid. Not one man was found wanting. Not a vehicle moved.

We had to set up rapid organisation and find our way as we went along. But the Methil Trades and Labour Council, of which I had been elected chairman in 1925, took control of the whole of the strike activity in the area. We set up various subcommittees to control different aspects of activity.

We had probably as good working-class organisation as any that was set up. Due to the efforts of the Miners' Reform Union leadership, which was in the main led by active members of the Communist Party and the Minority Movement, we had given a lot of thought to organised working-class activity. Prior to the General Strike there had been thought out what action should be taken. So that when the strike took place an immediate meeting of the trades council was called and the plan for action was laid down. The Methil Co-operative Hall, with its ante-rooms, was taken as the strike headquarters. It was continuously in use, even during the night.

The Communist Party had had a pit paper, "The Spark" being circulated at the Wellesley Colliery, which meant that there was typewriting and duplicating machinery, and a considerable stock of paper had been secured prior to the General Strike. This technical equipment, which had been in the personal possession of David Proudfoot, was put at the disposal of the Council of Action central strike committee, and played a very important role in as much as speakers' notes could be run off, and daily bulletins of events as known to the committee could be run off in considerable numbers. These bulletins were carried to other strike committees by the despatch riders or couriers.

The Council of Action or General Strike Committee was formed by means of having a central strike committee under a convener, and each sub-convener had a department to look after. There was a subcommittee that was in charge of transport permits, and this was under the control of the N.U.R. delegate to the trades council, a lad by the name of Harry Ewing.

There was also the question of defence and organisation of pickets. We set up for the first time a youth committee as part of the General Strike organisation, and from this youth committee there was a real backbone developed of the picketing, of the hard routine work. The embryo Young Communist League leaders also developed from this youth committee.

There was built up a communications group and the East Fife Motor Cycle Club in Leven approached us and offered their services as couriers and despatch riders. This augmented the push-bikes and one or two cars that were made available to us.

There was the committee set up to deal with entertainment, so that there would be adequate means of keeping people entertained, preventing boredom. We tried to get built up concert parties and groups that would do concerts and entertainment in halls or, when the weather was suitable, outside as well. In fact, we had concerts every night.

Then there was the question of publicity and propaganda and here a team of speakers was built up and whenever a meeting was being arranged it was felt that each trade union aspect should be provided for. In the team of speakers there would be a miner, a railwayman or bus worker, and a docker. So that the people mainly concerned in the strike would show their identity of interest and their unity before the people as a whole.

In addition to doing meetings locally we had requests from outside of the mining areas, especially for a miners' speaker to be sent. Perth became one of our main centres at which miner speakers from our area put the case. I remember one of the motor cyclists coming in with a request that there was a big strike organisation in Perth but they had no miners in their area and would like to have a miners' speaker. The only way to get up to Perth, because there were no buses and no trains, was on the back of a motor-cycle. I was allocated to speak. This was the first time I had ever been on a motor-bike. It happened to be a racing cyclist that was my driver. I think my hair was standing on my head all the road up to Perth. The only vehicles we passed on the way were military vehicles that were apparently touring around to give a demonstration of force. We held an extremely successful meeting. The boys at Perth were overjoyed to hear the miners' case and they booked the biggest hall, the City Hall, in Perth for a big meeting run by the N.U.R. We had been accustomed in my own area to hard, matter-of-act meetings. But when I, accompanied this time by Proudfoot, went back to Perth to speak in the City Hall, there was a wonderful atmosphere in the hall. There were musical turns. We put the case for the miners. It was one of the most responsive meetings that ever I had the experience to address. This was typical all over, because other local comrades were speaking in other areas.

In the days of routine discussion at Methil Trades and Labour Council before the General Strike, the Communist and Minority Movement supporters were always anxious for a more militant line, and the older, more sedate, cautious trade union officials such as were generally found leading the N.U.R. and the dockers were generally at loggerheads with us younger, more vehement comrades who were in the Minority Movement section. One would have imagined it very difficult to get joint activity from these previously almost warring elements. But the trades council decided that the transport and permits should be under the control of the N.U.R. and the dockers. The N.U.R. delegate at the trades council, Harry Ewing, was made convener. When the actual issue came, the lads who had been against rigid militant action as proposed by the Minority Movement elements were actually more rigid in the application of strike rules than we were.

I remember being present at one or two applications for permits to transport goods that came before Harry Ewing's subcommittee. Harry Ewing had always a final question to ask: "How did you get your supplies before the strike?" If the lad said they got it by railway, that was it — no permit.

When the police chief called and threatened Harry that he was usurping the functions of the State by issuing permits, Harry was completely unruffled. He told the police he was doing his job as instructed by his membership, he was carrying out their orders.

The police were under Inspector Clark, who was notorious in our area for his brutality, and he had under him Sergeant Park, who was equally of this type.[1] Clark was continually pestering the strike committee. On another occasion, later on, when we had a mass march to a pit, Clark threatened to take action against us for illegal drilling on the king's highway. Almost every conceivable avenue that he could think of he was always threatening to use against the strikers, and particularly against the strike leaders.

The whole system of control over transport was most complete and effective. Even if an ambulance was needed to take a special case to Edinburgh Infirmary or hospital locally, they had to apply for permits. Permits were not readily granted by this committee either.

On one occasion I happened to be speaking at a meeting in Buckhaven along with the N.U.R. branch secretary, Sam Happle. A runner came down from Station Road, one of the main road junctions, to say that there had been an attempt to stop a beer lorry from getting through and the police had carried out a baton charge and three of our picket were arrested. When Sam Happle and I proceeded to the scene, men, women and children were running towards the area in hundreds, grasping whatever weapons they could get their hands on — some with fireside pokers, some with sticks, some with pickshafts, stones, bottles. There was a building site adjoining and the police that were left were getting stoned and were running for their lives. One policeman cleared a six-feet wall round the slaughterhouse non-stop. He would have been suitable for the Olympics.

There was an immediate demand that we assault the police cells in order to get the three lads out. This raised an issue that was new for us but which we felt we would have to cope with. So it was arranged that we would have a meeting immediately at the big strike centre in the Co-operative Hall.

The hall was packed to suffocation. Our meeting was taken charge of by Proudfoot, who was convener of the Methil Central Strike Committee. He said, "Well, we've now got to meet force with organised resistance. The picketing must be carried out, the strike must go on. We're in this strike for the purpose of winning it. We're not going to be diverted by police baton charges. That is a feature we'll just have to face and overcome."

So we agreed to get some form of organisation. We in the strike leadership started off by saying, "All right, every man look at his neighbour sitting beside him. If you can't volunteer or vouch for him let him be questioned to prove he is a genuine striker."

Then we set about setting up a properly disciplined organisation. We asked everybody who had had army or navy experience to move to one side of the hall. Then we asked if anybody had been an officer. We did not run to the extent of having an officer. But we had two sergeant-majors: Walter White, who subsequently became active in the United Mineworkers of Scotland, and Will McFadyean.[2] So these sergeant-majors were made corps commanders. Everyone who had been an N.C.O. in the army was given charge of ten privates, and each private was given charge of ten men who had had no army experience. These ex-servicemen had complete control of this Workers' Defence Corps. There had been a lot of the youth committee and others in a loosely formed picket or Defence Corps before the baton charge, but its ranks swelled to about 750 or 800 after the batoning.

We said, "Well, you can arrange now the main points where picketing has to be done and decide how many men you require in order to make picketing continuous, with men held in reserve." We organised cyclists who could act as couriers, and particularly valued were young lads who had motor-cycles.

At that stage the most fierce discussion took place: what were we going to do to get the three men out who had been arrested? There were immediate demands that we should march up to the police buildings and forcibly rescue these men. I am not sure what would have been the outcome of that discussion but for the intervention of the father of Barney McGrory, one of the lads who had been arrested. The family were Irish Catholics and were active militants in the labour movement. His father was old Mick McGrory.[3] He got up to say, "Look, we're in a strike which is equivalent to a battle for our lives and our livelihood and all that we hold dear. You can't have a battle, unfortunately, without casualties. But if the battle is to continue then you must accept the casualties and carry on. My son happens to be one of the first casualties. I am very, very sorry that that is so. But he along with me would wish that we don't do anything that would prevent us from carrying out the strike. So we carry out the strike and they'll bear the consequences of having been arrested."

That had a tremendous effect on the meeting and I think was mainly responsible for getting our policy accepted at that big meeting of men. So each man then went home, had a meal, and reported to the strike headquarters. I remember going back down to the headquarters when the first company were going to resume the picketing. As they came up with the sergeant-major in front, he saw me coming along and he shouts, "Eyes left!" You could see the arms swinging. The arms were rigid because they were concealing pokers, hammers, and what have you.

The important thing is they went back to the scene where the baton charge took place. By that time there had been busloads of police drawn in from every area. But the picket took up its post and I remember watching them working. There were three roads converging on to this corner where the baton charge had taken place. The non-commissioned officer in charge of the picket put twenty men on each road, twenty men stopping the main traffic, with push-bikes running back and forward in advance, so that they could get timeous notice of any vehicle that was proceeding in that direction. And then they had something like fifty men standing by in reserve in case they should be needed. In spite of the fact that there was a big contingent of police they stopped every vehicle that came along and continued this activity. It was a marvellous display of organised, disciplined activity. They did their work without looking at the police. Everybody knew, including the police, that if anything untoward had happened they would have had a real struggle on their hands; and while there might have been some casulaties amongst the strikers there equally would have been a number amongst the police.

I have heard it said that in some areas there was collaboration between the workers' pickets and the police in order to keep order. There was no such arrangement in the Methil-Buckhaven area. There the pickets went on duty armed with whatever they could secure: pickshafts, pokers, railway distance pieces, and anything that would be useful in a dust-up. They all also were under instructions to wear their pit boots. They also would be handy in a dust-up. A number of them even used the hard hat they had in the pit at the time, but this was not common. From the time that the Defence Corps became an organised body there was no more police interference with the pickets.

But that night the midnight or overnight arrests started. Proudfoot was arrested, Sam Happle was arrested, and one or two others. These arrests were carried out at two o'clock in the morning. And that became the fashion. If you were going to be arrested, you were arrested when they thought everybody else was in bed. So that double precautions started to be taken, and those that were recognised as leaders had a protection squad allocated to them. I remember an amusing development. The lads would approach you and say, "Look, make sure you're not going to be arrested at night, make sure you're not sleeping in your own house." Ordinary miners would come forward and give you a key to their house, and you had to put their name on it. I had a pocketful of keys for houses that I could go into without warning.

My older brother George was very like me in appearance and build. He volunteered that he would hop in and out of my house, wander in and wander out, so that the police would not know if it was me in the house or not. Whether it worked or not I was one of the lucky lads: I was not arrested during the nine days of the strike.

21

SOME LESSONS FROM
THE '26 STRIKE

I REMEMBER a development in picketing during the General Strike at Buckhaven and Methil which demonstrated just the amount of discipline that existed among the strikers. A motor-cyclist coming along from West Fife intimated that there was a McEwan's brewery lorry breaking through the picket lines and coming right down to the east. He had got special wire protection round the cabin. The fellow was refusing to stop and barging right through the pickets. Our lads made sure that when the lorry approached they stopped it all right, though the police were there. But worse than that, they rolled the beer barrels off. All these lads were in the habit of taking a drink of beer, and while they had been on strike they had probably never had a taste of beer. But we thought it was the best demonstration we had seen when they knocked the bungs out of the beer barrels and ran it down the gutter without anybody making an attempt to take a drink.

One other subcommittee that we set up during the General Strike was a form of organisation that was brought in mainly from the continent but spread over here. That was the International Class War Prisoners' Aid.[1] The job of this subcommittee was to provide legal and monetary aid in the event of anyone being arrested who had dependants. We used the funds that were collected for that purpose when a number of local leaders, including David Proudfoot, were arrested.

When Proudfoot and one or two of the others were arrested, a local lad said, "The best thing we can do is to get along for our father confessor, Willie Dunbar." So the young comrades who had been attending Dunbar's lectures decided to invite him along. He was put up to speak at a very well-attended meeting.

At that time we were demanding the release of the local lads, and we were demanding an investigation into the actions of the police, the baton charges and the unnecessary arrests that were being made. So the agitation was a very strong one. However, Mr Dunbar in his usual sardonic manner said, "You're wasting your time. Your fellows have been arrested and you'll no' can do anything about it. The best thing to do is to get the best lawyer you can get and put up the best defence you can get. Make sure that you contribute to the lads' wives and family" — and so on.

The local lads who had looked on Dunbar as a father figure were stunned. As one who had been closely associated with Dunbar for many years I also was shocked. The moment he had finished, though I was not down as a speaker for that demonstration, I said, "I'm speaking next." I went up and went hell for leather for Dunbar, and told him that what he was proposing we were already doing but didn't want to limit ourselves to such proposals and if that's a' he could advise us it was the last time he would speak at a strike meeting. And so it was: he never got back.

Proudfoot's case was found not proven by the sheriff. There was a development attached to this. We were unused to court cases. Proudfoot's workmate, who worked as a checkweigher along with him, was an old socialist by the name of Alexander Gillespie.[2] He came forward to us and said, "Ye've got to get the best legal defence ye can get. There's nae use getting somebody that's the stereotyped, establishment lawyer. The best man that I know is Burke, a lawyer in Dundee." We said, "Well, we dinnae ken nothing aboot it, but we'll take your advice." So we engaged Burke.[3]

He was a big, powerful man, a very hectoring attitude. But he came down and into the place. We booked the big room in the White Swan Hotel. He had his clerk invite us all in, and as each witness came in and he took his evidence, Burke would say, "Do you smoke, sir?" If the lad said, "Aye", Burke would say to his clerk, "John, give him twenty cigarettes. Do you take a drink?" If the boy took a drink, he got a glass of whisky or a pint of beer. All the boys went round saying, "This is a great lad. This is some lawyer, this boy."

When Burke was trying to prepare his case he was not very particular. If he should say to a witness, "Did you see this happening?" the boy would say, "No, no, I didn't see it exactly."

"But you could *say* you saw it this way?"

"Oh, well, if you want me to say that I'll say it."

This was the type of defence Burke worked up. So when we got up to Cupar to the trial — the trial, of course, came after the General Strike was over — Burke used to personally browbeat the policemen witnesses, march up to and stick his face in front of the witness and say, "What were you before you joined the police force?"

"Oh, I worked on the farm."

So he would conduct this questioning, and make out the policeman was just an ordinary ignorant plooman. Well, it maybe took a trick with our supporters who were in court but I'm not sure it had any influence with the judge.

The N.U.R. had decided to stand the legal expenses for Sam Happle's defence. But when the accounts came in we found that we had to pay for all that whisky and cigarettes that Burke had been dishing out. The N.U.R. sent us up a communication; they said in the circumstances they might feel obliged to pay this legal account but they thought we could have got Sir John Simon, who was a leading K.C. at the time, cheaper.[4]

The thing so influenced our people that during a later period when I was arrested myself our lads said, "We're not getting Burke again." So they engaged a K.C., paid a fee of £10 or ten guineas, but he was immeasurably cheaper than Burke.

Like some others, Burke had wanted to arrange all the sentences of the lads arrested by having private talks with the procurator fiscal. So that when the prisoners walked into court the fiscal would have arranged it all through the defence lawyer and the sheriff would act accordingly. This kind of advice was given to another lad at the same time in Kirkcaldy. He was an Austrian named Kitchen or Kirschner, but we always referred to him as Lewis Kitchener. He had made a foolish speech during the strike. He was impulsive, was carried away with his own words, his English was not too good, and he was arrested. The lads who were in control of the defence organisation were concerned about what was going to happen to him, because he was not a recognised leader of the strike or the trade union movement. Although he was married locally and had a family, he was not naturalised, and the question was to avoid deportation. Those lads in charge in Kirkcaldy arranged with the fiscal that Kitchener should get a nominal fine and there should be no question of deportation. But the authorities went back on this. He was jailed for three months and ordered to be deported. This was one of the tragedies in this area, because this lad was deported, wandered about Europe for a time, and finally committed suicide.[5] This was one of the mistakes that was made by trusting behind-the-scenes arrangements with the fiscal when cases were coming up into court. It was a valuable lesson to those of us who had no court experience up to this time.

The period of the General Strike was very enlightening and educative. As the strike developed and all loose edges were being tucked in, a feeling of elation, of new-found strength, the solidarity of the workers created an extraordinary atmosphere among working men, their wives and families. There was therefore considerable difficulty when the call came by means of telegrams to the respective trade union branch committees that work was to be resumed. The bus people, dockers, and so on, refused to accept the telegrams that were sent out. Methil N.U.R. were also inclined to refuse to accept the notification in the telegram. But generally this had to be accepted and the General Strike petered out.

There was a general feeling of stunned shock and no one could really understand why this decision had been taken. It was not because there was any weakening in the ranks of the strikers. They were going from strength to a continued feeling of greater strength. They could look ahead and see that the only result could be one of a climb-down on the part of the Government and of the coalowners. They were certain that if the unity and determination that was being displayed was continued the result would be inevitable. It was only subsequent to that we discovered how the sell-out, as it was understood, was actually arranged.

I think on reflection the General Strike was called off because the leadership did not believe in it. In point of fact they had had the General Strike forced on them. It was not of their preparing for, arranging for, or deliberately planning for and calling. They were prepared to conduct negotiations ostensibly to try to get some support for the miners, but it was the Government, particularly Churchill, who was leading the fight against the miners, that forced the issue.

But as the struggle continued, it was becoming a struggle between an embryo workers' political state that was being set up and the power of the capitalist state. This was the issue that frightened the T.U.C. leaders. They wanted to get the strike called off before it went any further.

Inside the labour movement there has always been this right-wing argument that it is wrong to use political action for industrial purposes, or industrial action for political purposes. I think it was this general conception of working-class activity that was the main reason activating the General Council leadership. Whereas we used to argue at the time that we did not know where industrial action ended and political action started. It seemed to be one and the same thing.

22

SOUP KITCHENS

DURING the whole of the General Strike the only miners who were active in Fife were members of the Reform Union. There was no activity by the officials locally of the Adamson organisation. The political explanations were all made by the other trade union leaders — the Reform Union leaders — and Communist Party speakers. So that the general atmosphere was one favourable to the proposals of the Reform Union officials.

Because the M.F.G.B. Executive were still carrying on the struggle after the General Strike was called off by the T.U.C., we had to settle down to decide how best to organise effectively the lock-out activity of the miners. There was no sign of the miners giving in, and we were not prepared to accept an increase in hours and a reduction in wages.

I have already said that in the 1925 Parish Council elections we had run a Labour panel, as a result of which thirteen out of fifteen of our candidates had been elected. The remaining two elected were officials of the Wemyss Coal Company. The Wemyss Parish Council covered the area of Methil, Denbeath, Kirkland, Methilhill, Buckhaven, and the three Wemyss — East, West and Coaltown of Wemyss.

There were two of us who were Communists on that Council — John O'Neill and myself, both miners. The chairman, an old left socialist, William Phoenix, was also a miner. He was one of the early S.D.F. speakers and activists in the area. He was a very efficient representative and always took a leftist line on questions that were coming up. He was amenable to working with O'Neill and me in the Parish Council and using the Parish Council to the maximum in the interests of the miners' lock-out.[1]

The Parish Council clerk was rather a different type. He was elderly, gruff in his approach, and before we went on to the Parish Council we thought he was a hostile opponent. But once we were elected and worked with him, we found that this was not exactly correct. If there was any loophole that he could use in the law covering his job he was prepared to use it. I have known cases where he could not officially or legally make provision for a claimant, but where he actually paid some out of his own pocket.

Thus we had a fairly favourable chairman and clerk, and if there was any way of getting round the regulations, we were prepared to do it. So O'Neill and myself proposed that it was the Parish Council's responsibility to see that no one suffered from hunger or destitution in our area; and that the Parish Council would be responsible for feeding the strikers' wives and children.

In our view, relief would be more effective if it was organised on a communal basis, instead of giving each claimant who applied a chit in money or a chit to the Co-op for supplies. And as the miners were experienced in running soup kitchens during the 1912 strike and the 1921 lock-out, they would readily apply themselves to running one again in this 1926 lock-out. It was pointed out that the Parish Council had not got the means of running soup kitchens. If they were to do so it would be a costly business. They would have to pay personnel for cooking the food. They would have to pay for the site, for the use of boilers, and so on, and it was therefore not a practical proposition. O'Neill and I countered that by saying, "All right, why not approach the trades council and ask them to undertake the organisational work of running the kitchens but that the Parish Council would be responsible for providing the finance?" I moved this and we carried it by a vote, and asked that they should send a deputation to request the assistance of the trades council. All this had been worked out with the leadership of the trades council prior to this. A deputation was appointed by the Parish Council and I turned my hat and appeared as the chairman of the trades council. We got down to agreement.

The system that was to apply was first that we would organise everybody to apply for public assistance. This meant continuous meetings and whipping up round every street in the area of the Parish Council. We had to get the maximum number of people to apply for relief. This was not easy because a number of people were afraid of what their position would be legally if they had their own house, such as many of the miner-fishermen had. Some had money in the Co-op, some had other members of the family working. All these difficulties had to be overcome. And it was quite a sight to see this queue lined up at the Parish Council, including a number of well-dressed, respectable miners, applying for public assistance. This showed that they accepted leadership on this question.

The fewest possible particulars were asked on the Parish Council and once we got that done we then got down through the trades council to divide the whole of the area into kitchen areas, that is, areas that could be easily supplied from one kitchen. Then we would know how many we could supply, street by street; their names would be secured and a register prepared, checked with the Parish Council list, so that we would get to know exactly how much money was to be allocated by the Parish Council weekly to the trades council for relief. A survey was made to try to find a suitable house-kitchen that had big boilers, or boilers had to be secured and additional cooking facilities provided. In some places small halls were secured, in others outbuildings or huts, where the services of water and drainage would be arranged. In some places we had to build a hut and lay on the services, so that we could cover every part of the area for which we were responsible.

The women who were volunteers would be regular members of the cooking staff. But every male on the register had to take his turn of doing the labouring work, see that the fires were kept going, get coal, wood, do any heavy lifting needed, clean potatoes, prepare vegetables, and so on. Each man had to take three days at a turn, or longer if he volunteered.

A convener was appointed for each kitchen, with regular daily meetings of all the conveners, so that the menu could be worked out, the cost that would be permitted for each kitchen. The orders were placed with the local Co-op butchers and other suppliers. The strike committee had interviews with them and explained what they wanted, and how payment was to be made. The convener for each kitchen would collect the invoice from the supplier, take it to the central conveners' committee, this committee would then draw up the chits from the Parish Council and the cheques would be made out by the Council to the supplier. This meant that the Parish Council had a check on the allocations they were making. And they paid the bills.

The job of checking up as far as our own strike committee was concerned was undertaken by the branch secretaries who had knowledge of bookkeeping and secretarial work. Those who were taking an active part in mass activity — lock-out pickets, speaking, and so on — were relieved of the detailed responsibility of running the kitchens.

Once the kitchens were established then it was a question of augmenting what we could get from the Parish Council by whatever voluntary means were available, checking up on all the lads with gardens, so that all surplus vegetables would be secured. That was the job of the men attached to the kitchens. If they could secure other supplies then these were secured without any questions generally being asked. So that hens, chickens, rabbits, hares would find their way into the kitchens, just as fish would be handed in as well. We tried to arrange that at the beginning of the week a half-pound of margarine would be issued; tea and rolls every morning; then in the afternoon a very substantial thick soup, whatever meat was available, and bread. In the evening, again it would be bread and tea. If the funds could stand jam, then jam would be supplied. Sometimes we went to the extent of buying kippers on a big scale.

In Fife the Reform Union was not part of the M.F.G.B. Adamson's union was part of the M.F.G.B. and of the National Union of Scottish Mine Workers. All the money for miners' relief that was contributed nationally and internationally went to the M.F.G.B. and was distributed by them. So none of these funds were given to the members of the Reform Union.

It seemed paradoxical that the biggest support received by the miners in Britain came from the miners of the Soviet Union. They had levied their membership one per cent of their wages, and the Central Council of Soviet Trades Unions, anticipating the collection they would get from that, sent it to this country from their central funds. The Soviet Union created a very favourable impression amongst the miners at this time with their liberal support. They contributed over £1 million to the relief of the miners, which was two-thirds of the whole of the money that was collected outside of this country, including the big trade unions in the United States.

In addition, there was the Workers' International Relief organisation which collected money in this country and abroad and distributed it. They gave more in ratio to Fife than to others because they knew there were two unions and that the Reform Union members were excluded from the official hand-outs. They generally distributed relief in the form of parcels of goods, groceries, children's clothing, and so on.

Money was also raised from collections from factories and workshops. Organised collecting teams went out into non-mining areas. Dundee was a particularly warm-hearted supporter of the miners. There had always been a very, very close, friendly relationship between the workers of Dundee and the workers of the Fife coalfield, and generally when we were in industrial trouble, teams would be organised to get amongst the Dundee factory workers, who were mainly women.

We also organised bands, musicians, and so on, to tour these districts and raise as much money as they could for the soup kitchens. One of the lads who got a lot of prominence nationally and internationally afterwards was actually introduced to his full-time profession in that way. I refer to Jimmy Shand, who now is known all over Scotland and elsewhere as the bandleader of Scottish dance music.[2] Jimmy Shand came from East Wemyss. His father was on the Parish Council along with me. Jimmy was a very good player of the melodeon and he was used to tour the area to raise funds. He was playing in Dundee when his value was recognised by one of the big music shops that specialised in selling melodeons and they asked him if he would take a job with them. He took the job and from there eventually built up his dance band. You could ascribe his ultimate success to the introduction he got while playing during the miners' struggles in 1926.

As well as the soup kitchens for feeding miners and their wives, we had arranged through the education committee that school children should be supplied with meals at the school. This was also organised on a big scale. Curiously enough, in our area, quite a number of the Adamson local officials managed to become kitchen functionaries during this period. It meant of course that they were being very well fed, they were not running any risk from the mass agitation, but were still keeping contact with the people of the area through the children being fed at school.

There was another aspect that I discovered by chance. Those of us that were engaged in the mass acitivity always lived on the barest kitchen fare. But I remember when the municipal elections came along in November, one of the conveners of the kitchen was the Labour candidate in one of the wards. He asked me if I would speak at a meeting on his behalf. I said, "Oh, aye, I'll do that."

So after the meeting was finished, he said, "Well, will you come up and have your tea?"

"Tea?" I said. "No, I'll go up to the kitchen."

"Aye," he said, "ye'll no' have been able to use a pin for a while to pick your teeth?"

"No," I said, "it's a hell of a long time since I picked my teeth."

"Well," he says, "I telt the wife tae have something ready for ye when we come up."

So out of curiosity I said I would go and see. I was certainly surprised. I got steak, fried steak, that day — the first time for months. The wife brought out an ashet of butter and he gave me a twenty-packet of Capstan.

I said, "Hey, sir, would you mind telling me how the hell you can do this?"

"Oh," he says, "it's the branch manager at the Store. He's dead keen to make sure that I place the orders, to get his sales up. So I place the orders, and when the wife gauns tae the Store she gets that in her basket."

I said, "Oh, is that hoo it's done?"

That may have been the sort of backhanders that were given to get the lads to place orders, but certainly nobody who was active in the lock-out organisation mass activity had any necessity to use a pin to clean their teeth after any of the meals they got.

There was one very important aspect of this. A boot supplier, Wilkie, with a wholesale and retail shop in Methil and Kirkcaldy, approached the central lock-out committee to say he would be prepared to give a pair of shoes or boots to all of the workers vouched for by the strike committee. This was a wonderful offer and the strike committee decided who was to get the chits to call at the shop.

Boots and shoes were a problem as the lock-out continued. We actually took over one of the small halls in the central committee rooms and asked for volunteers from all the kitchens to repair shoes. Anyone that volunteered was guaranteed food and a packet of ten Woodbine per day. A quota was then allocated to each kitchen and the convener of the kitchen would give a note from the register of those who could call at the central repair depot to have their shoes or boots repaired. This was strictly controlled by the kitchen committee to make sure it was fairly distributed.

A second question that bothered us eventually was the necessity for haircuts. Here again we got amateur haircutters employed in the central hall and a chit for anyone who desired a haircut was organised also through the central kitchens.

As the lock-out dragged on and we came into the longer dark nights, another problem presented itself to us. It had not bothered us till then because we had had the benefit of extraordinarily good spring and summer weather. It was one of the best summers I can recollect. So that the question of lights late at night did not worry people much during the long summer nights. But as the autumn wore on, and it was getting dark quicker, the problem became of money to put in the gas. After serious discussion we decided we would allocate so many pennies per week to each household because they did not have a claim on money through the method of feeding that we had.

23

'A SPLENDID BODY OF MEN'

THESE were practical problems that we had to meet and we tried to meet them as best we could. The whole feeding, successful or otherwise, depended on this regular income from the Parish Council. But just as we were aware of that, our opponents were also conscious of it. And all over the country, systematically, continually, campaigns were being run by the Press, by the Tories, by Government speakers, that public assistance should not be paid to those that were on strike.

We campaigned against this continuously. I remember the Reform Union asked, as a miners' organisation, that Labour Party national leaders should actively associate themselves with our campaign to raise money for miners' assistance. Ramsay MacDonald particuarly, as leader of the Labour Party, was asked, but he never could find time to devote to that. As a matter of fact he went off to North Africa for a holiday in the sun.[1]

In order to keep regular counter-opposition to this propaganda, it was decided that we should run a big campaign on the need for public assistance, and that to show up what our entitlement was, that we would have a mass demonstration to the nearest poorhouse and for the males to demand admission. This was on the understanding that we could show up how impossible it was, and that the alternative to admission to the poorhouse was the continuation of payment by the Parish Council.

The campaign was organised on a wide scale, but in our area it meant that we had got to organise the whole of East Fife for a march on the poorhouse which was situated in Thornton, about a mile and a half down the main road towards the station from Thornton village itself. Keeping in mind what had happened in Thornton in the 1921 lock-out, this time we were concerned to make it an absolutely disciplined, organised march, and in the early part of the day instead of at night. We ran a series of meetings to explain the purpose of the demonstration and how we wanted this demonstration to be under the control of the Workers' Defence Corps that had been set up during the General Strike and had continued in being.

I remember speaking at a big meeting in Buckhaven. There were police there, and I was trying to get across the message without saying it in too crude a fashion. All the other fellows were saying something of the same kind, so it was not anything special that I did.

I said: "Well, you know that the police have been active in a number of places, according to the Press. We want to make sure that this demonstration goes off without any trouble at all. We therefore want to be a well-organised, disciplined force. Everybody that attends this demonstration will be under the control of their appointed marshals. No one is to act on their own. And you know that we are asking you to march a considerable distance. It may be that you are not as fit as you were before. You have not been doing hard work around the pit, so to help you along that long road each of you must come with a stick. It's much easier to march with a stick than it is to march without one. In addition to that, your shoes are getting worn. Better to gie yer pit boots a grease up, better break in the pit boots: you'll never know when you'll need to use them again. You'll get supplied with sandwiches at the kitchen. It's all right to take your piece-box. But I would not advise you to take your water can. Your water can will be getting rusty by this time. You'll enjoy a drink better out of a bottle, so that every one of you bring a bottle with you. This is compulsory equipment. And if you are a disciplined force we are quite sure that we'll march to Thornton and back again."

Nobody in that audience needed to be told what that message meant. And it was obvious that they understood it when you saw the lads on the march on the actual morning. Every one of them was fully equipped. The defence team, as I said, were in charge, and they used their old army experience: the column marched fifty minutes, the whistle blew and everybody fell out for ten minutes. At the end of that time the whistle blew again, up you got and away you went.

The leadership of the march fully expected that there would be trouble and in no circumstances did they intend to run away from it, while they would not provoke it. One incident sticks out in my mind about this. On the road to Thornton to the poorhouse, we travelled via Coaltown of Wemyss, the top end of West Wemyss, up through Boreland and then to the Gallatown road, and then up the Thornton road. The whistle went for the ten minutes' break just before we came to the road end at Gallatown. So the army lay down.

Looking ahead we could see row after row of police, big crowds of them waiting at the T-road junction. So the boys were looking along at the array of blue and saying, "Aha, this is it." There was a discussion about how we were to get round that corner, because it was a difficult location. We were coming up a slight hill into a blind end, as it were. We were at a disadvantage.

There was one lad, Aitchison, who had given us a wee bit of bother through indiscipline on the march.[2] He was getting on in years and was well known to us because of his activity in the concerts. He was the church organist and the choirmaster at West Wemyss, and he got his choir girls to sing at a number of these money-raising ventures. He had never played any part in union activity prior to the General Strike and the miners' lock-out. He associated with a different sphere: very friendly with the heads of the coal company, and staying in West Wemyss under the shadow of the Castle, he was well known to the lady of the Castle, Lady Wemyss.[3] It was therefore with a sort of amused smile that we used to look on his activities in this strike period, although we were quite pleased and gave him every assistance because of the work he was doing. Our friend Proudfoot used to tell us some stories about him when he had been in his unit during the war. He was the type that would accept no discipline but seemed to have such a hard neck that he got away with things that no other body could have got away with. So that when this fall-in was whistled prior to meeting this solid phalanx of police, we were wondering who should be in the leadership and who should be behind, when this lad moved off.

We shouted to him, "Come back, come back into line." He never answered us, he kept moving off.

We shouted to him, "Hey, you silly bugger, come back!"

He went on, and to show the remarkable character of this man, he walked right up to the police superintendent and police inspector that were in charge of this police unit, the lads who had silver braid, and said: "You know who I am and these are my men. I am in charge and responsible for this body of men you see in front of you. They are a splendid body of men and they are going to pass here without any trouble."

Actually, we did get past without any trouble, to our surprise. And Aitchison stood with the police until the last marcher was past safely and then fell in behind.

The column marched off into Thornton, the bulk of it swung into the public park. A deputation went to the poorhouse to demand admission and that was rather an interesting thing. It rather tickled us at the time that these lads, some of them tall and well built, fine-looking men — one of them had a gold chain across his belly — were demanding admission to the poorhouse because they were starving miners.

We ran a big meeting, kept this up, got the deputation's report, pulled back out of Thornton in a disciplined manner, and passed all the police again without trouble. The result of the demonstration was that the poorhouse said they had no room for us. The Government did not order the Parish to stop relief.

This was the real organised activity that kept our organisation active and alive.

As the lock-out dragged on, and coal was getting very scarce, it was like diamonds, and anything black could be kidded on to be coal and sold at fantastic prices. We had organised a team of roughnecks to stop the filling of coal on the beach. One of them came to the lock-out headquarters to report that he had found out that some miners from the Kirkcaldy end were working an outcrop in the area, and were selling the coals to carters. They were doing this during the night and clearing off when it became daylight.

We said, "All right, that's got to be stopped. Put out a few men tonight and check their activities, spy out the land and see that you stop them the next night." Well, this team, along with one or two lads in the second line of leadership, visited that place where the boys were working, closed the mouth of the inlet to the workings, fixed up a small escape hole with the branches of wood and anything they could get about them, and then shouted, "Are ye coming up?"

The boys who were working getting coal, well, I understand that they were not keen to come up. They had coal stacked waiting on the carter coming. They had also got some explosives with them that our boys got possession of, and one of them fixed up a small charge of explosives, chucked it down, and said: "That's a sample. Are ye coming up?"

Each one of our lads had armed himself with a piece of wood and made these lads run the gauntlet. They gave them a real smacking, and told them that if they came back they would get worse. They got a solemn assurance they would not come back.

But to reveal the general outlook, when they had chased these lads away and before they left themselves, our lads were wondering what to do with the coal. It was there. They said, "Well, we'll take it doon tae the kitchen." But they had no conveyance. Then the carter appeared. He said, "I'll pay you for the coal." So they had a huddle. What were they going to do? "Well," they said, "we're just as well to sell it to him. If not, some other body will pinch it if we gang away."

So they sold the coal for £4.50 to the contractor and then came down and handed every penny over to the strike committee, and asked if they had done the right thing. They were rewarded each man with a ten-packet of Woodbine, and given a special breakfast of tea and rolls.

These were real tough lads. They had been out and in the jail for various minor offences, but when it was necessary to show working-class solidarity they were not found wanting.

Coal became worth its weight in gold. We had effectively stopped anyone getting it from outcrops. There was nothing to be got out of the pit. But over many years coal in the stone had been washing up on the beaches at Buckhaven. This had come from the redd that was being discharged on the bing, washed away by the tide, and subsequently flung up on the beach. Generally, you could get, at certain times, plenty of small coal, at other times it would be mixed with stone; then you might get a period of stone covering up the coal that had been unpicked on the pit. So it was a regular habit of the people who resided in the area to go to the beach to try to gather coal to keep their house warm. No one had any objection to that until carters with a horse and cart started to go down, fill up whatever they could get if it was black, and then sell it at ransom prices outside.

There was a group of people on that beach who were good solid supporters of the lock-out activity, and they approached the committee and said, "This has got to stop. We don't mind anybody gathering coal for their own use. But we are not going to allow people to gather coal to sell in order to make money."

We said, "All right, you go ahead and stop it."

So the lads gathered together, armed with their shovels, and would play at quoits until the boys with the carts appeared. They adopted a most novel method of stopping these boys from filling coal. They would take up their position and start to dig a trench right round the horse and cart. The carter would be filling away to fill his cart, and the lads would dig a deep trench round about it so that he could not get his loaded cart out nor his horse.

There were altercations, threats, and scuffles, and so on, but these lads remained adamant. The only way the carters could get out of this island was to empty the coal they had dug, and fill up enough of the trench to let the cart out. They were told: "Don't come back."

On one occasion a local carter who had four horses and four carts on the scene, knew the boys who were digging the trench round his carts and he threatened them that they had no right to be there because they were drawing dole money and could not be genuinely seeking work when they were digging holes on the beach. So he threatened he would report them to the Labour Exchange.

Whether he did I do not know, but it is a fact that the following week their bureau money was stopped on the ground that they were not genuinely seeking work.

That night another coincidence occurred. The carter's stables went on fire, the carts were burned and the horses were lost.

I was out on bail at the time, and had been told I had to keep clear of pickets and so on. I remember going down with Jimmy Hodgson, a son-in-law of Bob Stewart of Dundee, who was acting Communist Party organiser in Fife at the time and was staying in my house.[4] We had gone down to post some letters. The police must have been keeping tabs on me, because they approached me next day to say, "We know that you were out. We saw you going down to the post and going back home again."

I said, "Aye."

They said, "You're bound to know who set fire to those stables last night."

"Me? I don't know the first thing aboot it."

"See, you're out on bail on a very serious charge. You'll get six months at the very least. If you were to tell us wha set fire to the stables we'll be able to put in a good word for you to the fiscal."

I said, "Well, if I have to get out of going to jail by that means you're barking up the wrong tree, sir. I'd rather go to jail. But first of all I don't know if anybody set fire to the stables."

They said, "Ye mix wi' them. Ye should find oot."

I said, "I'm no' going to try to find oot. And I'll no' gaun tae jail because I'll get aff."

However, this picketing on the beach continued and the next day the carters came down they were accompanied by a force of police. Undaunted, the lads still dug their trenches. The police threatened what they were going to do, but it had no effect. So they had to give in again. A third attempt was made, and this time the police drew their batons but the lads simply turned their shovels edge on and said, "Right, you can have it any way you like." So there was no baton charge.

But the police resorted to summoning the lads to court for conduct likely to create a breach of the peace. There were forty-five of the lads. Again we trooped up to the Sheriff Court at Cupar. Their bail was fixed at £5 per man, and we had one devil of a job trying to raise that money at that time. One of the methods of raising it was to gather whelks and sell them. By hook or by crook we raised the money, but to their credit the lads told us we had made a mistake. Lying in jail would not have bothered them. They would have been fed and they were all tough enough lads, it would never have troubled them. But eventually, when the case was tried, they were fined £3 each.

The lads again had got Burke as their lawyer — they had forgotten about the General Strike cases he had handled. And after we had finished congratulating one another that we had got them off with a £3 fine and that none of them had gone to jail, we said, "Oh, here, we've got £2 to come per man from the bail money." So we made tracks for the sheriff clerk's office. But he said, "Ye're ower late. The lawyer's clerk has been here and he's nailed a' the £2s himself." We never got these £2 but we said to Burke, "We're no' paying you any mair. You pinched that."

As the lock-out dragged on there was another incident that comes to mind. At some of the pits in East Fife, coal had been stacked on the bing prior to the lock-out. This was a tremendous bait to the coal company if they could get it filled off, because of the famine prices. As the struggle went on into October, there was obviously a number of people who began to feel the pinch of starvation and were anxious to get started to work if possible, or get money of some kind somehow. We were informed that a few men had turned up at Cameron Colliery and were filling coal off the bing. We decided that had got to be stopped. The Defence Corps organised pickets, they were called out at five o'clock in the morning and made their way towards this pit, which was about two miles from Buckhaven.

We had reconnoitred the whole area beforehand and knew that the police were in strength on the approaches from the main road to the pit and there were police billeted in the pit buildings. On the main road out of Buckhaven towards the pit there was a dip in the road. Farm cottages were between this dip and the pit, so that the police could not see from the pit what was happening in this dip in the road.

We arranged that thirty hand-picked men would lie back in this dip when the main body walked on under one of our best leaders, with instructions that under no circumstances was anybody to proceed past that spot to the pit. The main picket went on, flung their pickets round each road that approached the pit, and marched past the police. It was rather amusing to watch the police with their glasses searching the roads approaching the pit. There was nobody appearing. They used all kinds of threats towards the pickets around the pit. They said to David Proudfoot and myself that they would have us arrested for illegal drilling on the king's highway. But nobody got to the pit that day.

However, they must have called at the houses to find out why their potential workers did not turn up. They then resorted to putting their policemen on bicycles so that they were on the move the whole of the time and the element of surprise could not be repeated by us. But the boys countered this by arming themselves with packets of tacks. The whole approach to the pit road was simply littered with tacks and the police were getting their cycles punctured.

But because these lads would not be persuaded by ordinary picketing, the traditional method of dealing with blacklegs soon developed. Night visits were paid, windows and front doors were smashed in. The lads who were working found it would be better policy to stay at home. So that blacklegging at Cameron Colliery was nipped in the bud.

There was another occasion when our active lads in one of the outlying areas, Balgonie — about five miles from Buckhaven — found they were having difficulties. They were not covered by the same kind of feeding arrangements as we had devised in Wemyss parish, and were left individually to their own resources. They were having a difficult time. The terrain suited some of those that wished to work getting to work quite easily, because while there was a pit shaft there was also a number of surface mines, or as the miners called them, "in-gaunees", which were right around the village. The lads could get down into these pit workings without travelling over the surface to the pithead shaft.

The active elements that still remained in Balgonie requested assistance from us. We first of all sent up an organised team of canvassers, leaders, who visited every house, argued with the men that they should stick it along with their comrades. The main difficulty undoubtedly was the isolation and sheer starvation that was forcing men to go back to work. Next day we followed this up with a mass demonstration. Again we had to have it organised by the Defence Force, and while there was a big contingent of police on duty, they again decided it would be preferable to leave things as they were as long as we were not creating any breach of the law or riotous conduct. We certainly stopped any work that day.

But Balgonie was an isolated outlying area. We could not have pickets marching from place to place every day, and as the local lads were unable to hold the position once we got the rest of the blacklegs out, Balgonie gradually deteriorated. This was a sad business for us, because Balgonie had always been in the leadership as a progressive branch of the miners' union. They had been active before the war, during the war, immediately after the war, and in the whole period of the '21 lock-out, the Reform Union and the '26 struggle, and it was sad for us to see their morale being undermined and broken. It had a very serious retarding effect on that village for a long time afterwards. Those who had gone back to work were not happy about the position they had been forced into. They were conscious of it and the active elements felt under a cloud that they had failed to keep their village intact. It took a lot of work and water under the bridge before this village came back to its former progressive attitude, which it did of course during the Second World War, and in the building up of the National Union of Mineworkers after the war it again took its pride of place as a progressive branch.

24

VICTIMISATION

WHILE we had been able to keep our ranks intact and prevent any further baton charges in the whole of East Fife area, this was not the picture that was developing in other areas. Particularly from central Fife we were getting reports regularly of police batoning, police intimidation, police brutalities, and so on. It was claimed that many of the ex-Black and Tans, who had got their training in Ireland, were being recruited as special police and sent to Central and West Fife. They were billeted in the Co-operative Hall, Lochgelly, and other main centres. But Lochgelly had the name of having a brutal bunch of policemen.

On one occasion when the Fife Co-ordinating Council of Action was meeting, word was sent in to us that an ugly situation had developed at Glencraig Colliery in which men and women were facing rows of policemen. They asked us for assistance. A group of us went down to the pit and it certainly was a tense situation when we arrived. There were two rows of police drawn up facing men and women within about six feet of one another, the police with their batons out and the men armed with all kinds of improvised implements. Neither side would turn or give in to the other. It certainly looked an ugly situation. After consultation we said, "Look, we better get this thing calmed down." We said to the police, "You behave yourselves and we'll get thir lads away."

I remember Abe Moffat addressing them and saying, "All rights, lads, keep facing the way you are, but when I say 'one!' you take one step backward; when I say 'two!' you take another step." And we did that, with the leadership standing in the gap between the police and the local people until we got sufficient space between them to say, "All right, now we can break off."

We were informed that the night before the police had run amok in Glencraig, batoning everyone that was in sight, chasing people into their houses and following them. There was the story of one lad that ran into a house and the woman took the top off the boiler, the lad jumped in, she put the lid on again, and when the police came charging in they could not find the lad and went out. But women were being batoned, youths, and anybody else. It was alleged by the local people that these lads whom they referred to as the Black and Tans had been filled with rum and were running berserk through the village. In consequence, it was decided to organise a series of protest meetings about police brutality and to demand an investigation, a public enquiry, by contacting all sympathetic councillors of the county council on the police committee. It so happened that a whole series of lads were being arrested for the speeches that were being made following this. Jimmy Stewart of Lochgelly was arrested and eventually, after trial, was fined £10.

I was charged and finally arrested on a similar charge of sedition and utterances likely to cause disaffection among the king's lieges. I had just come back as a delegate from a Communist Party conference in London and was giving a report to the Party branch when the policemen knocked at the door and asked if I was there. I went out and they told me they had a warrant for my arrest. I looked at the policemen and said, "I'm surely a hell of an important man. Does it take fourteen of you to arrest me?" They had only about fifty yards to go from there to the police cell. Next morning I was shackled and taken off to Cupar.

I remember the old fiscal saying to the sheriff, "Your Lordship, this is a very dangerous person. He is a very fluent speaker, has a powerful influence on his fellows and must not be allowed at large for the safety of the country." When he described me as a very dangerous person I think he was right, because while it was Sunday night and I had been dressed as well as it was possible to be dressed, when I came to put on my clothes that morning in the police cells, my tie could not be got. David Proudfoot's wife had brought down breakfast to me, and when they were giving back the basket to her they put my tie and collar and so on in it. So I went to the sheriff court without a collar and tie. There was also no comb and brush, and my hair was hanging over my head unbrushed and uncombed, so I could certainly be looked on as a very "dangerous" person.

However, the fiscal was arguing for no bail, and that they could not afford to allow me at liberty. The old sheriff says, "Bail at £10", with a condition that I was not to participate in picketing and lock-out activity till I came up again to court. Ten pounds was something at that time. Well, as I said earlier, the committee that we had established for protecting people that were arrested decided they were not going to have Mr Burke, the Dundee lawyer, and got a K.C. named Watson in his place.[1]

When I went up for trial at Cupar we found that another comrade was on trial for a similar speech. He was a young lad, Jim Watt from Lumphinnans. He was a close colleague of Alex Moffat. They were both in the Young Communist League and they were as close one to the other in their work as Proudfoot and I were in East Fife. When Watt was being tried he repeated all the things that he was charged with, and the old sheriff said, "OK, three months." There was a sequel to that. Watt was full of bravado at the trial and at going off to jail. But apparently while in jail he was persuaded to become interested in some religious organisation and formed connection with them. So when he came out of jail they sent him to their special schools and trained him to be a preacher and sent him on the special mission to try to convert his old pal Alex Moffat. So we lost an active militant in Jim Watt.[2]

So as I said he was tried in the forenoon, and my case was continued after lunch. It so happened that the sergeant and constable who were the witnesses against me had only managed to get one civilian witness for the prosecution. He was a lad employed as a ganger for the firm that was uplifting the old disused tramway lines between Leven and Kirkcaldy. He certainly had been at the meeting. The police, however, made the mistake of allowing him to mix with the lads who were appearing as witnesses on my behalf. One of the principal witnesses for me was an Irishman from Southern Ireland and so was this lad who was the police witness. They got chatting at lunchtime and went and had a drink together. The militant Southern Irishman said, "What the hell are you thinking about, going to give evidence for the police against an active workman?"

"No," the other lad said, "I don't want to do that. I was forced into it."

But my witness said, "If you tell the truth as we see it there'll be nothing wrong with that."

So when the police had finished their evidence and called on this big Irish ganger as their civilian witness he had not been speaking long when the sheriff interjected and asked the fiscal, "By the way, Mr Fiscal, is this a witness for the prosecution or is he one of the defence witnesses called before his time?" The fiscal had to admit ruefully that he was a prosecution witness, but he was an excellent witness for the case that we were putting up.

When I went into the witness-box I said we had been repeating the stories as we knew them in order to make clear what the facts were as compared to the wild rumours that had been multiplying about the baton charges in Central Fife, and that we had been anxious to get contact with all county councillors to support a demand for an investigation by the police committee into the conduct of the police at Glencraig. Before our evidence was completed, however, the sheriff said, "I find that there is no case to answer here, and the prisoner is discharged." So I was discharged without a stain on my character, due in the main to a very good Irish witness.

As I mentioned, I had been arrested on my return from a Communist Party conference in Battersea Town Hall in London. When I was going into the conference, Mrs Helen Crawfurd, who was very prominent in the Workers' International Relief organisation, was waiting in the vestibule of the hall and having a look at the people coming in. When she saw me she said, "Ah, here's a lad that'll do. I want to see you. We want you to go to Europe and do a tour to raise money for the miners."

"Good God," I remember saying to her, "I cannae even speak English never mind speak other languages."

"Oh, don't let that bother ye. Ye'll get interpreters with you," she said. "Are you game to do it?"

I said, "I'll do it on one condition: that the boys back home gie their permission."

So we phoned back or sent a telegram and got word back we had that permission.

I remember going to France and Germany, and was to go right on to the

Soviet Union. But by that time it was into November 1926. The lock-out of the miners was weakening. I had only been in Germany a short time when I was recalled because of the deteriorating situation in the coalfield, and had to come back and get into picket activity to try to stiffen the struggle.

Our area was still holding firm but the position was deteriorating, partly collapsing, in other areas. The National Executive of the M.F.G.B. decided to recommend the calling off of the struggle. This was a substantial defeat. The miners, when they went back to work at the end of the six months' lock-out, this long glorious struggle, had to face the question of increased hours, reduction in wages, district negotiations. They had got no guarantee about getting their work back, and victimisation for the active elements was the order of the day.

Almost every one of our local active people was barred. There was a scattering of many of the best elements in the struggles that had developed. Many of them were induced to become insurance agents, shilling-a-week clothing salesmen, door-to-door visitation. A number of them left the district. One lad, for example, who had been extremely active in Denbeath, had a big family, and could not get employment here, decided to emigrate to Canada. He was Julius Cunningham — we called him Caesar Cunningham. He and his brother-in-law, Danny Ward, were curious characters.[3] One was Catholic, the other Orange. When they were sober, they were the closest of pals and fellow-workmen. When they got drunk, which happened occasionally, they would forget that, and the old Catholic-Orange difficulty would loom large and they would probably finish up with a real battle between them. But when they sobered up they were good working-class comrades again. We eventually heard that Caesar Cunningham had knocked around Canada looking for work and moving from place to place. Finally, he contracted pneumonia and died. There were stories of this kind turning up all the time.

Will McFadyean, one of the two sergeant-majors in our Workers' Defence Corps, did not get back after '26, went north to the hydro-electric schemes, and finished up as a foreman ganger.

Another lad who had been quite outstanding in the youth activity at the time of the General Strike and the miners' lock-out, and was a very fluent speaker, was Jimmy Duffy. He came from Denbeath from a family that was quite well known. His father was Frank Duffy, who was active in the trade union and took a very left attitude, more of an anarchist attitude, that everybody was out of step but himself. Frank Duffy was one of three brothers. Pat Duffy, one of the brothers, was a great football manager of the Wellesley Junior Football Club, a paid scout for the Glasgow Celtic, and produced many leading internationalists from this area — O'Donnell, Fagan, and so on. The other of Jimmy's uncles, Peter Duffy, was delegate in the Adamson union.[4]

Jimmy did not get back following '26, and went through to the Lothians to try to get a job. He got a job there but came up before the famous Mungie Mackay and his green table at Lady Victoria pit at Newtongrange. The green table was the manager's table. The famous Mungie Mackay

113

got a reputation for being the boss not only in the pit but out of the pit. You could only go to the Lothian Coal Company's pub, their shop. It was truck, though it was the 1920s. Any misdemeanour and you were told you had to go up and see Mr Mackay. You went in to see Mr Mackay and you had to take off your hat and say "Sir", and then he read out what the crime was, sat in judgement on you and gave you his decision. The decision always if you were a militant was that you had to clear out, and out of your house as well.[5] So that Jimmy Duffy had to leave. He was dismissed there because of his talk among the workers in the pit. He got a job at Lochhead Colliery, near Buckhaven, and settled in Coaltown of Wemyss for a period. I used to say jokingly he reminded me of an arab: he was always on the move, just up with the tents and away. Without any known reason he again upped his tents and away and finished up in Kent. Years later, when the National Union of Mineworkers was formed, and there was a ballot vote for the national officials, it was a surprise to me to see Jimmy Duffy's name on the ballot as contending against Bill Lawther for national president.[6] He got some 10,000 votes. I have not heard about Duffy since then and I do not know what ultimately happened to him.

Two other lads, Chick Watson and his pal, who had got involved in the trench-digging incident at the beach during the lock-out, also got a job in Mungie Mackay's pit in the Lothians.[7] They did all right till they drew their first pay. There was another lad from this district with them. When they drew their first pay, naturally they wanted to have a drink. Their old working-class background came up and they started to sing *The Red Flag*. They sang a lot of the strike ditties and songs when they got merry. Again they were up before Mungie Mackay and the green table on Monday morning and had to come back into East Fife.

Jimmy Hope of East Wemyss was another militant who was shut out, like most of the others, and could not get a job anywhere. He was persuaded by one of our old Marxian tutors, Jimmy Birrell, who had opened a draper's credit business in Dunfermline, to take on as an agent. To get a livelihood, Jimmy became what was then termed a shilling-a-week man. He was an extremely popular man amongst the miners and their wives. But he was not the most successful as a collector, because in those difficult days the woman of the house would say to him, "I'm sorry, Jimmy, I haven't got much this week."

"Oh, that's all right, lassie," he said, "ye'll just pay me when ye're able."

I could never bring myself to accept Mr Birrell's attitude to Jimmy, because he never put Jimmy on a set wage but paid him solely on commission. For what he had done to build up Birrell's business in this area, the time spent on it, devoting almost half his house to stock and so on, there should have been far better recompense for him than what there was.

Another man who was associated with the militant movement but also used them following '26 was Willie Dunbar. He was manager of the Liverpool Victoria Insurance Society. Every active miner that was victimised carried tremendous local sympathy and support. So that Dunbar visited these people and said, "Why not become an insurance agent?" There was some great conflict of ideas as to whether a lad who believed in socialism should become an insurance agent — why should we worry about what happens when a man dies and not when a man's alive? But Dunbar expressed his cynicism again and said, "Well, if Henry won't wake up, Henry must pay up." So that eventually many of them were persuaded to become insurance agents, and they made very good insurance agents. Many began to realise that it was easier to get a very nice livelihood that way than it was to be active in the labour movement as they had been in the past, and many of them became quite successful businessmen and so on. But it also meant that Mr Dunbar, the district manager, had the highest increase in business and was very successful too. So that while he had sympathy and help for the young lads who were being victimised, he also turned it into a profitable business for himself and the firm. And the Liverpool Victoria almost swept the boards in the mining areas for new business.

Among the many others who were victimised amongst our local militants were Willie "Mosie" Murray of Leven, who ended up as a scavenger with the town council, Peter Hastie of Windygates, who became a very successful insurance agent under Mr William Dunbar, and Jimmy Ord of Gallatown. Jimmy had to eke out a livelihood whichever way he could. He used to sell for a book club and also sold home-made clothes that were made by his wife.

Bert True of West Wemyss also did not get back. But, as I have said, he was not made of the same material as the rest of us. For following '26 there was an attempt to establish a miners' non-political union in Fife like the one formed in Nottinghamshire by George Spencer, M.P., who was expelled from the M.F.G.B. conference in October 1926.[8] A group of ex-Adamson people started this non-political union in the Lochgelly area, and at a time when I was unemployed and we had trouble with rent arrears and shortage of everything in the house, Bert True called at the house and asked if he could speak to me. Then in the course of the discussion he said he had been asked to take on an organiser's job for the non-political union and he was recommending that I should be given a leading job. He was empowered to offer me, he said, £6 a week as an official of the non-political union. True went out of the house quicker then he came in, and I have never seen him since, so I don't know what ultimately became of him.

I personally was barred after the lock-out. My father and brother George also were victimised: they were kept out of the pit for two years.

When the bar was put up against me being employed we had to try and live on sixteen shillings (eighty pence) for a husband, six shillings (thirty pence) for a wife, and two shillings (ten pence) for each child. By that time we had two daughters, so our total income was twenty-six shillings (£1.30) a week. We had been unable to get a house until the town council built a new housing scheme, and by that time, having two of a family and living in sub-let conditions, we qualified for a new three-apartment house. That was in 1926. It so happened that the house became available for occupancy during the period of the miners' lock-out. So here again we had a problem. Here was a house which we could occupy, but we were in the midst of a lock-out. I did not know when I would be able to resume work and get an income in order to pay the rent. But we decided

115

to go ahead, take the house, and if we were going to be short then the town council would be short of its rent for a period. So that this was a lovely break-in for Mrs McArthur, who had had no idea of what it was to live as a miner's wife, who had had reasonably comfortable circumstances when she had married me, and now, with two of a family, taking over a house without any income and not knowing where it was to come from.

I can remember making a decision and saying to my wife that our income was inadequate, that we could not meet all our commitments. Something would have to go short, but looking to the future, for the sake of the children, whatever we could spare would go on food, in order to build up healthy bodies. The debt arising from clothing or rent could be met sometime but you could not meet the effects of underfeeding in subsequent life. So it was a conscious and deliberate decision forced on us because of the circumstances and I have never regretted this, although it meant a completely changed life, not only for me but especially for Mrs McArthur. While my parents were anxious to assist us in every way possible, they were also obliged to sign on at the dole instead of being employed. It meant that my wife was compelled to learn the trade of make-do-and-mend, making down clothes for the youngsters, and making sure that they were reasonably well turned out. She was amazingly successful in this, and was always commented upon by some of her friends. But the problem was shoes. You could not make down shoes and I have seen her in tears many a time when she tried to cut pasteboard to fit into the shoes if it was raining or damp. That was the most difficult thing to overcome. We were so hard up that from 1926 until 1928 my wife went without teeth as she could not afford a set of false ones.

So I was unemployed almost all the time from the end of the lock-out in November 1926 until I commenced work in February 1928 as a full-time agent for the reunited Fife miners' union at the Dunfermline office.

I was still on the Wemyss Parish Council. We decided there that we should develop some form of relief work for men who were victimised by the coal owners. The Parish Council were in charge of a cemetery, and the only thing they could do was to excavate the roadways or runways into the cemetery, bottom them with a new bottoming, and put a tarmacadam surface on them. This would be a means of paying wages for a fortnight each for the men who were not finding work. The clerk to the Parish Council approached me and said that the architect who was doing the work would need a man on the job to check on the material coming in and going out so that they could have a check on the charges of the carters and other suppliers, and the time work. So I became checker-timekeeper to the architect and got a few weeks' work at that. But the powers that be got to know about it and claimed that I could not carry on as a parish councillor if I was being employed by means of the Parish Council. So I had to resign from the Parish Council.

The only other work I could get during those months was a temporary job track-laying for an electric power company which was laying a cable from Kennoway to Windygates. I was employed there for three months until I commenced work in Dunfermline in the Fife miners' union in February 1928.

There the salary was fixed at £4 a week and this was certainly a tremendous change. We had to use the good offices of Jimmy Hope, who was a shilling-a-week man with Birrell, in order that I could get clothes to be presentable to take on this union job.

25

A MOST FANTASTIC
SITUATION

THE efforts to get unity between the Reform Union and the old union, or
Adamson's union, had been considerably strengthened during the period
of solidarity, the General Strike and the miners' lock-out. As I have said, the
Communists and Minority Movement groups in Fife had, in and after 1922-23,
swung in wholeheartedly behind the fight against Adamson, when we had been
forced into forming a rival organisation, the Reform Union. But while this
fight went on there came to develop, as a result of persistent agitation amongst
us by national leaders such as Nat Watkins,[1] Harry Pollitt and Arthur Horner,
and of regular discussions, a split even within those giving allegiance to the
Communist idea in Fife. A small section, including David Proudfoot, started
to argue on the necessity for getting one union and resolving the split between
the Reform Union and Adamson's union. This argument went on fiercely
amongst us up to 1926 when the General Strike developed. Mass
confrontation with the Government and the long drawn-out struggle of the
miners meant that all argument about the necessity for one union was
conceded, and the Communist members, Minority Movement group and the
other active elements in the Reform Union actively participated in the fight for
the amalgamation of the two unions. So while the Fife Communists had more
or less ignored, or did not pay enough heed to, the general guidance of the
Communist line on split organisations, it was the insistence of members of the
Communist Party within the ranks of the Reform Union that led that
organisation into leading the fight for amalgamation.

Prior to the General Strike itself, as I have said, this agitation for unity
had been very powerful, very widely supported. In a number of areas in Fife,
ballot votes had been taken by the men at the pit as to whether or not they were
in favour of the two unions being merged into one. In Leven and Kelty and
some of the West Fife pits the support was almost unanimous in favour of the
one union being formed, the healing of the breach. And then the feeling was
that it was the officials in Dunfermline of Adamson's union that were
preventing the merger. It is a matter of history that Adamson fought this tooth
and nail. However, the Miners' Federation of Great Britain put pressure on

the National Union of Scottish Mine Workers, and with Robert Smillie, who was then president of the N.U.S.M.W., himself in favour of the merging of the two Fife unions, consultations between them took place in July 1926, and amalgamation was agreed on. I was one of the team representing the Reform Union in these negotiations. It was agreed that Philip Hodge, who had been general secretary of the Reform Union, should be taken over into the reunited union as a full-time agent. It was also agreed that Jimmy Cook and Sandy Smith, the two agents of the Adamson union, would continue in office pending new elections.[7] These elections for the two agents would be carried out as soon as possible, and there would also be elections for branch officials of the amalgamated membership, as well as elections of representatives from Fife to the N.U.S.M.W.

Again Adamson tried his utmost to prevent the amalgamation taking place even after it was agreed to, and it was only under last-minute pressure from the General Council of the Scottish T.U.C. that it was eventually put into operation by March 1927. The Reform Union was dissolved.

We found that Jimmy Cook, who had been an agent in Adamson's union, was in a curious position. He had been the agent for the Clackmannan part of the coalfield. It was a small county, and in the process of growth it had been agreed to amalgamate the Fife and Kinross miners' union with Clackmannan miners' union and form the Fife, Kinross and Clackmannan Miners' Association. This amalgamation had taken place in 1917. As Cook was already agent for the small area, he was taken over as agent into the Fife, Kinross and Clackmannan Miners' Association. When the General Strike took place and the miners' lock-out followed, whether or not he felt that the future was not very bright, Cook had left this country to go to Canada for an appointment in the Civil Service. It appeared that there had been some mix-up in the arrangements, however, because it was found when he got to Canada that he was over age for employment in the Civil Service. He had resigned from his appointment as agent, or financial secretary, in the union but he wrote to Mr Adamson and Adamson had agreed he should come back and resume his old post. I remember towards the finish of the miners' lock-out he was down to speak on the difficult termination negotiations. In reply to questions from his members, he was saying that he was not there to explain the reasons why the National Executive of the M.F.G.B. were advising the miners to accept the terms to go back to work. He was in the position of a soldier carrying out his orders. I could not help interjecting and saying, "Did I understand him correctly—that he was in the position of a soldier carrying out his orders? If he was, it was not a happy simile, because a soldier who was engaged in a battle as the miners were with the employers, who deserted the fight and cleared off to Canada, who deserted in the face of the enemy, could only get one punishment — and that was being shot at dawn as a deserter. And if he claimed that he was a soldier that's the fate that awaited him." The meeting broke up in disorder.

Cook was the agent therefore who was occupying a temporary post in the Adamson organisation but for which he was to stand election after the amalgamation. The other agent was Alex or Sandy Smith, as we used to call him. Sandy Smith was the delegate for the small branch of Methilhill. He was an out-and-out Adamsonian supporter. He had an extraordinarily loud voice. I remember one occasion when were were in the office at Dunfermline after amalgamation, awaiting the results of the ballots that were going on. John Bird, noting the loud voice of Sandy Smith on the phone, said, "He reminds me of the story about the Prince of Wales. He went into the Colonial Office and said, 'What's that noise?'."

" 'Oh,' said an official, 'that's Mr J. H. Thomas talking to India'."

" 'Talking to India? Can't you tell him to use the phone?'."

So Sandy Smith would remind you of much the same. He was an out-and-out constitutionalist and stood rigidly by that, was unbending.

The choice was a clear-cut one as to what was to be the eventual position in the Fife union and in the N.U.S.M.W. The General Strike, the political mass agitation that had been done, the publicity gained by the militants as against the staying-in-the-background role of the old union officials, the sell-out by the General Council of the T.U.C., the feeling at the finish that the miners had been betrayed and were being forced to go back into terrible conditions, the victimisation, the unemployment and underemployment that existed in the coalfield — all that meant that there was a very strong support for the militants in Fife and also in the Scottish coalfield. When the two unions were merged in Fife, ten of us who were Communists had been appointed as delegates to the Central Delegate Board in Dunfermline, including myself from Buckhaven branch, Proudfoot for Methil, Jimmy Stewart for Lochgelly, and so on. But there were no steps being taken to have the agentships filled, and it was on instructions from my branch that I moved suspension of standing orders at the Delegate Board at Dunfermline to have this matter discussed. It was finally agreed that we should have nominations sent in from the branches to fill these two positions. As we were due to make appointments to the executive of the National Union of Scottish Mine Workers, and as Fife had five representatives on that, it was also agreed that nominations should be asked for these as well.

A series of meetings was held amongst ourselves as Communists, Minority Movement men and Leftists, and finally, on votes being taken, it was agreed that the Minority Movement would support David Proudfoot and myself for the two positions as agents in the Fife union. While a number of other people had been nominated for these positions it was also agreed that we should let their nominations remain on the ballot paper but urge supporters to vote for Proudfoot and me. Thus John Bird, Jimmy Stewart and Andrew Jarvie had been nominated, but they agreed to try to swing their votes wherever they could to Proudfoot and myself.

On the position for the representatives on the N.U.S.M.W. from Fife, it was agreed we should try to get support for myself, John Bird, David Proudfoot, Jimmy Stewart and Philip Hodge. Again a number of prominent lads — Tommy Miller, Andrew Jarvie, Pat Connelly — had been nominated from their own branches, but it was agreed to try to swing the votes to the five agreed-on representatives.

In addition to that it was felt that as far as the four positions of office-bearer on the executive of the N.U.S.M.W. itself were concerned, that we should put up nominees for each of these positions. As a result of consultations with all the militant lads from the other counties, it was agreed that John Bird from Bowhill should be put up as the representative for the presidentship against the sitting president, Robert Smillie. It was felt that Smillie was a mere shell of his former self and was no longer fulfilling a satisfactory role as president. The sitting vice-president was Hugh Murnin of Stirling, who was also, like Adamson, an M.P. We agreed to put up for the vice-presidentship a good militant lad who was well known in Stirlingshire, Alex Thomson, a working miner.[3] And for the general secretaryship, there was put up my old Labour College colleague, Willie Allan from Blantyre, who had been elected to the executive of the N.U.S.M.W. from the Lanarkshire miners' union of which he had become general secretary. Allan was fast gaining a Scottish reputation.

It was also agreed that another lad who had been active with us, Dan Sim from Ayrshire, would be put up as treasurer. Dan Sim had been in the Ayrshire Reform Committee and then the Minority Movement. He had been meeting with us during the First World War, and at the meetings with A. J. Cook, Arthur Horner and the others subsequent to that, he had always been a leading representative from Ayrshire. So he became the natural choice for the treasurership of the N.U.S.M.W. Dan Sim eventually became an agent for the miners' union in Ayrshire and for many years later on was convener of Ayr County Council.[4] All these four offices in the N.U.S.M.W. were part-time jobs only.

When the ballot was taken in Fife, it was obvious that the sitting members — Adamson and his supporters — got a shock. Everything possible was done by them to prevent the ballot vote from being declared. First of all it was said there were not enough people in the union, so the announcement of the result of the ballot should be deferred. Proposals were made by Adamson that we should not disclose the ballot vote but instead go in for a recruiting campaign: everybody in the union — and then we would take a ballot vote. This was Mr Adamson.

Nevertheless Adamson was forced to give way by the pressure from the rank and file, and when the ballot was declared we could see the reason for all the manipulation to try to prevent it being disclosed. Proudfoot and myself were at the top of the ballot for the Fife agents' positions, and I was top of the ballot for the Fife representatives to the N.U.S.M.W. executive, with John Bird and Proudfoot following, Adamson fourth, and a long string of others.

When this ballot was declared those of us who were regarded as left wing proposed that we should reduce the nominees to a short leet and have a straight vote on four from whom to elect two as agents; and as five positions were vacant on the N.U.S.M.W., that we should again reduce the list of nominees for that to ten and have a straight vote for the five seats.

But this did not suit Mr Adamson and his friends. So that they proposed that we chop off the tail-end and have a second ballot, with six nominees for the two agents' positions, and thirteen for the five N.U.S.M.W. Executive seats. The second ballot was taken, on the basis of Adamson's proposal, and again there were attempts made to nullify this ballot. Suffice to say that this ballot was even worse for Mr Adamson and his friends. Whereas Mr Proudfoot and I were still top in the Fife agents' ballot, Mr Hodge now topped the ballot for the N.U.S.M.W. Executive. Adamson remained in fourth place, with the other four of us from the top five (including Hodge) beings Lefts. But again Adamson refused to accept this as a final ballot and finally accepted the proposal that the Left had made much earlier, that we should have a third and final ballot.

Again every possible attempt was made to prevent this ballot from being disclosed. There had been a tremendous press barrage working up for this ballot. The usual anti-Communist "Moscow gold", "representatives of foreign alien power" propaganda had been trotted out. The campaign had been particularly vicious in the *Glasgow Times, Glasgow News*, and the *Dundee Courier*. They were out to prevent, as they called it, the Communists getting control of the union.

Adamson tried to upset the ballot by means of this previously mentioned undemocratic method of delegate representation at the Delegate Board at Dunfermline, and a majority of the delegates supported his plea that the ballot be not disclosed. But when this decision came back to the branches, the membership in their meetings simply revolted and demanded that this ballot result be declared. It is quite easily seen why they had been so anxious to prevent the disclosing of the results. Myself and David Proudfoot were easily at the top of the agents' ballot by a bigger majority than in the previous two; and whereas Adamson had been fourth in both the first and the second ballot for the five Fife representatives to the N.U.S.M.W., this time the complete panel of Lefts were easily elected. Hodge, myself, Proudfoot, Stewart and Bird received the highest votes, with Adamson's panel of himself, Cook, Alex Smith, Jimmy Potter and Charlie Toner being heavily defeated.[5] Not only that, but the proportion of votes cast was very heavy — more than ninety per cent of the membership recorded votes. I should have imagined that everybody who was a democrat at heart must have been overflowing with joy about democratic recording of their wishes.

However, along with that were the branch financial votes being taken in Fife and in Lanarkshire for the office-bearers in the N.U.S.M.W. We had carried the panel by our Fife votes, while a similar thing had happened in Lanarkshire. But where in Fife it had been by branch financial vote, in Lanarkshire it had been a delegate vote. The other districts, so far as I know, did not consult their membership at all. But on a proportional representation basis it meant that there was a majority of the membership of the N.U.S.M.W. with Fife and Lanarkshire combined, voting for the Left panel, which meant that they would be automatically elected when the N.U.S.M.W. delegate annual conference was convened.

It was quite clear that those who were in control of the N.U.S.M.W. saw their control being challenged, and if the ordinary democratic methods of control were to be operated then the policy of the Union would be completely changed. So the obvious thing was either to accept the will of the majority, to become real democrats, or to think up all the excuses possible, invent them if they did not exist, in order to refuse to operate democratic decisions. This is what happened.

First of all, when the decisions in Fife that David Proudfoot and I had been appointed agents were intimated to the existing executive of the N.U.S.M.W., they decided that they could not accept our appointment. They used the fact that Fife was in arrears with its dues. This created a further row in Fife and the branches there decided that we were to take up office because otherwise it would have meant that two who had been appointed as agents were not to take up office, while two — Jimmy Cook and Sandy Smith — who had been rejected in a series of ballot votes were to continue in office. So the branches decided that Cook and Sandy Smith should demit office and that David Proudfoot and myself should take up office, and if the N.U.S.M.W. were not going to meet our salary, that that would be met from the Fife funds.

Accordingly, Mr Proudfoot and myself went in as agents to report for duty at the Dunfermline office of the Fife miners' union in the middle of February 1928. It was not a very pleasant atmosphere, but Mr Adamson as general secretary was a wily old bird. At the time there had been a new Trades Disputes Act passed. Those who wished to pay the political levy to the Labour Party had to contract in instead of having to contract out as had formerly been the case, and when we went into the office there were the branch returns sent in with the names and addresses from each branch of their membership that was to contract in. Mr Adamson felt that it would be a good break-in to put Proudfoot and myself in a room by ourselves with this mass of paper and prepare in handwriting a register of all those who had contracted in. So we were expected day in and day out to undertake a clerical job that we were not suited for and had no time for, and the membership out in the coalfield was wondering when we were likely to show our faces as the new leadership. We stuck it for a short time then said we had not been elected to do that, that any schoolboy or schoolgirl could do it. Our job was to give leadership and to deal with the grievances of the men.

The lads were still organising the big mass meetings outside and we had one big central demonstration at Cowdenbeath on a Sunday. We had bands out and we had a remarkably well-attended and fine demonstration at which, amongst others, Proudfoot and myself spoke. We were dealing with this question of the N.U.S.M.W. and the refusal to operate democratic decisions. We were very well received.

The next day Adamson came into the office in the most towering rage, objecting to us criticising him at meetings. He said that was all right arguing that way before we got into the office, but now we were into the office we could not expect to carry on as we had done before.

Proudfoot was no small lad — he must have been five feet eleven, and well built. But Adamson himself was a big man. He was in such a towering rage that he gripped Proudfoot by the shoulders, lifted him up in the air and shook him.

He said to me, "You," he says, "you should look to your future. You're a young man. Play your cards right and I'll get a safe Labour seat for ye. Ye'll become a respected Member of Parliament, and at your age, with your ability, there's no saying how far you could go in the Labour movement." But neither Adamson's attempt at browbeating Proudfoot or his cajolery with me had any effect and we carried on in this activity.

The whole question of what was to happen to the union in Scotland, as well as in Fife, was being actively discussed. There was a big conference in Falkirk, convened by the Minority Movement, in which all the elements that were active in the coalfield attended. It was called a "Save the Union" conference, so that we could get down to the job of building the N.U.S.M.W. into a powerful weapon, following the General Strike, the long drawn-out lock-out and the non-unionism that was prevailing as a result of the schism in both the Fife union and the N.U.S.M.W. But we had reckoned without the officials, who refused to call the N.U.S.M.W. conference. The reason they gave was that districts were in arrears with their dues, but the real reason was because the militants had won the elections. And as long as the officials did not call the conference obviously they remained as the officials.

There had not been an annual conference of the N.U.S.M.W. since 1925, although the rules said it should be held annually. There maybe was an excuse in '26, but there was no excuse in '27 or in '28. But finally the officials decided to play their main card and that was they set up a finance committee to report on the finances of the N.U.S.M.W. This committee, which included one representative from Fife — Jimmy Cook — finally reported that all county unions that were in arrears with contributions to the N.U.S.M.W. would not be eligible to attend the conference.

It so happened that both Lanarkshire and Fife were the outstanding districts for arrears. In Fife the arrears had accumulated in the main because of the bad management on the part of Adamson and his friends. While the split was on in Fife, while the Reform Union was in existence, the Adamson-controlled union had maintained its affiliation with the N.U.S.M.W. on a fictitious basis. That is, they were affiliated for 25,000 members while they did not have half of that actually in membership. Apparently nobody bothered about that, it was a paper recording. Then there was the period of the General Strike and the lock-out, and although they reduced the affiliation numbers to 12,500 after the lock-out, due to the men who were still unemployed, the disgust with the union and the growth of non-unionism meant that when work was resumed after the lock-out, the finances were very low. It was only after the amalgamation of the Reform Union into Adamson's union that the monthly returns started to grow and rose from £400 a month to over £1,000. The affiliation fees to the N.U.S.M.W. were being paid, plus something to arrears.

But this was used by the officials of the N.U.S.M.W. then in office to prevent the newly elected men from taking up office both in the N.U.S.M.W. itself and in Fife. A conference was called at the Christian Institute, Glasgow, at which the officials of the N.U.S.M.W. were not prepared to allow representatives from Fife to attend. There was a row at the conference. Hodge resorted to legal action against the N.U.S.M.W. officials, and so on. Finally, it resolved itself in that in February 1929, the Fife organisation, under its new leadership, was expelled from the N.U.S.M.W. because of arrears created under Adamson's leadership.

Just before that happened, the branches in Fife were in revolt because of Adamson's actions. The Lumphinnans branch moved a vote of censure on Adamson and demanded his dismissal as general secretary of the union. He was actually suspended, but before a ballot vote could be taken on the question of his dismissal, Adamson and his friends walked out of the Fife, Kinross and Clackmannan Miners' Union. He formed a new union and tried to confuse the issue by saying that they were the Fife, Clackmannan and Kinross Miners' Association, so that a lad hardly knew the difference between one and the other as far as titles were concerned.

Adamson and his new Association applied for affiliation to the N.U.S.M.W. and were accepted, while the elected representatives of the Fife, Kinross and Clackmannan Miners' Union were expelled because of the arrears of dues created by Adamson himself. It was a most fantastic situation.

26

THE U.M.S.

WHEN in the summer of 1928 Adamson and his supporters hived off from the Fife miners' union and formed the Fife, Clackmannan and Kinross Miners' Association, and within a few months were recognised by the M.F.G.B., on whose executive at that time there was a majority of members sympathetic to Adamson, we were back again in the old position of two rival unions for miners in Fife.

Shortly after Adamson's breakaway, there was another important development. Militants, mainly from Lanarkshire and Fife, formed in April 1929 the United Mineworkers of Scotland. It was formed as a unified national militant union in place of the various county unions and as a rival body to the N.U.S.M.W.

In Fife Philip Hodge was in difficulty. He disliked having any association with Adamson, but he did not like the developments that those who were more to the Left were taking. He refused to join up with the United Mineworkers of Scotland on the ground that he thought the whole situation in Scotland and in Fife could be retrieved, that the M.F.G.B. nationally were bound to look at the situation more favourably and that they would in the end come to support the line taken by himself. Hodge tried everything he could within the M.F.G.B., used every contact that he had. He still had the illusion that they would see the light of day and come down against Adamson and in support of his own attitude. But Adamson had plenty of contact with the right-wing section in the M.F.G.B. Executive.

Hodge was left in mid-air. He could not see his way to support Adamson. But he could not associate himself with those of us who were going into the new Scottish organisation, the United Mineworkers of Scotland. He came to oppose us as much as he opposed Adamson.

Alongside of this the rank and file in Fife were getting restless. We were still in the old Fife, Kinross and and Clackmannan Miners' Association while the rest of Scotland was developing the U.M.S. In consequence of a branch officials' conference held in Lochgelly in June 1929, it was decided that we should go ahead and officially introduce the U.M.S. into Fife. Hodge did not attend the Lochgelly conference. I did, along with Proudfoot. Proudfoot was appointed an official in the Scottish office of the U.M.S., while I was to remain in charge of the U.M.S. in Fife. When I went into the Fife miners' union office in Dunfermline next morning, after the Lochgelly conference, Hodge was there, accompanied by his wife. They asked me if I had attended that meeting at Lochgelly. I said yes, and told them what was decided. Hodge and his wife then physically tried to eject me from the office. They both laid hands on me, his wife especially, but I left the office of my own accord.

Because of Hodge's refusal to come in along with the Minority Movement lads who had decided it was necessary to form the U.M.S., he claimed he was carrying on the old Fife organisation and that he had the right to the union office in Dunfermline. We were forced to get other premises. And for a short period we had Adamson's breakaway organisation with an office in one part of Dunfermline, the U.M.S. securing offices in another part of Dunfermline, and Philip Hodge sitting in the old union offices there. So that for a period we had in fact three rival organisations in Fife.

There was little or no support for Hodge once the Adamson supporters were away and once the militants in the U.M.S. were away. It was only a rump that was left supporting Hodge and that was how he finished up. In desperation he went to Adamson to see if he could be taken under Adamson's wing. But Adamson refused, so Hodge went out of the organisation entirely. His wife went back into school teaching to get a livelihood. Hodge reserved his animosity and bitterness for those who had been associated with him all the time, rather than for Adamson. I believe in the main it was because his association in Fife was more or less at the union office level, instead of being down at the pit level fighting for improved conditions for the miners, that he got so little support at the end. He finished up in that insignificant way and died soon after the U.M.S. was formed.

In the U.M.S. we tried to carry out a lot of the theories that we had been propagating. One was that we should have women interested in the miners' union and its activities. We tried to form a women's guild organisation where the women would have the right to send representatives to the branch meetings of the miners' union, and the women's guild would appoint two of their number to sit on the miners' branch committee. We managed to get some guilds set up. We had a good functioning one in Buckhaven. But generally we did not entirely succeed, because we were in many cases merely duplicating the Co-operative Women's Guild of which most of the women were already members, and it meant that we were hauling women out of their houses for another night of the week, or we were in competition with the Co-operative Women's Guild.

We had advocated special youth organisations. We tried to form youth committees. But here again we did not succeed entirely, though there was one interesting development in the Buckhaven area. We wanted to set up sports committees, hiking committees, cycling groups and cultural activity groups as well. We looked at the question of a football team: would there be teams based on each pit, and would we form a league, would we enter the Scottish Football Association? The question of having a league depended on uniform development taking place in other areas and at other pits. Eventually, because we could not get support in other areas, we decided to go ahead on our own and form a juvenile football team which entered the local football association and affiliated to the Scottish Football Association. So we competed just as any other ordinary juvenile team, although our team was known as the East Fife U.M.S. In order to finance it we also organised raffles and started Saturday night dancing, known as the U.M.S. dancing. This was a successful venture.

So a U.M.S. organiser, such as myself, had to spend activity at the pit, recruiting members to the Union where possible, carrying out Union activity in regard to disputes, and so on, then be active in the women's organisation or guild, try to engender enthusiasm for youth activity, travel with the football team on a Saturday afternoon, and then officiate at the dancing. The work of a full-time agent for the U.M.S. was certainly a very varied one in this area. But it kept the Union, which was not distinguished in many cases from the Communist Party, always to the forefront.

Because the coalowners, in alliance with Adamson's union, were trying to ostracise the U.M.S. activists, most of whom were Communist Party lads, it was felt that one way to beat that and yet to give service to the miners would be to deal with the question of safety in the pits — run a campaign on the need for improved safety measures, and argue this could best be done by the appointment of worken's inspectors. Here of course we came up against the usual difficulty that the colliery owners would not let us near the pits. They would not allow us to be appointed as workmen's inspectors, and we had therefore to make serious study of the Coal Mines Act and to use the Act in its completeness, and also to use the Mines Inspectorate Department. As a result of this we were able, if we carried out the legal procedure, to hold statutory meetings at the pit, call them in accordance with the regulations, and in closely following out the regulations, were able to insist on a ballot vote being taken at meetings for nominations, a proper voting register being prepared by the colliery manager, actual voting booths being erected, and the ballot being carried through and the declaration made. This was going ahead simultaneously also in West Fife.

The first attempt we made resulted in a fight at Lochhead and Victoria pit. We felt that was a good place to start, because Willie Drylie, who was checkweigher there, was chairman of the Adamson union.[1] We created the utmost concern among the colliery officials when they were compelled to carry through the ballot on the lines I have suggested, and even worse when the ballot resulted in a majority for Bob Eadie, a full-time U.M.S. official, and myself. They tried everything possible to stop the appointment from being carried through. But we insisted and we thus operated as workmen's inspectors at Lochhead and Victoria pit.

This was immediately followed by similar tactics at Michael Colliery, which was the biggest colliery in the Scottish coalfield. Again the same kind of opposition was met with. We, by the same means, defeated this opposition, and in the ballot Bob Eadie and I again were successful.

We tried the same tactics at Wellesley, which was much more under the direct control of the Wemyss Coal Company and the police, and of Peter

Henderson for Adamson's organisation.[2] While we were able to compel a ballot vote, the police were at the door to keep us out from the actual counting. So that while the lads in the pit swore by all that was holy that we had won the ballot hands down, from their knowledge of what the men in the pit were saying, the manager published figures and said, "That's the figures." We were narrowly defeated by the two representatives of Adamson's union, who afterwards carried out one inspection and then did not carry out any more. I do not know if we had a majority of the Wellesley men or not, but it is true that we had a fair degree of support, and in keeping with the attitude and general feeling amongst all the other pits I think we were entitled to assume that we did have a majority in that pit.

The Fife Coal Company appealed to the Minister of Mines that we were using the Mines Regulations to get appointed as workmen's inspectors solely for political reasons, and that it was simply to further the aims of the Communist Party that we were carrying out this line of activity. But the Mines Department replied that they had studied the report of the workmen's inspectors referred to, that they had instructed their own inspectors to visit the collieries immediately following an inspection carried out by us to check on the veracity of the reports. They said they had come to the conclusion that they were the most helpful reports they were getting of any examinations carried out in the British coalfield. They could find no grounds at all for interfering, but on the contrary they hoped that every other pit would go and do likewise. So that avenue of opposition to us was closed.

But even then the coalowners were not finished because they claimed that as we were acting on behalf of all the men in the pit — trade unionists as well as non-unionists, members of the U.M.S. and of the rival organisation of Adamson, and of the tradesmen's association, all of whom had a right to take part in our election — in consequence the payment for the shift's work on taking an examination should be a responsibility of all workmen in the pit. We therefore proposed that U.M.S. branch committees would take a collection of twopence per man per inspection, to pay for the shift's work. But in order to block this, Adamson's union sent out directives that their union was against any of the members contributing to this payment, and appealed to them not to make any payment.

Our experience was that in the beginning the safety inspections were a new experience to the men in the pit, and they were able to see the tremendous difference the inspections were making in the pit — the extensive preparations made to improve the safety conditions prior to our visit, what was done following our visit, and the visit of the Government inspectors resulting from our visit. The men readily responded to these examinations, which were made regularly once a month. But, as is usual, as the months went past and it became established procedure, it became increasingly taken for granted.

When I had become a full-time official in the old Fife union in 1928, I was asked to take over responsibility for files of compensation cases and new cases. I had not handled detailed compensation before other than for a short time as a branch secretary, so I had to start on a completely new basis. In consequence of the dilatory methods of Jimmy Potter, the previous compensation official, who was a supporter of Adamson, there was a colossal backlog of cases. So that overnight I was plunged into this detailed work. I had to start making a special study of compensation procedure. As time went on I got a good working knowledge of it, again applying the experience I had gained at the Labour College. I decided to help the branch secretaries who had to handle compensation cases by organising schools at which we discussed compensation procedure and drew up directives along the lines of questions and answers. This created a very good basis for future work also in the U.M.S.

A lot of the compensation work meant appeals to the court of referees. As part of the struggle against the U.M.S., the doctors at that time were demanding payment for issuing lines to their panel patients if they were going before a medical referee. This was something new to us because the miners had always had a deduction made from their pay packet which still continued whether the man was in Adamson's union or the U.M.S. or was a non-unionist. The deduction was made from his pay each working week, and this entitled him to free medicine, which was charged against the medical fund.

When the doctors tried this move we fought back. I remember a young doctor in my area who had set up practice on his own, and we in the U.M.S. canvassed our members because he said he would give us the certificate without charge. So by carrying out these kinds of tactics we managed to break this attempt by doctors to defeat us in the U.M.S.

The majority of miners supported the U.M.S. in Fife and in a number of districts in Lanarkshire. But, unfortunately, this support was not uniformly spread over Scotland as a whole. The U.M.S. was much stronger in Fife than elsewhere but even in Fife it started to experience considerable difficulty. First of all the coalowners made it quite clear that they were recognising Adamson's organisation for negotiation purposes and were instructing their managers not to deal with the U.M.S. Not every manager carried out this instruction. But where they did it meant that we had to battle at every pit. In consequence of this the wages and working conditions of the Fife miners were not as good as they ought to have been.

Unfortunately, too, after 1930-31, a period of depression started in Scotland and pits were closing, running down in manpower. This was one of the biggest difficulties we had to overcome. Double shift production pits were being reduced to single shift production. For example, at the Wellesley at Methil, where a high proportion of the East Fife men were employed, production was reduced to a single shift, and 500 men were dismissed. In connivance with the Wemyss Coal Company, the Adamson organisation refused to take any steps to oppose this but arranged that their membership should be given priority in getting the jobs that were left, and most of the militants were eased out. This happening on a county scale made things very difficult. At least two miners in five became unemployed, and the screw was applied by management on the men that were left. Always there was this threat of the unemployed man at the door.

The two organisations — the U.M.S. and Adamson's union — spent a considerable amount of time fighting for membership, to the detriment of the working conditions of the Fife miners. Because of the strength of the U.M.S. in Fife, however, conditions were much better there, bad as they were, than they were in other parts of Scotland. That was a time when trade union leader after trade union leader would point out that the miner was getting less for his work than it would take to keep an inmate in the poor law institution; that there was the speed-up, the pressure on the men to get the maximum output for the lowest possible wage. I remember the Fife Coal Company introduced a fixed rate for strippers at that time and they got a pay of one shilling a shift if all the run was stripped off. We used to say that the Fife Coal Company was gambling a shilling a day that you could not do it.

This was a really difficult time for the miners. It was a difficult time to build and establish a fighting trade union. When working conditions were under continual attack from the mineowners it became increasingly difficult to carry on the expansion of the U.M.S.

One of the ways of maintaining contact in the pit was to extend the appointment of workmen's inspectors. While we were carrying out regular pithead meetings, the company tried to carry out an interdict to prevent us as U.M.S. representatives going on to the colliery premises. We were able to circumvent this easily enough because they could only take out an interdict for each pit for each man. We simply allocated a different U.M.S. speaker there and followed it up with one after the other, which meant that for all their pits there was a group of lads who were prepared to go on and do pithead meetings. There would have had to be a continual stream of applications to the court for interdicts.

The coalowners and managers resorted to quite a lot of other tactics to keep the U.M.S. out. I remember holding a big meeting at Michael Colliery. Between the meeting place and the pit siding on the railway there was only a corrugated iron fence. So what the company resorted to was to place an engine alongside this fence and start blowing its whistle continuously. At that time we had not the benefit of loudspeaker equipment so that you could not carry on long before your voice gave way.

In Glencraig colliery, while Abe Moffat and Alex Moffat were holding meetings, the manager used to blow the colliery horn continuously in order to drown out their voices. There was quite a humorous anecdote about that because the man who was checkweighman at the pit heard the horn blowing, said, "That's a fire!" — and sent for the fire brigade. Cowdenbeath Fire Brigade appeared at the pit to deal with the fire and discovered that it was simply a device to prevent the U.M.S. speakers from speaking.

At that time we had a whole team of lads who did meetings at the pit and also we had a flood of Communist Party pit papers. There was "The Spark", "The Flame", "The Torch" and "The Lamp" in East Fife, and "The Panbolt", "The Mash", "The Hammer", and so on covering West Fife.[3] So there were these pit papers, regular propaganda meetings at the pits, the work as workmen's inspectors, and the attempt to deal with grievances at the pit — all these were part of the struggle carried on by the U.M.S.

131

I remember the big question that arose when the M.F.G.B. managed during the second Labour Government in 1930 to secure that the spread over of eight hours, imposed by the Tory Government in 1926, should cease, and that we should have a seven-and-a-half-hour day. In Scotland, in spite of the M.F.G.B. decision, and in spite of a special letter sent by Shinwell, who was again Minister of Mines in the 1929-31 Labour Government,[4] telling the N.U.S.M.W. officials that this was a decision and the law, Adamson and his friends all over Scotland still played the coalowners' game of keeping the Scottish miners not only working for the lowest wages in the British coalfield, but also continuing to work eight hours while the remainder of the coalfields had stopped the extended hours.

As a consequence we had a strike in Fife in 1930 in order to come in line. The strike was very successful. It was on that occasion that, at the Mary Colliery at Lochore, our old friend Jimmy Stewart tried to provoke the police, as I have already described.[5] But we managed to bring Fife in line with the rest of the British coalfield, and the U.M.S. was almost entirely responsible for that success. It was their leadership and the backing of the other men that got the results.

At the same time there was another big issue that we had continually to fight, and that was the question of overtime. While many men were unemployed, men down the pit were set on tasks they could not perform and were being obliged to work overtime. Therefore the fight against excessive overtime became one of the key fights in Fife and outside of it. Again we had very considerable results.

These continuous efforts meant that management, while officially they declared that they would not recognise the U.M.S., had to take into account the fact that the U.M.S. was there, and the fact that there would be action at the pit helped to prevent Fife being dragged as far down as actually took place in the outside areas. It meant that many managers who wanted their pit to work would say, "Do you know, I can't recognise you. I make no attempt to recognise you. But if you come in we'll try to settle this case." If, on the other hand, they were adamant, we used to arrange meetings with the men, have a resolution prepared telling them that a deputation of the men concerned was calling on the manager and they were expecting the manager to resolve the grievance. If he did not resolve the grievance there was a meeting the following morning. So that by this sort of threat of action, again we were able to settle many outstanding cases.

This power to negotiate even unofficially at each pit was varied in its effects. It depended on the strength and the willingness of men in a given pit to make a stand on the points that were being raised. So that in some pits we were able to get more done than in others. I have already mentioned one outstanding case at Kinglassie Colliery, which was more or less under the control of the agent for Adamson, Mr Peter Ness, and where there was a particularly difficult atmosphere prevailing. That was the occasion when because we would not give in and go away, the exchanges became heated, and Abe Moffat took full in the face a blow that was aimed at me by one of Ness's supporters. In consequence we marched back to Kinglassie with our supporters from all over Fife the next Sunday and, as I have said, Jimmy Stewart said that if they wanted a fight in Kinglassie they could have it either on the platform or down on the greensward that was in front. Kinglassie subsequently developed into a fairly strong supporter of ours. This was typical of some of the tremendous difficulties we had to overcome.

While in Fife we wanted, because of our background and tradition, to give service to the membership, I am afraid that in Lanarkshire particularly the same attitude was not always in existence. It seemed to me that far too much emphasis was laid there on getting a pit idle, that a strike had taken place at a pit on a given date, rather than that benefits had been secured for the men working in the pit arising out of the activities of comrades in the coalfield. In Lanarkshire any kind of issue, real or imaginary, was good enough in some cases for the local U.M.S. leaders to get the men to walk home, so that they could report that a strike had taken place. This brought its inevitable result and support for the U.M.S. in Lanarkshire gradually fell away and it became a difficult job to organise it. As for Ayrshire or Stirling, we never really got building the U.M.S. there, though we had contacts with some semblance of organisation in parts of the Lothians.

We regularly carried out propaganda in the Lothians, and Fife speakers had to make regular weekly visits there. One of the places that we concentrated on was Newcraighall. The influence of the U.M.S. there became greater and greater, although the area was under the control of the Mid and East Lothian Miners' Union, with Andrew Clarke as its secretary.[6] Our agitation at Newcraighall induced the miners there to appoint workmen's inspectors — and they appointed two Communists. These two men carried out their inspections, but because one of them — Joe Swan — had been squeezed out of his job and was unemployed, the Lothian Coal Company took action to have him evicted from his house.[7] But the U.M.S. had built up a very decided influence and we were able to pull the men out on strike at this pit, in spite of Andrew Clarke's efforts, to stop Swan from being evicted. But subsequently, when Swan was down the pit actually making an inspection of the whole of the mine, the bailiffs and police put his furniture out on the street. This was typical of the kind of atmosphere that prevailed.

But in Lanarkshire gradually things got to a stage where it was felt necessary there should be a change. Willie Allan of the Lanarkshire miners, who was the first general secretary of the U.M.S., resigned to take up work elsewhere and David Proudfoot from Fife took over as general secretary. In my view, Allan, in spite of his enormous ability, suffered from what I always felt was a weakness common to most people that I knew in the Lanarkshire movement. That was a lack of serious sense of responsibility, a go-easy, devil-may-care, sometimes flippant and jocular attitude to organisational questions and the solving of problems. The old idea of a shrug of the shoulders, what-does-it-matter-there's-another-day-coming sort of business, meant that organisational problems were not tackled and solved as they should have been. It showed me the big difference in the mental approach to trade unionism, to organisation, to strike activity and so on, between the Fife comrades and many of our Lanarkshire colleagues. In later years I found the approach of Jimmy McKendrick and John "Dabs" Miller, who were also from Lanarkshire, to be like Allan's.[8] Allan lost interest in the continuation of the U.M.S. He later left Scotland on the winding up of the U.M.S. and went down to work in Northumberland. But it was not possible to keep a good man down. Before long he was appointed checkweigher at one of the collieries there and with the passage of time became an agent of the Northumberland miners' union and representative to the National Executive. He was nominated for the presidency of the National Union of Mineworkers in 1960 and came second in the ballot.

Allan was replaced as general secretary of the U.M.S. by David Proudfoot in 1930. But Proudfoot found that the task was greater than he could continue to face up to, particularly the Lanarkshire situation and having to travel to Glasgow to the head office. By that time debts were piling up, income was being reduced, and a difficulty in getting adequate wages compelled Davie, who had one of his periodic bouts of depression, to pack in. It was at that stage, in 1931, that Abe Moffat took over as general secretary. Bob Eadie, who had been a full-time U.M.S. official in Lanarkshire, was directed to come through into Fife because of the situation in Lanarkshire, and came to stay in my house until he could get alternative accommodation. Therefore it became a rearguard action to build up U.M.S. organisation in Fife and to consolidate.

In addition to these difficulties there was, in my opinion, another serious mistake made in the U.M.S. That was that in some cases there was the mechanical acceptance of directives, that in the international field the Red International of Labour Unions might be coming to certain decisions that were not applicable to the situation prevailing in Scotland. On many occasions mechanical attempts to apply these R.I.L.U. decisions did not work out. I had the feeling that our Lanarkshire comrades were more concerned to get a strike than to settle the issue in the men's favour, and were operating decisions without the men having a say first.

The U.M.S. period I regard as the most difficult in my whole industrial and political life. The formation and struggles of the U.M.S. took place at the beginning of the gathering economic crisis, continued during the early thirties — these were years of low wages, of being castigated as the Red Union, the hirelings of Moscow, in receipt of Moscow gold, etc., etc. I felt many a time that I would have welcomed any distribution of Moscow gold, because as things got worse, many times there was no money in the U.M.S.'s hands to send out our wages, although we were full-time officials. We had been on a nominal salary in the Fife amalgamated union in 1927-29 of £4 a week. When the U.M.S. was formed we voluntarily agreed to take a wage nearer to what the miner himself was getting: £3 a week. But in subsequent periods we were lucky if we got anything like that and many times we got similar to what could have been paid as unemployment benefit. At times there was not sufficient in the hands of the U.M.S. to pay salary at all. You would expect your salary to come by post, instead you would get a note saying there was nothing in the kitty and to go round some of the branches and see if you could collect sufficient to give you your salary, and send in receipts. In these circumstances it was not surprising that a number of people gradually ceased activity.

A considerable amount of our time as U.M.S. leaders was taken up with activity amongst the unemployed — fighting for more adequate maintenance for them, the abolition of the Means Test, the fight in the County Council for increased scales of public assistance. The work at the Labour Exchanges, court referee work, organising mass demonstrations and marches to the public assistance office, marching against threatened evictions, hunger marches, marches to the centre of the County Council at Cupar — all that meant a regular form of activity outside of the actual pithead activity. In addition, as I already sketched out, we tried to develop organisation amongst the women and women's guilds, organisation amongst the youth, the formation of a football team, and financing these and popular dancing, and so on.

It was at that time, in 1932-33, that I was asked to stand for Buckhaven Town Council, and was duly elected for Ward One in November 1933. I was in turn duly elected to Fife County Council as well, as a burgh member. To be a member of the Town Council and pay attention to it, and to participate in the County Council, meant that more and more time was being used up and it was less possible to continue the direct pit work. But this pit work had to be carried out in the shape of safety inspections — and I was a workmen's inspector at a number of pits. So that my time was certainly fully occupied.

But eventually, by 1935-36, it was felt that the question of protecting the working and living conditions of the miners was so important that we should solve the problem of divided organisation. The U.M.S. by then was still strong in the Fife coalfield, and its influence was much stronger. Adamson's organisation had had to take on two extra organisers. These acted first of all as parliamentary election agents for Mr Adamson in the general election of 1935. Peter Henderson was to organise East Fife in Adamson's interest, and Peter Ness West Fife. After the election was over they were asked to carry on as union organisers, recruiting for Adamson's organisation. So that the battle was almost a continuous one. But eventually those in the U.M.S. who were also in the Communist Party decided, as a result of regular negotiations, that they would be better to try to get unity, unity even at all costs.

But every attempt at trying to get a meeting was being pushed aside by Adamson's union. Ebby Edwards, who by that time was general secretary of the M.F.G.B., was most favourable to building up a powerful union on a united basis in Fife and was extremely friendly to those of us in the U.M.S.[9] After unity was won he still remained one of our best friends. But anything we did to try to get unity by agreement was simply turned down by Adamson. Consequently, we had got to look at the whole question whether or not it would be advisable to carry on the U.M.S. or to voluntarily liquidate the union.

This question was most seriously discussed. It was eventually agreed, but only after tremendous difficulty, to liquidate the U.M.S. I remember many miners who had stuck by us in the Reform Union days and the whole period of the U.M.S. were so incensed that they said we were betraying them and that they were finished with the militant movement because we had sold the pass by giving up the U.M.S.

When we did decide to liquidate the U.M.S. it was not because we were forced to do that by financial circumstances or lack of response. Rather the contrary, that after the very difficult period had been surmounted we were actually organisationally and financially better than we had been for a long period beforehand. Under Abe Moffat's leadership as general secretary from 1931, and with the able assistance of Miss Morton, his secretary,[10] the debts had all been paid off, there was a comfortable balance built up, we were able to assure all compensation cases and old lads who had entitlement to funeral benefit that these would be safeguarded, and we officials were getting our salary, small as it was, regularly. But liquidation of the U.M.S. was felt essential in the interests of the broader movement. We had seen the advent of fascism in Italy, the Nazi movement in Germany, the growing resistance that this had entailed, the attempt to get a united front in France — and as Communists we felt it was a difficult time to argue for an attempt to unify all the forces of the working class if we kept this internecine struggle among the miners going mainly in Fife but also in other parts of Scotland. In Lanarkshire, Ayrshire, etc., after the U.M.S. had gone out, there had been a growing militant movement and many lads who were Communists and militants had actually come forward into the leadership of the county unions. It meant that we were isolated from them in Fife, which was the strongest militant section of the Scottish coalfield. For these reasons, we argued that even although liquidation meant a period in the wilderness, it would be for the ultimate good.

While we put these arguments forward we urged our members to apply for membership of the county unions, and it was at this stage that they came to a decision that they did not want most of our members, and tried everything possible to keep them out. With regard to those of us that were in the leadership of the U.M.S., the leaders of the county unions came to a hurried decision that none of us was to become a member of the county union unless actually employed in and about the industry. Then they came to a second agreement with the coalowners in Fife and elsewhere that they would make sure that none of our leading men got employment. So they were trying to make doubly sure that the leading elements in the U.M.S. were not allowed to come back into the county unions and bother them. They took other measures with regard to county union elections, conditions of membership, and so on—so that every step, within reason, as far as they were concerned, was taken to try to keep us out.

So on the voluntary liquidation of the U.M.S. in 1936, and the merging of its rank and file membership into the county unions, it was difficult for many of us to get jobs in the industry. The coalowners claimed that we were not wanting work in the industry, we were only wanting to get into the county union. Consequently the bar was up against the two Moffats, myself, and other U.M.S. leaders. I was kept out of employment in the pits and out of membership of the Fife county union for about eighteen months, between 1936 and the beginning of 1938. During that period, for the first time in my life, and against my wishes, I was a non-unionist.

27

THE COMMUNIST PARTY
IN FIFE

IN looking at my experiences in the working-class movement, obviously my coming into political life and joining the Communist Party played an important and almost dominant role. I remain a founder member of the Communist Party and, in fact, I have had an unbroken membership of a political party since I joined the Kirkcaldy branch of the British Socialist Party in 1916.

I have mentioned the conference I attended in Glasgow in 1920 when I was at the Scottish Labour College. It was held to discuss what steps should be taken to try and get a unified Communist organisation in this country. It was rather a stormy meeting but finally finished up with support for the proposal for one united Communist Party for Britain. A Provisional Committee was elected from that meeting to meet the other sections of the movement in order to try and get an agreed-on basis. The next we heard was that there was to be a conference called in Leeds in January 1921. I was not a delegate to that conference because I was at the College in Glasgow, but our branch of the Fife Communist League was represented and supported the formation of a United Communist Party for Britain.

One of our branch representatives at Leeds was a young pal of mine, Bobby Venters, and he appears in the photograph of delegates taken at the conference. Venters shortly afterwards emigrated to the United States but later returned to Fife and remained a member of our local branch of the Communist Party until his death in 1976.

The Leeds conference decided on one Communist Party for Britain. I can recollect when the information and decisions were being sent out there were again the fiercest discussions about what should happen. While many of those who had been opposed to parliamentary activity passively accepted the new decisions, there was always a reluctance or hesitancy on their part — and of which I was not entirely blameless myself — to participate in any local election activity. However, our branch of the Communist Party at Buckhaven did apply for affiliation to the local trades and labour council at Methil. We were accepted and played a part in that council.

But a number of our colleagues took the view that it was asking far too much from a pure undefiled revolutionary to associate with the Labour Party, to associate with parliamentary or local authority election activity. A number of them resigned from the Communist Party rather than participate in this activity. One of them, Jimmy Clunie of Dunfermline, who had been one of our main lecturers in Marxian economics, had resigned from the Fife Communist League when it decided to become part of the Communist Party and to apply for affiliation to the Labour Party. The passage of time does strange things because, subsequently, friend Clunie developed into a prominent local Labour Party councillor and then, in 1950, became M.P. for Dunfermline Burghs when Willie Watson died.

The period in which the Communist Party was being developed was one in which amongst the active elements in the progressive movement there was a very strong feeling of hatred against those leaders of the parliamentary and trade union movements who were regarded as having acted in a treacherous manner and betrayed the active workers. In consequence, there was this combination of Socialist Labour Party sectarianism, syndicalist approach to trade unions, and a strong feeling of opposition to the social democratic leaders. So that while we had accepted that there should be a united Communist Party that should be part of the Communist International, we did not fully accept the decisions that were being arrived at higher up. An example I have already given was the part played in forming the Fife miners' Reform Union in 1922-3 by Communists and other militants.

Many instructions were very confusing for us, for most of us Party members in Fife were just ordinary workers, mostly miners. We had left school at fourteen and the only knowledge of economics or politics we had was what we had gained in the classes that we ran amongst ourselves. When we started to read documents coming out from the Communist International we were learning a new language. They were talking in terms of bourgeoisie, proletariat, lumpenproletariat, nuclei, fractions. It was like going back to school. We had difficulty in knowing what some of the phrases implied. Some of us were inclined to forget the original teachings we had that if we were to express our thoughts and hope to influence others we should do it in the simplest words possible. I can recollect when Bob Stewart from Dundee was lecturing us in our class in Buckhaven in 1918 and asked each one to give a contribution, I talked about the domestication of animals, to show how knowledgeable I was. Stewart immediately stopped me and said, "Isn't there a simpler way to express it than that?" For the life of me I could not understand what he meant until he said, "Wouldn't 'taming of animals' express it more effectively?" So that lesson stuck with me — until we started to read those Communist International documents.

Again, there was the emphasis that we were in a revolutionary period, and all activity should be devoted to furthering the revolution. This emphasis on the revolution being round the corner and it was our job to devote all our time to advancing it meant that you had got to take up a very rigid and even sectarian line with people who were not in the Communist Party, even if they were active trade unionists. So, we were most vicious in debates with lads on the trades council who happened to be members of the S.D.F. and the Labour Party.

This question of working within the Labour Party was a difficult pill for us young lads to swallow. The Trades and Labour Council at Methil, instead of being a place where we met to discuss our differences and reach agreement with friends of the Labour Party, right-wingers, and so on, became a battleground, with some of our young lads threatening what they were going to do when the revolution came to some of these old fogies they claimed had betrayed the movement. So, instead of building unity with the other elements of the working class, because we had not fully understood how to work inside the Labour Party, we took up a position of opposition and started firing all the adjectives we could think of at the right-wingers. We developed a feeling towards ourselves of hostility which if we had known more about politics we could have avoided. It was only when we got into a real battle like 1926 that these real hostile differences disappeared for the duration of the conflict and a much better basis of understanding was developed between us Communist Party members and the non-Communists. By that time of course we had reached the position where we and the non-Communist elements could run a joint campaign, and John O'Neill and myself, who were Communists, were included in the Trades and Labour Council panel for the Wemyss Parish Council election and were duly elected in 1925.

One Labour councillor objected to our inclusion in the panel. But on being remitted to the Trades Council branches, they endorsed the decision to include us. Out of the Parish Council's fifteen members, thirteen were elected from the Labour panel and these included the two of us as Communists. Up to then there had not been a bar against Communists participating in the Trades and Labour Council acitivity. We participated in that activity quite openly and had at least a very powerful influence in the activities of the Labour group on the Parish Council.

In the forming of the Communist Party locally in Fife, most of the work was done round miners' problems, the agitation in the miners' union. Members of Communist Party branches would be appointed as miners' union branch officials, and it was difficult to tell where trade union activity ended and Party activity commenced. This was one of the factors in all probability that militated against the building of organised Communist Party branches. The generally haphazard approach in the Fife coalfield to Party organisation was really due to us seeming to think that trade union branch activity was the same as Communist Party branch activity. The whole industrial and even political-social life in the mining villages generally centred round the miners' trade union branch activity. So that when the Communist Party membership wished to carry out a given line of campaign, it was the simplest thing in the world to get it carried out by the mobilising of trade union branches, co-operative women's guilds, and so on. It was also a feature in Fife that the trade union leader in a particular village was generally regarded as almost the uncrowned king and his word was more or less law in most matters of politics that came up. So that when the Communist Party started to be active in the 1921 miners' lock-out, carrying through to the struggles of the miners in the Fife coalfield that led up to the Reform Union being formed in 1922-3, the fight from 1924 to bring about amalgamation, and then 1926, the General Strike and the miners' long drawn-out struggle — the work of the Party was identified with the struggle of the miners mainly.

It was at this time, in 1925, that we thought it would be a good thing to commence a pit paper. I remember the lad, by the name of Ernie Woolley, who came up from London to urge our Party branch to start a pit paper.[1] Ernie was a very effective mass-meeting propagandist. When we told him that we were a bunch of miners, we had never seen a pit paper before, we could not type, we did not have a typewriter, we said: "How do you go about this thing?" I remember Ernie looking at us so blandly. "I don't know," he said. "All I know is you have to start a pit paper."

That was the limit of the advice we got. But we managed to acquire an old second-hand typewriter, got some stencils, and found lads who could do drawing and sketching. They were asked to turn out cartoons reflecting the struggle in that pit. It was to be a paper for the Wellesley Colliery at Methil and the other pits in East Fife. It was called "The Spark", and the first issue was in July 1925. Proudfoot was checkweigher at the Wellesley, we felt he was most secure in his employment, and therefore his name would appear as editor, to whom all correspondence should be directed. That first issue was done on a flat copying machine, with a roller which we rolled by hand. We did not have any Party premises at the time, so we produced the first issue in the house of a comrade named Young Pattie.[2] I remember the mess which the table and bedclothes were in after the first issue, and the row there was in the house when the wife discovered the mess we were making. But from such very modest beginnings we developed probably one of the most successful pit papers published at the time. It was merely the forerunner of a number more. Outside of West Fife, where other papers were being run, such as *The Justiceman* at Bowhill, "The Torch" at Cowdenbeath, "The Hutch" at Kirkcaldy, and "The Picket" at Lochgelly, we managed to run three other papers in East Fife.[3] We carried on for a while with me as the chief factotum, doing the writing up and cutting the stencils and running them off. Women comrades and whoever else we could get did the selling of these papers. So that that background, as well as regular propaganda meetings, helped to develop the line of the Party in East Fife.

In 1926 the only active political organisation in Fife during the General Strike and after was the Communist Party. All other organisations had folded up. The local Communist Party spokesmen and those who were associated with them were in the miners' Reform Union. Regular meetings were held by the Party, with huge attendances.

The experience gained as a result of discussions amongst ourselves was responsible for the Communist Party locally being able to put forward positive proposals on how to organise the workers when the General Strike actually did materialise. I can remember we discussed on many occasions what form of organisation we should seek to adopt. It meant that when the General Strike burst like a bomb on some folk it did not catch our local Communist group unprepared. It was our sketch plan submitted immediately the strike took place that was like a lifebelt flung out to lads who had been chucked into the sea. They clutched it and enthusiastically endorsed it. This working in groups representing all the various trade union organisations helped to give the feeling that they were all pulling their weight in a joint effort. Those who had been almost strenuous political opponents prior to the General Strike were given positions of definite responsibility and reacted in an excellent manner. There was no attempt at division during the whole period of the General Strike and the very extended activities that were carried out in East Fife.

When we started a recruiting campaign we actually recruited 600 new members in Buckhaven and Methil. This was typical of what was going on in the mining areas. It was difficult after a bit to meet some young lad that was associated with the mines that had not passed through either a brief or extended period in the Communist Party. Our difficulty was that we did not know how best to retain them in membership and to build around them. We still had the old rigid, and in many cases sectarian, approach. I remember when we had our first meeting of recruits. We had to take the biggest hall in Methil. It was bigger than a normal mass meeting. My old friend David Proudfoot opened the meeting. He had the most awkward way of attracting people to the Party. He told them that this was a Party of a new kind that they were joining. It was not a Party that was interested in having socials and dances and tea parties. It was a Party in which everybody had to do work and devote themselves entirely to the work of the Party. They had got to participate in strike activity, go on picket work if it was needed, organise meetings, raise funds, participate in the communal feeding activity, sell the Party organ, and attend regular classes. Unless they were prepared to do all these things the door was open and they would be better to go away. Proudfoot laid down all the rigid rules that were to be carried through until he had even the old Party members wondering where they were. I remember having a first-class row with him when he finished, and telling him that that was not the way to treat people who were anxious to become members of the Communist Party. "Ah," he said, "if they cannae stand up to that they'll be nae guid to us in the Party." And that was generally his attitude. It was no surprise that many of the recruits vanished like thieves in the night. But even then we still had a big Party membership at that time.

Even when the General Strike was called off the workers in East Fife still gave one hundred per cent loyal support to our strike leadership, which was under the leadership of Communist Party members. It was only the Communist Party and Minority Movement representatives that carried through public agitational work. Organised picketing was left in their hands. The Party played a prominent part in organising supplies for the soup kitchens and the children's relief fund. When the police arrested workers for picket duties or other lock-out activity, again, without question, the support, legal aid, and assistance to the womenfolk was organised under our Communist leadership. The allied organisation of the International Class War Prisoners' Aid came to their assistance. That is why there was this tremendously ready response to Communist leadership during that period — and not only in the Buckhaven-Methil area. We used to joke among ourselves that workers were not asking to join the Communist Party — they were breaking in. This was taking place all over the Fife coalfield. That is why following the General Strike our campaign to get the split amongst the miners healed, to get this unity going between the Reform Union and Adamson's union, actually succeeded.

I remember in Valleyfield, in West Fife, we had a similar experience. A whole lot of immigrant labourers had come in there from Lanarkshire and Ireland over a number of years, and there was a very strong Catholic tendency. There had been a colossal influx into the Party branch in Valleyfield during the miners' lock-out. This so alarmed the authorities in the Catholic Church that special priests were sent up, special campaigns conducted. And those Party recruits also vanished like snow off a dyke.

So there was this huge influx of new members into the Party in Fife, this tremendous fund of goodwill, this appreciation by the miners and particularly by their wives, of the work, the unstinting efforts that were being put in by the Party comrades during this period of struggle in 1926. But the defeat of the miners, the return to work under worsened conditions, the victimisation of all known Communists, gradually weeded out a whole number of people from membership of the Party.

It was the general attitude on the part of some Communists of sectarianism and rigidity, and the lack of a properly organised Communist Party, that led to a weakening, I think, of our influence amongst the organised workers in Fife. This was happening all over the country. There had already arisen the idea that we should develop an entirely different kind of Party from that which we had been accustomed to in the loose, propaganda, free coming together groups. We had then to get down to looking at what the Communist International said. There was a special commission set up in this country, in 1922, consisting of Palme Dutt and Harry Pollitt.[4] Their report said we were to transform the old basis of the Communist Party. We had got to organise on the basis of wherever we worked. In the pits we had to form pit groups, in the factories factory groups. There was this whole duplication of organisation: trade union fractions, Co-operative fractions, street nuclei. When we endeavoured to carry this form of organisation into effect, it meant that we were spending almost every night sitting discussing reports, discussing the work of subcommittees, instead of conducting mass agitational work amongst the workers. We used to joke and say that you turned your cap when you wanted to move from one committee to the other. Over it all was to be a grouping of the most effective comrades into our leadership, and this was to be known as the Local Party Committee. So we got into using terms such as agitprop, politbureau, L.P.Cs. We were in a state of mental confusion, stringing around, using these terms to show how well up we were in the Communist administrative jargon. All these changes meant a complete change in our Party work. It was also laying down an emphasis that, as we were in a world revolutionary situation, we had got to develop Party organisation that would be able to exploit that situation and that nobody was of any use to the Communist Party unless he was an active member.

I was used fairly extensively, because I had been to the Labour College, to do educational work in the Party branches. I used to give a lecture as to what we expected from people who joined the Communist Party and how Communist Party members should conduct themselves. Joe Stalin subsequently became known for the phrase that Communists were people of a new kind. But before we had read anything from Joe Stalin we were trying to get across similar ideas to our Party recruits. Probably it was because of our Calvinistic Scots upbringing, and the early association with leaders like Bob Stewart and Willie Gallacher, who were temperance advocates, and the incorruptible John Maclean, that we said that we were not free to conduct ourselves as Communists in exactly the same manner as ordinary workers. Ordinary workers or trade union officials other than Communists could get away with bad behaviour, excessive drunkenness, kicking up rows, in some cases beating up the wife or womanising. But we claimed that members of the Communist Party should keep in mind that the Party's prestige was all-important, and how they conducted themselves in their private life had its reflection in the support or otherwise for the Communist Party. Therefore we should, like Caesar's wife, be above suspicion. In addition to that, if we were to win support and if our leadership was to be accepted where we worked, we should take every step possible to acquire the highest skills in our work. We should be all-round, thorough, competent miners, so that if we were advocating a line of policy it would not be open to the management, or even to some workmen that disagreed with us, to say we were arguing that way because we were unable to do the job. If we were arguing that working conditions were deficient, then if we were known to be good capable workmen our arguments would be accepted more readily than if we were not.

I remember in my own case one occasion after the '26 lock-out, when we in the U.M.S. were trying to stop the pits in East Fife. I was speaking at Muiredge Colliery to the back shift workers before they went on work. The Wemyss Coal Company agent, David Gemmill, interrupted the meeting and told these lads that I was a paid agent of Moscow, that I did not want anybody to work because I could not work myself. A really bad situation developed because the lads were going to manhandle this Wemyss Coal Company agent. But it so happened that the colliery manager, Mr Mercer, was standing there too. I said, "Just a moment, we'll clear that point up. Mr Manager, I worked for years in your pit. You've heard what Mr Gemmill has to say. Do you agree with him?"

Mercer said, "No, no, Johnny. I cannae agree with him. You worked wi' me and you were one of the best workmen I had in the pit. As far as work's concerned you could start back in here tomorrow."

That was a minor thing but was proof of what I had been advocating in our Party classes. We did set a very rigid standard of conduct. It was not uncommon in those difficult times for men with families to use trade union or other working-class funds when they were in difficulties. But while we could understand that, it was laid down that this would not be tolerated inside the Communist Party — and quite a number of members at one time or another were expelled because they had mishandled Party funds or dues, monies from pit papers or Party organs.

I remember too that at this time, about 1928 or 1929, we had a young miner who was doing work for us as a cartoonist on "The Spark". He was quite a young lad but had exceptional ability and political understanding. His cartoons were attracting considerable attention. Peter Kerrigan, who was a national leader of the Party, visited us to find out who the cartoonist was.[5] Kerrigan suggested that, if the young lad agreed, the Party would send him out to Moscow to the Art School for tuition in art, drawing, cartooning, and political education, and thereafter he might be most useful on the *Daily Worker*, which was soon to begin publication.[6]

It was arranged therefore that at the beginning of the new session in the autumn this young lad should go to the Art School in Moscow. In the interval, however, a group of Party lads were working on fretwork and required some chisels and other tools. They thought the easiest place to get them was from the school they had just left, so they went into the school and acquired the tools. But they had been spotted, were apprehended, and our young artist got a fortnight in jail. In consequence, our branch decided they could not support the idea he should be sent to Moscow and informed Kerrigan. So a very promising young artist spoiled himself with the Party. He lived this incident down, subsequently volunteered to fight with the International Brigade during the Spanish Civil War, came through that, and is still a member of the Party locally.

That was the general approach we took in order to try and build up a reputable Party in Fife. At the same time, we were having difficulty in building the Party due to the whole economic circumstances. After 1920, as unemployment had become more rampant, the Communist Party had undertaken to organise the unemployed in order to win the best conditions for them, and the best maintenance they could get, and to use them to assist the employed worker rather than be used as a threat against him. As people who had become unemployed included the active Communists in the pits and industry, most of the Party members at that period were in the ranks of the unemployed. It had meant that it was possible to build up an organisation amongst unemployed people, that we struggled to raise funds, and the building up of the Party itself was thereby made more difficult. Unemployment also lent credence to the general line of the Press and the capitalists against the Communists, that they were a bunch of work-shys, and did not want any other body to work because so many of themselves were unemployed. This capitalist propaganda was intensified in later years in the "hungry thirties".

At the same time as we were compelled to develop activity amongst the unemployed, there was another development. At international level it had been felt that there should be industrial organisation built alongside of the political organisation of the Communist International. There was therefore built up the Red International of Labour Unions, the R.I.L.U. This was set up in Britain, its main purpose being to co-ordinate the activity of reform committees, shop stewards and workshop organisations, and Left trade union leadership. Harry Pollitt was secretary of the R.I.L.U. in London. In Scotland the full-time organising secretary of the R.I.L.U. was William Leonard. Leonard was also secretary of the Scottish Labour College, and was an active Co-operator and an official in the furnishing trades union. He subsequently became Labour M.P. for St Rollox division in Glasgow.[7]

In 1924 the Reform Committee movement amongst the miners was merged into the Minority Movement, and became known as the Miners' Minority Movement. The Minority Movement was the trade union or industrial expression, while the Communist Party was the political expression. I attended the national conference of the Minority Movement in Battersea Town Hall in 1927, and got to know Pollitt and the South Wales representatives, particularly Nat Watkins, who was in charge of the Miners' Minority Movement.

So that back in the coalfield there was this Miners' Minority Movement, unemployed activity, Communist Party activity, and as the Party in Fife was centred on the mining industry, it meant that most Party and Minority Movement members were one and the same people. It was bound to be difficult for the average worker to distinguish between these organisations. We were busy speaking each weekend, and sometimes at mid-week meetings as well. On most of these occasions we would be speaking for the Miners' Minority Movement, urging action in the miners' union, and participating in the fight for greater democracy and to get rid of the reactionary leadership. Hostility to, and arguing for the removal of, reactionary trade union leaders was part and parcel of the general propaganda attitude of the Communist Party as well, particularly following the Datum Line Strike in 1920 and the sell-out of the miners and the other trade unionists as their turn came in 1921. This meant, however, that while there was Communist Party organisation, in many cases it took second place to activity amongst the miners and the Miners' Minority Movement.

From the 1920s the Communist Party in Fife, in addition to its other activities, was putting up candidates in the elections to the parish and burgh councils and to the county council. I have mentioned how John O'Neill and I became Communist parish councillors for East Wemyss in 1925. Abe Moffat was elected to the Parish Council at Ballingry about the same time. The local comrades in Lumphinnans were successful in electing Bruce Wallace as a Communist councillor — the first Communist to become a county councillor in Fife. Thus when we came into 1926 there were already a number of Communist councillors in the Fife coalfield.

When Bruce Wallace was squeezed out after '26 and resigned from the County Council when he got a job at Glenfarg reservoir in Perthshire belonging to the Fife Water Authority, Alex Moffat, one of our young comrades at Lumphinnans, was elected in his place as the only Communist county councillor. One of the most outstanding opponents that Alex was meeting in the County Council was a Labour representative from Buckhaven burgh, Tom Kirkcaldy, a miner, who was always supporting the side of reaction, particularly on the question of unemployment and public assistance.[8] To get support, Moffat requested in 1932 that I should make an effort to win Kirkcaldy's seat in Buckhaven. Alex Campbell, the Fife area representative of the Communist Party, came down to see me and said, "We've got to get Kirkcaldy removed from the County Council."[9]

But I was very reluctant to stand against him at the election because his ward was not one that I had been reared and brought up in. I had been born and brought up and had had most of my activity in Ward One, while Kirkcaldy represented Ward Three. However, I was persuaded to make a fight in Ward Three. I might have won but for one or two of our lads who attended Kirkcaldy's meeting on the eve of poll, in spite of instructions they should stay away, and rather misbehaved. This influenced just sufficient votes that we were beaten on the tape.

The following year the Scottish District Committee of the Party again said I would have to stand for Ward Three. I argued that if I was to stand for the Town Council I would only stand in Ward One, in which I resided. I was certain that I could win Ward One. There was a long argument about this. Big Peter Kerrigan was sent in from the Scottish District to try to persuade me to stand again for Ward Three, but I was adamant. Big Peter said, "All right, be it on your own head. We'll deal with you if you are wrong."

It was a good campaign. At the end of the day I won the seat quite easily, so I was spared the strictures of Comrade Kerrigan.

In 1935 we recorded a very substantial advance: we broke through in the parliamentary sphere and got Willie Gallacher elected as M.P. for West Fife. It was the first real breakthrough as far as direct Communist parliamentary representation was concerned in this country, and was a fairly positive demonstration of the support there was for us in the Fife coalfield.

In the 1920s, Gallacher had more and more come to visit Fife as a propagandist. The Fife lads were adamant that we could break through with him as a parliamentary candidate in West Fife. We had seen the possibilities when we had put Philip Hodge up to oppose Adamson for the seat in 1923. Gallacher associated himself very closely with the miners' struggle in Fife and the rest of Scotland. He associated himself with us in the Reform Union and in the efforts to get unity towards the end of that struggle, and in the fight for democracy and the appointment of alternative leaders in the miners' union in Scotland. He was in the thick of that fight all over Scotland as he was a Scottish propagandist, as well known in Lanarkshire, Ayrshire and the Lothians as he was in Fife. When the U.M.S. was formed he closely associated himself with its struggle. As well as being intimate with those from East Fife, he became intimate with the Moffats at Lumphinnans in the struggle for the U.M.S. It was this close association with the miners' progressive movement that I think helped to get him elected to Parliament and to beat his opponent, our old friend William Adamson, as well as the sitting Tory M.P.

Prior to the election there had been one or two issues at the pits in Fife, and in particular at Valleyfield over the dirt scale.[10] Valleyfield at that time was a stronghold of Adamson's organisation. The U.M.S. had no organised branch, although there were a number of influential people and their representative on the County Council, Andrew Jarvie, was a Communist Party member. But when this fight took place it was an attempt by the Fife Coal Company to impose a dirt scale which the men resisted and which we had always claimed was illegal. The pit was on strike, although Adamson and his officials tried their utmost to get the men to return to work, the men stood solid and refused to work under a dirt scale. We immediately, as the U.M.S., jumped in to help these men, gave them every possible assistance we could and conducted solidarity with them all over the coalfield. If the Valleyfield men sent out collectors, we openly allied with them at the pits, and urged the men at the pits to collect contributions. Gallacher of course took full advantage of this and openly identified himself with this struggle of the men in Valleyfield and campaigned for support for them in the coalfield. The refusal of Adamson and his officials to actively assist the men, meant that a number of people refused to vote for him in the general election and transferred their votes to Gallacher. That, allied with the general situation and the activity of Communist Party members established in most of the miners' union branches, was sufficient to tip the balance against Adamson.

Before the election there had been very fruitful work done all over the West Fife constituency by the Communist Party. There had been successful local election results. Alex Moffat and Andrew Jarvie had been elected to the County Council, as well as Bob Selkirk to Cowdenbeath Town Council; while in East Fife, Jimmy Hope had been returned for West Wemyss and I for Buckhaven. This meant there were outstanding local people supporting Gallacher's election campaign.

I remember when Gallacher came out immediately after the declaration of the result and did a tour of the voting areas, he came down to East Fife. There were tremendous scenes of jubilation. He was carried shoulder high to the election rooms and when he called at my house for a meal he signed one of the window display photos for my two oldest girls. He said that was the first time he had signed himself as an M.P.

That result actually was the beginning of the end for our old opponent, Mr Adamson. This was a tremendous psychological shock to him and you could sense it when you came in contact with him. By that time Adamson was beginning to feel the strain. Although I stayed in Buckhaven, which was in the Kirkcaldy Burghs constituency, one side of the street I stayed in was actually in the West Fife parliamentary constituency. I remember Adamson had an election meeting arranged for Methilhill and I thought I would go along and see if I could upset the old man. For an old seasoned campaigner he was easily disconcerted. The meeting was started when I got there. I walked down the passageway slowly. He got his eyes on me. I walked right down to the front seat, sat down very determinedly, took out my notebook and pencil, and looked up. The old man could not get his eyes off me. He was more concerned about that notebook and pencil, and he kept stuttering and spluttering and hardly completed a connected sentence. I was surprised at the change that had come over this man who had been a real vigorous, tough old campaigner.

The fact that he was defeated by a Communist, by Gallacher, was surely more than he could stand. He claimed a recount at the election, it was not possible that he could be beaten, but he had finally to accept the result. A few weeks afterwards he gave up the ghost entirely and passed away.

In the early 1930s, at the same time as we were winning seats in the local councils, the Communist Party had decided we should have to strengthen our hands in the Co-operative movement. Again it was myself that was to be put up first to make the breakthrough. The first time I was nominated, in 1933, I got a letter from Buckhaven Co-op saying that I did not qualify according to rule. I went down to see the manager. It turned out the reason was that, being a good Co-operator, I had gone to the Co-operative and had been measured for a suit of clothes. So I had a suit on order. They had not been supplied and the practice was that you only paid for a suit after you had got them. So the Co-op manager argued that I had this commitment against the Co-op, I did not have enough untraded upon capital, and so was ruled out from standing for election to the Board. This was only a pretext of course. So at the next meeting I made sure that I complied with the rules, and I was duly elected to the Board.

There followed a regular sequence of lads who were in the Party or associated with us being elected to the Buckhaven Co-operative Society, until we were able to play a very influential role in the Society, right up to the outbreak of the Second World War. There were also other Party lads being elected in other Co-operative Societies, so that the Communist Party in Fife had come to have a very decided influence in the Co-operatives. At this time it was also possible to form men's guilds alongside the Co-operative women's guilds. We took the initiative and formed a men's guild in Buckhaven, and a colleague, Bob Eadie, was appointed chairman. In the course of time he became chairman of the Scottish Committee as well. So that the Party locally was able to play a very influential part in the broad sections of the Labour movement.

At this time as well, there was the most important question of carrying on the fight for a United Front against Facism. This culminated in our efforts to get support for the Republican Army in the Franco invasion of Spain. We conducted a tremendous public campaign in support of the Spanish people and the Republican government, and for the first time in my experience met with real organised opposition in some areas in Fife.

Bowhill had always been regarded by us as one of our strongholds. For years and years Bowhill had been solidly supporters of a militant policy, before the First World War, during it, and after. I was speaking there one Sunday night on aid for Spain when there was a sudden growth to the meeting and continual interjections, insults and threats were being flung at me. Altercations broke out amongst the crowd, who were objecting to the behaviour of this section. After the meeting was over I discovered that the section that had interrupted the meeting had come down from the Roman Catholic chapel. They had been advised to support Franco on religious grounds, to oppose the Communists, who were agents of an atheistic power, and so on. That was the first real taste of religious opposition that had expressed itself in my activities in the Fife coalfield. It was obvious that the Catholic Church was being used increasingly against the progressive movement, and this experience that I personally had in Bowhill came to be expected wherever we entered an area where there was a number of practising Catholics.

However, there was very, very strong sympathy amongst miners and their womenfolks on the question of Spain. We conducted meetings night after night, collected food and money, and even had to deal with applications by people who were anxious to join the International Brigade. A number of comrades actually left East Fife to fight in the International Brigade. We laid it down that whether we granted applications to go depended on their domestic circumstances; if the applicant was married, if his wife was willing to agree he should go. On that basis, we refused quite a number of applications. For those that did go, we were able to get enough funds to see that their dependants were given a weekly allowance.

Out of the group who did go from East Fife all but one came back. David Donald, a young lad who resided in Methilhill, was killed and was buried in Spain.[11] Some of the others were wounded. From other parts of Fife some of the lads who had gone to the International Brigade did not return. One of our real bright lads, John Penman from Bowhill, contracted kidney trouble as a result of his experiences in Spain, and succumbed from a lingering illness after he came back.[12]

In East Fife we had probably the opportunity of contacts that were not got elsewhere in the county, because there was contact at Methil Docks with sailors in the Spanish ships that called. The sailors got to know our Party rooms, and regular meetings took place. We arranged functions for them, discussions, social evenings, and generally fraternised with them.

So that, at that time, we kept up a continuous programme of political discussion. The big question was the danger, as we saw it, from the growth of Fascism, the threat from the Chamberlain Government to make its peace with Hitler, and the need for a United Front to overthrow the Chamberlain Government and make common cause with the Soviet Union, and with Czechoslovakia and France.

I remember carrying this fight even into the Co-op, where I was a member of the Buckhaven board of management, and getting resolutions agreed to for the Co-operative Congress in support of the policy of a United Front and opposition to the Chamberlain Government. Some thirty-odd Co-operative Societies had resolutions on this subject for the Co-operative Congress at Scarborough in 1938. Most of the resolutions were of a similar nature. I recollect some of the London Co-operative Society delegates, who were arguing the same line as us, said that the principal opposition would come from A. V. Alexander, who was a Co-operative M.P.[13] He was the only man they were afraid of in the debate. Some bright spark made a suggestion that the best way to silence A. V. Alexander would be to take advantage of his love of booze. The London Co-op delegates said they were staying in the same hotel as him, so the boys had a whip-round to get a kitty and said they would spend all night trying to fill A. V. Alexander that drunk that he would not be able to speak the first thing next morning. I was not sure I thought it was a good idea. But they tried it. They spent all the money that was in the kitty and boozed all night. But the brightest spark of the lot next morning was A. V. Alexander. He was as bright as a linty and was the principal speaker for the opposition to the United Front and, sad to say, managed to carry the day.

Once again the policy which the Communist Party had formulated and was trying to get carried, which we were popularising and fighting for, was being opposed by Labour and Co-operative leaders. Our policy became eventually, fairly late in the day, the policy of the labour movement. But by then it was one for which Britain was paying a tremendous price.

Events were moving swiftly and automatically. At each change in the European or world situation the people used to crowd along to the Ness braes at Buckhaven in the better weather, or to the miners' institute, when political meetings were arranged with whichever speaker was available. It was on this basis that we kept up the agitation on the eve of the sell-out at Munich. We were able to explain what was happening, and that in our view it was a danger. There was tremendous exasperation with Chamberlain's policy of trying to isolate the Soviet Union. As I say, we had fairly good attendances and political discussion and awareness locally.

28

COUNCILLOR

IN 1933 I commenced a lengthy period as a councillor on Buckhaven and Methil Town Council which I continued without interruption until I was again appointed a miners' full-time agent in 1946. Buckhaven, as a small burgh, was allowed six representatives on the Fife County Council. I was in turn duly elected in 1933 also to the County Council as a burgh member and thus became the second Communist county councillor along with Alex Moffat. That was at the time we were conducting a campaign in the County Council with regard to the unemployed and public assistance, at the time of the hunger marches to Cupar and the tremendous effect that these marches had on the County Council and the obtaining of relief.

One of the things that probably helped me to win the election to Buckhaven Town Council was that I had a visit from my brother-in-law a couple of days before polling day. He said, "Do you want information that would make you a sure winner in the elections?" He then told me that meat condemned as unsuitable for human consumption had nevertheless been going out from Buckhaven slaughterhouse to local butchers. Some of it had been made up in cheap parcels for the unemployed. Other condemned meat had been going out to supply the boats that were coming in at Methil Docks. So at the election I made a point of saying that I would be responsible for an investigation into rumours about where the cheap parcels were coming from. Because at that time almost every second family was unemployed, sheer economic necessity was compelling a wide section of the populace to buy the cheap parcels. It was a serious threat to the health of the people.

When I was elected I submitted a motion right away demanding that a committee of investigation be appointed. I can remember yet the consternation that developed amongst the older members of the council. When we brought in slaughterhouse employees they said when they had finished work at night there were condemned carcases left, but when they went the next morning there were no traces to be found. The meat had not been put through the digester because if it had there would have been traces of bone and so on.

Because the slaughterhouse employee we suspected had smelt a rat in time to save himself, we could not get a conviction. But we were able to get a decision that the slaughterhouse superintendent should be dismissed, a new man appointed, and much more rigid control operated. So my very first action as a Communist councillor was to ensure that a better class of meat would be brought out for the people. This was an action that gave me good standing even with the butchers who were dealing with first-class meat, because of this unfair competition being removed.

The practice in the Town Council was the oncoming councillor should take over the committees of the councillor whom he had unseated. Thus I became Public Health Convener, and a member of other committees. As Public Health Convener I was responsible for initiating schemes of house building. As a working miner I knew next to nothing about housing construction, layouts, and so on. I had therefore to start a crash programme of acquiring knowledge. Fortunately I found that if you showed a keen interest in the work that the officials in charge of these schemes had to do, and were prepared to co-operate with them, they were anxious to assist you by giving as much information as they could. Although I had been anti-official, when I went on the council I found that by the correct approach to these people it was possible to work harmoniously with them. I was able therefore rapidly to acquire a working knowledge and came to be accepted amongst my colleagues as an expert on housing.

As a result of the development of the local authorities, more and more power was being vested in the County Council and fewer direct powers were invested in the burgh. The questions of housing, interior roads, playing fields, and drainage, however, still remained with the burghs. But it was evident that Buckhaven and Methil Town Council required considerably more space if they were to embark on bigger schemes for housing the people. This meant the burgh had to go in for burgh extension. In order to do this there had to be an application to the Court of Session in Edinburgh, at which parliamentary commissioners would be appointed, and if there were objections they would hear the objectors. As could be expected, there were objections from the County Council, the Water Trust, and the landowners — the Wemyss Estate, the Wemyss Collieries Trust, and so on. This meant that K.C.s and parliamentary agents had to be appointed, and we appointed representatives to speak for the Town Council. I happened to be one of the witnesses by being convener of the Public Health Committee. Having to formulate proposals for additional housing, it was up to me to argue why we required additional land.

I remember in the preliminary discussions with the K.C., who was a lad by the name of Duffes, he said, "Oh, you'll be our main witness."[1] I had never been at the Court of Session before. On the morning we turned up for the hearing our senior K.C. was in a terrible stew. He was most upset. The other side had been poking fun at him on two grounds. First, that one of the parliamentary commissioners had been taken ill and he was being substituted for by Joe Westwood. They were telling him that Joe Westwood was a county councillor and would therefore be more sympathetic to the County Council's case than to the burgh's. Second, he said, "I want to know, is it true that you are a Communist?"

I said, "What the hell's that got to dae with this enquiry?"

"Oh," he says, "this is terrible: my star witness, and I've found out that he's a Communist."

I said, "You go on, sir, and carry out the case. Never you mind what my politics are. We're no' interested in my politics. And secondly, you should congratulate yourself that Joe Westwood is on this parliamentary commission. Joe Westwood is a native of Buckhaven. It's true he's now residing in Kirkcaldy and represents it on the County Council, but that's no reason why you should be worried about him being on this commission. Because if there is one man that canna tolerate the Fife county clerk, Mr J. M. Mitchell, it's Joe Westwood.[2] The two of them can hardly look at one another without casting out. So if Mitchell is representing the county, Joe Westwood is a friend for us. So buck up, my lad, you've got a friend in court, and that's worth a lot of argument."

We proceeded with the enquiry, and Westwood made no bones about it that he was favouring the application by Buckhaven for burgh extension.

I remember there was another commissioner, Lord Belhaven.[3] He put the point, why did we waste time negotiating with the land superior, Captain Wemyss.[4] If we could not get suitable land we should apply for a compulsory purchase order. That was right up my barry. I had been arguing in the council on many occasions before this that we should stop feuing land and take away any power of the landlord to decide our housing programme, our layout, and so on. So with the advice of the parliamentary commissioners we managed to get two things. First, a substantial extension of the burgh and an off-the-record recommendation that we should consider compulsory purchase. Immediately following the grant of burgh extension I succeeded in getting the council to agree they would not in future feu any ground from laird Wemyss, the landowner, but that we would apply for a compulsory purchase order, the price to be fixed by the Government authorities.

If there was one thing that upset old Captain Wemyss it was that somebody dared to suggest taking the ground from him without considering his wishes on the matter. This was the biggest blow that he had got for a long time. The land was his as it had been acquired from his father, and he hoped to give it to his oldest son and nobody had any right to interfere.

In consequence there were long drawn-out battles. It was a complex situation. The Wemyss Estate were the owners of the land surface in the whole of the area covered by Buckhaven and Methil Town Council, as well as the surrounding area. The Estate also had become the principal owner of the mines. There had been financial jugglery carried through. The Wemyss Estate had sold the mineral rights to the Wemyss Collieries Trust, which was Wemyss Estate's man Friday. And the Wemyss Collieries Trust sold to the Wemyss Coal Company the right to exploit and develop these mineral deposits. Then over and above all, for general development the Wemyss Estate had formed the Wemyss Development Society.

I remember passing scathing remarks about the intellectual ability of Captain Wemyss. But the county clerk said: "Don't make any mistakes. This is a dead fly and very skilful owner." Subsequent events bore that out. An example was that I had got the Town Council to agree we should develop the lower part of Buckhaven and extend the layout of the new housing to the beach and the braes to the westward, which was controlled by the Wemyss Estate. Wemyss Estate adopted a blocking tactic. In the old part of the town, where we were carrying through slum clearance, we were anxious to acquire the site on which these houses stood so that we could use it for future development. But the architects employed by the Wemyss Estate would visit these owners, advise them that the Estate was also interested in acquiring these sites, and when the Town Council had given them their final offer to make sure to come and see the Estate and they would give a little extra. They succeeded in getting a house here and there in the lower part of the town, or, if a house had been demolished, ownership of the site, and said that as owners of these sites they would block any proposal the council put forward.

When we applied in 1938 for a compulsory purchase order to acquire the whole area for house building we were of course in the hands of lawyers. Finally, the Court of Session granted permission to the Town Council to proceed. The Town Council direct labour squad entered the area, mapped it out, and started to excavate the soil for the purpose of laying bottoming for the streets and putting in main drains. But we then had an interdict slapped on us by the Wemyss Collieries Trust. The lawyers, when they drafted the long legal documents to acquire the land for house-building, had forgotten the Wemyss Collieries Trust. The Trust said they were the owners of the minerals, which included the common clay and that when we cut the subsoil we were cutting into the clay which was their property and we had no right to interfere with it. So we were again landed in a beautiful legal wrangle. Was common clay a mineral? The housing programme had to stop until it was decided whether common clay was a mineral or otherwise. This question was still unsettled when the war broke out. When the war finished we proceeded to build houses without ever bothering about whether common clay was a mineral or not.

There was another illustration of Captain Wemyss' obstructive tactics. As part of the development of the burgh a broad highway was to be built by the council from one end of the burgh to the other, and traffic would go right through without becoming a menace in the older, narrower streets. The council proceeded to build their housing schemes in accordance with this highway, Den Walk. But in the middle of it there was the railway line coming down to Methil Docks, which was used by the Wemyss Coal Company. They also had a brickworks there and they proposed to extend their brick-making capacity at Denbeath brickworks. They could have extended to the south, east, or west, but they decided to extend it to the north. This meant that the extension, including a chimney stalk that stretched up into the sky, was planned for right in the middle of Den Walk. On the Town Council we tried every legal trick we could resort to to alter the site for extension of this brickwork. We held up the plans for it in the Dean of Guild Court, we appealed to the Scottish Office — but we were told we had no legal powers to stop the extension. The building went ahead. So even to this day Den Walk is not a completed throughroad: it is a beautiful road that extends on either side of the burgh but has this monument, a brickwork chimney, stuck in the middle.

I remember shortly after the war broke out a knock came to my door. My wife came up and said, "There's a funnily dressed man and I canna mak oot a word he's saying." I was surprised when I went downstairs and found it was the laird, Captain Wemyss. He was dressed in one of those old highland capes and a deerstalker's bonnet. He had come along to try to get my support for certain projects he had for his estate. It appeared that he had gone to the county clerk and he had advised the laird that if he wanted to get his projects through without opposition he had better convince me.

Captain Wemyss explained to me what he was after. I advised him that this was an opportunity I had looked for for a long time — to get him by himself without his legal advisers and just tell him what I thought of him. So I did just that. I ended up by saying to him, "When you are kidded on to make a legal fight you involve the Town Council in legal fights as well. Far better if you would come and meet the council and let both sides try to work out some policy that is going to be advantageous to both and so avoid acting as a milch cow for the legal fraternity."

Funnily enough, he agreed at the time. But after the war was over I only served a short time on the Town Council and we were not able to follow that up.

I never had any illusions about the power of landlordism, but my experience on Buckhaven Town Council and with the restrictive powers of Captain Wemyss made me a firm believer in the idea that a local authority should have the power to take over from the landowner whatever land was needed to satisfy the needs of the people. It was a question of the people against the landowner.

When I was first elected in 1933 as a representative from Buckhaven Town Council to Fife County Council, the only other Communist county councillor was Alex Moffat, who represented Lumphinnans. There was a number of Labour councillors with whom I was on good enough relations. I managed to get on to the finance committee, and also subcommittees for property and works. But I could never understand why I should be shifted without my consent on to the police committee. I wondered what kind of progressive political activity I could carry out as a member of the police committee.

The committee had about thirty members. Most of them were real die-hard Tories. But I began to understand that there were some grounds on which I could carry out effective work. I discovered that the police service in Fife was riddled with complaints, grouses and dissatisfaction. The old Chief Constable was one of the old army officer type, and anyone in the police force who kicked over the traces or showed any sign of a rebellious spirit was disciplined by being sent to a rural beat where the housing conditions were atrocious. This policy, by punishing their wives and families, was able to keep most of the young policemen quiet — either that or they packed up and left. Another

155

source of complaint was that senior officers who had reached the retiring age were hanging on like limpets to their posts, preventing promotion for young men, and thus there was continual division amongst the policemen on this matter. So I submitted notice of motion that in view of the need for moving police around from beat to beat, the County Council, through the police committee, should prepare standard plans for police houses throughout the county, and we should start building these houses immediately. The standard plan would mean that the household fitments — curtains, carpets, and so on — of a constable who was shifted from one beat to another would fit also into his new house. This gave me ground for an agitational issue on the police committee, allowed me to carry it on in the County Council and to get publicity in the Press on it. Before long I had become the unofficial champion of the policeman in Fife. Policemen with grievances would make a point of visiting my house after dark and, generally, inside information fell into my lap.

I made a great point of fighting to get all the men who had reached retiring age to be compulsorily retired to make room for the promotion of the younger men. This was the most beneficial argument I could use with the policemen. It had its good aspects outside as well, because at the time we were having difficulty in the U.M.S. with the Fife Coal Company in holding pithead meetings. Every possible scheme and device was being used by the company to block these meetings. Dr William Reid, the son of Charles Carlow Reid, managing director of the Fife Coal Company, having completed his college training, had been sent for managerial experience to Frances Colliery at Dysart.[5] He said he was not going to tolerate these lads from the U.M.S. speaking in his pit. Bob Eadie had been along at a meeting, had been set on by the watchman, and had got a bit of a drumling up. So we decided we would follow this up with a meeting held by myself and Abe Moffat. I acted as chairman and opened the meeting. Abe Moffat was in the course of his speech when the village policeman from Boreland was seen coming down on his bike to go into the colliery office. After a short time he came out to speak to me and said Dr William Reid was complaining that we were creating a breach of the peace. The policeman said, "He wanted me to chuck you off, Johnny, but I said, 'I'm no' doin' that'."

I said, "No, no, that's quite right. You know the law, and he doesn't. The law says you can't put us off here unless you've got an interdict. You go back in that office and tell him that if he does not behave himself you'll arrest him for a breach of the peace."

The policeman said, "I'll be bloody quick and dae that." So he went back into the office and did it.

Moffat afterwards said to me, "How did you manage to stop that policeman?"

"Because," I said, with a grin, "I'm the policemen's advocate. I'm their senior K.C., with the result that you can't get them taking action like that."

I remember another occasion when I was in the midst of an election in Buckhaven. It was the practice on the night before the poll for the election committee to go out and whitewash the town with slogans and tell voters why they should vote for McArthur, and so on. The committee were gathered together discussing the work, where they were going to get the pails of whitewash, and so on, when a policeman approached them. He said, "Are you lads going out whitewashing tonight?"

Naturally, they were suspicious. "Why? Why did you want to know that? You're going to stop us?"

He said, "No, no, I'm not going to stop you. I'll go wi' ye." So the policeman went on the rounds whitewashing.

When I stood for Parliament in 1945 in Kirkcaldy Burghs, the same lad was one of the policemen looking after the door at one of the polling booths. When I appeared he said, "Well, you've got your first vote today, Johnny."

So that even policemen, provided correct work is done on their behalf, can be won for a militant policy just like any other worker.

The County Council was a much wider field for debate. Being a burgh member I was permitted to speak only on certain subjects. I was not allowed to speak on matters, such as landward housing and drainage, that were purely the concern of the landward members. But if working-class issues were involved I always made a point of trying to get a few short sharp sentences in, and then when the chairman said I was out of order as a burgh member, I would apologise and say, "All right, I accept your ruling." But by that time the Press had caught the main points that I was after. I employed that tactic quite frequently in order to give support on landward issues to Alex Moffat, who was at that time the only Communist Party councillor apart from myself.

Gradually, however, our numbers increased and we became a very influential section on the County Council. Alex and I were followed by Jimmy Hope from East Wemyss. Jimmy was an excellent county councillor. He was the most painstaking individual I have known. He made a point of being conversant with all items that were coming up before the County Council. He had got every document, minute and memorandum read, marked off, and notes taken, so that if we other Communist councillors had not had time to read them because of pressure of work, we could always depend on Jimmy having his notes prepared and the points ticked off that were to be raised. This was of tremendous help to the remainder of us who had so many other activities that occupied our attention. Then we were also supported by Andrew Jarvie from Valleyfield until he left and Abe Moffat became councillor for that area. So we gradually built up a good fighting unit on the County Council. By the time I retired from the council in 1946, Mrs Maria Stewart had come in from Methilhill and Bob Selkirk from Cowdenbeath.[6] We had in 1945 a really smart young lad who came in from Thornton, George Sharp.[7] Sharp was a young railway driver and a keen lad in the Communist Party. After the war he left the Party and became a Labour councillor and ended up in the 1970s as convener of Fife County Council and then chairman of the Convention of Scottish Local Authorities. He became Sir George Sharp. This was quite an effective debating team and on most items could play a fairly important role.

To start with we had to make our presence felt on the question of public assistance, because of the tremendous poverty and misery from unemployment and low wages. This fight on the question of public assistance, school meals, and so on, was a very vital one. We followed that up with hunger marches which were being undertaken by the National Unemployed Workers' Movement at that time, marching to Cupar on more than one occasion from West and East Fife, and supporting the line that the Party was taking at the County Council. In these agitations Alex Moffat played a remarkable and solid role. All of us Communist councillors in Fife were also marching on one occasion to Dundee, on another to Edinburgh — a famous march that got wide publicity — and we were also on the big march led from Scotland by Alex Moffat to London, to protest against the Means Test.

I remember one occasion when the fight was taken up on Fife County Council and a deputation was accepted. The marchers were outside shouting slogans. The question was how were they to get home. The Co-operative in Cupar supplied meals to the marchers and did an excellent job. One retired jute manufacturer who represented Newport on the County Council wanted to show his magnanimity and said he would pay for buses to take all the lads home. We were so pure that we had long arguments as to whether we should accept this wealthy man's gratuity, or walk home. Some of those present said, "No matter a damn who it is, if this boy is going to get us home, it's better than marching." But that was typical of the atmosphere prevailing at the time.

Fife County Council at that time was dominated by representatives of the landed Tories. Due to the election set-up predominance was given to landward members as against the industrial or burgh members, and the Tories retained the voting majority all the time that I was on the County Council. These landed Tories were a real hard-faced unsentimental bunch. No matter what hard-luck plea we tried to put up it was impossible to make them feel any emotion for hardship cases brought before the council. They had one main object: to cut expenditure to the limit and only pay what they were forced to pay.

The leading spirits among them were Lord Elgin, who was chairman of the County Council, and Brigadier-General Crosbie, who thought he had achieved a certain amount of notoriety by having been in charge of a brigade in the Archangel landings against the Bolshevik Revolution.[8] Some of us made sure that in subsequent debates he did not get any chance to forget it.

There was also Sir Robert Spencer-Nairn, who had an estate at Leslie, and whose family owned the linoleum works in Kirkcaldy.[9] His son Douglas was also a member of the council.[10] Another Tory member, from East Fife, was Sir Thomas Erskine.[11] Allied to all these was a whole host of hangers-on who supported them on every occasion.

The convener of the finance committee was a key post for the Tories. They made sure that no matter who controlled the other statutory committees of the council they controlled the finance committee. The convener of this committee was a real hard-faced Tory, Mr David Bonthrone, a landed proprietor but also the owner of the malt works at Newton of Falkland.[12]

On one occasion, when I was a member of the property and works committee of the County Council, there was a dispute as to where a new proposed library should be erected — in Cupar, or in Kirkcaldy. There had always been that division in the county. The landed Tories preferred Cupar as the centre, while the industrial workers preferred Kirkcaldy because of the better bus service, and so on. This division reared its head again on this issue. It so happened that Mr Bonthrone's daughter was an applicant for the chief librarian's job. He was therefore concerned to obtain the new library for Cupar, as it was in that area that his daughter lived. At a meeting of the property and works committee it was agreed that the question be referred to a subcommittee. The chairman of the property and works committee and Sir Robert Spencer-Nairn and Brigadier-General Crosbie pleaded that I should go on the subcommittee. I had plenty of commitments and was reluctant to undertake any more, but because of the special pleading of the committee and that the meeting of the subcommittee would be arranged to fit in with another commitment I had, I agreed to serve.

But lo and behold, when we all met on the subcommittee, Mr Bonthrone as its convener entered the meeting and claimed it was out of order as the former remit had not been exhausted. So the meeting broke up and no business was conducted.

At the following meeting of the finance committee I got up in great dudgeon to object that the time of the council had been wasted by the convener. I reminded the members that I had been very reluctant to go on the subcommittee and had only agreed after special pleading, and that then to be insulted by the convener when I got there and told I had no right to be there — I was not prepared to accept that from him and demanded an apology.

This was the first time they had had a real issue of this kind and while they tried every manoeuvre possible, I remained adamant that the meeting would not be allowed to go on until we got an explanation and an apology to the rest of the members. Mr Bonthrone was too important a lad for that. To apologise to a Communist was outwith his code of conduct. So he picked up his papers and walked out.

It created an extraordinary situation because he was the convener of the finance committee, and the estimates had to be submitted at that meeting, which was a statutory meeting. When he walked out in great dudgeon he took all his papers with him. So the finance committee could not complete its business. It meant that the statutory meeting of the County Council was due to be held without the estimates having been passed by the finance committee. All of us were quite tickled to death as to how we were going to get out of this difficulty.

When I went to the County Council meeting following the finance committee meeting, one of the permanent staff advised me that Lord Elgin was in his room and wished to see me. I went up the stair to the cloakroom and there was another official standing to advise me of the same thing. I went in to sign the sederunt book and there was again advised that Lord Elgin wished to see me. I went to my normal seat and the deputy county clerk came to advise me that Lord Elgin was waiting on me.

I said, "Hey, sir, it's Lord Elgin that wants to see me, isn't it?"

"Oh, yes, oh, yes."

"Well," I said, "if Lord Elgin wants to see me, tell him to come and see me. This is my meeting here. I'm no' gaun tae his room. I don't want to see him."

"Oh," the clerk says, "I cannae tell him that."

I said, "You go and tell him that. That's what I say."

Everybody by this time was aware there was something on. Lord Elgin finally came. I said, "What is it you want, sir?"

"Aw," he said, "it's this trouble with you and Mr Bonthrone. I want to know, will you be raising it here at the County Council today?"

"Oh," I said, "if Mr Bonthrone's there I'll certainly raise it. He's no' getting away with it."

"But," he said, "I understand that Mr Bonthrone is not coming to the meeting."

"Oh," I said, "that's a different story. If he's no' coming to the meeting, I'm no' making an attack on him in his absence. But I assure you if he comes into that meeting I'll raise the question again."

Mr Bonthrone did not attend the meeting. He did not attend any more meetings of the County Council, as a matter of fact. He resigned. Not long afterwards he passed away. I do not know whether it was because he lost his position on the County Council or not.

There were one or two curious incidents while I was on the County Council. I remember another new Tory appeared on the County Council, Brigadier-General Lefanu.[13] He did not know much about council affairs and was very impulsive, would speak on the spur of the moment. Generally, if he was at a meeting at which I would be trying to wheedle the birds off the trees with a case, he would jump in and second. So that on many occasions we had this curious combination between myself and Brigadier-General Lefanu.

One day he approached me on the street, with a face as red as a beetroot, spluttering with annoyance. I said, "What's wrong wi' ye?"

He said, "You would hardly credit it. Sir Robert Spencer-Nairn and Sir Thomas Erskine have been at me. They tell me that I'm too friendly with you and I'll have to stop it. I've got to realise that I am a Conservative with different politics from you altogether. I told them where they could get off."

"Good for you," I said, "I'm glad to hear that. I wouldn't let anybody tell me what kind of politics I have to pursue. If you think the proposals I make are good for the people by all means you support them."

That may have been his view that day, but he was a very careful gentleman after that and very seldom jumped in to support proposals I would be making on the various committees. He may have felt indignant, but he bowed to the pressure of the Tory group.

Sir Robert Spencer-Nairn used to approach me and say, "I can understand your attitude and can respect it. We know on every issue that is coming up where you are likely to stand and you inevitably take up that stand. And you can't be induced to change it for any consideration. We've no time for these Labour people. They start off the argument, shouting like wild lions.

When the debate finishes and the vote's due they generally finish up like tame rabbits."

Another time he approached me and said, "I would like to go to the Soviet Union for a visit."

I said, "Good for you. That's a good idea."

He said, "If I go to the Soviet Union on my own there are only certain things they'll allow me to see, and things I want to see I won't get the chance to see. What about you coming with me?"

"Oh, lord," I said, "that's a different proposition."

He said, "I'll pay all your expenses if you come."

I said, "Look, I'm desperate to get the opportunity to visit the Soviet Union. But if I do, I'm not going as your guest. That would be entirely misunderstood and I would never be happy."

There was a real character on the County Council by the name of Willie Duncan.[14] He represented Kennoway. Duncan was a working miner, getting on in years. He was that early type of miner, a Liberal in politics. But at the County Council he always voted with the Moderates or Tories. I never heard him speak for or against any proposal. He used to say to me: "I work in a different manner from you. You get up and fight for every proposition that you consider worthy. You draw attention to the points you are raising. But I go about things quietly. If I want something for my constituency I go up early in the morning of a council meeting and have a chat with Mr J. M. Mitchell, the county clerk. I can generally arrange to get things I want without having to say a word on the County Council."

Duncan had a very close friendly attitude towards myself. He had known and worked with my father in the pits and that leant him towards me with a certain sympathy. We used to travel on the same bus to or from the County Council meetings at Cupar and often we would chat together. One day he approached me while we were in the bus queue and said, "Have you any objection to me sitting beside you on the road back?"

I said, "Oh, no, that's all right, Wullie. What's on your mind?"

"Oh," he said, "I've been talking to Sir Robert Spencer-Nairn. He's asking me if I knew you. I said aye, I knew you. I knew your father and worked with him when you were a boy. Sir Robert was anxious to know if I could guarantee that you are an honest man and I said I guarantee that all right. I told him I dinna agree with your politics but you're an honest man. I said, 'Why are you wanting to know that?'."

"'Well,' said Sir Robert, 'my grieve's leaving and I would like to get a man to act as my grieve. I wonder if you would speak to Mr McArthur and see if he's interested? I would like him to take over the job as grieve on my estate. But of course he would have to give up County Council work'."

"Well," I said, "Wullie, thank you for being the message boy. You can go back and tell Sir Robert that I am not interested in becoming his grieve in order to give up work on the council."

I was unemployed at the time, and it was just one of the baits that were being flung out to me.

The atmosphere on the County Council was a peculiar one. I remember the first meeting I attended. During the course of the meeting, the chairman said, "We'll ask Mr Mitchell's opinion." Mr Mitchell was of course the county clerk. I got up and said to the chairman, Lord Elgin, "Mr Chairman, I'm new here. Will you please inform me which constituency does Mr Mitchell represent?"

Lord Elgin looked at me so pityingly and said, "Mr Mitchell is the county clerk."

I said, "Yes, I know that. I'm aware he's the county clerk and I'm aware that on matters of legal importance and of order he's entitled to give us his opinion. But to enter into the merits or demerits of a case under debate is only the right of the elected members of the County Council. I repeat, what constituency has Mr Mitchell been elected for? If he is not an elected member, he has no right to participate in the formulation of policy as a non-elected member." However, this was heresy, and Mr Mitchell, in spite of my protests, was allowed to speak.

I was always amazed at the deference shown to Lord Elgin by the Labour councillors. They would get up and address Elgin as "My Lord". To break the tradition, we Communists would get up and say "Mr Chairman" or "Mr Convener". While we were prepared to acknowledge the chair, never once did I or my Communist colleagues refer to him as "My Lord".

One of the controversial issues at the time of my early days on the County Council was whether or not a road bridge should be built over the Forth, and if so where. The Communists and the Labour group had been arguing for a long time the necessity of a road bridge to span the Forth, and we had argued that it should be built at what was then known as the McIntosh rock site at Queensferry, nearby to the existing railway bridge. But the Tories, under the leadership of Lord Elgin, always opposed this. When pressure for the bridge became strong they suggested an alternative site — it would be cheaper, and so on — in the Kincardine area.

I remember at that time being surprised to get a fancily embossed large envelope addressed to Mr and Mrs Mc Arthur, informing us that "Viscountess Elgin would be at home in Broomhall" on a certain date. After talking it over, my wife and I felt the best thing to do with that was to return it marked *Mrs McArthur's at home any day*. Elgin never spoke to me again after that.

But all the Labour group attended the garden party at Broomhall. Curiously enough, when a vote was taken at the next County Council meeting in favour of the crossing at Kincardine it was carried by a majority. It was merely coincidental that the building of the bridge there considerably enhanced the value of the land in the surrounding area, which just happened to belong to Lord Elgin. That we were right in urging that the road bridge should be built nearby the existing railway bridge was borne out subsequently — the new bridge has actually been built there. But I presume that it would be at least twenty times the cost when it was built than it would have been at the time it was suggested.

It's always a matter of amazement to me that working men who take an active interest in politics, who take the socialist ticket, by the very nature of their upbringing and background should ever fall for this blandishment of invitations. I remember another occasion when I was present at a committee meeting of Buckhaven Town Council. Ex-Provost Mackay was preening himself and advising the committee that his good lady and himself were going to Edinburgh.[15] He came over this once or twice, and I said, "Oh, by the way. Is it the Royal Garden party at Holyrood that you're gaun tae?"

He said, "Yes, how did you know?"

"Och," I said, "the last two or three invitations I got to it I flung in the fire. If you want another one to mak sure ye get in, here's one. You can tak that one wi' ye."

But, unfortunately, most of my Labour colleagues seemed to feel honoured that they were getting the limelight be basking in the sunshine at Holyrood, or when they got the minor honours flung at them — J.P., O.B.E., and so on. From my earliest days, before the First World War, when these things were being dished out, the early socialists used to say that when O.B.E.s were bestowed upon trade union and political leaders, it meant "Our Bloody Enemy".

29

A JOB IN
THE PIT

AT the time that the bar was up against me at both the pits and the union after the liquidation of the U.M.S. in 1936, and I could not get employment of any kind, I remained a county councillor. But being a councillor presented a problem for me. When I attended meetings of the County Council I was not eligible to claim for loss of work, since I was an unemployed person. On the other hand, the Labour Exchange tried to claim I was not available for work because I was at a council meeting and so I was not entitled to unemployment benefit. But in a way the problem was overcome by me saying that I was employed by the workmen's inspectors' committee in the pits to make inspections on their behalf and I was fully occupied in that. A certificate was signed by the secretary of the workmen's inspectors' committee and I went to the County Council and claimed for loss of work. At that time we were paid twelve shillings (sixty pence) for loss of work at the County Council. This was my means of sustenance, twelve shillings for a meeting of the County Council and a collection at the pit, when an inspection of the colliery was carried out.

In this situation, with four lusty growing children, I do not know how my good lady managed to put up with the hardships, the difficulties, the complete change in the life that she had been accustomed to before our marriage. My children could not have been more attached to us than they were. They were uncomplaining, and right throughout all the years they were growing up there was a very helpful, happy relationship. Our oldest girl, Ellen, was being asked by a chemist to work at the weekends and during her holidays; and when it was near time for her sitting her Highers at school he wanted her to start work full time with him. We were in a quandary, because we were anxious that she should have the opportunity to take her Highers. But she was sufficiently understanding to know the circumstances in the home, and said she was willing to start work and forget all about her Highers. I remember going down to have an interview with her headmaster. I told him my problem, that I was unemployed, that we were anxious that Ellen should take her Highers, but we had the offer of apparently suitable employment for her. Could he give us an assurance that she had a reasonable chance of passing her Highers? I was shocked when he opened up and said it was the most hopeless class he had. Not one of them, he thought, could pass their Highers. In these circumstances I told Ellen that if she wanted to start with the chemist, that was all right. After she had started work we were approached by her teachers as to why we had withdrawn her from school. We told them what the headmaster had said, and they replied he did not know what he was talking about, that it was an exceptionally good class. In point of fact, all of Ellen's class passed their Highers, except two. So that this stupid old headmaster was completely out of touch. Funnily enough, I had quite a number of chances after becoming a member of the education committee to put this same fellow through his paces, and I took a delight in doing it.

When our second daughter, Margaret, left school, she had difficulty in getting employment but managed to get a clerical job with the gas company. The same thing happened with our third daughter, Isobel, and with our boy, George, when in later years they left school. The applied for numerous jobs. Their school records were excellent, their appearance and handwriting were quite reasonable. But when the name McArthur was mentioned, that was sufficient, the bar was put up. Isobel managed to find employment on the clerical side of the Co-operative Funeral Department, and George with the Fife Electric Power Company. All other avenues had been closed. This was a general experience for leading Communist Party lads when their families came to try to get employment.

Meantime, I got a job myself at last. In 1938, when we were in continuous conflict on Buckhaven Town Council with the Wemyss Estate because of the spoliation of the beach and silting up of the outfall of the sewers by redd from the bing being washed out to sea and washed up again to a depth of twenty or more feet, we had to enlist the assistance of our M.P., Willie Gallacher. We had a meeting on the beach, at which were present the town councillors and officials, Gallacher and myself, and Dugald Baird, general manager of the Wemyss Coal Company. After the meeting, Gallacher said to Dugald Baird: "Why don't you find a job for Mr McArthur here? He's been unemployed a long time now. He's a married man with four of a family and he'll do a good job in the pit. Why don't you see he gets one?"

Dugald Baird, to my surprise, said, "I've no objection to him getting a job."

So the next day I decided to put it to the test. My wife raised one serious objection. "If you are going back to work at the pit it is only on condition that you get a job at a pit where there are pithead baths, so that you leave your pit clothes at the pit and no' bring them back to my fireside." I thought that was perfectly reasonable, and consequently I went along to the Michael Colliery at East Wemyss, where I was a workmen's inspector. I knew the officials intimately. The manager was Willie Galloway. I remember yet the look of incredulity on Mr Galloway's face when I said, "I'm along for a job."

He said to me, "What job?"

"Oh," I replied, "a job in the pit."

After a period of contemplation, he said to me, "Hey, Johnny, ye're not serious, are ye?"

I said, "Of course I'm serious. I've got to get a job, I've got to get work. This is the nearest pit. I thought I'd get a job here."

After a period of humming and hawing he came away with some bright advice. He said, " I'll tell ye what. When I'm due to retire, I'll let you know. You can come along the day before and I'll start you so that I can retire the next day."

I had to assure him that I was perfectly serious, and that Mr Baird, the general manager, had said he personally had no objections.

"Oh," said Willie Galloway, "that's a different matter. If that's so you'd better come back. Come back on Saturday and ye'll get the answer."

So back I went to Michael Colliery on the Saturday. Galloway was accompanied by James Keir, the agent, another Buckhaven townie. Galloway said, "What jobs can you do in the pit?"

I said, "I can do any job in the pit. The only job I don't want to go to is on a coal-cutting machine."

Galloway says, "But you're a member of the County Council, aren't you? And you have to attend meetings during the day, so that you are not available for work every day?"

I said, "I'm in exactly the same position as any other member of the County Council, that when I have a meeting on I presume I would get attending without objection."

"Ah," he said, "that's not the point that's bothering us. If you're employed as a stripper we look for continuity of attendance. On face work or as a brusher or any job that requires regular attendance it would not be possible for us to give you a job. There are not so very many jobs you could do which would also allow you to attend the County Council. But," he said, "would you take any job?"

I knew it was a question of getting a job of some kind so that I could get joining up again in the union. Mr Keir said, "Well, we've thought this over. I'm in charge of two pits, Michael Colliery, which is a big one, and Lochhead Colliery, which is not so important. At the moment we get on very well with James Smith, who is union delegate for Michael Colliery.[1] If you started in the Michael, we presume that the first thing you would do would be to join the union?"

"That's right."

"Yes," he says, "that's what bothers us, because at the first election we could expect that you would be appointed delegate. You would be coming in here representing this big colliery. And as we are getting on very well just now with Mr Smith we don't want to see any change. Consequently we would not like to offer you a job in the Michael. But we will offer you a job in Lochhead."

"Oh," I said, "what kind of job?"

"Well," he said, "there are two jobs vacant. One is to go labouring to the bricklayers." This was one of the toughest jobs in this pit because it was a pit very much subject to underground fires, and in consequence there was a lot of building of brick stoppings, which meant you were working in a fire area most of the time, dealing with tremendous heat that gave off obnoxious gases.

The other job was to work on a German pneumatic stowing machine. I had seen this machine in operation while I was making examinations as workmen's inspector and I certainly preferred to work as a bricklayer's labourer.

I said, "All right, then, if that's the only job available at the moment. I don't like it but I'll take it."

Mr Keir then said, "Ah, but there's another condition we wish to lay down. Willie Drylie is the delegate at Lochhead Colliery, and as you know he's chairman of the Fife miners' union. He is checkweigher, and again we get on very well with him as the men's representative. We want you to agree that you won't seek to join the union at Lochhead Colliery, because you might unseat Mr Drylie and create trouble for us at that pit. But we have no objections to you becoming a member of the union in the branch where you reside in Buckhaven."

Again, I was not going to raise any difficulty or give them the excuse to continue keeping me out of the industry. I felt the most important thing was to get a job no matter what kind it was, in order that I could continue my activity within the miners' union. I said, "All right, I'll take on this job and join the branch at Buckhaven."

As they had anticipated, at the first election I stood for the position of delegate and became the delegate of Buckhaven branch. I continued as a delegate until I was elected a full-time official of the National Union of Mineworkers in January 1946, except for a couple of years in 1939-41, when there was a backlash against Communists arising from the Press barrage against the Soviet Union on the Nazi-Soviet Pact and Finnish War issues. So that when I finally retired at the age of 65 in February 1964 I could say that, apart from that period, and the period in 1936-7 following the liquidation of the U.M.S., when I had been kept out of the pits and out of the union, I had been continuously in office of some kind in the miners' union in Fife for almost half a century.

NOTES
THE RECOLLECTIONS OF JOHN McARTHUR

CHAPTER 1

1   John Maclean, 1879-1923. See above, pp. 33-48.
2   The Social Democratic Federation was formed in 1880-4, the first socialist party in Britain and Marxist in outlook.

CHAPTER 3

1   This incident is referred to in H. W. Lee and E. Archbold, *Social Democracy in Britain* (London, 1935), 154.
2   No copies are known to survive.
3   The British Socialist Party was formed in 1911-12 from the Social Democratic Federation plus some branches of the Independent Labour Party and other socialist groups.
4   Henry Mayers Hyndman, 1842-1921, leader of the Social Democratic Federation and until 1916 of its successor, the British Socialist Party.
5   Independent Labour Party, formed 1893, was parliamentary socialist.
6   John O'Neill (O'Neil), "about fifteen years older" than J.McA. Bobby Venters, c. 1898-1972.
7   The Industrial Workers of the World was formed in U.S.A. in 1906 as a revolutionary socialist and unionist organisation.
8   William Gallacher, 1881-1965, British Socialist Party, a leader of the shop stewards' movement and from 1920 of the Communist Party; M.P. for West Fife, 1935-50.
9   For Scottish Labour College, see above, pp. 30-48.
10 William Dunbar, "much older" than J.McA.
11 Bob Lamb, himself a miner, had worked in America for about two years but had returned to Fife about 1910; he died in March 1939, aged 67.
12 Lewis Henry Morgan, *Ancient Society, or Researches on the lines of human progress from savagery, through barbarism to civilisation* (London, 1877); another edition, ed. by Leslie A. White (Cambridge, Massachussetts, 1964).
13 Joseph Dietzgen, *The Positive Outcome of Philosophy*. Translated by Ernest Unterman (Chicago, 1906).
14 Thomas Johnston, *Our Scots Noble Families* (Glasgow, 1909).
15 Robert Blatchford, *Merrie England* (London, 1894); *Britain for the British* (London, 1902).
16 The Socialist Labour Party was formed in 1903 as a breakaway from the Social Democratic Federation; *The Socialist* was published from 1902.

17 The *Labour Leader* was published as the official organ of the Independent Labour Party from 1894, continued from 1923 as the *New Leader*, and later as the *Socialist Leader*.

18 *Forward*, 1906-60, was an independent labour paper founded and for long edited by Thomas Johnston.

19 *The Call*, published 1916-20 by the British Socialist Party, then in 1920 incorporated in *The Communist*.

20 See p. 95.

CHAPTER 4

1 Rt. Hon. William Adamson, 1863-1936, General Secretary, 1908-28, Fife, Kinross and Clackmannan Miners' Association, and 1928-36 of Fife, Clackmannan and Kinross Mineworkers' Association; Labour M.P. for West Fife, 1910-31, Secretary of State for Scotland, 1924, and 1929-31.

CHAPTER 5

1 Karl Liebknecht, 1871-1919, German revolutionary socialist.

2 Rosa Luxemburg, 1870-1919, Polish revolutionary socialist.

3 The Clyde Workers' Committee was formed in 1915 as a rank-and-file organisation of delegates from several industries and included leading shop stewards such as William Gallacher.

4 For the rent strike in Glasgow in Oct.-Nov. 1915, see, e.g., James Hinton, *The First Shop Stewards' Movement* (London, 1973), 125-7.

5 *The Worker*, 1916-33, published in Glasgow, originally the organ of the Clyde Workers' Committee, later of the National Workers' Committees and Shop Stewards' Movement, then of the British Bureau, Red International of Labour Unions, and of the National Minority Movement.

6 Theobald Wolfe Tone, 1763-98, Irish republican, founder of the United Irishmen, 1791; sentenced to be hanged by the British authorities but committed suicide.

7 Constance Georgine, Countess Markiewicz, 1868-1927, daughter of Sir Henry Gore-Booth, married a Polish count. She was a Sinn Fein leader, twice imprisoned in 1916-19; elected to the Westminster Parliament in 1918 for a Dublin constituency — the first woman to be elected to Parliament — but refused to take her seat; a member, 1921-27, of the Irish Dail, and Minister of Labour, 1921-22.

8 James Connolly, 1868-1916, born in Edinburgh of Irish parents, founder, 1896, of the Irish Socialist· Republican Party, a leader of the American Socialist Labor Party and an organiser for the Industrial Workers of the World, executed by the British authorities for his part in the Easter Rising in Dublin.

9 James Larkin, 1876-1947, Irish labour leader, sentenced to ten years' penal servitude in U.S.A. in 1920 for "criminal syndicalism", later a member of the Irish Parliament.

10 John Boyd, "much older" than J.McA.; David Proudfoot, 1892-1958, above, pp. 52-324; Gardner, no further details available; Peter Hastie, "about twenty years older" than J.McA.; Tom Smith, Methilhill, born c. 1897 and understood to be still alive; William Kirker, "ten years older" than J.McA.; Jimmy Galloway, "much older" than J.McA., died c. 1950s; John Bird, 1896-1964, began work in the pit at Bowhill at age 14, active in the miners' union from about age 17, victimised after the 1921 miners' lock-out, imprisoned twice — in 1921 for three months for incitement and in 1926 for six weeks for sedition — employed for a time as miners' checkweigher but "felt he had lost the confidence of the men" and

resigned, subsequently became tenant of Bowhill Hotel, and later of George Hotel, Burntisland, and on retirement from that became a sub-postmaster and newsagent at Musselburgh, Midlothian, served for many years as a parish and county councillor in Fife. Tom Smith, Lumphinnans, "at least fifteen years older" than J.McA. Andrew Jarvie, "about ten years older" than J.McA., emigrated with his family to Canada because of victimisation by the coal company after the 1926 miners' lock-out, returned to Fife in the early 1930s, became a county councillor but was later badly injured in an accident at Lindsay Colliery, and moved to Edinburgh (see Angela Tuckett, *The Blacksmiths' History* (London, 1974), 254-5). Peter and William Swain were "twenty years older" than J.McA.; the Thomson brothers were "more than twenty years older" than J.McA.

11 The National Union of Scottish Mine Workers, successor to the Scottish Miners' Federation of 1894-1914, was a loose federation of the half-dozen autonomous county unions in Scotland, including that of Fife. The N.U.S.M.W. was replaced in 1945 by the National Union of Mineworkers (Scottish Area).

12 The Miners' Federation of Great Britain was founded in 1889 as a federation of the various district miners' unions, such as Yorkshire, the Scottish Miners' Federation or National Union of Scottish Mine Workers, etc., and was reconstituted in 1945 as the National Union of Mineworkers.

13 See above, Chap. 14.

14 Arthur James Cook, 1883-1931, a leader of the Miners' Minority Movement in 1923, was General Secretary of the Miners' Federation of Great Britain, 1924-31.

15 James MacDougall, 1890-1963, a bank clerk, member of the Social Democratic Federation and British Socialist Party.

16 James Maxton, 1885-1946, schoolteacher, I.L.P. leader, M.P. for Glasgow Bridgeton, 1922-46. Campbell Stephen, M.D., B.D., B.Sc., 1884-1947, M.P. for Glasgow Camlachie, 1922-31 and 1935-47. Stewart from Edinburgh has not been further identified.

17 J. R. Campbell, 1894-1969, wounded and decorated in 1914-18 war, member of British Socialist Party and Communist Party, editor of *The Worker, Workers' Weekly* and *Daily Worker*, principal in the "Campbell case", 1924 (see Chap. 16, Note 1). Tommy Clark (?-1943), Socialist Labour Party, Clyde Workers' Committee, Communist Party.

18 R. Foulis, no further details available.

19 Captain J. R. (Jack) White, D.S.O., organiser of the Irish Citizen Army, arrested in 1916 for attempting to persuade Welsh miners to strike in protest against the execution of the leaders of the Easter Rising. General Sir George Stuart White, 1835-1912, besieged in Ladysmith, 1899-1900, during Boer War; later a Field Marshal.

20 Irish Citizen Army was formed as a result of police attacks during the Dublin transport workers' strike in 1913, and took part in the East Rising, 1916. Every member of the Army had to be eligible for trade union membership.

21 Tom Bell, 1882-1944, editor of *The Socialist*, later a leader of the Communist Party. Arthur McManus, 1889-1927, Clyde Workers' Committee, later a leader of the Communist Party and Communist International. James Clunie, 1889-1974, housepainter, author of *First Principles of Working Class Education* (Glasgow, 1920), Labour M.P. for Dunfermline Burghs, 1950-59. Daniel De Leon, 1852-1914, a leader of the American Socialist Labor Party and a founder of the Industrial Workers of the World in 1905.

22 Extensive mutinies had taken place in the French army in May and June, 1917 — see, e.g., Alistair Horne, *The Price of Glory: Verdun 1916* (Harmondsworth, 1964),

322-5. Mutinies, though on a very much smaller scale, had taken place also in the British army, e.g. at Etaples in Sept. 1917 and at Calais in Jan. 1919 — see D. Gill and G. Dallas, "Mutiny at Etaples Base in 1917", in *Past and Present*, No. 69, Nov. 1975, 88-112.

23 Bela Kun, 1885-1937, leader of the Hungarian Soviet Republic of Mar.-Aug. 1919.
24 Jack Villiers Leckie, Chairman, Communist Labour Party formed in Glasgow in Oct. 1920 (see above, pp. 46-7, and also Walter Kendall, *The Revolutionary Movement in Britain 1900-21* (London, 1969), 260, and 418 n.22). Leckie was Communist candidate at Dunfermline Burghs in the 1929 parliamentary election. Rt. Hon. Thomas Kennedy, 1876-1954, *Clarion* lecturer on socialism, Scottish organiser from 1903 and General Secretary from 1919 of the Social Democratic Federation, M.P. for Kirkcaldy Burghs, 1921-22, 1923-31, 1935-44; held junior office in Labour Governments, 1924 and 1929-31.
25 Jimmy Birrell, "twenty years older" than J.McA.
26 The Communist or Third International was founded at Moscow in Mar. 1919 and was dissolved in 1943 during the Second World War.

CHAPTER 6

1 Bob Beattie was killed in an accident at Lumphinnans No. XI Colliery early in 1924, when he was about thirty-seven years of age. He left a widow and five children.
2 Joe Westwood, 1884-1948, Industrial Organiser of the Fife miners' union from 1916, Political Organiser, 1918-29, of the National Union of Scottish Mine Workers, Labour M.P. for Peebles and South Midlothian, 1922-31, held junior office in Labour Government, 1929-31, M.P. for Stirling and Falkirk Burghs, 1935-48, Secretary of State for Scotland, 1945-7, killed in a road accident.
3 No further information about Neilson is available.
4 Robert Smillie, 1857-1940, President, Miners' Federation of Great Britain, 1912-21, President, National Union of Scottish Mine Workers, 1894-1912, 1922-8. Herbert Smith, 1862-1938, Yorkshire Miners' Association, President, M.F.G.B., 1922-29. Frank Hodges, 1887-1947, General Secretary, M.F.G.B., 1918-24, Labour M.P. 1923-24, Civil Lord of the Admiralty, 1924. Sir Leo Chiozza Money, 1870-1944, author and journalist, Liberal M.P., 1906-18 and junior minister; joined Labour Party, 1918. Professor Richard Henry Tawney, 1880-1962, economic historian, a leader of the Workers' Educational Association, 1905-44. Sidney Webb, 1859-1947, social scientist, author, Fabian Socialist, Minister in Labour Governments, 1924 and 1929-31.
5 Alan Ian Percy, eighth Duke of Northumberland, 1880-1930.

CHAPTER 7

1 David James Williams, 1897-1972, educated at Central Labour College and Ruskin College; National Council of Labour Colleges tutor in east-central Scotland, 1924-30; Secretary of Fife, Kinross and Clackmannan Council of Action, 1926, and charged with incitement to riot but found not proven; returned to South Wales, 1931; Labour M.P. for Neath, 1945-64.
2 William McLean Watson, 1874-1962, Labour M.P. for Dunfermline Burghs, 1922-31 and 1935-50.
3 John Briggs, "thirty years older" than J.McA.
4 John Welch, son of a Cardenden, Fife, miner, began work in the pits at Cowdenbeath at age 14; died 1948, "aged between 50 and 60" (*Scotsman*, 9 January 1948).

CHAPTER 8

1   James Cook, 1878-1955, General Secretary, Clackmannan Miners' Association, 1895-1917, Fife, Clackmannan and Kinross Mineworkers' Association, 1936-44, and of National Union of Scottish Mine Workers, 1939-46.

2   William McLaine, 1891-1960, in 1920 a member of the Central Committee of the Communist Party but later left the Party; became Assistant General Secretary, Engineering Union.

3   Andrew Fagan: James Jack, retired General Secretary, Scottish T.U.C., "sat at Fagan's feet" in later years, and recalls him as "a remarkable man" who "suffered quite a lot of intimidation and victimisation". Fagan ultimately found work as foreman with a public works contractor and held that job until he died at the age of 91. Between the wars Fagan "did a lot of lecturing for the Lanarkshire Labour College and carried his 'magic lantern' throughout the mining villages". William Allan, 1900-70, began work on the surface at Greenfield Colliery, Lanarkshire, from the age of twelve, worked underground from age fourteen at Craighead Colliery, was elected Workmen's Local Inspector at Loanend Colliery at age nineteen, organised study classes among young miners on industrial and trade union history and economics before himself going to the Scottish Labour College, worked for a time as a stoneman in Yorkshire after being victimised at the end of the miners' 1921 lock-out, was elected branch delegate at Cadzow Colliery, Lanarkshire, on his return, and, at the age of twenty-four, a member of the Executive of the National Union of Scottish Mine Workers; he was elected checkweigher at Tannochside Colliery shortly before the 1926 General Strike; in 1934 he went to work in Northumberland, became checkweigher at Cambois Colliery and in 1937 was elected to the Executive of the Northumberland Miners' Association then in 1944 he became the Association's treasurer. See also above, p. 133. About William Crawford and James Hunter no further information has been found. Robert Spence, 1879-1965, a Clydebank engineer, Labour M.P. for Berwick and Haddington, 1923-24; secretary and parliamentary agent of the Scottish Temperance Alliance.

4   *Science of Understanding*: no trace of this publication has been found and it may be merely another version of the *Positive Outcome of Philosophy* (see above, Chap. 3, Note 13).

5   Paddy, or Peter, Lavin apparently emigrated to Canada, c. 1970.

6   Formed in 1924, the Minority Movement contained the militant sections, under Communist leadership, in the unions. It aimed to resist wage cuts, achieve reformation of the unions as industrial unions, extend democracy within the unions and, in the long run, make them revolutionary bodies. See R. Martin, *Communism and the British Trade Unions, 1924-33. A Study of the National Minority Movement* (Oxford, 1969).

7   See pp. 121-5.

CHAPTER 10

1   Omar Khayyam, c. 1048-1122, Persian poet and scholar, author of the *Rubaiyat*, translated and published by Edward Fitzgerald in 1859.

2   Published 1918, 119 pp.

3   Presumably so called after Henry Bradbury, 1831-60, writer on printing, including printed notes.

4   Harry McShane, 1891-, engineer, British Socialist Party, Clyde shop steward, a member of the Communist Party, 1922-54, a leader in the 1920s and 1930s of the Unemployed Workers' movement, remains politically active at the age of 88.

5   Sandy Ross, "thirty years older" than J.McA. Ross later emigrated to India and worked in a Calcutta jute mill. Nan Milton, *John Maclean* (London, 1973), 277.
6   Peter Marshall, "ten years older" than J.McA.
7   Sir Edward Carson, 1854-1935, Conservative Unionist M.P. for Dublin University, 1892-1918, and Belfast Duncairn, 1918-21; member of War Cabinet, 1917-18; a leading opponent of Irish Home Rule or independence. ·
8   The Black and Tans, so called because of their khaki uniforms with black police caps and belts, were raised in 1920-21 in Britain as reinforcements for the Royal Irish Constabulary, and acquired notoriety for ruthlessness and brutality.
9   Ford was head of the Safety Department, Fife Coal Company, from 1910. A. Muir, *The Fife Coal Company* (Leven, 1953), 77.
10 Abe Moffat, 1896-1975, General Secretary, United Mineworkers of Scotland, 1931-36, President, Scottish miners, 1942-61. Alex Moffat, 1904-67, younger brother of Abe, President, Scottish Area, National Union of Mineworkers, 1961-67. John Wood, 1900-76, Vice-President, 1947-56, and General Secretary, 1956-65, Scottish Area, National Union of Mineworkers.
11 John S. Clarke, 1885-1959, Socialist Labour Party, writer, lion-tamer, Labour M.P. for Glasgow Maryhill, 1929-31.

CHAPTER 11

1   William Spalding, agent, Fife Coal Company.
2   William Easton was sentenced to a year's imprisonment. R. Page Arnot, op. cit., 165, 336.
3   James Henry Thomas, 1874-1949, General Secretary, 1917-18, and Parliamentary General Secretary, 1919-31, National Union of Railwaymen, Labour M.P., 1910-31, National Labour M.P., 1931-36, Minister in Labour Governments of 1924 and 1929-31, and in "National" Government, 1931-36. Croncemore Thomas Cramp, 1876-1933, Industrial General Secretary, 1919-31, and General Secretary, 1931-33, of the National Union of Railwaymen. Harry Gosling, 1861-1930, Transport Workers' leader.
4   Alex Gordon and Bob Thomson were both "about ten years older" than J.McA.

CHAPTER 12

1   Jimmy Hope, 1890-1948, born in Ayrshire, professional footballer with Raith Rovers, 1911-13, and Stoke City, 1913-15, returned to the pits in Fife in 1915 on the suspension of football at Stoke due to the war; Fife county councillor for West Wemyss and Coaltown of Wemyss, 1938 until his death.

CHAPTER 13

1   Bob Mercer, "much older" than J.McA.

CHAPTER 14

1   Philip Hodge, 1872-1936, began work in the pits as a boy, attended evening classes and gained Honours in Principles of Mining in 1893 and a silver medallion in Honours Mining in 1897-8 from the West of Fife Mining School. See also above, p. 69.
2   Mick Lee was the grandfather of Jennie Lee, Labour M.P., now Baroness Lee. Jimmy Robertson, agent, Fife miners' union for "about sixteen years" until his death in Apr. 1926.

CHAPTER 15

1 Formed in Moscow in 1921, the Red International of Labour Unions was the trade union organisation of the Communist or Third International.
2 *The Miner* was published from Sept. 1922 to Oct. 1926. A file of the paper is preserved in the National Library of Scotland, and another in the British Library at Colindale, London.
3 Willie Thomson, "about twelve years older" than J.McA.
4 Joe Corrie, 1894-1968, author of over eighty published one-act plays and several volumes of poetry.
5 Pat Connelly, "about twenty years older" than J.McA.

CHAPTER 16

1 The law officers of the Labour Government in Oct. 1924 began a prosecution of J. R. Campbell, acting editor of the *Workers' Weekly*, for an article appealing to troops not to shoot workers in industrial struggles. Because of widespread protests from the labour movement the prosecution was abandoned. The Tories and Liberals then combined to defeat the Government and bring on a General Election. The "Red" or "Zinoviev" Letter was alleged to have been sent by G. Zinoviev, President of the Communist International, and purported to urge British Communists to do all they could to ensure ratification of the Anglo-Soviet Treaties then being debated in Parliament, but also to prepare for an insurrection in Britain. The letter was generally regarded in the labour movement as a forgery and as a classic election scare.
2 An article by Philip Hodge in *The Miner*, 25 Oct. 1924, headed "The Defeat of Adamson means Progress. Vote against him this time again", argued that industrial unity in Fife would be brought nearer by Adamson's electoral defeat.
3 Charles Augustus Carlow, c. 1876-1954, managing director, Fife Coal Company, 1917-39, chairman and managing director, 1939-52, chairman, Shotts Iron Co. Ltd., 1939-52.
4 "The Spark", fortnightly duplicated organ of the Methil Communist Pit Group, then from Oct. 1930 of the Militant Section, Wellesley Colliery, Methil, ran from July 1925 until Dec.1931.

CHAPTER 17

1 Harry Pollitt, 1890-1960, General Secretary, 1924-29, of the Minority Movement, and, 1929-56, of the Communist Party, whose Chairman he was from 1956-60. Arthur Lewis Horner, 1894-1968, President, South Wales Miners, 1936-46, and General Secretary, National Union of Mineworkers, 1946-59.
2 Harry Hicken, 1882-1964, General Secretary of Derbyshire Miners' Association, 1928-42. Jack Williams.
3 Stanley Baldwin, 1867-1947, Conservative Prime Minister, 1923, 1924-29, and 1935-37, latterly Earl Baldwin.

CHAPTER 18

1 William "Mosie" Murray, "about the same age" as J.McA., and still alive; James Cation, "older" than J.McA.; Reddie Henderson, 1882-1936; Bert True, "about the same age" as J.McA; Jimmy Ord, 1902-61, a founder member of the Communist Party, organiser of the local Spanish Aid Committee during the Spanish Civil War; Davie Martin, "ten years older" than J.McA.; Johnny Moir, "twenty years older" than J.McA.; Jimmy Stewart, died 1937; Jim Gourdie,

"three or four years older" than J.McA.; Bill Crooks, "about the same age" as J.McA.; Bruce Wallace, born in Glasgow, came to Fife as a boy, died c. 1973; Peter Venters, died 1958; John Gordon, "about fifteen years older" than J.McA.; Jimmy Jarvie, 1919-70, General Secretary, Associated Blacksmiths' Society, 1960-70; Tommy Miller, "three or four years younger" than J.McA.

2   A third Communist, Richard (Dicky) Wilson, also stood for election with John McArthur and John O'Neill as a member of the Trades Council panel, but was not elected. See "The Spark", No. 3, n.d. (Aug. 1925).

3   The National Unemployed Workers' Committee Movement was formed in 1921, with Wal Hannington, Communist Party and Amalgamated Engineering Union, as its principal national leader. The N.U.W.C.M. conducted demonstrations and hunger marches against unemployment.

4   Robert Thomson, "about fifty years older" than J.McA.

5   Tom Thomson, died c. 1948.

6   Walker Thomson, killed c. 1936.

7   Peter Thomson, died c. 1948.

CHAPTER 19

1   John Sutherland, Fife county councillor, 1935-52, died 1961.

2   Davie Martin, "twenty years older" than J.McA.

3   Bob Eadie, 1894-1956, organiser for the United Mineworkers of Scotland, workmen's inspector at Michael and Lochhead Collieries, President, 1930s, East Fife Spanish Civil War Relief Fund, and, 1940s, of Scottish Co-operative Men's Guild, Labour councillor at Buckhaven and Methil, 1945-56, killed in an accident at Wellesley Colliery, Methil; father of Alex Eadie, Labour M.P. for Midlothian since 1966.

4   Peter Ness, died 1971.

5   Bob (or "Rab") Smith, "about the same age" as J.McA., and still lives at Lumphinnans.

6   Alice Brady Moffat, died 1928.

7   Jimmy Moffat, 1892-1973, went to U.S.A. in early 1920s to work in the coal mines of West Virginia and Indiana, later moved to New Jersey as a heating engineer; returned with his family to Scotland in 1932, then worked as a door-to-door clothing salesman "but couldn't stand having to take the people's last shilling to pay their debts". He worked first as attendant, later as superintendent, at the pithead baths at No. 11 Peeweep Pit, Lumphinnans, until he retired in 1960.

8   Dave Moffat, 1902-.

9   Bob Selkirk, 1887-1974, born Arniston, Midlothian, son of a miner. His autobiography is *The Life of a Worker* (Cowdenbeath, 1967), 47 pp.

10   Proletarian Schools and Socialist Sunday Schools were flourishing in the 1920s.

11   Jim Connelly, "ten years older" than J.McA.

12   Aitken Ferguson, a boilermaker, a leading Scottish Communist, parliamentary candidate at Glasgow Kelvingrove, 1923, Aberdeen North, 1928 (by-election) and 1929, and Greenock, 1931, died 1975. Shapurji Saklatvala, 1874-1936; he remained M.P. for Battersea North until 1929.

13   Bob Stewart, 1877-1973, son of an Angus farm worker, Scottish Organiser, 1921, and Acting General Secretary, 1925, of the Communist Party. Willie Joss died 1967, aged 88.

14   Founded originally in 1921 in Germany to provide help for the Soviet Union against famine and aid its reconstruction after the civil and interventionary wars,

the Workers' International Relief soon began to organise aid for workers in need all over the world. It was supported by many who were on the Left but outside the Communist Party.

15 Mrs Helen Crawfurd, resigned from I.L.P., 1921, and joined Communist Party, of whose Executive she was a member in 1923-25; hon. secretary, Workers' International Relief; five times imprisoned for suffragette activities before 1914, and was charged several times during the 1914-18 war with anti-militarist activities; died 1954, aged 77.

16 Mrs Isabel Brown, 1894-. Ernest H. Brown, 1892-1960, a full-time organiser of the Communist Party from 1921, member of the Political Bureau of the Party from 1925 and of the Executive in 1924-26.

CHAPTER 20

1 Inspector Andrew Clark (Clarke) and Sergeant George Park. A motion by John O'Neill calling on the Chief Constable to transfer Clark from Methil because of incidents during the General Strike was adopted by Wemyss Parish Council. *Fife Free Press*, 22 May 1926.

2 Walter White and Will McFadyean were both "about fifteen years older" than J.McA.

3 Mick McGrory was "about twenty-five years older" and Barney McGrory "about five years younger" than J.McA.

CHAPTER 21

1 The International Class War Prisoners' Aid was founded in 1922 to raise funds for strikers, political prisoners and other victims of class war. The British Section was formed in 1924 and was supported by Left Wing elements in the Labour Party and I.L.P., as well as by the Communist Party.

2 Alexander Gillespie, J.P., was "about thirty years older" than J.McA.

3 A. Fordyce Burke.

4 Sir John Simon, K.C., 1873-1954, Liberal or Liberal National M.P., 1906-18, and 1922-40, member of Liberal Government, 1910-16, Foreign Secretary, 1931-35, Leader of the Liberal National Party.

5 Lewis Kitchener, 1874-1926, born in Austria-Hungary, interned as an alien in Britain during the 1914-18 war; worked in the Pannie pit, Kirkcaldy, from about 1906 until 1914, and after 1919 in Frances Colliery; union branch delegate in Fife miners' union; joined Communist Party c. 1920; in 1926 strike he told crowd of around 200 that "there was only glass between them and the food they wanted". He committed suicide at Strasbourg in Sept. 1926 after his deportation. *Fife Free Press*, 5 Jun. 1926, and information from Mr F. Kitchener.

CHAPTER 22

1 William Phoenix, died c. 1970, aged about 84.

2 Jimmy Shand, 1908-.

CHAPTER 23

1 Rt. Hon. James Ramsay MacDonald, 1866-1937, Labour Prime Minister, 1924 and 1929-31, and of "National" Government, 1931-35.

2 Aitchison: no further information available.

3 Lady Victoria Alexandrina Violet Cavendish-Bentinck, 1890-, daughter of the Duke of Portland, married Captain Wemyss, 1918.

4 Jimmy Hodgson, about "ten years older" than J.McA.

CHAPTER 24

1   Watson has not been further identified.
2   Jim Watt, 1906-, became a Church of Scotland "home missionary" at Valleyfield, and later studied at a Quaker college in England. Around 1930 he joined and became a leader of the Oxford Group, but quarrelled with Dr Frank Buchman, its chief leader, and left the Group in 1936. Watt then became a Church of Scotland minister in British Guiana, joined the Black Watch at the outbreak of war and was invalided home from France in 1940. He married the daughter of a president of the British Medical Association, but after the death of his wife in 1947 emigrated with his daughter to Australia where he worked as a postmaster, and where he still lives.
3   Julius Cunningham and Danny Ward were both "about fifteen years older" than J.McA.
4   Jimmy Duffy was "three or four years younger" than J.McA. Frank, Pat, and Peter Duffy had been born in Lanarkshire but moved to Denbeath in 1902, where they worked in Earlseat, Muiredge, Wellesley and Michael Collieries. Frank Duffy died in 1962, Pat in 1957, and Peter in 1955. The brothers Frank and Hugh O'Donnell, who played first for Wellesley Juniors then for Preston North End, both played for Scotland in the 1930s; W. Fagan played for Celtic, whose captain he was in 1945 when he was transferred to Liverpool, and he also played for Scotland.
5   Mungo (Mungie) Mackay, agent and general manager of the Lothian Coal Company, was an Ayrshire man who worked at Auchinleck Colliery before moving to Polton pit, Midlothian, about 1894. He seems to have been an unusually capable mining engineer and was made a director of the Lothian Coal Co. in 1927. He was also an outstanding autocrat and paternalist. James Jarvie of the Blacksmiths' union wrote in 1920 of Mackay and his control over the mining village of Newtongrange: "This is a village where the firm own all about the place — dwelling houses, picture-house, public-house; in fact, everything from the cradle to the grave. The General Manager acts as the Lord Mayor." (Angela Tuckett, op. cit., 201-2). Mackay died in 1939, at the age of 72.
6   Sir William Lawther, 1889-1976, President of the Miners' Federation of Great Britain and National Union of Mineworkers, 1939-54.
7   Chick Watson, "about ten years younger" than J.McA.
8   George Alfred Spencer, 1873-1957, President, Nottingham Miners' Association, Labour M.P. for Broxtowe, 1918-29, opposed to the 1926 General Strike, expelled from Miners' Federation conference, 8 Oct. 1926, led a breakaway union from the Nottingham Miners' Association.

CHAPTER 25

1   Nat Watkins, a South Wales miner and member of the Communist Party, was National Organiser of the Miners' Minority Movement formed in 1924. He died in 1952.
2   Sandy (Alex) Smith, "about thirty years older" than J.McA.
3   Hugh Murnin, 1865-1932, agent of Stirlingshire Miners, President of National Union of Scottish Mine Workers, 1920-22, and Vice-President from 1922, Labour M.P. for Stirling and Falkirk Burghs, 1922-23, 1924, 1929-31. Alex Thomson was "about ten years older" than J.McA.
4   Dan Sim had entered the pits as a boy, was for many years secretary and agent of the Ayrshire miners' union, represented Kilmaurs on the county council for

thirty-eight years, and was county convener from 1957-67; he became a labour relations officer with the National Coal Board, was awarded the C.B.E. in 1965, and died in 1967 at the age of 66.

5   Jimmy Potter, "thirty years older" than J.McA., died 1959. Charlie Toner (or Tonner), "thirty years older" than J.McA.

CHAPTER 26

1   Willie Drylie, "fifteen years older" than J.McA.
2   Peter Henderson, who was "about fifteen years older" than J.McA., was President of the Scottish Trades Union Congress in 1943, and died in 1969.
3   "The Spark", see above, Chap. 16 Note. 4. "The Flame" has not been further identified, and no copies are known to survive. "The Torch" was issued by the Militant Section, Frances Colliery, Kirkcaldy, and nos. 1-6, 18 Oct. 1930-31 Jan. 1931 survive. No issues of "The Lamp", published in East Fife, have been traced; there was a duplicated weekly sheet with the same title produced in 1927 by Cowdenbeath Branch of the Communist Party, and a copy of this for 20 Aug. survives. "The Panbolt" was issued by Peeweep Pit Cell at Lumphinnans, and a copy for 29 Aug. 1930 survives. "The Mash" and "The Hammer" have not been further identified and no copies of either are known to survive. For some other Fife pit papers see I. MacDougall, op. cit., 131, 289.
4   Emanuel Shinwell, 1884-, Labour M.P., 1922-24, 1928-31, 1935-70, Parliamentary Secretary to the Department of Mines, 1924 and 1930-31; a Life Peer from 1970.
5   See above, p. 83.
6   Andrew Clarke, 1868-1940, Secretary, Mid and East Lothian Miners' Association, 1919-40, President, National Union of Scottish Mine Workers, 1932-40.
7   Joe Swan was "ten years older" than J.McA.
8   Jimmy McKendrick, Lanarkshire District Secretary, National Union of Mineworkers, died 1962. John "Dabs" Miller, agent, Lanarkshire District, National Union of Mineworkers, died 1961.
9   Ebby Edwards, 1884-1961, General Secretary, Miners Federation of Great Britain, 1932-44, Labour M.P. for Morpeth, 1929-31.
10 Peggy Morton.

CHAPTER 27

1   Ernie Woolley, a leader of the Young Communist League, was a member of the Executive Committee of the Communist Party in 1925.
2   Young Pattie was "about five years older" than J.McA.
3   *The Justiceman* was a printed paper, unlike all the other Fife pit papers; the first number, 17 Apr. 1926, survives. Four issues of "The Torch" for 1926-27, Nos. 2-9 of "The Hutch", Jan.-10 Apr. 1926, and two issues of "The Picket", 1926-27, survive.
4   Rajani Palme Dutt, 1896-1974, a graduate of Oxford University, imprisoned in the 1914-18 war for refusing to serve in the forces, founder member of the Communist Party of Great Britain, founder, 1921, and first editor of *Labour Monthly*, editor, 1923-24, of *Workers' Weekly*, and, 1936-38, of *Daily Worker*; lived in Brussels for several years from 1924 because of a breakdown in his health; member of the Central Committee of the Communist Party, 1922-65, and Vice-Chairman for twenty years until his retirement in 1965.

5 Peter Kerrigan, 1899-1977, a Glasgow engineer, member of the Executive Committee, Communist Party of Great Britain, 1927-29 and 1931-65, leader of hunger marches from Glasgow to London, 1934 and 1936, successively Scottish Secretary, National Organiser and Industrial Organiser of the Communist Party; a Political Commisar in the Spanish Civil War.

6 *Daily Worker*, Communist newspaper, Jan. 1930-Apr. 1966, then continued as *Morning Star*.

7 William Leonard, 1887-1969, a cabinetmaker, emigrant in Canada, 1907-13, Secretary, Scottish Labour College, 1918-20, Scottish Organiser, National Amalgamated Furnishing Trades Association, 1921-31, Labour M.P. for Glasgow St Rollox, 1931-50, President, Scottish T.U.C., 1925 and 1931-32.

8 Tom Kirkcaldy, "about thirty years older" than J.McA.

9 Alex Campbell, "about twenty years older" than J.McA.

10 The dirt scale represented deductions made by the coal companies from the miners' tonnages to allow for "dirt", e.g. stone, filled into the tubs or hutches with the coal.

11 David Donald was "five or six years younger" than J.McA.

12 John Penman, 1908-54, active in the Reform Union, U.M.S., and Communist Party, visited Russia in 1931 and stayed on for five years, working in the pits in the Donbass, as well as on building of the Moscow underground, and at Novosibirsk in Siberia; joined the International Brigade in Spain, 1937, by crossing the Pyrenees on foot, captured and imprisoned at Burgos and San Sebastian, returned to Bowhill in Feb. 1939, and worked for some years in Dundonald pit, suffered from Bright's Disease after his return from, but apparently not as a result of his experience in Spain, and was an invalid for the last four years of his life.

13 Albert Victor Alexander, 1885-1965, Earl Alexander of Hillsborough, co-operator, Labour M.P., 1922-31 and 1935-50.

CHAPTER 28

1 A. P. Duffes, 1880-1968, M.C., LL.B., K.C.

2 John Methven Mitchell, 1887-1959, M.B.E., J.P. Fife county clerk until his retirement in 1952.

3 Robert Edward Archibald, 11th Baronet Belhaven, 1871-1950.

4 Captain Michael John Erskine-Wemyss, 1888-, of Wemyss Castle, East Wemyss; Captain, Royal Horse Guards; Director, Wemyss Coal Company Ltd. and Wemyss Collieries Trust Ltd.

5 Dr William Reid was an official of the Fife Coal Company from 1929, and Director from 1942; he became the Chairman of the Scottish Division, National Coal Board, from 1952. Sir Charles Carlow Reid began as a clerk in the offices of the Fife Coal Company in 1893; became General Manager in 1939; Production Director of the Coal Board in Scotland 1942-43, and 1943-48, in Britain.

6 Mrs Maria Stewart, represented North Wemyss on Fife County Council from 1945 to 1952.

7 Sir George Sharp, 1919-, O.B.E., J.P., D.L., Fife county councillor, 1945-75, Convener, 1972-75, of the County Council, and, 1975-78, of the Regional Council; President of the Convention of Scottish Local Authorities, 1975-78.

8 Edward James Bruce, 10th Earl of Elgin and 14th Earl of Kincardine, 1881-1968, Chairman, Fife County Council, 1929-38. Brigadier-General James D. Crosbie, 1865-1947, base commander at Archangel from Nov. 1918, Chairman, Fife County Council, 1938-45.

9 Sir Robert Spencer-Nairn, 1880-1960, Director, Michael Nairn & Co. Ltd., linoleum manufacturers, Kirkcaldy.
10 Douglas Leslie Spencer-Nairn, 1906-70, Conservative M.P. for Central Ayrshire, 1955-59.
11 Sir Thomas Erskine, 1880-1944, D.S.O., of Cambo, Kingsbarns.
12 David Bonthrone, 1873-1937, head of Alexander Bonthrone & Sons, Newton Maltings, Fife; a county councillor for over twenty years, finance convener from 1930, vice-convener of the county from 1932.
13 Major-General Lefanu, of Freuchie, Fife, member of the County Council, 1945-55.
14 Willie Duncan was "about the same age" as J.McA.'s father.
15 Ex-Provost Mackay of Buckhaven was "about thirty-five years older" than J.McA.

CHAPTER 29
1 James Smith was "about twenty years older" than J.McA.

Left: John McArthur as a young man.

Bottom left: John McArthur, aged seven, with his mother and elder sister Betsy.

Bottom right: Four generations of McArthurs. *Left to right:* John's grandmother, his eldest daughter Ellen, himself, and his mother, in the mid-1920s.

Above: John Maclean with full-time students and staff at the Scottish Labour College, Glasgow, session 1920-21. Front row, left to right — William McLaine, tutor, John Maclean, William Leonard, secretary. Middle, left to right — William Allan, Lanarkshire Miners, Andrew Fagan, Lanarkshire Miners, John Welch, Fife Miners, John McArthur, Fife Miners. Back, left to right — R. Hunter, Ayrshire Miners, William Crawford, Lanarkshire Miners, John Bird, Fife Miners, and Robert Spence, Toolmakers' Union.

Below: Bowhill mineworkers' strike paper money; signatories — George Stott, George Lamb, John Bird, James Galloway.

Bowhill Mineworkers' Strike

The Mineworkers of Bowhill
Promise to Pay the Bearer

August 1920 · BOWHILL · August

1/ ONE SHILLING 1/

For the Bowhill Branch Fife Miners' Union.

George Stott .... Chairman.
Geo M Lamb .... Treasurer.
Bird .... Delegate.
Galloway .... Secretary.

No. 1241

August · BOWHILL · 1920

For recognition of Minimum Wage.

Buckhaven Branch, Fife Miners' Reform Union, 1924 (John McArthur, front row, third from right).

John Bird disguised as a special constable in the General Strike, 1926.

Philip Hodge, General Secretary of the Fife Miners' Reform Union.

Above: East Wemyss Gala Day, June 1926 (David Proudfoot seated, wearing bonnet and grey suit). Standing, left to right — unknown, unknown, J. Burt, unknown, D. Grant, unknown, J. Grant, G. Johnstone, J. Davidson, six unknowns, J. Moodie (with trilby), unknown, D. Provan, J. McColl, unknown, P. Lindsay, rest unknown. Seated, left to right — R. Cuthill (bareheaded, open-neck white shirt), J. Venters, S. Jinks, unknown, unknown, G. Gorrie, D. Proudfoot, unknown, A. Rodger (arms folded), D. Lennard, unknown, J. Goodfellow, unknown, unknown, J. Adamson, C. Webster, J. Wilson, I. Izatt (on floor, arms on knees). Foreground, left to right — unknown, unknown, J. Smith (bald), D. Wilkie (lying), J. Hope, J. McLean, W. Lindsay.

Below: Miners at work underground at Wellesley Colliery, Methil, in the 1920s.

Above and below: Miners at work underground at Wellesley Colliery, Methil, in the 1920s.

Above: U.M.S. Gala, 1930s.
Back row, left ro right: third
and fourth from left, Alex and
Abe Moffat, then William
Gallacher, John McArthur,
F. Moone, Bob Eadie,
unknown, Alex Campbell.
Seated, left ro right: Tom
Mann (with hat in hand), Tom
Whittaker (with bowler hat).

Left: William Gallacher
speaking at an open-air
meeting in Fife, with John
McArthur (centre) and Abe
Moffat.

G. Allen Hutt, chief sub-editor of the *Daily Worker*, in the 1930s.

David Proudfoot addressing a meeting in Methil, 1920s.

THE LETTERS OF
DAVID PROUDFOOT
to
GEORGE ALLEN HUTT

1924

21 Durie Street,
Methil,
Fife.
Tuesday, May 6th, 1924.

Dear Comrade,

Received your note of 26th April and also figures bearing on Fife Coal Company and Wemyss Coal Company. These figures will be published in the issue of *The Miner* for May 10th.[1]

Send on 1½ dozen copies of *Labour Monthly* for May.[2] I think I can dispose of that number. Comrade Hope of East Wemyss has agreed to canvass for readers but up to the present I don't know what success has come his way.[3] However, if we require more I will immediately let you know. Will remit monthly accounts.

A joint meeting of East Fife and Kirkcaldy groups of the Communist Party was held on Sunday to discuss the advisability of sending a delegate to the annual Congress. Comrade Dick of Kirkcaldy was appointed and will raise the question of Central organisation and need for a campaign in Fife during the summer.[4]

At the Annual General meeting of Kirkcaldy Divisional Labour Party resolutions were passed demanding an Inquiry into Police spying on Labour organisations, protesting against the action of Labour M.P.s who voted against Lansbury's amendment to the Army Annual Bill,[5] demanding the Labour Government to pass legislation for a national holiday on May 1st, and condemning A. Henderson for refusing to remit sentence of 6 months passed on a worker for stealing 3/-.[6] Comrade Wright of Kirkcaldy agreed to send those to *Workers' Weekly*.[7] Methil Branch, Reform Union,[8] also passed these resolutions.

At present I haven't had a case reported to me that would be of sufficient interest to write the *Workers' Weekly*. There are cases in plenty but we cannot get sufficient evidence due to the individuals concerned not being prepared to report. As you know I am in a position where I am more out of touch with happenings underground than previously.

The Old Association[9] on Saturday had our Labour Secretary for Scotland[10] present at their monthly meeting and unanimously decided to recommend their members to ignore the Reform Union ballot. We are making the most of it.

182

Hope you and Page got back all right.[11]
                    Yours fraternally,

                                        David Proudfoot.

                                        Monday, May 19th, 1924.
    Up to the present I *have not* received the May issue of the *Labour Monthly*.
You might please see to it that at least 1½ dozen copies are sent on as some of
those who ordered them are making inquiries as to the reason I haven't
delivered them. Should you have more than 1½ dozen to send on you might
extend the order to 2 dozen as I haven't seen J. Hope as to how many he will
require. If it is possible you might send on the June issue so that I could have
them for the Gala at Burntisland on Monday, June 2nd. A few dozen extra
could be disposed of then. Could you send on particulars of profits and
dividends of other Scottish Coal Companies — Wilson and Clyde, Baird and
Company, etc.? Hoping to get this month's issue this week.

                                        June 8th, 1924.
    Received your note of 23rd May, also facts about Wilson and Clyde, and
Nimmo and Company. These have been published in *The Miner* of 7th June. If
you can manage you might send for next issue facts relating to the Lochgelly
Iron and Coal Company and Edinburgh Collieries.
    I made an attempt to get something done at Methil on behalf of the Ruhr
miners but managed nothing.[12] The Dockers were greatly concerned about the
result and findings of the Court of Inquiry into the Leith dispute,[13] the
railwaymen are practically immovable and the split with the miners has tied
matters up in the pits. Locally the Dockers and Railwaymen are keen
opponents due to poaching members. You will have some idea of the spirit
prevailing in the pits when I tell you that it requires the services of the
Government Inspector to stop the wholesale and excessive overtime that has
been going on for the past few weeks. Excusing means accusing oneself but
that is the local position. Enclosed is a copy of the history of the Union
dispute.[14] As I indicated to Page and yourself, I suspected some of the leading
Reformers were opposed to the suggested ballot [and that] has been
demonstrated by the decision of the last Executive Board meeting — 19 against
and 10 for an immediate ballot. The excuse being Adamson and Company
recommending their members to ignore the ballot. Yet we are a rank and file
organisation who *act* independent of officials.
    Pollitt and Watkins and Steve Lawther were the speakers at the Reform
Union Gala Celebrations, and made a good impression on the crowd who
attended.[15]
    I received the June issue of the *Monthly* yesterday — 26 copies — and will
manage to dispose of the lot. I almost forgot to mention that the Sub Executive
of the Reform Union have recommended the branches to support the
affiliation of the Reform Union to the Labour Research Department.[16]

July 16th, 1924.

Many thanks for your letter of 21st June. Since last writing you I have resigned from the Reform Union Executive and Sub Executive Boards as I have been feeling rotten and wasn't prepared to "carry on" as an active unit in what is to me developing into a farce. When business of any consequence which meant a new departure from the old style or which required action on the part of the local committees was submitted it was "snowed under", not by direct opposition but by the time-worn platitude "we agree in principle but the time is not opportune to put it into operation".

Bird and Kirker have been appointed to represent the Reform Union at the National Minority Conference to be held in London next month.[17] The Reform Union has (as far as I can gather from my successor) decided to affiliate to the Labour Research Department. No action on part of local officials necessary to do so. I can't see how H. Pollitt arrived at the conclusion that some of the leading Reformers were only waiting for an opportunity to lead the Reform Union back to the Old Association assuming that they could save their faces, other than Bird and myself taking up the position "that should the suggested ballot be adverse to the Reform Union's proposals the only course was to get back and carry on an intensive propaganda inside the Old Association for these proposals". The others are "all out" for maintaining the present position.

I don't know (other than the report in the *Workers' Weekly*) how Joss got along in Fife.[18] We were unfortunate in having a heavy rainstorm when he was with us but he stuck 2½ hours on the box at Leven. I understand Bob Stewart is to be in Fife for a month, commencing immediately after his return from Russia.[19] We had a brief report from the Comrade who acted as delegate, but it was accepted as satisfactory by the group, who by the way have gone to sleep for the summer.

The Fife coalfield has now entered into a "slack period". We have been on 3 days per week since 14th June and "how the hell" some of them are getting along beats me. Men with families going home with 10/- a week and stating when advised to apply to the Parish (Guardians) "that they would rather die than accept charity". You have possibly heard about that curious item — SCOTTISH INDEPENDENCE, which when demonstrated in your locality is expressed as damn ignorance. Well, it is very much to the fore here at present but by all indications will get a severe knock during the next few weeks. We are "signing on" at the Labour Bureau but nothing has as yet been paid and the majority are sceptical as to any payment being made. I am going to try and get them to make a kick on Friday if no money is forthcoming as we are on "holiday" next week and rumours have been going around that the money will be paid on Friday. The clerk in charge of the arrangements told me that he knows nothing about it. We have written the School Management Committee pointing out the necessity for getting the school children fed, also the Town Council to extend their Child Welfare scheme. "Henry" himself can live as long as he can manage on his INDEPENDENCE, which will not last long and then we will manage to get him to move.[20] Some of them have been suggesting getting communal kitchens started but "nothing doing". They were useful in preventing scabbing during the 1921 lockout but as the Boss has nothing to offer this time Henry will have to stand up and fight.

Rathbone's article on the Budget was the goods, as also is Dutt's Notes in this month's issue.[21] No petty attacks on individuals but a scientific analysis of the present position and future results of the policy of the Labour Government. I managed to get 32 copies of this month's issue sold between Saturday night and Monday. Have ordered 3 dozen of August issue. 75% of those who have ordered it regularly are chaps between 20 and 28 years of age who are beginning to take a keen interest in the movement, which should reap the benefit in the near future.

Notice by the Press that you have been having a "hot" time in London as far as climatic conditions are concerned, so much so that Tom Kennedy has been "overcome" whilst attending to his duties as an apologist for Capitalism.[22] He will have a "hot" time whilst giving his constituents an account of his "stewardship". As far as our position is concerned I can't see any other course than that of open hostility to any member of the present Government.

July 27th, 1924

Many thanks for your letter of 24th. Noticed the extract in the *Workers' Weekly*. Some people are born famous, others have fame thrust upon them. I appear to be in the latter category as I have been accused of being the author of the paragraph.

Despite all our scepticism re payment of dole we were paid last Friday. What a scramble for 2/6d. per man per day, 10d. per wife and 2d. per child. It wasn't looked at in the light of an insult to a man's intelligence but — "something for nothing". I have been trying to weigh it up and have come to the conclusion that the Labour Government have played a cute card. As most of the mining constituencies are Labour, and owing to the Labour Party "ratted" so far as Nationalisation of the Mines is concerned, and also the servile attitude they took up during the threatened crisis in the coalfields in April they can now state, "Why, we gave you the dole"; and as the average miner's philosophy is "Talk's cheap but it takes money to buy beer", the Labour Party can face Coal Jock without fear of getting his back up. It's a great game. Wife and kiddies assessed at nothing when working and only become valuable (2 pints for 1 wife and 1 child per day) when on the dole.

By adverts in the local press we have caused a flutter in the dovecote of the Education Authority. We asked for applicants to give us (Reform Union) particulars about their kiddies at school with the result that one called Baird, Secretary for the Education authority, has written the local authority notifying him about Section so-and-so, Clause so-and-so re procedure. This procedure is as follows. Applicant must get special form from Clerk of School Management Committee, fill it in, hand it to employer to certify wages, hand it to Clerk, and then face the School Management Committee to be cross-examined re particulars on form. This is to be rigidly enforced owing to what they are pleased to term "looseness" in 1921. We have appointed a deputation to act as K.C.s for the applicants at that meeting. I am one of the deputation representing Methil. If the crowd rolls up as we expect either red tape or the School Management Committee will be broken that night. We are also advertising in the local Cinemas, Pierrot stands, Collieries, and sending the Union collectors round on a door-to-door campaign, and getting at the women. At the same time we are advising all and sundry to roll up to the Welfare Centre of the Town Council to get the youngsters under school age catered for. Milk and Soup Commissars.

We have been on "holiday" since July 17th and commence work tomorrow, Monday; and as only 3 shifts will be worked for and paid at the end of the week business should be brisk at both offices.

Give my best wishes to Comrade Budden and also tell her that I hope she isn't giving you regular doses of "kosa", as I was getting a bit fed up after a few weeks of it.[23]

Do you get *The Miner* regularly? If not, I can send it on to you. Not comparable with the *Workers' Weekly* but it plays its part. No further developments re Reform Union and Old Association. No official intimation has been received at Reform Union Central Office from Scottish Executive[24] re Committee of Inquiry. Position of stalemate, both sides "dug in" and not even signs of a raiding party other than local bickerings re unemployment dole, personal attacks on local officials on what they have or haven't done.

If you can manage you might send particulars of Lochgelly Iron and Coal Company and Edinburgh Collieries Ltd.

Could you find time to read *Bunk*, and if possible give a review?[25] If so, let me know and I will send it on when I get it back. It has been "out" since you were here and everyone is tickled with it.

I expect Page will have been notified by this time that the Reform Union has affiliated to the Labour Research Department.

August 25th, 1924.

Received your letter of 19th. Hope you had a good time during your holiday in Kent.

Re the matter of the suggested Left Wing and its personnel, we up here are out of touch of those individuals but reading between the lines of some of their articles some of us had come to the conclusion a short time ago that all was not as it should be. However, let the scrap come as soon as it may and after the dust has cleared away the Party will be all the better. I have always contended that as the social conditions grew more and more acute the Party would receive a generous purging, as the sort of individuals you describe would show their hand and get what they deserve. Better to find what strength and/or weakness is in the organisation before it is engaged in a critical action than to go in with what is really tripe, imagining it to be the real meat.

We had 2 anti-war meetings here under the auspices of the Labour College. The speakers were 2 Kirkcaldy comrades. From the point of view of numbers none of the meetings could be termed successful but the discussion that ensued at Methil was certainly the goods as we had some Social Democratic Federation members showing their gums (I nearly inserted teeth, but as they were intended to bite and hold on with it would be a libellous statement to make regarding those chaps), and the Party policy re the Labour Government and British Imperialism was clearly put to the meeting. 5 dozen *Record of the Labour Government* sold at Methil meeting in addition to 1½ dozen sold 2 days before.[26] Kennedy will get more than bouquets when he next appears.

I had a meeting last Saturday with a few Leven (place on east side of Methil — golf links, promenade, and Fife Coal Company compounds) chaps who assured me that they could get a group of 12 members for the Party. I wrote the Organising Bureau and have had a note from Comrade Inkpin granting the formation of a Party Group in Leven.[27] I expect another group will be formed in East Wemyss (3 miles west of Methil) shortly. There are also fair prospects of a group in Methil, as I have approached a few young chaps who are at present considering the position.

We have been working steady (full-time) for the past 4 weeks. You ask if we have stirred Henry to any extent. We must plead guilty to failure so far as getting him to move re the feeding of schoolchildren or the Parish. I think I informed you in my last letter that the Reform Union had appointed a deputation to meet the School Management Committee. Comrade McArthur[28] and myself met the Committee. When we entered the room I noticed that only a few application forms were in front of the chairman. In stating our case I anticipated their plea (that, judging by the number of applications made, there appeared to be little or no cases of necessitous children) by stating that the average worker would not apply to any full-time official for relief due to the treatment received from these officials for generations and the only alternative was to grant us (the local Union officials) the forms to distribute. A joker who wears his collar arse for elbow[29] asked me if it was my intention to feel all the school children in the Parish. I replied, certainly if they all required it and in my opinion very few were in the position of not requiring it. He then went on about those who paid taxes being in as bad a position as those who didn't. I told him that made the position all the more critical if he meant those who paid Income Tax, etc., were in a necessitous condition — then the need for getting the feeding started was greater than I had thought; but if after being in possession of those facts he didn't favour an immediate start then he had no right to be in the position he occupied. As only 11 applications had been made in a Parish of 25,000 you will understand we had to make some show. I can assure you that both McArthur and myself felt a bit disgusted at the poor response made to our appeals, but after some consideration one arrives at the conclusion that that same doggedness that is Henry's make-up will be a necessary virtue in the near future. When he gets going he will stick it but the present problem is — how can he be started?

If the statements attributed to T. Bell and J. R. Campbell in the Press are correct, viz., "that they expected arrests to follow the publication of the articles to the Forces", I think it was an error to make those statements.[30]

Enclosed are cuttings from the *Edinburgh Evening News* on the case.

Enclosed also is a copy of the Mineworkers' Reform Union balance sheet. 40 copies of August number of *Monthly* gone in 4 days. Will possibly require 4 dozen of September issue.

September 9th, 1924.

Enclosed is *Bunk*, which I have just received after it doing a tour of this district. No two have the same opinion of it, justifying my opinion as to it being subtle. You might send it on after Page and yourself have had a go at it as there are a few "marking time" on it.

Newbold and Company have taken the plunge and the announcement has caused some discussion here.[31] Some of them (who by the way are not attached to any political party) are declaring this to be "a tactical move on the part of the Communist Party to institute a Communist cell in the Labour Party". Others of the S.D.F. extraction assert "that it was inevitable, as people possessed of the commonsense of Newbold were bound to discover that the Communist Party was composed of adventurers and would leave it sooner or later to join the Labour Party". Others who are in sympathy with the Party policy and are at all times prepared to assist financially state that they are almost dumbfounded as in their opinion Newbold and Company are now shown up to be a crowd of opportunists; and are wondering how many more are left in the Party. I get it slung at me at every step, but owing to lack of information I point out that the *Workers' Weekly* will publish the affair so far as the Party views it, and also to bear in mind that those people are of bourgeois extraction and that the only way to prevent similar occurrences in the future is for every worker who accepts the Party policy to get inside the Party and take an active part in the carrying out of the policy and not leave it to be played on by bourgeois adventurers. I expect a few members of the Party will follow these jokers but that again will prove whether we have reliable members who are in the Party because of its policy or whether they are like the idol-worshipping crowd who are "leading" the local Labour Parties.

Our group is about as dead as the "dodo" as we cannot get a meeting to discuss local business, and I have up to the present been unsuccessful in forming a group in Methil. If I cannot manage it this month I intend joining the Leven group.

As far as I can gather there are no developments further than the Scottish Sub-Executive meeting the delegations from the Reform Union and the Old Association (separately). The local newspapers published a report that a meeting between the 2 was to be held before the end of September.

Received the postcard from Paris. Hope you had a good time.

We are working full time at present; in fact Methil Docks have been full up with boats waiting for coal for the past few weeks, and wages at the minimum 9/4d, and likely to remain so until the termination of the agreement.

Have been having a rotten time recently with recurrences of "dingy" every 3 or 4 days.

Expect to manage sale of 4 dozen *Labour Monthly* this month. If you can you might see that they are sent on earlier in the month as it was during the 3rd week when I received the August issue.

Sunday morning,
October 12th, 1924.

Received your letter of 27th September. Sorry to see by it that you are kept grinding away for 12 hours per day. Great life — when one is at work one gets too much of it and when out of work worrying like hell to get back again to keep life in by knocking it out.

The Newbold affair has simmered down here and the general view taken and expressed by those who take some interest in political affairs is "Newbold is a fool if he has been on the 'make' as he is now discredited by both Communist and Labour Parties". Even if sincere (which is doubted) he will require to make better and clearer explanations re his position.

Price has some wriggling to do before he can get out of the corner he has got into by his articles in the *Monthly* and *Plebs*.[32] Both Dutt and Rathbone have got him "by the bo-yank" (to use a local expression meaning down and out).

We have Bob Stewart in Fife at present and I think a few groups will be formed. I managed to get the Reform Branch (Methil) at their last meeting to invite him to come to the next meeting (Sunday week) and have a talk with them about the formation of a group in Methil. Those who attend are all sympathetic, read the *Weekly* and the *Labour Monthly*, assist financially, and when a crisis arises are to be depended on, but seem to think it a joke when I ask them to join up. Bob Stewart will possibly manage to get some of them. Every one is a worker and should we be successful in getting a group formed we should manage to give this man's town a bit of a shake up. The group that has gone under was East Fife group.

The Labour Party Conference has certainly played up to the lead given by the Labour Government. They have developed the habit of passing resolutions of "far reaching consequences" but this year's will travel further than some of them anticipate. "MacDonaldism" has won this round but at the price of "MacDonaldism". I am judging by some here who were good workers for Labour but have declared that they have no intention of moving a finger to help Kennedy at this election. Kennedy will get a stiff fight this time as it appears (at present) that he is to be opposed by an experienced politician, and success or defeat lies in the hands of the few local workers. Our position is a delicate one and after talking it over with Stewart he stated that he would raise it at the Executive meeting. Kennedy is an S.D.F.er and is a declared Anti-Communist. He is also a member of the Government. We have a decided influence with a considerable number of the young chaps who will act on our lead. We cannot do any other than adversely criticise the Government and by doing so will give the impression that we are opposed to their actions, which, without further explanations, will in all likelihood be interpreted to abstain from voting. If on the other hand we make our criticisms and then advocate active support it will take some explaining away. To me the latter appears the only course but I wish we could go bald-headed for the rotters.

These are the conclusions I came to on *Bunk*: None of those who have read it agree with me. All have different opinions. Do these coincide with yours? It is a dangerous book to hand to a raw hand. Because it is the embodiment of "MacDonaldism", "Change of heart". Interests don't count. Webb moves in Bourgeois Society, talks *at* them and shows up their position but unlike Everhard in London's *Iron Heel* does not challenge them.[33] Does not move amongst or even suggest organising the workers but suggests that Trade Unions and Corporations are anti-social. Similar to MacDonald's Preface. No lead given. Some trite sayings but so has Jack Jones.[34]

Enclosed is James Cook's (Adamson's successor) reply to Reform Union circular.[35] Speaks for itself and Cook. Reckoned in Methil to be so dangerous to Reform Union and Communist Party that Reform Union members distributed copies of it, suggesting that any Reform Union member who was weaned over was a good riddance.

Coal trade in East Fife (Wemyss Coal Company) is and has been very brisk since end of July. Bings at pit heads have been filled to supply the shipping at Methil Docks, where ships are waiting for coal. But in Central and West Fife the pits have been idle 2 and 3 days per week since June.

To me the Factory Group is absolutely essential and we will be compelled to form them because of the tendency of the present time for "Part Control of Industry by the Workers". Group could act as ginger group. I believe that the Political Mass organisation of workers must be preceded by and assumes its form from the Industrial organisation, which will necessitate the formation of Factory Groups of the Party to popularise the idea of Industrial Unions with Pit and Factory Committees as the unit of organisation. This will mean scrapping the existing machinery of Trades Unionism (residential branches), but who will try and defend it against organising at the point of production. The initial groups will have plenty of work but it will have to be met if we are to have a *Mass* Party. Regarding Fife, I think we should manage to get considerable numbers *after* the Amalgamation of the 2 Unions (which at present appears a long way off), as in my opinion Pit Committees will be the basis of the new organisation due to the exorbitant expenses incurred by both Unions in trying to maintain their respective memberships by door-to-door collection of subscriptions. "Money talks" and Coal Jock will look at the economy in finances 1st and 2nd and all the time.

(Sunday evening): I understand that Bob Stewart has been nominated to contest Dundee, although I haven't noticed it myself in the Press. It is to be hoped that someone is sent immediately to Fife as some immediate results to the Party could be obtained.

Am getting the *Monthly* away "like snaw aff a dyke". 52 copies of this month's issue away in 2 nights and other 2 dozen ordered. Seem to be developing "intellectuals" but no Party members, at least so far.

November 6th, 1924.

Many thanks for your letter of 18th October. Page will have told you of his meeting with the members of Methil Branch, Reform Union. His efforts have not been fruitless as we have a group of 6 enrolled but due to various causes not yet got down to business. Page made a good impression, especially the way he tackled the S.D.F.ers. We managed to dispose of 10 dozen of his and 10 dozen of Campbell's[36] pamphlets and are getting away other 5 dozen of each.

I wasn't on Kennedy's committee this time, although Comrade O'Neil of Buckhaven was Convener (in name only) of a Ward Committee.[37] We had a solid wallop at him (Kennedy) and heaven knows what kind of a Party member would not, after listening to the following. "Campbell had an unblemished military and civil character, lost parts of both feet during the war, and *possibly his war experiences have affected his mind.* Campbell wasn't responsible for the article,[38] and to have prosecuted a man for something he wasn't responsible for would not have been *British Justice.* Besides, had the prosecution failed, as it was bound to, *people* would have felt nothing but *contempt for the Law of the Crown and Constitution.*" "Russian loan a good business proposition.[39] Glad to see that the Russians were learning sense and Bolshevism had failed because the Russians were now coming to Capitalism for assistance." "MacDonald had created a peace atmosphere by bettering relations with France and Britain and France and Germany. Dawes Plan might injure the workers but the Committee appointed would soon stop that."[40] And so on. He lost his rag at me and advised me to vote for Murray.[41] I then advised the workers (over 1,000 at the meeting) to vote for Kennedy and make him fight, and explained the Party position. It caught on and Kennedy saw he had made a bloomer and explained that he had been longer in the movement than I, etc., etc. He had a debate with Murray (Capitalist) on Nationalisation of Mines. It started by Kennedy giving statistics re Accidents, Production, Wages, Profits, etc. Murray made criticisms and it ended by both being on the same platform — We are anti-Communists and stand for British Institutions. We sold 14 dozen *Weekly,* which was certainly some solace for the insults received to intelligence. Kennedy was emphatic that the alleged "Red" letter was a forgery.[42] He had bills posted all over that it was an election "stunt" started by the *Daily Mail* and that it was a fraud and a forgery. Almost 400 votes less were cast in this Ward on this occasion, due to lack of canvassing and also wet weather from 5 p.m. to 7 p.m. on Polling day.

Comrade O'Neil, Buckhaven, was Labour candidate for No. 2 Ward in the Municipal Election. He opposed a Colliery Agent, nominee of the Wemyss Coal Company, but was defeated 495-292. What a spectacle was presented. O'Neil was nominated and adopted on Thursday, 23rd October, at the Trades and Labour Council, despite the fact that nominations were asked at the April meeting of the Trades and Labour Council. Not a "moderate" Labour man would stand against the Colliery Agent and this is a Socialist stronghold. We raised the matter on 23rd October and on O'Neil's name being put forward the question of Party members was raised. One S.D.F.er suggested that, to save the Labour Party's prestige, O'Neil be adopted and the question of relationship of Communist Party members to the Labour Party be allowed to lie on the table. We opposed this and forced the issue, with the result that only 2 voted for upholding the Conference decision.[43] Kennedy advised his committee to work for the Labour candidates but none of them would assist O'Neil. The Provost (a Labour renegade) would not sign a permit to hold a Sunday meeting in the biggest hall in Buckhaven, so in addition to back court meetings we had to go to a small hall in another ward. 2 Labour Councillors were approached and asked to sign O'Neil's nomination form but they both refused — one, Farmer, "because he was a Councillor", the other because "he was in a hurry". Another prominent Labourite and ex-S.D.F.er said he had a touch of the 'flu and couldn't be bothered doing anything. We also had a young railwayman (and a prospective Party member) opposing the chief of staff of the opposition in No. 4 Ward, and despite the fact that our candidate is almost unknown he polled almost as many votes as the sitting Labour member — 445. The results here leave the position unchanged, my butty[44] being returned by almost 300 of a majority.

What do you think of P. Hodge's article on Adamson in *The Miner*?[45] He has raised hell against himself this journey. The Sub Executive met before the Election and repudiated his article. Reform Union local committees were active on Adamson's behalf but this action of Hodge has made matters more complicated than ever. Methil Branch moved that a vote of censure be passed but I understand that some in West Fife are out on a campaign, the slogan being "Hodge must go". If that was going to clear some of the mess it would be quite a simple matter but it would mean a big breaking away from the Reform Union — not to the "Old Union" but more non-unionism, and if and when we amalgamate it would be better to have the Reform Union solid than having a few amalgamating and a big percentage non-unionist. The dismissal of Hodge would in my opinion mean more chaos, as many Reform Union members are Anti-Adamson and Pro-Hodge. Methil Branch's decision to move a vote of censure and instruct the Sub-Executive to scrutinize any article before publication during a political or industrial crisis should prevent anything of a like nature again.

What do you think of the Election results?[46] Severe blow for MacDonaldism. Sort of convinces one about the impossibility of ever getting a Labour majority without a suppression of the Capitalist Press, which action would mean end of Parliamentary Democracy.

If you can you might see that the *Monthly* is sent on as I haven't yet received November issue. 7 dozen this month. Hope you have all recovered from the Election.

November 30th, 1924.

Thanks very much for yours of 23rd November. You are correct when you state that we had a good time at Kennedy's meeting. Lost 3 orders of *Labour Monthly* but gained about 20 through it. The purging process goes on. November sales 102.

We are in some mess in Fife at present. The Hodge article and now Kirker's stunt,[47] also the prosecution of a local secretary for dipping into the funds of the Reform Union. You would notice in the letters denouncing H. Pollitt veiled attacks on another individual — J. Bird. In my opinion something is going to come out of that correspondence that will cause a split in the Reform Union ranks. I am not sufficiently informed as to some of the games behind the scenes so have kept out of the debate ? at present. I think H. Pollitt was badly advised to suggest the liquidation policy at present. We will require to have a few groups established before a move can be made with any success. In the meantime I intend raising the matter of an all-in ballot vote of the Fife coalfield on 1 Union for the coalfield with some of the Reform Union's "reforms" as the ballot matter, with the suggestion that if the ballot tells against us that we go back to the Old Association. Also having a short article in *The Miner* to open up discussion. If the Reform Union Executive Board adopt their previous attitude we will have good grounds for giving them a knock. Of course I intend raising the matter at the next District Party Committee meeting and so ensure some organised support in other branches. One letter denouncing Harry Pollitt and the Party requires special mention. I refer to "Some Plain Speaking" signed by Robert Beveridge, Cowdenbeath. By all that one holds sacred Robert Beveridge was and is the Robert Beveridge appointed to the Fife District Party Committee to represent the Cowdenbeath area. How's that?

The Kirker stunt is some business coming immediately back of the Hodge article. As far as I know he is still at large. Pity we couldn't deal with cases such as his without having to rely on the Boss's courts of "justice". I may state I had no suspicions until I was informed about the audit, but I now believe that he has been "at it" since the Union started and has gone undetected until now due to the neglect of the Finance Committee, *who have not* (only disclosed since discovery) *examined the Bank Book this year*. Booze and living above his income are the explanations offered by the Executive. In addition most of the delegates looked at the organisation from the viewpoint of a Mutual Admiration Society. Everyone was bound to be an Anti-Adamsonite and those prominent more so than the lesser fry, and therefore should not be embarrassed in the good work of slaying Adamson with their verbosity.

I have already stated that the sales for November *Labour Monthly* are 102. Page surely wakened the manager up as he sent me 104 instead of my order of 7 dozen. What do you think of the following? In 2½ hours I sold 54 *Labour Monthly*, 7½ dozen *Workers' Weekly*, 1 dozen 10 *Worker*,[48] 5½ dozen pamphlets, and 8 3/- copies of Bogdanoff's *Economic Science,*[49] without moving from the corner where I took my stance. The roads were dry and I laid them on the kerb with the result a few curious people gathered and then the sales commenced. Of course one wouldn't manage it in crowded streets without interference from the police. I also sold 2 dozen Party *Training Manuals* and 2 dozen *Historical Synopsis* the same weekend.[50] Along with Bogdanoff's *Economic Science* we are getting the Party *Manual* used as the text books at the local class of the Scottish Labour College. Most of the *Monthly* readers whom I have asked how they liked it are greatly impressed with the "Notes of the Month". They are becoming Duttites but show no inclination to join the Party. However, all is not exactly lost. We can boast of a bigger sale than any Labour daily, weekly or monthly in this locality. We are now getting sales amongst the Railwaymen and are likely to get a few recruits from them. Methil Branch N.U.R. voted £1 to the Party Election Fund, which action is almost one of revolution when looking at their record during the past few years.

I could have been at the Party Council meeting this weekend but owing to having an abscess on my gums and a dose of cold I declined. Comrade Dick, District Party Committee Secretary, was appointed. It was a good job I declined as my "butty" has been off work all week and will be unable to work for a few days yet due to an attack of the 'flu. I have been at it every day for the past week from 6 a.m. to 10 p.m. and am absolutely fed up with figures, tubs, and weighing machines. I think if I were to snuff it and a post mortem held on me QTS and CWTS would be found deeply imprinted under my skull.

Let Page know if he can "put me up" and also "put up with me" I will accept his offer of a few days in London at New Year.

Enclosed Ku Klux Klan statement on Immigration which might interest you, also statement to Reform Union members on Kirker case. Marx states in his introduction to *Capital* that the "English Established Church will more readily pardon an attack on 38 of its 39 articles than on 1/39th of its income". It has still to be learned if the Reform Union members have objected to Kirker's action and shown their dislike by leaving the Union. So far we in Methil have only lost 8 out of over 500. P.S. I assume you wrote the review of Fimmen's book in the *Monthly*.[51] There is a word that I can't get the hang of — *coquecigrues*.[52]

December 16th, 1924.

Many thanks for your letter of 6th inst., also your telegram. Thanks for explanation of word "coquecigrues". I assumed the phrase meant "till doomsday" but as I couldn't get the word in the dictionary that I possess I wrote you.

Possibly a good thing that the trouble at the *Daily Herald* has died down a bit by giving your groups more time to organise. It would cause some "stink" to have a strike of the employees of "Labour's Own".[53]

I intend leaving Leven on Wednesday, December 31st with the 7.3 p.m., arriving King's Cross at 6.40 a.m., January 1st.

My butty started work last Wednesday and I can assure you I was delighted to see him. 16 hours per day almost out-Dubbs Dubb himself. You bet I was paid for the extra time: time and third for the second shift — Coal Jock's own terms.

Is the *Monthly* out this month as up to the present I haven't received my order? It is to be hoped I receive them this weekend as next week is my dud week, backshift, when very little can be done by way of sales, after which only 3 or 4 days are left before the New Year celebrations commence in real earnest, when it is next to impossible to get anyone to take an interest in anything other than pantos, football matches and shortbread guzzling.

I have sent a rambling letter to *The Miner* dealing with a suggested ballot vote. I think it will cause some discussion and if not I will come out with other suggestions that will compel some of the Reform Union diehards to show their hand. Will explain when I meet you. Methil Branch, Reform Union, had a full dress debate on a resolution for the Union agenda re a ballot, and after 1½ hours' discussion it was agreed to practically unanimously, only 1 objecting to what he considered the "crawling attitude being adopted to get back into the Old Union". Only about 2 dozen out of a membership of slightly over 500 were there but they have some influence with a big proportion of the local membership, although that influence will be severely tested when it comes down to the proposition of "going back". Everyone who spoke realised "that the position of the Reform Union was unsatisfactory, *that we had now reached a point when it was absolutely necessary that a determined attempt by the rank and file should be made to bring about fusion*". It was agreed that the ballot (if agreed upon by the majority of the branches) should be taken before February 28th, 1925. That should provide time to get some propaganda across. I brought the proposition before the District Party Committee and it was agreed to without any discussion, there being only 3 of us present.

J. Bird has resigned his positions on the Reform Union Sub and General Executive. He hasn't attended a District Party Committee meeting since Bob Stewart was here immediately after the General Election and didn't notify us as to his intended resignation from the Union positions. As far as I can gather his action is due to his and Kirker's delegation expenses to the Minority Conference held in London during August. They travelled excursion fare and charged the Union ordinary, another neglect of the Finance Committee by reporting it after the Kirker disclosures. However, I think there are some other explanations, but I can't get the information. It certainly hasn't "boosted" Bird's prestige and will certainly not do the Party any good if Bird is put prominently forward as a Communist. I intend raising the matter at the next District Party Committee meeting (Saturday first) and inviting Bird (if he isn't there) to give an explanation of his action at a special meeting.

I understand from the chap I introduced you to at the Wellesley check box that he had ordered *Oil and Politics* by Page immediately he received the Labour Publishing Company's Autumn publications but up to the present he hasn't received it.[54]

Expect to have a cheery Trades and Labour Party meeting on Thursday night due to the Labour Party Conference decision re Communists,[55] despite the fact that 2 months ago they decided against the Conference decision. It was raised last month by the chairman, an S.D.F.er, but we managed to get him removed from the chair, and a Party sympathiser installed. Since then a Labour Party has been set up in Denbeath with my "butty" as chairman and I expect an attempt by the *Denbeath Branch of the Reform Union* (and the Reform Union is alleged to be an appendage of Moscow) to try and burst the existing Trades and Labour Council. It is part of a move engineered by the

Labour Town Councillors ("who are not desirous of being associated with the Communists as it might spoil their chances with the ratepayers"), of trying to work on the free lance ticket, because we are beginning to dominate the Trades and Labour Council. Will give you result later.

1925

Sunday, January 18th, 1925.

I arrived back home A.1 after a pleasant holiday. Have had an exceptionally busy week which has terminated tonight with some of the vilest, slimiest anti-Communist propaganda from T. Kennedy. He has adopted a new style of attack. Says he is opposed to the Communists and by suggestions and inference opens his attack. Admits without being challenged that he has no evidence. His case is built on the past expressions of the Communist Party *vide Morning Post* and *Daily Record*. Russian gold, secret society, etc.

You will be delighted to know that we have managed to get a group set away in Methil, 6 in number.

I sent on the book I promised you with the Miners' stuff to Page. You ought to have a look at some of the reports of Executive Board meetings and Conferences between the Union officials and employers in Fife and Scotland.

Enclosed is my suggested reply to the letters replying to mine which have appeared in *The Miner*, issue of January 17th. It has to be endorsed by the District Party Committee on Saturday first. If you can find time and have any criticism to level at it you might send them on as I want to give a complete knockout to some of the Diehards of the Reform Union.

P.S. We are now getting it in the neck with short time at the pits. The coaltrimmers at both Methil and Burntisland are working 50% of staff for 2 weeks and 2 weeks on the dole alternately. West and Mid Fife pits are practically idle, although up to the present only 2 days were lost by a few pits in East Fife last week. 1 pit, "Klondyke" (you remember it), has been posted with a notice that it will be shut down after Saturday first, also back shift at Wellsgreen — both Fife Coal Company health resorts. Over 150 men in Klondyke and 60 in Wellsgreen. Looks very healthy.

Am sending on *The Miner* of 17th January, also enclosed copy of Scottish Miners' Rules[56] for Page to add to his collection. Those rules are scarce, only 2 being issued to each branch in Fife.

[No date.][57]

Dear Comrade,

Comrade McArthur asks "Why a Ballot"? The reasons are obvious to those who desire unity.

1st. To ascertain what the mineworkers of the three counties think about those points which are the bone of contention between the two organisations.

2nd. To determine by result of ballot whether or not the Reform Union has a majority of the mineworkers sympathetic to their policy and programme. Wise leaders at all times desire to know the strength or weakness of their forces.

If the majority are in favour the obvious course is *to get into the union with national connections (Old Union) as an organised body where those points coula be carried into effect.* If on the other hand the result of the ballot is against, then as class-conscious workers *we must get into the Old Union as an organised body for the purpose of actively propagating our policy until it is realised.* Although the *Reform Union is liquidated* it does not mean that the *policy* of the Reform Union is liquidated, providing that those responsible for carrying out that policy are determined *fighters.* The policy practised by the Adamsonian school is still in operation and will have to be fought. At present it is going *unchallenged,* and is assisting to *form wages and conditions* of Reform Union members who have no voice in preventing it, however much they *detest* it.

Comrade McArthur does not openly oppose the ballot (which if taken *will not* be unofficial, as by the time this letter appears [it] will be decided upon by the Reform Union branches) but suggests as a reason for it not being taken the refusal of the Old Union officials to assist the Reform Union with the suggested ballot of May of last year. He along with other Reform Union speakers and writers (see Reform Union pamphlet *The Fife Miners' Union Split*)[58] denounced that attitude as an example of the Old Union's desire to keep the breach open. Now it appears the Reform Union should show its desire for unity *by following the example of the Old Union.* He also states that the Old Union officials local and central are not disposed to co-operate with those of the Reform Union. If the non-co-operation of officials means that a ballot cannot be taken because of the fact of them belonging to different organisations the only logical conclusion is to *liquidate one* and that one, the Reform Union, and so demonstrate by deeds and not words our desire for unity. If the Reform Union cannot take a ballot at the pits it is a useless machine.

Possibly Comrade McArthur might remark that I have stated that we should be in one Union, fighting the anti-working class policy as expressed by Adamson, which does not bespeak unity, but he will agree that *no* mass organisation has unanimity of opinion, and also after the experiences of the past two years that the most effective fight can be made *inside* instead of outside mass organisations. He also draws attention to the fact that the spirit of non-co-operation is developing amongst the Reform Union officials, and also "that policy (liquidation of Reform Union) is absolutely unthinkable to most of our active spirits and would mean the domination of reactionary officialdom in Fife for a long time to come". Does the non-co-operative spirit exist amongst the rank and file? I think not. One can see the spirit of *co-operation* demonstrated into *action* at the pits. Take the Valleyfield case reported in *The Miner,* issue of January 3rd.[59] Those actions in themselves should give a *lead* to "most of our active spirits" *who* are animated with the desire for working-class progress and a quick finish would be put to reactionary officialdom.

Comrade McArthur takes up a rather curious position for an advocate of rank and file control. He states after quoting A. J. Cook[60] re 100% organisation: "if they (Miners' Federation of Great Britain Executive) are sincere in their desire for a 100% organisation then *they* ought to tackle the dispute here right away. The path is now clear for them in view of the failure of the Scottish Executive and *we have nothing to fear from an examination of our case*".

If "we have nothing to fear from an examination of our case" by the M.F.G.B. Executive then as workers who have beliefs in rank and file control, why *not submit our case* (which we claim is the Fife, Kinross and Clackmannan mineworkers' case) *to the rank and file for examination* and submit it by ballot?

Comrade Kitchener's[61] letter only proves some of the statements made by Comrade McArthur re the spirit of non-co-operation developing amongst the Reform Union officials. For instance, "We in Dysart did dare to approach the officials of the Old Union for a much less thing than this . . . and now, comrade, you would come forward with a suggestion that we ought to do our best for men who declared they were going to have nothing to do with us." I expect Comrade Kitchener approached the Old Union to assist in something affecting the workers which the Reform Union were unable to perform successfully by themselves, or *why ask for assistance*? His action in doing so demonstrates that he realises that so long as two organisations operate it is next to impossible to achieve any important working class success without both participating. But he shows a lack of perception when he suggests that nothing should be done towards assisting those who *at present* declare they will have nothing to do with us.

Do not low tonnage rates, low brushing rates, low shift rates and bad working conditions imposed on Old Union members react on Reform Union members? I think they do, and if only from the viewpoint of "himself" Comrade Kitchener will be compelled "to do his best for those men". Bread and butter interests being identical, why not one Union?

I haven't suggested "going down on our knees"; instead I advocate *getting up, standing on our feet and opening our eyes*. At present the Reform Union *is "on its knees"*, worshipping at the shrine of a Constitution to the exclusion of everything. They are like the Lamas of Tibet, praying and meditating on seclusion. If the Reform Union Constitution is a desirable thing to attain (I admit it is) let us spread it through the national machinery and not confine it to a section of Fife. Take the ballot vote and, realising our strength and weakness, let us get into the Miners' Federation of Great Britain and there carry out our policy.

Tuesday, January 27th, 1925.

Many thanks for yours of 23rd. Like yourself I am writing this letter at intervals (i.e., when I can find time) as my days (at present) would require to be of 48 hours duration and that without sleeping time, to try and give justice to the innumerable jobs I have managed to collect. What do you think of the following, more, what other idiot than your humble would have (in Coal Jock's parlance) "the bloody cheek" to try? (1) Group leader and Representative on District Party Committee; (2) Group Trainer (oh, hell); (3) Chief literature distributor (for January, 30 dozen *Workers' Weekly*, 10½ dozen *Worker*, 104 *Labour Monthly*, 4 dozen pamphlets *Towards Trade Union Unity*, 1 dozen *Slave Plan* (almost 25 dozen since General Election), 3 dozen *Young Worker*, and 100 *Mineworker*;[62] (4) Delegate for Union Branch to local Trades and Labour Council; (5) Delegate for Trades and Labour Council to Divisional Executive; (6) Collector of subscriptions for Communist Book Club; (7) Doormat for local industrial disputes; (8) Checkweighman in spare time. Since formation of group I have lost 1 job — Class War Prisoners' Aid, a new comrade taking over.[63] I am writing in this fashion not from a boasting point but for the purpose of demonstrating (a) the position (or should I rather say positions) some of us have to occupy in these districts; (b) the absolute need for more attention being paid by Headquarters to the provinces — speakers, etc., for the purpose of rousing some enthusiasm and possibly getting new members who would naturally have to take on some work. At present I am on the Rules Committee appointed by the Trades and Labour Council to draft new rules. Also in the storm centre of the Union dispute. How in hell's name can any one man do all of those jobs right?

Regarding my letter in answer to the 2 in January 17th issue of *The Miner*, it isn't exactly a case of the conditions as exhibited by the Reform Union diehards changing, but a case of the chief workers in Methil Branch, Reform Union, practically agreeing that it is the only course, also the District Party Committee members' desire that the controversy should be based on the lines suggested. In addition Methil Branch, Reform Union, have agreed to issuing a letter in *The Miner* inviting those of both Unions who desire Unity to write me so that a Conference can be arranged at an early date.

Since sending my letter to P. Hodge I have had a communication from him suggesting I should withdraw the letter as the Scottish Executive have again taken the matter up and in his opinion the letter would complicate matters by causing the Old Union crowd to hold back with the intentions of awaiting what they would and certainly will consider that a split had occurred in the Reform Union. I agreed to the delay of publication for a fortnight and if no move was made by the Scottish during that time the letter should be published. (Wednesday 28th January): After considering the matter more fully I have come to the conclusion that the invitation from the Branch should be published this week (February 1st) and should no success attend it (as I anticipate) by intimations from the Old Union then the letter should be published. In addition there might be a move made by the Scottish but I do not expect very much of a result if they do. You can judge by these brief explanations how hellish complicated and difficult a proposition it is. On the one side "honourable settlement only", while the fight gets closer, and the other "absolute surrender" — both parties agreeing verbally that Unity is desirous and absolutely necessary. McArthur, who asks "Why a Ballot?", is an ex-member of the Party who left the East Fife local because of differences re the Union dispute. He stated that the Reform Union was of more consequence to him than the Communist Party. He is also a product of the Scottish Labour College. Kitchener is an Austrian with an imperfect grasp of English. One of Guy Aldred's bunch.[64]

Let Comrade Budden know that I think I will manage to get along with the programme she gave me. We are getting a few copies typed for nix but at an office in Dunfermline, 28 miles away. Some promise of a daily sheet in Methil at present? We have the raw material to work on but a lack of technical advisers and due to that, lack of apparatus. However, that deficiency is on the road to be made good as one or two young intelligent chaps whom I have been "nursing" for a few months are on the verge of "coming in". I "addressed" a meeting of railwaymen on Sunday past and after raving for 1¼ hours had a rousing reception but no offers for Party membership. Had its recompense — 1 dozen 3 *Workers' Weekly* sold and 1 dozen *Slave Plan*, 3 copies *Path to Power*.[65] Also had digs at Kennedy's remarks re Party, Dawes Plan, and Minority Movement, which was very well received by audience of between 20 and 30. According to expressions at meeting the Reserve Force stunt is to be scotched by local men, although it will require more meetings of a like nature before we can report success.[66] The bonus offered is certainly a spicy bait to those who are always on hard tack. Has the Party Headquarters considered the advisability of issuing a pamphlet to the Railwaymen on this subject?

My holiday was the kind I needed as, since coming back, I have been in the pink and am tucking more grub under my skin than I was previously doing. In addition it was profitable from the point of view of coming into contact with comrades, which certainly dispels the impression sometimes forced on one in this kind of a place — that the Party only exists in one's own imagination.

Enclosed are cuttings re Trotsky,[67] Kennedy's Methil meeting (which I was unable to attend, being on backshift) and Sir Adam Nimmo's recent speech.[68] The impression I got from Reade re his position was to the effect that Trotsky's Preface was his defence, which justified him in Reade's eyes.[69] I at that time pointed out that although not having read the Preface, still Trotsky's previous erratic actions were sufficient in themselves to condemn him, although at that time I hadn't exactly made up my mind as to how I stood owing to the fact that I had read very little of the discussion. Since then I have definitely taken my position against Trotsky. The movement is greater than any individual, immaterial who he is or what he has been, and the fact that Trotsky's attitude is a defiant and deliberate act of indiscipline puts him "out of court". It is certainly good for the Party, from the point of view of another test, that there are Reades who try to kick up a noise, and by doing so focus party members' attention on those things, and afterwards those who remain are certainly to be reckoned as of some use. A somewhat similar but more important and far reaching test than that of Newbold's resignation. It is part of the process (in the words of a circular issued by the Party on Leninism) "of hammering out a party which must be of steel, and all of one piece, incapable

201

of splitting into sections and groups in the current of the *intellectual* and petit bourgeois stream". I think you could manage a good article from the *Glasgow Herald* leader re Trotsky.

Also enclosed demands of Trawler Coalies in Methil in strike of last year.[70] I promised to send them to you. I was chairman of strike committee and "drew up" their demands. None of them were granted due to Houghton, an organiser of Transport and General Workers, ratting.[71] Not such a "comprehensive" document of demands as that of National Union of Railwaymen.

Friday, 30th January: Have just seen a report in the Press "that all affiliated organisations to Scottish Miners' Federation[72] must enforce subscriptions of 1/- per week on or before February 1st (tonight is subscription collection) or be expelled" — which means no contact with Miners' Federation of Great Britain, T.U.C., and Labour Party. As the "Old" Union is at present affiliated (although a few thousand £s in debt to Scottish) they are only collecting 6d. per week subscriptions (because Adamson will not allow *his* connections to be broken). Should they (as I expect) try to raise the subscriptions, the position in Fife will be further complicated, as by increasing subscriptions at present the result will be a good number of members leaving the "Old" Union, some joining the Reform Union (who charge only 6d. per week); but I expect the major portion will become non-unionist. Of course the Reform Union will try to make capital out of it, which of course will mean denouncing 1/- per week subscriptions and comparing (with a localised argument) the Reform Union position of 6d. per week. As the Reform Union has no affiliation fees to pay, the "direct" financial benefit bait will have some effect but in my opinion not sufficient to ensure victory for the Reform Union by having a majority. On the other hand, should the Old Union not try to put the decision of the Scottish into effect and suffer expulsion it will mean intensifying the struggle in Fife because Adamson and Company would be compelled to come out and fight, which would certainly (in my opinion) have the effect of bringing the dispute to a quicker finish (but not before June). However, if the latter position results the Miners' Federation of Great Britain would be compelled to take action, because of the importance of the Fife coalfield.

I understand from our Branch delegate that the suggested Ballot was overwhelmingly defeated at the Reform Union Executive meeting on Wednesday, on the grounds of "Impossible to take at Pits" (Christ, what a heap), "No more crawling" (and they haven't even learnt to toddle yet). I feel like smashing (or at any rate trying) Methil Branch, Reform Union, and trying to get them over to the Old Union, although at the same time I realise the almost impossible task it would now be, should subscriptions be raised to 1/- per week. However, if it has to come to that I won't be shy in having a go at it and besides I don't think the position would be any worse.

You might let Page know I am on the track of more stuff re Fife and Scottish Miners. Will send on when I get a batch. Haven't got February issue of *Labour Monthly* yet. Am trying 9 dozen this time. Have mailed you this week's *Miner*.

I am sorry I have overlooked a few important points in your letter re the Factory Groups and given so much prominence to the Union Dispute, but I think you will understand how I feel about this matter. Glad to know you are getting along so well with the Factory Groups. The pioneer work is usually hard, with very little signs of success for the amount of energy expended but the fact that 8 have shown themselves at least ready to come together and discuss a policy is certainly very gratifying. All of them *will not* be duds, and that being so it means that where only 1 previously existed there are now at least 4 or 5 "live wires".

I act as a sort of 1 man Pit Group in so far as sticking up Posters, chalking slogans, distributing handbills, and selling literature is concerned. Dished out of weighbox the Party pamphlets for Lenin week. At the present time I have the weighbox decorated with Lenin stick-a-backs, the front page of the January issue of *The Young Worker*, with Lenin's portrait and cuttings relating to mining conditions and policy from the *Worker's Weekly*, *Worker*, and *Mineworker*. Should one of the young chaps I have referred to join up we can then get a group of 3 started — 2 on pithead and 1 underground and that amongst over 2,100 men, women and boys. But we will not separate from the existing group for some time as to do so at present would in all probability mean its demise, and concentration on 1 Pit instead of as at present "contact" with other 2 and also the Railway Depot.

Re the notes I sent you and to which you refer, the position of the coal trade has slightly changed, at least so far as East Fife is concerned. Methil coaltrimmers only put 25% of their number on the "dole" for fortnight stretches and since doing so those who are left have been employed "steady", with the result that only a few of the pits (in East Fife) have lost more than 1 or 2 days per week. "Klondyke" is closed down and Wellsgreen backshift has been elevated to those dizzy heights of "State beneficiaries". A peculiar situation is now on in Fife, so far as demand for certain qualities of coal is concerned. At present there is a bigger demand for splint coal (the best for domestic purposes and incidentally costliest) than others, with the result that "sections" working those seams are in some pits working almost "full time" while others working in other seams are only getting 2 days per week. As nearly all of those orders are "land sale" it doesn't require a Sherlock Holmes to arrive at the conclusion that it isn't the workers who are buying, but some others who are in all possibility "laying up" stocks against something that is coming along, i.e., strike or lock-out. Wouldn't you suggest the latter after "sizing up" (1) The publicity campaign of the owners for the 8 hours day and their tactics in closing various groups of collieries and then reopening them when they considered that the Coal Jocks in that part were sufficiently demoralised to accept almost any terms, but were now rallying to A. J. Cook's appeal to fight against any increase of hours; (2) That being class-conscious members of the Boss class they have given the tip to the others as to their intentions in the near future, owing to some of their plans (guerrilla warfare) miscarrying, and that it will be necessary for a general attack, owing in some measure to their inability (at present at least) to nobble the M.F.G.B. with tales about "the industry". You will be almost bored to death by the time you have read this so I will close. P.S. I have almost forgotten to mention a very important matter re the Methil coaltrimmers. They have the job on the co-operative contract basis and when agreeing to put 25% of their number on the "dole" they also agreed that the proceeds of the "pool" and the "dole" (and in the event of those who were suspended for a fortnight getting employment at some other job) and those wages would be "pooled" and equally divided. Not at all a bad idea if the *Un*employment Exchange Authorities do not try and scotch it.

Demands of Trawler Section (Methil Docks)

For Crane Work only: from 8 a.m. to 5 p.m., Monday to Friday, both days inclusive, also Saturday 8 a.m. to 12 noon, 2/- per ton. From 5 p.m. to 8 a.m., 2/6d. per ton. From 12 noon Saturday to 1 p.m. only, 2/6d. per ton and 5/- per hour or part of one hour per man.

We desire to avoid basket work as far as possible, but when cranes are required for discharging other cargoes we are prepared to work baskets at the following rates: From 8 a.m. to 5 p.m., 2/9d. per ton; from 5 p.m. to 8 a.m., 3/3d. per ton; from 12 noon Saturday to 1 p.m. only, 3/9d. per ton and 5/- per hour or part of one hour per man; from Saturday midnight to 8 a.m. Monday and holidays, 4/9d. per ton.

Before any additional workers are engaged they must produce their Union card and satisfy the Works Committee appointed by the men. Before any man can be discharged for any alleged misdemeanour, his case must be thoroughly investigated by the Works Committee. The brokers must consult with the Works Committee on any point regarding the bunkering of trawlers affecting the men employed.

March 25th, 1925.

Am commencing this letter today on receipt of yours of 18th-24th, for which many thanks. The Wellesley is "idle" today as are a few other pits. We are now getting the benefits of the Dawes Plan in Fife, although we in the eastern portion of the coalfield have not got it in the neck to the same extent as those in West Fife. But that, as you know, does not mean that we are having an exceptionally fat time. 4 pits within a 3 mile radius of Methil have been closed down during the past 9 months in addition to a back shift at another. Roughly 1,400 men involved. 2 are closed down for good and the other 2, one of which is almost 50 years old, are being reconstructed — new roads, cross cuts (mines driven at level through the strata from one seam to another) to replace existing braes and dooks for haulage purposes. (Reported in last week's *Workers' Weekly*.) In fact, modernising those 2 pits which as you know does not by any means augur "prosperity" for the mineworker, especially after a prolonged period of semi-starvation as the slowing down has meant for those involved. In addition, the short time prevailing at the other collieries has had the effect on those employed of submitting to "partial" reductions without any real attempt at opposing the management, with the result that the managers have in a good number of cases put their heels on the neck of Coal Jock.

One would think that the oft expressed phrase "the more oppression will breed more resistance" should now show itself by a determined if not thoroughly organised resistance in Fife, but at present it is the reverse. To give you an illustration which only occurred here last Sunday. For some considerable time the Wellesley management have complained that the amount of coal weighed at the pithead weighbox has not coincided with that weighed by the pit dispatcher (Coal in waggons); and they accordingly demanded that a tare of the hutches be taken. A tare is the average weight of the empty hutches ascertained by taking the average weight of a number of tubs — usually over 100 at the Wellesley. The tare was taken a week past Saturday and resulted in an increased tare of ¾ cwts. As I wasn't informed of the tare and wasn't present I refused to accept it, as although I knew that an increase was inevitable due to the gradual supersession of steel hutches over wooden I was not going to be ignored in such a manner by the management. It also meant a reduction per shift of from 2/- to 4/-. My mate was there at the tare but on my refusal to accept he also would not agree to accept. A special meeting of the Checkweighman Committee was called on Sunday. I suggested a morning meeting at the pit head on Monday morning and volunteered to picket the pit at 4 a.m., but was defeated. It was agreed to send a deputation to the manager right away, and along with 2 others I met him. He at first refused to meet us because of my presence but after I closed the office door he lost some of his bluster. He accused me of going to "bayonet him", Russianise the Pit, etc. It was then agreed that another tare would be taken on Tuesday night, when a deadlock occurred. We stood for a flat tare, the manager for two separate tares. The flat tare meant 6½ cwts, the 2 separate tares 5¾ cwts wooden and 7¼ cwts steel. As the ratio of steel tubs to wooden at present is 2 to 1 we were making a good thing for the men, as although we were giving away ¾ cwts on the wooden we were actually getting 1½ cwts with the steel, an actual gain of ¾ cwts on 1/3 of the tubs weighed; and as the steel is increasing and wooden diminishing, a growing gain. The management, manager and agent threatened to allow the pit to stand idle if we didn't accept their offer. My mate and I were aware that this was one piece of bluff, and accordingly were going to get off the pit head and then address a meeting of the men on Wednesday morning, when the Committeemen who were present suggested that we should accept the manager's offer "under protest" and call a meeting for Sunday and then get the men's opinion.

The meeting was held and only between 30 and 40 attended out of over 800 affected and by Christ their decision was to "leave the checkweighmen with full powers" as it was considered that a pit head meeting would not be successful. I pointed out to them that all we could do was to interview the manager and if he refused to accede to the flat tare it would mean we would have to call a pit head meeting, and in addition were we to operate the two tares and if not were they prepared to stop work and try by that means to make the manager sit up? No reply was given. They applauded *me* when the chairman reported that the manager stated that he would not receive me on a deputation, but when I told them it wasn't for them to applaud but to hide their faces for shame that they allowed such a state of affairs to exist they sobered up. They gave one the impression that they were frightened to speak in case anything said was reported to the manager.

However, on Monday we were received by the manager and agent, who both agreed to our demand, at least to give it a trial for a week. They received us cordially; good heavens, a stranger looking on would have thought we were all bed mates — "Davie this" and "Davie that". Makes one think. My opinion was that they had not got a report of Sunday's meeting and were a bit off as to what would happen were they to refuse our demands. In addition they received a resolution passed by the meeting that I was to be recognised as the men's representative by the management.

But at present I can assure you, George, I don't place much reliance on the men so far as being prepared for action. They are frightened at the unprecedented unemployed. The lesser officials have been sticking their chests out and if a man shows any spirit he is told "if you are not prepared to do it for what is offered there are plenty who are", with the result that very few cases are reported and no stand is made. But the short time should and will make them realise their position more.

We have appointed a comrade worker correspondent to the *Weekly*. He receives reports written and verbal from us so should be supplying some matter. In fact he was rather annoyed last weekend because none of his stuff was appearing.

Had a postcard from Page. Let him know I am now at or almost at the end of my local resources re minutes, etc., of Old Union. I have approached some of the local men who were delegates before, during and since the war but have drawn blank, they having burnt everything.

I am sorry I didn't address my last letter to your parents' address but I thought you would possibly be back with Page as I had allowed 3 weeks to elapse before I answered your letter. Hope you get along all right with your new job but as you remark it means to a great extent losing personal contact with the workers and their everyday troubles; but the contact you will now have, reports as to activities not in a local aspect but national and international, should to a certain extent compensate you for the change. It is necessary someone should be there and why not you?[73]

A. J. Cook must have been carried away and I grant he has some excuse by the meetings he held if the two in West Fife were like the one in Methil. He had an audience of over 700, the majority of whom were Reform Union members, and his advocacy of Reform Union members getting into the M.F.G.B. was applauded but he has to realise he was talking to men who have during the past 6 months had it drummed into them the need for unity even if, from the Reform Union standpoint, unconditionally. That has been the Methil Branch, Reform Union, standpoint but it has been entirely different in some of the neighbouring branches whose officials are of the diehard pattern. In fact some of them (and ex-Party members at that) have stated that Cook had no business to mention the dispute from the College platform[74] and that he only did so on pressure from me and other members of the Party — *another Communist plot*. This viewpoint was stated at the East Fife Area Committee of the Reform Union and they have minuted "that the pronouncements made by A. J. Cook was likely to prejudice the Reform Union position but it was decided to employ energetic measures to combat the *reaction* which might ensue from his remarks". And they — some of 'em — call themselves revolutionary, live, intelligent, studious workers. Well, well. At our local group meeting it was decided that the matter of "back to the M.F.G.B." should be discussed and a circular drawn up by the Fife District Party Committee advising Reform Union members and non-unionists to get into the M.F.G.B. The matter was discussed last Saturday and a resolution was agreed on to be submitted to Reform Union branches on Sunday where we had Party members. The resolution was "that a ballot vote of the Reform Union membership be taken before the 19th of April on the following question: Are you in favour of rejoining the M.F.G.B. if admitted as a full member?". An aggregate meeting of Party members in Fife [is] to take place at Bowhill on Sunday. As the Party is in a precarious position in Fife it was decided to call the aggregate meeting so that we could get the feeling of some of the recently joined members who are or were recently Reform Union diehards. We do not want to unnecessarily jeopardize the party's chances in Fife with precipitate action, although the members of the District Party Committee with one exception were prepared to force the issue on Reform Union liquidation. Methil Branch, Reform Union, passed the resolution unanimously and in the discussion which ensued it was agreed that if the Executive board at its meeting today voted against the resolution no contributions would be collected for the Reform Union in Methil on Friday and that a special meeting be called to wind up the branch. I expect we will ultimately have to adopt that course but it would be infinitely better if we could get some influence over and get some sort of organised body to go over.

If P. Hodge made an admission to Cook that he was agreed to go back, his press reports and his phone conversation to me on the day following Cook's meetings do not convince me of such a desire on his part. He accused me of "being on the same platform as Adamson", "only being able to fight when the band is playing", "only fight when I am getting scalps", "me and my kind not worth fighting for", etc., etc., and his position as expressed by a press report — "that unity could be achieved by the Old Union members joining the Reform Union" — is of a very dubious quality of bluff, if he is prepared to rejoin the Old Union. Cook made a great impression and will certainly get bumper meetings should he come back.

We advertised the *Sunday Worker*, of which we could have disposed of dozens if we had had them available.[75] Like you I wasn't greatly impressed with the 1st issue but as "hope springeth eternal from the human breast" expect it to get better. We haven't received last Sunday's issue yet due I suspect to sabotage by some of the locals, possibly directed from the other Sunday papers. The difficulty here is that we are not on the main line, all English

Sunday editions being dumped at Kirkcaldy for the East Coast and only 2 newsagents in Methil sell Sunday papers. We managed to get a considerable number of orders (myself over 50) to those newsagents, but the difficulty of getting them to Methil seemed to be the only excuse from the newsagents. That being their particular business I haven't interfered.

No, I haven't read Dutt's article in the *International*.[76] In fact I only get it occasionally, not having time to read it and also not having at a given time the necessary cash to buy very much of that which I do not require or cannot consume immediately. But I get from your expressions on it what is and has been the fault of a great number of Socialist and Communist speakers and writers — a well written or spoken, closely knitted speech or article dealing with the general development of Capitalism, its general trend and ultimate development and an ideal form of society to take its place, with a general statement on the need for organising to meet that situation. It is necessary that a certain amount of that kind of propaganda should still be carried on to give a sort of wide vision for those who are compelled to do the "local" fighting but it can be carried too far and tends to develop that kind of "revolutionary" who can talk big and denounce "reformist" tendencies in other countries and neglect immediate "home" issues. Talking to British workers about the duplicity of the Social Democrats in Germany does not cut much ice as the insular British mind conceives that the German brand of Social Democracy is like everything else of German origin — different from that of the British. We have got to get down to a criticism and attack on the British brand with only an occasional reference to the Continental brand, and push our alternative for all we can.

We are getting along fairly well in Methil — no increase in membership over last month but a more steady and increased regular sale for literature (130 *Labour Monthly*). Comrade O'Neil has been elected Chairman of the local Trades and Labour Council and Comrade Duncan Secretary.[77] I am a delegate to the Divisional Labour Party Executive.

A rather unique position has just been exposed here. The local tramway workers have been paying members of the Transport and General Workers but have not held a branch meeting for over 2 years; but due to the victimisation of the branch secretary (a report should now be in the *Workers' Weekly* editor's hands) a meeting was held on Sunday 15th March and another Sunday past, to both of which meetings I was invited and attended. 10.30 p.m. to almost 2 a.m. isn't exactly an ideal time to hold a branch meeting but it is the only time they can arrange to get a decent turn-out. The Secretary has been reinstated but they have hell of conditions: 1/- per hour for drivers, with 60 hours and over per week. They have decided to affiliate to the local Trades and Labour Council and by their present expressions will certainly not add much in the way of revolutionary enthusiasm but we (the Party) are getting the grip as we are now looked on by them to be their advisers, although it isn't all acted on. We managed to dispose of 2 dozen *Workers' Weekly* at both meetings in addition to a number of Party pamphlets. But if it is at all possible for the 2 delegates appointed to attend the Trades and Labour Council we are assured of 2 more votes for the Communist Party policy as both delegates are sympathetic or at least have professed themselves to be. Will now close, hoping you have completely recovered from your recent 'flu attack.

P.S. Have just received a report from our Branch Delegate re the Reform Union Board meeting of today. The resolution I have previously mentioned was under discussion for over 3 hours and no vote was taken but it was decided to put it to the branches via the Executive minutes, instead of arranging special meetings — which means that it will be impossible to take the ballot on the suggested date. It was also decided that meetings be addressed by Hodge and other members of the Sub Executive in the "affected areas", viz., the branches where the resolution had been sent from. We are to have P. Hodge and James Stewart (who was in Russia with me in 1921)[78] at Methil on Sunday week. Will see to it that this meeting will be advertised widely enough to ensure a big turn-out to view the "gloves off". It appears that I am to replace Adamson as the central figure for Reform Union shafts. I am confident that I can manage to face the "storm" at Methil and come out on top. To demonstrate the Reform Union's desire for unity and their foresight as to its immediate need, they had under discussion today the appointment of an assistant secretary (full-time). 13 applications were in and are to be submitted to the branches to be voted down to a short leet of 6 who will then be submitted to the members to vote on by ballot.

P.P.S. I almost forgot to refer to the circular issued by the Party Headquarters re the Fife Dispute. They advocate the Unity Conference method but do not provide or suggest an alternative when one of the parties in the dispute refuses to meet the other, as is the case with the Old Union bunch. The rumoured conference under the auspices of the Scottish has not happened and the Reform Union has not as yet received any communication, and they today at the Executive meeting have decided that the only conference they will attend will have to be suggested by the other side. I am now more than ever convinced that only by liquidation of the Reform Union (and that means a decidedly unpopular attitude) will this be healed. However, I do not intend making any move until the aggregate meeting on Sunday which will be a rather stormy one but will have to be faced, not on any sentimental or sloshy grounds but on the facts of the position. It is a case of surrendering the viewpoint of working class unity for a doubtful Party membership or facing the real situation and losing a few members whose entry into the Party wasn't exactly to work for the Party. Comrade Joss is to be there so that the meeting will have advice from one who isn't blinded with partisanship, in this case Hodge v. Adamson. Excuse the length of this epistle.

March 27th, 1925.

You will see by this issue of *The Miner* what the Party is up against in the "leading lights" of the Reform Union. Thomas Smith, the author of the front page article, is President of the Reform Union and became a member of the Party when Comrade Joss formed the group at Cowdenbeath. "Fifer" is P.

Hodge but I don't know who "Philemon" is but suspect it is Hodge also. "Communism is impracticable", "is a long way off", according to some of those gentry but it seems the Party that stands for it is a very useful one to try and scare the Fife miners with. Adamson and Company used it and we now get our "progressive" crowd Hodge and Company doing the same. I intend having a wallop at the whole crowd and if it is refused publication will get the Branch to meet the expense of printing a circular dealing with the situation.

April 5th, 1925.

Am writing this note in haste. Many thanks for *Communist International* but I am not exactly in circumstances where I cannot manage to spring a tanner, but I assure you I appreciate the spirit in which the *Communist International* was sent. Up to the present I haven't managed to get time to have a look at it. Sold 24 dozen *Workers' Weekly*, and 3 dozen *Worker* this weekend, breaking new ground in 2 places, viz., Wellesley Pit 5 dozen 4, and Leven (door to door), where another Comrade and myself sold 8 dozen under 1½ hours. We doubled our order last week [to] 40 dozen and are going to tackle 50 dozen next week. Prospects are good. We are now 10 but no prospects at present of formation of pit groups. Perhaps sale at pit which I intend to carry on weekly will give the necessary jab.

Enclosed find cutting from *Edinburgh Evening News*,[79] Reform Union subscription card and last year's stamps for Page, also a short paragraph for *Weekly* dealing with recent tare at Wellesley. Am addressing this note to Labour Research Department, assuming you have taken up your new duties. Will write you later regarding aggregate meeting of last Sunday and P. Hodge's meeting today. A Conference under Scottish auspices of the 2 Union Executive Boards is to be held at Dunfermline on Saturday 1st.

April 24th, 1925.

A hurried note with *The Miner*. You will notice that P. Hodge has inserted the Political Bureau decision in this issue instead of a fortnight ago when it would have appeared *prior to* instead of after *Unity ?* Conference. I sent in a letter a fortnight ago dealing with the Trade Union Delegation Report on Russia[80] and it also is kept out of this issue. However, Hodge can "carry on" with the crowd he has at his back. He won't get far. I wrote Page re the meeting held in Methil last Sunday when we formed a Joint Committee. Enclosed find newspaper cutting dealing with same. I notice you have "dressed up" the skit I sent on. Anything I send in future you might also do it up as the published one is certainly more intelligible than the "raw material".

How are you getting along in your new billet?

As you will see by *The Miner* we have Nat Watkins in Fife for a fortnight commencing Sunday, April 26th. We are getting fairly steady work here at present, 4 and 5 days per week.

We are getting Methil fairly well organised with the *Weekly*. 2 of us manage to dispose of 27½ dozen. I have managed to get a chap in Leven to undertake 5 dozen weekly, another in Methil has agreed to distribute 2 dozen after we have organised the district. But only 4 out of the 10 members of the group are active in the distribution. Got a fairly decent sale at the Wellesley Colliery. 7 dozen last week and 4½ dozen this week due to my being on fore shift. Conditions at the collieries are against us, especially the Wellesley as it is a double shifted pit where the men on each shift are partners and the back shift going on (when I sell the papers) usually have no money as their fore shift partners are on the pit head with the pay line and cash and after getting their share go down the pit. The fore shift is usually dirty (as barely 50% use the baths) and are anxious to get a bus or car home. No signs as yet of establishing pit groups but the sale of the paper is causing talk and it isn't confined to 1 village as the men at the Wellesley are drawn from over a dozen places.

May 3rd, 1925.

Enclosed find a report which you might condense and if at all possible get into this week's *Weekly*. I think the report is self-explanatory without my stating much more here other than I called and addressed the meetings referred to along with Nat Watkins at the meeting between 1 and 2 o'clock on Thursday. We had a May Day Demonstration here today and I again raised the question of the Wellesley reductions and appealed for volunteers for a picket for tomorrow morning to stop the day shift for a meeting. I expect we will have some trouble but I intend holding meetings morning and afternoon every day this week until we get the men on the move. I had a sale of 10 dozen 8 *Weekly* at the Wellesley on Friday, so if a report, however small, of the Wellesley dispute appears we should knock Friday's sale into a cocked hat. Nat Watkins will give a report to Headquarters when he gets back.

What do you think of this sale for one: 30 dozen 7 *Workers' Weekly*, 3 dozen *Worker*, and 6½ dozen *Sunday Worker*? Mine for this weekend and no *Workers' Weekly* at the Demonstration (which by the way was fairly successful, although no recruits came in), in addition to a few pamphlets.

I acted as arbiter in the dispute I referred to before and gave my decision as follows. Owing to the Dockgatemen, 15 in number, being in 2 organisations — Transport and General Workers and National Union of Railwaymen — I decided that a meeting of them should be called and a vote taken as to which of the 2 organisations they desired to belong to. The decision of the majority to be binding on the minority and that the joint Committee set up by both organisations see to it that that decision be enforced.

Will have to close as it is now past 11 and I have to be at the pit gates at 4 o'clock. Hope to be able to report successful attempt to get the Wellesley men to move.

May 8th, 1925.

A short note with *The Miner*. Notice paragraph re Wellesley. Sorry I did not exceed last week's sales at pit due to my being on fore shift and therefore had an hour less to sell the paper. As the night shift men come at 12 for their pay and are not in their working clothes I get away a good number amongst them on my back shift week. However, I did fairly well — between 7 and 8 dozen.

Re the dispute: it is going to be (by present indications) a fiasco as the following points can bear out. I have held 8 meetings in all, 6 at the pit, 1 at Denbeath, and 1 in Methil but there is no response. A week past Wednesday a deputation of 6 was appointed to interview the manager. I was on the deputation and after waiting almost ½ an hour for the manager "coming up" the pit he refused to meet the deputation because I was on it. We met him at his office door and after stating his reasons (as above) for not receiving the deputation he rushed into the office. I followed him but he went into the agent's room and shut the door. After knocking twice and receiving no reply I opened the door and then "the lid of hell was removed". Both agent and manager rushed at me with their arms swinging — the agent partially pushed and punched a member of the deputation in the chest, sending him reeling. He rushed at the agent and threatened to clout him one but as it would have meant the man (who by the way has this week taken 1 dozen *Weekly* to dispose of) being rushed and victimised I got between them. The result was I had both manager and agent buzzing round me telling me I was a Communist agitator, etc. They refused to discuss anything and we left. Later in the afternoon the agent came to me and told me "that he hoped I didn't think he was uncivil (Oh, Christ), but I didn't approach him in the proper manner by trying to force myself into his office". I told him that I wasn't going to stand on ceremony with him or any colliery official when men on a deputation were standing in the cold with damp clothes on. He agreed that such a position wasn't "fair" and he would, if he had known, have received the deputation.

I was at the pit head at 4.15 on Thursday morning and by God you ought to have seen the fore shift. Machine guns couldn't have stopped them from going to work. I managed to get between 150 to 200 to stand and put the case to them and advised them to appoint a pit committee to deal with this dispute and in the event of the manager refusing to withdraw the notices that the pit should stand. The manager appeared on the scene and began howling "that the men shouldn't listen to me, that I was a Communist and not recognised by any Labour organisation; that he didn't care whether they went to work or not, he wouldn't suffer", and finished with a screech — "get to your work". In the stampede a few were nearly hurt.

We held another meeting between 1 and 2 o'clock and after again repeating how the deputation was received got no indication of support. We got a few to volunteer to act as a Pit Committee but only 1 Old Union member is amongst them and practically none of them have any influence amongst the men. We had the matter at our May Day Demonstration last Sunday and it was well advertised at the Wellesley, but only a few Wellesley men turned up. We managed to get a few volunteers for a picket for Monday morning and although we managed to get a better hearing then still no response was made to our appeal for a United Colliery front. The Denbeath "Loyal" officials after I had taxed them with wilfully ignoring the dispute agreed to co-operate and called a meeting of the Sea Mine men for *3 o'clock* on Monday afternoon. The section affected is double shifted and the back shift commence at 2 o'clock. However, the meeting was held and you ought to have heard the 2 "loyal" officials state their terms of united action. "Prepared to co-operate with any deputation appointed by the men, but couldn't deal with Reform Union members' complaint." "Couldn't see the manager today as it was absolutely necessary to make arrangements with him as to what time would be most suitable for him." "Not to assume that we could successfully fight the partial reductions at the Wellesley as they were being imposed all over the coalfield." I received one of the worst slaps in the face of my life. The men appointed a deputation and left me out, which action, although not done intentionally, certainly played into the manager's hands. I suggested that no miners' agents should be asked to intervene until the deputation had interviewed the manager and it was agreed to unanimously. My reason for so doing was to make it more apparent to the men that the "Loyals" were out to sabotage united action at the pit and my suspicions were well founded. As soon as the meeting was finished one of them went to East Wemyss and got in touch with Adamson, who came to the Wellesley next morning and without seeing the men of the Sea Mine Section, along with some local "loyal" officials and 2 men (loyals) interviewed the manager. The result was — postponing of notices for a week and Adamson to get pay lines from men.

No meeting was held to inform the men but one of them conveyed the result to the others as he met them. We held a meeting next day and exposed the treachery of Adamson, the uselessness of pay lines if it was a case of maintaining "no reductions", and the reason why Adamson wanted the pay lines, viz., to ascertain if the average wage prevailing in the section was above the county average, and if so then a compromise would be effected. To counteract that we appealed for a strong Pit Committee to be set up and solidly supported by the whole pit on "no reductions of present standard rates". But there was and still is "nothing doing". Others in different sections here received notice of reductions. 5 in one section [received] notice of dismissal without any reasons — and no signs of a kick. I have almost lost my voice and have a rotten cold but by Christ can make more noise than the bundle of them. It was suggested by the "loyals" that a meeting would be held at the weekend but no notice has been posted at the pit today, and tomorrow (Saturday) the pit is "idle". It is some job, not like pits at Bowhill, Glencraig and the other mining centres where the men are all drawn from the same village. The Wellesley employs about 2,200 drawn from 13 or 14 villages, with the result that it will take something in the form of an earthquake to shake them up. In addition meetings can be held inside most of the pit premises but that is impossible at the Wellesley. However, a move might be got next week but I am not very hopeful.

Our group is on the verge of a crisis due to the usual — no activities on the part of some and others being overworked. We have also received the resignation from the Party of our newsagent who was informed by the Wellesley manager on Monday morning that if he was seen with a *Workers'*

Weekly in his possession on the pit head he would be dismissed. As he has physical disabilities and has to support his parents, who are old, he has decided to resign from the Party. I don't in any way blame him for his action as he would be losing his job, be thrown out of his house — a Wemyss Coal Company one — and, as already shown, he would get no support from those at the Pit.

I was appointed to act as delegate to the Party Congress but will be unable to attend as my mate will be at the Co-operative Congress at Southport the same weekend. I am going to try and get a comrade who has only been in the Party since the formation of the group to go as he is one of the best workers we have and it will give him some idea as to what the Party is. We have some bright lads here in the group. Out of 40 dozen *Weekly* another Comrade and I dispose of 30 and sometimes 34 dozen, the others doing some "chinning" at the group meetings about the Labour Party reactionaries and their cowardice, but that is all we get from them. It is about time they were drawn up and it might mean a few expulsions but that will do us some good as the inaction of those chaps has caused dissatisfaction amongst the active comrades.

You will notice my letter in this issue of *The Miner.* P.S. The local Trades and Labour Council have decided to call a Conference for the purpose of forming a Joint Committee of Miners, Dockers, Engineers and Railwaymen.

May 10th, 1925.

Am enclosing this hurriedly written note in *The Miner.* I didn't write a reply to the articles appearing in last issue as I understood from Comrade Joss that the Political Bureau were to insert at advertisement rates their decision, which would have been sufficient.

I have read Comrade Dutt's article and have come to the following conclusions. 1st: He asks "What is to be the line of the British working class in the *new* period?". But although making a good analysis of the failure of the Labour Government and also the composition of the left leaders, he still fails to give an "immediate" lead other than "unceasing ideological warfare" against those "left" leaders. Hasn't the Party been doing so? Wheatley, Maxton and Company, although the Trade Union leaders Cook, Purcell, etc., have been more or less left alone.[81] 2nd: He states: "The Communist Party must press forward every direct expression of struggle to the practical tests of immediate action or preparation. And alongside of this the Communist Party must the whole time . . ." etc. Are we or are we not at present trying to do so? United Front of Miners, Railwaymen, Engineers and Dockers. But the response to the Communist Party as such re new members isn't as big as it might be, but "persistent dripping wears away a stone". Those who are dubbed "Henrys" can see through the idea of "if there is to be a strike we'll all require to be in it" but are still obsessed with the Westminster Gas Shop and the Labour Party, although MacDonald, Thomas and company are now at a discount.[82] "That man Parliament gets aw'thing tae dae" (as the illiterate Buckhaven man said), is the biggest obstacle to surmount and will mean more and still more propaganda to overcome it. The only way it can be overcome is by the establishing of strong Factory and Pit Groups with a direct bread and butter policy, who will awaken the dormant militant spirit at the place where it will be most effective — the workshops.

What do you think of the "One Red Union"?

Enclosed is a short skit for the *Workers' Weekly*. It happened at the Trades and Labour Council last night. I am the arbiter.

I have tackled some proposition this weekend — 30 dozen *Workers' Weekly* and 3 dozen *Worker*. But I think they will go. I wrote Page re the Party meeting at Bowhill and Hodge's Methil meeting.

May 20th, 1925.

Congratulations on your new adventure. Wish you and your partner best of luck. Sorry have been unable to reply earlier to yours of 10th May due to (usual excuse) excessive work, which of course demonstrates very forcibly lack of organising powers. An efficient organiser is one who can organise work for others to perform.

Had a letter from Nat Watkins in which he informs me that he had passed on to him from the Labour Research Department the last note enclosed in *The Miner* issue of May 9th. I replied to his and informed him to send it to you. Hope you have got it.

The Wellesley and Michael proposed reductions are still hanging fire, notices have been postponed for a week on 2 occasions. As I indicated in note which Nat Watkins received, the Rt. Hon. William Adamson, M.P., P.C., ex-Secretary for Scotland, had been introduced into both disputes. The result has been as usual — modified reductions offered and men affected to ballot on Company's offer. Reductions to operate Tuesday, 26th May. Wellesley men at present are hopeless. Possibly my methods in approaching them have been wrong or the circumstances are not ripe enough for those of their calibre to try and make a kick, but if the latter is the case then we are going down into servility worse than any previously known in the mining industry. An example of the Wellesley militant proletariat: last pay day one of them showed me his pay — 25/- for 5 shifts. I advised him to go to the oversman to get "made up" to wages (9/4d. per shift). He refused to go and told me that I didn't require to trouble about it as *he* wasn't going to. He was on the back shift but to record his protest against the Company, decided to do by himself what I have been trying the past 3 weeks to get them to do collectively — stop work until the notices of reductions had been withdrawn. Of course he "turned out" on Monday having penalised himself by losing a shift before he tackled the oversman.

You ask how can the owners make reductions of those kind under the agreement. In the first place the agreement has no "legal" status as we in Fife had proven to us in 1922 when we had a case in Court for a man to be "made up" to the minimum wage. The Sheriff turned it down on the ground that he had no powers to interfere in any arrangement come to between 2 Trades Union organisations. 2ndly Partial reductions such as the present have always been imposed in the Pits, the usual procedure being an attack on rates in sections where men are making more than the County average. I have seen cases where only 1 or 2 men (due to having "good" places) in sections employing 40 to 50 men have been earning 3/- or 4/- per shift more than the County average, the others earning "the bare wage", served with notices of reductions. Those few men's wages being quoted as the section's average. The result is that other sections take up this narrow view, "It's no business of ours and besides why should we do anything to assist those whoe are earning more than we are; besides, it's their own bloody fault, they knew they would be broken and shouldn't have filled so bloody much coal". We have tried without success to establish a "darg", that is, a limited number of tubs per shift. In almost every section can be found a man who is bribed by the manager with the offer of a "heading", "level" or some other job with perquisites who will "break the darg" by filling more coal and the inevitable result has been a visit to the section by the manager, individual interviews with the men — "So-and-so can fill a certain number of tubs, his 'place' is no better than yours, you had better get a move on — or move out." That and the aim "to get as much as I can" results in the serving of notices of reduction. I remember one section I was in in the Wellesley—we had 2/9d. per quantity of 23 cwts (with 10% of output deducted for dirt, unknown to us—only stopped after we were appointed checkweighers). I along with 2 or 3 others wanted 3/3d. per quantity and we, to force the manager's hand, agreed to fill only 16 tubs per shift. The section was double shifted and we on our shift, fore shift, did not exceed the agreed "darg"; but a bright lad on the back shift filled 24 tubs and busted the show. To conclude with this portion I cannot do better than quote an old agent who is still employed: "Give them 10/- a ton if they want it. They'll bloody quick mak a ton rate for themselves." No two section are alike and therefore have varying ton rates. The Coal takes "bends" hard and soft, and the result is that (outside machine runs) the men are not earning alike, with the consequent bitter feelings towards those who are more or less lucky with "good" places. Company's motto: "One section at a time". The average wage for the section affected in the Wellesley is 13/6d. Some of them had £2.5/- to £2.15/- last pay day for 5 shifts, so that any further reductions in the ton rate will mean a still further reduction in the "blue band margarine".

I was appointed by the Group to go to the Party Congress but as my mate at the Wellesley is going to the Co-operative Congress at Southport the same weekend, I declined and a recruit who is a *worker* had been appointed to go. I might be there on Monday as we in Fife celebrate our Gala on that date.

You will be kept busy at present with the new paper but Trade Union Unity is *the* first essential to any move.

Sorry to report a dropping off of sales of *Labour Monthly* due to short time at the pits. Will possibly have to reduce order by 30 copies at least. Rotten, but cannot be helped. I am agent for *Sunday Worker* — 6½ dozen last Sunday and an order for 8 dozen of next issue. "The Professor" is a big attraction. It might injure slightly the sale of the *Weekly* but I am canvassing it in districts in Methil where the *Weekly* has a small sale.

What do you think of the letter of mine in last issue of *The Miner*? It has caused some talk and due to my concluding remarks I am due on Sunday first to debate at Lochgelly with the Fife Independent Labour Party Federation Chairman "Can the I.L.P. Policy benefit the working class?". Will try my best (which isn't much) to do the Party Policy justice.

We have formed a Council of Action here. Dockers, National Union of Railwaymen, and Miners. Held a meeting last night in Methil where a Railwayman, Docker and Miner were to appear on the box. The Railwayman, a Party member, shied at the last minutes — stagefright — as also did the Docker, an S.D.F.er, with the result that I had to carry on myself. We had an audience of almost 100 but although the response wasn't particularly encouraging last night a series of meetings as arranged should help to stir up some enthusiasm. As I indicated in my last note I reckoned on expulsions from the group. 1 member had already resigned and the group unanimously decided to expel another. We are now 8 but more effective work should result from last Sunday's discussion.

A meeting of the 2 Union Executives under Scottish auspices is to be held in Dunfermline on Saturday. Something of a definite nature should result as the districts have been roused to some extent by Party and Reform Union propagandists and also by the reductions being imposed at nearly every colliery.

Enclosed find 2 copies of Constitution and Rules of local Trades and Labour Council, 1 of which you might give to Page. I expect he will be at the Party Congress. Tell him to get hold of our Delegate, who is green but anxious to get a grip of things. If he (Page) can find time and cares to write him, his name and address is Young Pattie, 55 Commercial Street, Methil, Fife. P.S. Let me know what you think of the Constitution and Rules.

May 22nd, 1925.

Enclosed Reform Union Balance Sheet, Ballot Paper on suggested Reduction at Wellesley and Verbatim Report of recent fiasco. Have written a short note to Page re some local developments, along with some matter for Labour Research Department.

May 30th, 1925.

Received your letter of 19-25th May. This note is enclosed in copy of *The Miner* with my letter or rather extracts from Delegation Report. Was at Lochgelly last Sunday and if previously I wasn't sure about the Independent Labour Party having a policy, Sunday's proceedings convinced me absolutely. Crooks[83] kicked off with 20 minutes and stated that POLICY meant A METHOD OF GOVERNMENT, read the Constitution of the I.L.P. and said it was necessary to replace Capitalism, i.e., the competitive system, with one of equal citizenship. Need for Democratic Political and Industrial Control. Workers should have some measure of Control. (Didn't say how much). Only 1 variety of Socialism (but didn't state how many varieties of Socialists in

I.L.P.) Believed in slow evolutionary process, not too slow (Exact speed represented by letter X), and then asserted need for transitionary period. Can you beat it?

I had 20 minutes and dealt with the positions taken up by I.L.P.ers in the Labour Government — Dawes Plan —Emergency Powers Act[84] — Bombing of natives in Iraq[85] — Snowden's Budget and his banquet with Bankers, etc.,[86] and how 2 Annual Conferences of the I.L.P. had treated some and all of those actions. How I.L.P., although having workers in its ranks, *was not a Workers' Party*, as shown by its facing both ways, etc. Crooks then had 10 minutes and stated *"that he wished the I.L.P. was as well disciplined as the Communist Party and also wished the average I.L.P.er was as active as the average member of the Communist Party"*. He did not support Dawes Plan, etc. As he had put nothing of any importance up re the subject of debate I occupied my 10 minutes with a brief outline of Communist Party Policy. Questions and discussion were then allowed and a few questions not on I.L.P. policy but Russia were asked by a few I.L.P.ers. I then had 5 minutes and made an appeal (you possibly cannot visualise me making an appeal) for recruits to the Party, especially those I.L.P.ers who considered themselves Left Wingers, as the I.L.P. was becoming more and more Liberalised and that their (Left Wingers') activities inside the I.L.P. were becoming more and more barren.

Crooks had last 5 minutes and if he had made any impression (which I doubt) beforehand, he threw it away when he accused the Greenock Comrades of assaulting Stephen Kelly during the last election,[87] accused me of "mental dishonesty" re Political Action (he really meant Parliamentary Action). A few Comrades in the Hall caused him not to exactly withdraw but to state that *he* understood it was the Communists who had assaulted Kelly. No Vote was taken. At least 200 to 250 were present. I wasn't in the best of fettle as I was in bed with "dingy" on the day previous and had only 1 slice of bread to eat on Sunday. However, George, I believe we had the best of the encounter but don't know whether any additions have been made to the Lochgelly local. I expect they will submit a report to Headquarters.

Must congratulate you on June *Monthly* (haven't had time as yet to read May issue) both for prompt delivery and good matter. Price's article: the concluding sentences are very well answered by both Dutt and W.N.E. in the *Review* and article.[88]

See Page and get a look at the Scottish proposals for Unity.[89] I expect they will get the dull thud from the Reform Union.

Can't get to the Branch meetings as I am selling the *Sunday Worker*. Have ordered 7 quire for issue of May 31st. Big demand but not enough assistance. "Professor" big attraction.

Could have managed to Party Congress as pit is idle today. Have a meeting at Leven tonight and if I manage to get away *Labour Monthly* will go to Glasgow on Monday. If not will go to Burntisland. Should get away fair amount of literature. Like you I believe the Press and Pamphlets, etc., are the strongest and best weapon we have got and incidentally I am beginning to think that my inability to rouse them in this locality is due to the fact that we are selling so much literature, and that my audiences are better acquainted with my subject matter than myself, they having time to digest it and me having to skim it, with the result that they come to the conclusion (and possibly with some justification) that I am a blethering kind of joker. However, as no other is prepared to face the music I suppose it is necessary that someone has to tackle it and I get it to do.

Re publication of threat of Wellesley manager to our late newsagent: don't publish names, colliery, individual, etc., as the manager is so damned rotten that the publication of those would cause him to put his threat into operation and at present we couldn't get a move on by the men at the colliery. Had it been anybody other than Frazer, who is a cripple in every sense of the word, we could have "gone the bundle" on this but if Frazer loses this job he is "out" for "keeps". Have to close as the meeting in Leven tonight is for our local Council of Action. Expect some of our aspiring speakers will take "cold feet" and again leave me the "baby to hold".

June 5th, 1925.
You will find the proposals of the Scottish Executive in this issue of *The Miner*. I was at Burntisland on Monday and the Party was well to the front, Mrs Crawfurd, Tom Mann and Saklatvala.[90] The latter made a great fighting speech. The goods. Battered the Social Democrats and put forward a strong militant policy. It was well received. Crowd of between 1,500 and 2,000, standing bareheaded howling (that's the word) *The Red Flag*. Tom Mann was his usual. I didn't hear much of Mrs Crawfurd's speech but from expressions I heard later she impressed very much. All of them *asserted* membership of Communist Party. Not exactly as per advertisements of Gala Demonstration —"Indian Orator and Patriot", etc. Received this week's *Weekly* too late to sell at Wellesley. Unfortunate, as with the Congress Report it should be valuable. Been working 3 days from 6 a.m. to 10.15 p.m., as my mate isn't home from Southport.

June 19th, 1925.
Short note enclosed in *The Miner*. In my last note I didn't answer 1 or 2 points you raised in your last letter, viz., Wellesley dispute, Union dispute and *Trade Union Unity*. The section in the Wellesley is now on 6d. per quantity reduction and some of the men are not making a minimum wage — 9/4d, although the majority are making over, due to increasing production. The few are growling and have been *at me "to get back the 6d."* but are not at present prepared to try and get a move on with a pit committee. We have had 3 shifts each for the past 2 pays so you will have some idea what it has meant to the majority of them, who reside in Company's houses: rent and taxes from 13/4d. to 19/6d. per fortnight in addition to Health and Unemployment Insurance, Doctor, Band, Hospital, Benefit Society, Coal, and Blacksmith docked off 30/- or less. How they are getting along is a mystery to me as appeals for them to make a stand at the Colliery, apply for Parish Relief, or get the children fed at school are not receiving any response. I have had a talk with Comrade Joss re attempt to form a Party Group at the Wellesley Colliery and he thinks it will

be necessary to get a paper going as a preliminary. As I am the only member employed the work would naturally fall on me, which would of course mean that I would require to chuck some of my present work, the main portion of which is distribution of the *Weekly*, and it would be foolish to do so as anything I had to supervise would not (even if sold) replace in value to the Party the loss of even a small number of the *Weekly*. I have an average weekly sale of 9 to 10 dozen at the Pit now. The Comrade who was at Glasgow and myself accounted for 145 dozen 11 copies during May. We had almost £17 worth of literature sales during May. Can't all be lost, but it at present appears that we locally cannot catch them so I have suggested both to Joss and Page that national speakers should be poured into Fife during the summer to rouse the feeling which is here at present dormant.

Re the Union dispute the diehards of the Reform Union have won this round, Methil being the only Branch to vote for acceptance of the proposals as a medium for further Conferences. You ought to have seen the monthly agenda: resolutions condemning "the Reform Union Executive for participating in a Conference without the sanction of the rank and file", which was BALLS as the branches have decided on different occasions to instruct the Executive to meet the Old Union. Another instructing the Executive not to meet the Old Union until all 5 points have been granted, and one from the Executive recommending Branches to vote against the proposals. It seems a hopeless mess at present but the only way out of the difficulty is Pit Committees which when being attempted are also a stiff proposition. However, that is our task and if our propaganda at present does not appear to be successful the Boss will drive them to us in the near future. You will notice in *The Miner* that Kirker has been arrested and a short leet of 3 has been drawn up to be balloted on to fill his job. 2 are Party members — McArthur and Smith.[91] The result of this short leet has not as yet been felt but a growing discontent from various quarters in the Reform Union because certain nominations were unsuccessful will cause a "stink" in the near future, and some of it from recently joined Party members.

I have only read a portion of the first issue of *Trade Union Unity* so can't express much of an opinion. Will you believe me, George, that it is sometimes Tuesday or Wednesday before I can get time to scan the *Weekly*.

I am not following the footsteps of our ? Covenanter forefathers in my observance of the "Scotch Sabbath" due to *Sunday Worker* (now 17 dozen sales) and meetings. Our Council of Action has not done much to qualify it for the abuse against it by the Boss Press. However, we are getting the idea popularised and by persistent propaganda should make it be felt in the near future.

I received 20 dozen *Problems of the Labour Movement*.[92] Afraid I shall have to return 10 dozen. Good stuff, but the cash is lacking.

I had a postcard from Reade when in the Balkans.[93] Is he still on the Trotsky business?

You will notice the "Unemployed Notes" in *The Miner* by R. Selkirk, a Party member in the Cowdenbeath local.[94] 1st class Comrade and a great worker for Party. Doing good work amongst unemployed in West Fife.

I hope by this time you have managed to get more agents in Fife for the *Monthly*. We have had to reduce our order for July — 8 dozen, but taking everything into consideration the sale isn't bad. As for boosting the *Review*[95] we cannot do that in Methil without injury to the *Monthly* and the same with the *Sunday Worker* and *Weekly*. We have pushed the *Sunday Worker* in streets where we couldn't or had not tried the *Weekly*, with the result that little injury has been done the *Weekly*. My candid opinion is that the Party machinery is being overloaded with so many publications, although 2 which we distribute locally — *Monthly* and *Sunday Worker* — are not official organs but here have to be "pushed" by us as nobody else cares to handle them.

Methil Branch, Reform Union, last Sunday unanimously passed a resolution for the Reform Union monthly agenda calling on the Reform Union to invest £50 in the *Sunday Worker*. Required certainly, and good enough in its way, but I would rather some of them had been prepared to assist in distribution locally. The idea is getting abroad here, and not without justification, that the chief qualifications of a Communist Party member are being a 1st rate newspaper seller and a soap box orator. Hope you are getting along all right in your job.

Thursday Forenoon,
July 2nd, 1925.

Received your letter of 29th June today and as the pit is "idle" today have commenced my reply. You seem to be collecting the jobs. Aren't there some members in London with the necessary qualifications and, what is just as important, time to take up some of those jobs that are being thrown at you? Here it is different: few members and plenty of work, with the result we have to get "dug in".

Sorry to have disappointed you re *Trade Union Unity* but the fact is that I only read a part of Will Thorne's article in No. 1 issue and haven't seen another copy.[96] I don't consider *that* sufficient to pass on an opinion regarding a magazine. However, George, I find it almost impossible to read the papers, etc., I am getting. This group leader business is knocking lumps out of me. By the way you will be delighted to know we enrolled 8 last Sunday — 5 Young Communist League and 3 Communist Party — with the promise of another 8 this Sunday — 4 Y.C.L. and 4 Communist Party. We start Party Training on Sunday 1st. Comrade Pattie is responsible for the Y.C.L. members. Should have 3 Pit Groups going in a few weeks. The new members are going to be fed on mainly importance of organising at pits, so that none of the quibbles re residential basis of organisation will arise. Enclosed new style of propaganda for the Wellesley. Don't understand how it never struck me before. About 300 of those weight slips issued weekly. Intend to give them something to occupy their minds. How does the first one strike you? Should impress some, with some relationship of 4 items mentioned. Specimen of 1 with weight.[97]

As you remark, Purcell should have a good show in Forest of Dean. I have some idea of the type you mention. They are not unknown here. In fact here is a short true account of what happened in "Klondyke" before the war. A section was threatened with a reduction in rates and a deputation was sent to interview the manager. As usual some greyhead (outside) was appointed. After putting their case to the manager, who looked at this elderly chap and said, "George, am sure you dinna need tae care aboot the reductions, you are no' like some o' them, you can howk coal. What you want is mair tubs an' I'll see that you get them. Awa' tae yer wark." The deputation went and so did part of their rates. Case of "support the man who gies wark tae the warkman", never mind a damn what the returns are. "Gie us wark and tell us we're braw wark chaps." Like discussing a horse — "Good 'puller' on a stey brae". But that's the material we have got to mould. Slow in results but sure.

Problems of Labour Movement going slow here. 5 dozen only out of 20 dozen received, but have to take into consideration a number of *Labour Monthly* sold with article. Should we get national speakers here and with fairly decent audiences should give them a shake up. Wish I could get someone to handle *Sunday Worker* and so allow me to attend Union meetings. Gradually getting some off my hands — 2 Comrades are now assisting in distribution. Knocked lumps out of my previous best at the Wellesley last Friday: 14 dozen *Workers' Weekly* — 1 for every 13 or 14 employed, sold at the pit and in addition some are distributed at the homes of those employed at the Wellesley. Of course, George, when discussing the Wellesley it is a case that doesn't have many like it — due to my being checkweigher and immune from victimisation by the management for those activities. We haven't many Communist Party members on a like job.

I am sorry if I have led you to think that McArthur and Smith (who are on the short leet for Kirker's job) are both good Party members. McArthur joined Methil local in February (he had the letter in *The Miner*, "Why a Ballot?"), since when he hasn't attended a group meeting and refuses to sell the *Weekly*, although he sells *The Miner*. He was a product of the Scottish Labour College, being 1 year (1920-1) at Glasgow. T. Smith is President of the Reform Union and is, along with some others of the Cowdenbeath local, opposed to Party fractions in the Reform Union as "we are all good Communists in the Reform Union". He is one of those I wrote you about when Joss formed the locals in West Fife who were only in the Party through curiosity. As they have a fairly good following it would not do the Party a great deal of good at present to declare open hostilities with them. They are gradually showing their hand and will either have to conform to Party discipline or get chucked overboard in the near future.

Re the Factory Paper, I think it will have to be shelved for a bit until we get some of the new comrades "going", when I will be relieved of some of my present work.

Going to Trades and Labour Party meeting tonight. Will write any item of interest.

Thursday night: Two decisions of Council merit some attention. 1st Unanimously agreed to write Leven (a neighbouring Trades Council) asking them to appoint 5 representatives to meet 5 Representatives from Methil for the purpose of discussing methods of meeting the impending industrial crisis.

Moved by an S.D.F.er who is gradually coming to us. He along with a left wing Trade Unionist (unattached politically), a Party sympathiser, Comrade O'Neil and myself represent Methil. S.D.F.er wasn't sure whether it was a Council of Action he had proposed. 2nd Unanimously agreed to send the following resolution to Secretary, Trades Union Congress: "Methil Trades and Labour Council calls on the special Trade Union Congress Conference to be held at end of July to grant full powers to the General Council to call out on strike all organised workers in the event of the Government refusing to withdraw British troops and warships from China."[98]

I had a letter from one William Nagle (I.L.P.), Old Union organiser and member of Scottish Executive, asking me to meet him for a private talk. As I met J. Bird on Sunday and was informed by him that Nagle had been at him trying to get Bird to break away from the Reform Union and join the Old Union and that he would like a talk with me on the same subject, I wrote Nagle to the effect that he could consider the suggested meeting as having taken place. None of this backdoor intriguing with that crowd at this time. Bird is in my opinion having too many of those visits from Nagle. The Political Bureau decision still stands, viz., no breakaway by individuals or Branches, and for anything like that to take place at present would let the Party down for a considerable time in Fife. We have a *good case* and can bear daylight.

Joss managed to form a group in West Wemyss and should compliment himself on doing so, as it is one of the most out of the way places imaginable. 5 members, 2 of whom I am acquainted with and have some influence in the village. If they display any activity they should rally good support as the 2 pits in which the majority of the village are employed have been getting it thick and heavy during the past 4 or 5 weeks, one of the pits being idle 4 days out of 6 for 3 weeks on end. J. Stewart of Lochgelly formed a group of 13 at Crossgates, home of President of Old Union.[99] I haven't heard what progress they are making.

Friday evening: I forgot to mention that the Trades and Labour Council agreed to invest £2 in the *Sunday Worker*. Had a good sale of 10 dozen *Workers' Weekly* at the Wellesley today. I reckon on a sale of 20 dozen in a few weeks' time. Have an up and down sale each week due to my being on backshift and foreshift each alternate week. Backshift week I commence sales at 12 o'clock and finish 2.30. Foreshift I am relieved from work at 1 and sell until 2.30, losing most of the nightshift (almost 400 men) and a good number of the backshift.

What do you think of the owners' terms? Seem very quiet about them. Very little appearing in the Press. The feeling here is — "7 hours is enough to work and Christ knows how we are to get along with another reduction in wages; something will have to be done". But that is where the shoe pinches. "Something" will have to be done by somebody — not "me". A chap today had a pay of 6/4d. for 4 shifts after rent and half (echo of lock-out and a period of sickness due to gas poisoning) and other offtakes to keep 7 for a week. Requires some ingenuity to "make that go".

Wellesley is working tomorrow, Saturday — first Saturday for months. A cage at the Rosie Colliery, Wemyss Coal Company, went down the shaft on Wednesday night. From what I can gather it was a case of overwinding and the overwinding apparatus worked but the rope became unhosed and the 4 safety chains broke. No men were on it. The pit was due to be idle yesterday but I understand the Government Inspector made it idle today also, due to the state of the shaft. The safety chains must have been neglected during inspections, if any. The nightshift were waiting to go down when the "accident" occurred, but nobody was on the cage. Carries 8 men.

Comrade Pattie informs me that about a dozen more are to join the Y.C.L. on Sunday. London had better look around or Methil is going to supersede it. Perhaps. You might tell Comrade Beauchamp[100] that I will distribute the unsold copies of the *Labour Monthly* to the new comrades. P.S. What do you think of Comrade Selkirk's letter in this issue of *The Miner*?[101]

July 17th, 1925.

A short note with *The Miner*. Received 3 copies of *Trade Union Unity* and *Monthly Circular*.[102] Will write you next week as we commence our annual "holidays" on Monday. 1 week "idle". Enclosed find pay line for 4 — 2 men and 2 drawers — for 5 shifts each, drawers' wages being 7/6d per shift — 6.6%. Sales of *Weekly* still going up at the Wellesley: 13 dozen 9 last week and 15 dozen 3 today, and 3 dozen *Bulletins* (International Class War Prisoners' Aid). Fife District Party Committee getting a move on — 9 or 10 meetings for Sunday. I appear at Lochgelly and Bowhill.

July 20th, 1925.

Have read June and July Numbers of *Trade Union Unity*. I like Fimmen's and Purcell's articles as they appeal to me as dealing more direct and giving more of an immediate lead than the others, Marchbank in particular[103] oozing with the usual platitudes — "It *must* be recognised" (no need to advocate Unity if that were so), "We hope" (no reasons given), "*Must now* be apparent", and of course J. H. Thomas's matter re railway unions. It is in my opinion a good little magazine, with more good points than bad and should assist (if circulated widely enough) greatly in bringing about the object for which it is being run. Regarding the photos: couldn't you publish them on one side of paper only as (judging by some chaps in this locality) some readers have them framed.

Had 2 meetings on Sunday, 1 at Lochgelly and 1 at Bowhill; between 3 and 400 at Lochgelly and almost 200 at Bowhill. Not much enthusiasm being shown at meetings but that possibly due mainly to speaker.

We, having made a momentous decision, have bought a duplicator today and are going to *try* and run a factory paper every fortnight. Our chief difficulty at present is to get someone to type the stencils, none of us having a typewriter or acquaintance with a local typist. However, I think we will manage to get over that before the weekend. We are aiming high, anticipating at least a 1,500 sale, as we were going to include notes from 3 or 4 pits in addition to the Wellesley. As they are all Wemyss Coal Company health resorts we should manage fairly well. In addition, we are on the idea of getting something better than a duplicator. What is your opinion of an "Adana"? The Kirkcaldy group are running a paper, "The Underworld", a copy of which I enclose.[104] You might send me a copy of 1 of the London papers to give us a lead as we desire to make a success of this venture. The group thinks very little of "The Underworld" and reckon they can knock lumps out of it. However, that remains to be seen.

Only 6 of the 15 or 16 who promised to join up are attending the Group training. However, that means 6 more than formerly.

What do you think of "our 'Erb"?[105] Is it bluff or has Cook shaken him up? Immaterial — he is taking up an attitude that deserves all support.

Tuesday evening: Have drafted for consideration of Local Party Committee 1st issue of "The Spark", official organ of Methil Communist Pit Group. 4 Pages, 13 inches by 8 inches. Will send on a copy when ready. Expect criticism, if you think it worth criticising, of the nature you gave Fimmen's book.[106]

Don't you think that there is at present some rotten "back-door" work going on re the Mining situation? We get very little information in the papers published here but I think the owners will unreservedly withdraw their terms, meet the Federation Executive, who at present are making a show of a determined united front; but having no definite claim to rally the coalfield behind them will go to pieces when meeting the owners in an "unconditional conference". We are keeping the Minority Movement programme in front and although not getting any opposition we cannot by any stretch of the imagination claim to be overwhelmed with demonstrations of enthusiasm for it.

Purcell made a good show and judging by the Press reports has more or less stirred the Boss. A good report appeared in the *Glasgow Herald* — "When news was known Back Bench Socialists demonstrated enthusiasm but the Front Opposition Bench looked glum, Mr MacDonald in particular realising that he was going to have another extremist to add to his troubles."[107]

We are on "holiday" at present — 1 week idle, the result of which will be shown in our sales of *Weekly* this weekend. Expect to get away remainder of 20 dozen of *Problems of Labour Movement* at weekend. Notice you had an advertisement in *The Miner*. I could have disposed of a good number of copies at Bowhill on Sunday, but thinking the Bowhill comrades would have some I didn't take any with me. They had none and a good opportunity was lost. I had to walk home from Kirkcaldy on Sunday night, a distance of 9 miles, having failed to get the last bus home. Although a strict believer in "3rd class riding being better than 1st class walking", I have to admit the forced exercise was overdue.

Had a note from Beth Turner re organising miners' wives.[108] Time *we* had some women organisers to give a push to that line. P.S. What do you think of our title block, copy enclosed?[109] Drawn by a local comrade. Give Page a copy of Wellesley Colliery Benefit Fund Rules.

July 29th, 1925.

Received your letter of 24th July today with Factory Paper enclosed. Am commencing this reply on Tuesday night so that I can manage to reply to some of the points in your letter and send it along with a copy of "The Spark", which we expect tomorrow, Wednesday.[110] We bought some wax stencils along with the duplicator (a flat one) and they turned out duds. I managed to get a chap to type them on Wednesday last but only lines and punctuation marks came through. Tried one or two places locally on Thursday and Friday but was unsuccessful in getting someone else to type, so sent a comrade to Glasgow District Party Committee office on Saturday, expecting to have them for sale at Methil during the weekend. They agreed to print 500 of them and to send them on for Tuesday. As I stated in my last letter, Methil Group isn't much gone on "The Underworld" — consider it has too much statistical material and without definite leads. It is printed in Glasgow on a Gestetner. Yes, there are a few pits in the near vicinity of Kirkcaldy, 1 practically in the town and 3 others on the outskirts, with a fourth — a mine, no shaft — being developed. Local name for latter, in-goingee. All Fife Coal Company.[111] There are 500 "Underworlds" printed, the copy you received being No. 2 issue, No. 3 not having yet come out.

I am responsible for the complete issue of "The Spark" and will probably have to tackle it myself for a few issues as some of the others are as yet a bit shy, so don't be sparing with your criticism. However, when they see a few issues from my pen it might compel them for the Party's good name to butt in and try their hand. Cowdenbeath local are running one, "The Torch".[112]

Re the Pay ticket. It was for 4 — 2 men and 2 Drawers — with 5 shifts each, total of 20 shifts on Pay line. Top entry is amount of coal filled in quantities of 23 cwts @ 2/6d. per quantity. 2/6d based on 10/- shift rate, which makes 2/4d. The next entry is for oncost work at shift rates, also based on 10/- shift rate. Next entry is 6.6% decrease, as minimum wage in Scotland under agreement is 9/4d. Drawers' wages in that section (Barncraig) runs between 6/- and 8/6d. per shift. Quality of coal — best Household, and fetches from 30/- to 35/- per ton *here* in Methil, so Heavens knows what you would have to pay for it in London. The method of ascertaining if their wages are correct on Pay ticket is to deduct 1/4d per £ on total before stoppages are deducted. Fife Coal Company do not work the %age trick. Will try and get a Pit-Head Worker's line for you with subsistence rates, etc. "The Adana" I understand (I haven't seen one) is a printing machine. Various sizes, ranging from £2 to £11. We were also advised to get a Polograph £20 to £25 new. However, the printing machine idea has been relegated to the scrap heap for the present as the comrade who visited Glasgow on Saturday has seen, and after seeing is full of, Gestetner. He was offered one for £10 so our next objective is a Gestetner. I forgot to mention our present one is a Red Seal, Remington, 2nd hand, and along with ink, 2 dozen stencils and 1 Ream of paper we paid £3.2/- in Edinburgh. As we are more at home judging picks and shovels we, after showing it to a comrade who is here on a campaign for the Y.C.L., are complimenting ourselves on our capture. We have made a slight alteration with the design. The one you refer to is bully. We are going to have cartoons, getting one ready for No. 2 issue which is intended to be out next week — Party Anti-War Week — and every fortnight afterwards, not to clash with *The Miner*. No use in creating antagonism with some of the Reform Union diehard element. You will be thinking, and rightly so, that I am full of "The Spark". Christ, George, I have had brilliant issues when lying awake in bed. Have got 2 pages of No. 2 issue ready.

Tomorrow, Wednesday, will be a critical day for the working class movement in Great Britain and what a bunch to depend on. After reading tonight's paper I am more than ever convinced that we are on the verge of a big sell-out. Vague suggestions are made in the *Edinburgh Evening News* that on pressure (?) from the Prime Minister the coalowners will withdraw their ultimatum on condition that the M.F.G.B. Executive will agree to carry on the present agreement for 2 months. Where will we be then? The German miners starved out and possibly on a 9 or 10 hours day, and some of the others on the Continent clubbed, then our turn. A somewhat similar tactic to that adopted by Lloyd George in 1919 and the weak-kneed attitude adopted by the M.F.G.B. Executive in the 1920 Datum dispute.[113] Hesitating and cowering, delaying notices, and working on day to day notices until the morale of the men is gradually broken. During the "peace" period new stunts arising in the Boss Press, completely knocking the guts out of the rank and file. You would see that "peace" period advocated by his most mighty F. Hodges during the weekend.[114] Frankie can voice the stuff.

I believe I notified you that our suggested meeting with Leven Trades Council did not come off. Owing to being on the backshift this week I will be unable to attend the Trades and Labour Council meeting on Thursday, but the Party fraction will raise the question of calling a special meeting as early as possible of the Trades and Labour Council, Labour Groups in the Parish and Town Councils, Co-operative Society, Labour Group in School Management and Education Authority and Benevolent Societies. Rather late, but due to the nearness of what might be a fight might make the meeting more successful, at least in numbers. You mention "if even Adamson shows fight he should be supported" — Every time.

You describe the spirit being demonstrated in Durham and Wales. It is here also but will require something like Old Arse for elbow collar Welldon's letter — something that attacks them all simultaneously — to get a real demonstration of that spirit.[115] In 1921 the women were not so militant as they are at present and they are some factor to be reckoned with. It is a great pity we haven't had any of the women organisers up here. I had one or two meetings during 1921 with the women but I am a "jibber" where they are concerned. When selling the papers I have a chat with some of them and they know no limits. Mention Royalties, Profits, Royal Banquets, Ascot, etc., and in most cases I am a lisping infant in profanity and in others a mild milk and water Sunday School teacher in methods to get Workers' Control. Re Welldon I recollect a letter in 1921 in a local paper owned by the Coal Companies advocating keeping the miners down the pit and only allowing them up twice per year — New Year's Day for a blow-out, and once during the summer months to see and bet on a local whippet handicap. It roused them. Demonstrations took place outside the newspaper office, the Trades and Labour Council declared a ban on the paper and instructed the Labour Groups in the Town and Parish Council to vote against the firm getting any printing work. It is only recently the ban was removed and the Labour Groups instructed to support the firms' quotations as the only other firm (a small one) quoting is a "black shop" on the Typographical Society books and the other firm pays Trade Union Rates and recognises the Society. The circulation of the paper is not increasing. They — the paper — won't repeat 1921 stunt, having learnt a lesson.

Have managed to get away over 16 dozen *Problems of Labour Movement*.

Wednesday night: Another day gone and "The Spark" not arrived. Some reliable crowd in Glasgow.

Nothing in tonight's paper re today's Conference[116] but Fife coalowners have posted their terms for August: 85.42% over the 1888 basis (4/-), which means 7/5d. — a reduction of 1/11d. for underground workers and 6/- per shift for adult *able bodied* surface workers. Along with the terms they have posted the following notice which for sheer bloody cheek takes the cake:

NOTICE

EIGHT HOURS DAY

If it had been possible to have returned to an eight hour day the Owners would have been able to pay a higher percentage on the 1888 basis than for a 7 hour day.

For the month of August, instead of 85.42% for 7 hours they would have been able to pay 123% on the 1888 basis, after the deduction of the extra percentage added to pieceworkers' rates to compensate them for the alteration of hours.

Wellesley, 29th July 1925.

In 1919 pieceworkers received 14.2% on rates for loss of hour, and of course it would be deducted if we reverted to 8 hours, which would mean on the 10/- shift rate a reduction of 1/5 + 5d. (123%) from July (133% above basis), with of course the extra hour to make it up. What inducements! Am going to post the following notice alongside Boss's terms tomorrow, Thursday:

WELLESLEY WORKERS

THOSE TERMS ARE NOT FOR MEN. ONLY SCABS WILL WORK FOR THOSE. LET NO SCABBING TAKE PLACE. FORM STRONG PICKETS.

On Behalf of Methil Communist Pit Group.

Dav. Proudfoot.

Enclosed is a cutting from tonight's *Edinburgh Evening News* dealing with the temper of the Fife Miner at present. Notice that trouble has commenced in

South Wales in the anthracite district.[117] The reasons are not stated but I expect it will have arisen due to the men on strike trying to get out the "safety men" according to their decision made during the weekend. Good move to force nationalisation and grant terms. Withdraw safety men and compel Government to bring pressure on owners. Would be more successful than in 1921. Reported in tonight's paper that that bum lot of Shirkie's, Colliery Winding Enginemen, Boilerfiremen and Mechanics, will remain at work "as they are not linked up with the M.F.G.B. and are not parties to the dispute".[118] Well, Well. But as they are not the only pebbles on the beach, we shall see. They have made that decision before and "the plans of mice and men gang aft agley".

Thursday forenoon: I notice by this morning's paper that yesterday's conference was abortive. Have been at a few Trades and Labour Council delegates (Dockers and Railwaymen) and they are at present full of fight.

Just received "The Spark" from Glasgow. They are some crowd, charging us £1 for 415 copies and in addition have left out some of the most important points — slogans — also mixed some of the stuff. However, there it is, George. What do you think of it? Will try and keep you posted as to events locally. P.S. Posted notice at pit head and left a crowd round about it. It is already causing talk. Intend holding a meeting at pithead tomorrow, Friday. The Boss's terms have roused them some.

July 31st, 1925.

A short note with *The Miner*. What do you think of today's proceedings? We here are in the dark; we only know that action has been postponed for a fortnight due to withdrawal of owners' ultimatum. The general feeling is one of disgust, and everyone I met tonight have freely expressed themselves — "Sold again", "No need to give the bastards another 2 weeks' coal", and "1920 and 1921 over again".

As indicated in my last letter the posting of the Boss's terms on the pit heads acted like cold water over a sleeping man. It roused them, so much so that a big number of the back shift refused to go down the Wellesley today. The night shift men were determined not to go down tonight — "To Hell with work for nothing", "Why aren't they straightforward and ask us to work for nothing?". The spirit was good today between 1 and 2 o'clock, now it is a case of "To Hell with the Union and leaders — they are all alike".

As I don't know the bait snapped by the M.F.G.B. Executive I can pass no opinion but I expect it will be on somewhat similar lines suggested by F. Hodges.

I was in a fair way to beat all previous records of sales of *Weekly* at the Wellesley today but rain commenced at 1 and continued with only slight breaks until 2.30. However, I managed 13 dozen 1 and 170 "Sparks". Due to the rain I didn't hold a meeting but it was unnecessary as a good strong picket volunteered and did turn up between 8 and 9 not knowing that action had been postponed. They turned a few men home and possibly some trouble will arise. There are usually bum suckers at every pit and the Wellesley is no exception to the rule. The manager has challenged 1 man and if he carries out his usual procedure that man will get 14 days' notice to quit. My impression at present is that this is a 2nd Black Friday. P.S. What do you think of our Glasgow comrades'(?) charge to us for printing "The Spark"? And Glasgow is *THE* Red spot against exploitation. Sales will realise 17/-. Their charge — £1. We sell the paper and (in addition to other charges) pay 3/- for doing so. 500 copies of "The Underworld" 10/- off the same machine. Glaswegian Aberdonians.

August 6th, 1925.

Enclosed No. 2 of "The Spark". Have had to draw it up myself, see to typing (which was done by a chap who has just started), and printed most of 650 copies myself. I have had a week of it. Will have to sell at least 75% of them, but that won't last long as keen interest is now being shown by other members of the group. If we could get a room it would solve a great many difficulties as at present everything (bar typing) is being done in my bedroom. What do you think of the cartoon? Enclosed is also a copy of "The Torch", issued by the Cowdenbeath local. They had 2,000 printed and gave them away *gratis*, getting Comrade Joss to stand the bulk of the expense. Received the *Labour Weekly* yesterday but haven't had time to open one.[119] Have a few 4th Pages to finish so will close.

August 13th, 1925.

Received your letter of 11th and 12th August, also *Economic Position of the Coal Industry*.[120] I have been trying to get one for the past 4 weeks but was unable to do so. Am commencing this reply tonight as I expect I shall be pretty well occupied this weekend and major portion of next week with No. 3 of "The Spark". We have some difficulty getting the stencil typed owing to the chap who does it being a railwayman and employed on various shifts, also being a "raw hand" at typing. It took 8½ hours to get the last issue, No. 2, typed. I was reading to him and was printing them until 3 and 4 almost every morning last week, so you can bet I was glad when our paper supply ran out. In all we have sold (at 1d. each) at least 500 copies. A good number were unsellable. Have got No. 3 already typed owing to our typist being on a different shift to me next week. We are on the track of a Rotary machine: going on Saturday to get a demonstration — 2nd hand at £3. Glad you think our attempt at the paper is promising. Contents of No. 3 will cause some stir amongst the Wellesley management. We have cartoons on front page, and intend making them a regular feature. I have to supply idea and a comrade draws them. Haven't managed to get contributions from any of the group yet but expect to get them to move for No. 4 issue. Re the title, I was for "The Lamp" but the comrade who draws the design and cartoons, along with one or two others, decided on "The Spark" and as you state — there it is. The N.U.R. branch here intend running a sheet and are not above asking our advice on policy so that we can get some knocks around though [it is] a non-party organ.

As I stated in my last letter the spirit shown on Friday, 31st July was great.[121] Everyone buoyed up and prepared to put up what they considered was inevitable — "a scrap like we never had before". A vague realisation that we were on the verge of something stupendous, no real idea how to meet what was coming along but the idea firmly fixed "we have got to scrap". That being so the news to "continue work" came like a thunderbolt causing them (and myself) due to our past experieces to think we had again been "sold a pup". The idea remained during the weekend because we had little or no information to go upon, but when the results were realised the general impressions can be divided into 2 categories — "We shall have 'peace' for a definite time and perhaps some way will be found to get things righted", and "We should have got dug into it. Best chance we ever had: Government unprepared and besides we would like to have tested the Alliance."[122] That roughly explains the position here with of course the usual apathy beginning, although more slow than formerly to creep in.

There are 3 Pit Papers in Fife: "The Underworld", Kirkcaldy Pit Group, "The Torch", Cowdenbeath, and "The Spark", Methil. I haven't any copies of the other 2 but will try and keep Page supplied with future numbers. Lochgelly intend running one also, and J. Bird of Bowhill when I last met him was talking about getting one in Bowhill. Fife should and will be within a short time a Party stronghold. What do you think of "The Torch"? Some bitterness expressed in it.

The Union dispute is still dragging along, in fact it appears to be getting worse. At their last monthly meeting a fortnight ago the Old Union Executive passed a resolution refusing to co-operate with the Reform Union on any question. If for no other purpose than compelling fusion it was a pity the lock-out didn't take place. The result would have been the Reform Union funds finished and with them a considerable amount of windy support. Methil Branch last Sunday decided to write A. J. Cook pointing out to him that the reactionary officials of the Reform Union, Old Union and Scottish were sabotaging every effort at establishing Unity, and referred him to a statement he made at Methil — that he, if invited, would come to Fife to help bridge the gap. The attitude of Methil active members is that the position is now reaching a point when it will be necessary to commence a break-away, either as branches or individuals, having tried the non-conditional Conference, and attempts to form Joint Committees, and failed. Adamson was in Buckhaven on Sunday and according to the local press report he was vomiting the MacDonald tripe — Public Opinion won this "victory", "*if* the two sides would get their heads together the Coal Industry could be saved", "Baldwin showed great statesmanship by his decision",[123] and last but not least, "the miner had given so much to the State during the war period that it was now time for the State to give the miner something in return because of the poverty existing amongst the miners". You wouldn't credit that sort of stuff would go down and it wouldn't have been allowed to go unchallenged, but Wullie[124] with his usual pawkiness had his meeting advertised an hour or so before it was timed to start and only his faithful henchmen attended.

What do you think of the Reform Union decision on Methil Resolution re investing £50 in the *Sunday Worker*? 8 branches for, the others against — "not on principle but sum named was too much". And the Reform Union has been called a Revolutionary Organisation. It would almost make you weep were you to read the Executive reports of business. On the verge of a big "do" and instructions issued in name of Executive that delegates must come to Board meetings to report as to number of Committees selling *The Miner*, numbers sold, number of members — Full, half, female, Underground, Surface, and Funeral, Numbers, lost or gained, probable causes, Canvassing activities, etc., those reports to take priority to any other business at every Executive meeting.

The ballot has not yet been taken for Kirker's successor but instructions have been issued to branches that every member, ½ member, funeral and female member must receive a ballot paper, not so much from the point of view of allowing everyone to vote for their choice but for the purpose of "showing at least a 9,000 membership". Some of us ought to be kicked for helping to throw up an organisation such as this one has developed into. However, George, all the regret in the world doesn't remove the cause or causes. We have got to get down to it and make some attempt to straighten matters out during the next few months.

On reading what I have written I discover that I haven't stated my opinion (which isn't worth much) on "Red Friday". Like most here I was disappointed at what was rather a tame ending to what [it] appeared was going to be a "big thing". But were we prepared? I wouldn't gull myself that we were but once we had got involved we could have managed to get a move on. Certain lines of action which I will let you know of later were discussed here. On the whole I still incline partly to my previous view — that this "victory" of "Red Friday" has not (unless we continually keep hammering at the value of mass action) been of great advantage to the workers, because this "truce" period will be used by the weak-kneed Labour and Trade Union leaders in frittering away the morale of the workers by the continuous Conferences with the Government and Employers and the usual verbiage of "Parliamentary majority", "Round Table Conferences", etc., with of course the confusion ladled out in the Press. The "wirepullers" get the upper hand at and during this "close fighting" and the Adamson type ("Compromise is the path of progress") manage to manipulate things. The "long range fighting" (as it was prior to the Government intervention) kept that kidney under. But I agree that a lesson has been taught which we as I have already stated should keep hammering home. Briefly, I think the line we have to take is — Not to minimise the "victory" but to point out that this massing of working class forces on the industrial field, even on what was really a *defence* without any real objective of immediate advantage to the workers, can and will be the right method of attaining lasting benefits if a well organised *attack* with *demands* easily understood by the average worker is initiated. To minimise the "victory" would in my opinion play into the hands of the MacDonald crush who would immediately quote us as having discarded mass action as being of no avail and therefore having no policy — that *the* only policy for the Workers to pursue is that of

Parliamentary action. I hope I have made myself clear because at present my think-box is a bit hazy with "dingy".

Saturday morning: Had a good sale of *Weekly* at the Wellesley yesterday — 17 dozen. There has been a big demand for "The Spark", now popularly known as "The Sparker", at the Wellesley. The Wellesley management have got their "backs up" at the Party Anti-War Literature which decorated the Pit head. The pithead back shift gaffer was employed for a few hours tearing and washing it down. He will be kept busy in the future. Lost one member last month but have got another this week.

If you can manage it you might send on another copy of *The Economic Position of the Coal Industry* for one of the Comrades here whom I want to get started writing some general stuff for "The Spark".

I haven't opened the August Number of the *Monthly* yet so can't pass on any opinion but have asked one or two readers what they think about it. They all consider the number one of the best issued, so that the eleventh hour scamper hasn't in any way hurt the contents.

Have you seen the joint report of the M.F.G.B. and the Mining Association yet?[125] I understand it has been issued but owing to our non-membership of the M.F.G.B. can't get a copy here.

The chap in the pit checkbox whom I introduced you to asked me to let you know that he compliments you on your article on the "Riff war",[126] and he considers "Student's" article good stuff from the angle of anticipation of Baldwin's speech in the House of Commons on the Coal Crisis, and that parts of it should be quoted in dispelling the effect in some Labour Party quarters of Baldwin's speech re "community anarchy", etc.

Has Comrade Beauchamp told you about my last account? I sent on £3.12/- [in] 3 £1 notes, 10/- note, and 2/- Postal Order — for payment of 8 dozen July *Monthly* and 16 dozen *Problems of Labour Movement*. She informed me a few days later that only 3 £1 notes were in the envelope. I sent on number of 2/- Postal Order a week ago but haven't received (at time of writing) a reply. Hope everything is all right now.

Have had an offer from a non-party chap to draw cartoons. Asked him to submit a few and if any good will get him to send on to *Weekly*.

I wasn't satisfied with our Cartoon in No. 2 "Spark". It wasn't as I wanted. My suggestion was to have 2 sections, the entire cartoon entitled "Peace in my time! Oh Lord.", 1 section sub-titled "The Coal Boss's Idea of Peace", and depicting a figure marked "Miner" crawling on hands and knees before another figure marked Coal Boss; 2nd section sub-titled "The Communist Party's Idea of Peace", with a figure of a MINER facing front with the COAL BOSS in his left hand and his right hand to his nose, asking "Whaur the Hell's the Midden?". As it was printed it in my opinion more or less depicts the wavering timorous attitude of the Trade Union leader at present — We would like to, but we might get contaminated if we look at it. However, as it was it passed muster with our readers. I have tried to mix the stuff in No. 3 —

Local, national and International — which should be more effective than cramming all those by themselves.

You will notice a skit in No. 3 which requires some explanation to one outside the district. I have used the names of those prominent in the Wellesley. "Gardiner" is a Brushing Contractor in the "Sea Mine" section. "Penman" is an oversman, "Marshall" backshift gaffer, "Kirkcaldy" a Contractor, "Beveridge" Colliery Agent, "White" an oversman, "Broon" or "Brown", Manager, "Baird" (local way of expressing Beard), assistant General Manager of Wemyss Coal Company. Baird is also an oversman at the Wellesley.

Sunday Forenoon: We bought the duplicator yesterday and it is a big improvement over the flat one. 2 of us ran off 600 1st and 2nd pages in 4 hours last night. Going to run off 3rd and 4th this afternoon.

4 of us have disposed of 20 dozen 7 *Sunday Worker* this morning, but I am seriously considering giving up this game of paper selling. Along with the *Weekly, Sunday Worker, Worker, Labour Monthly* and *Inprecorr*,[127] a few *International* and *Review*, I have to write, see to typing, print and sell "The Spark", act as Group Leader, Fraction Leader in Trades and Labour Council, Industrial Leader, Political and any odd job that comes along. In addition we get continually "dunned" by the Bookshop[128] for *accounts already paid*, which is making the chaps absolutely sick. What manner of Bookkeeping do they practise at No. 16?[129] If they "carry on" much more as they have been doing some of them will have to come here and sell the stuff themselves. All of us are out of pocket every week with the sales ("no change", or "broke") and one can't always refuse a copy and can do without having those letters and accounts for accounts already paid. 3 of the most active comrades have been doing what today's *Sunday Worker* poster states — "Grousing Again" — and threatening to pack up. One can't blame them. However, we will have a full dress debate tonight.

Sunday night: Had a good meeting of group and now count 16 members in Y.C.L., ranging from 14 to 21 years. Some good material — all working in the pit. No resignations. Have Saklatvala at Leven on Saturday first.

Enclosed 4 copies of "The Spark", 1 1st, 1 2nd, and 2 3rd issues. 1 copy of 3rd for yourself and others for Page.

Thanks very much for invitation but don't know when I can accept. Hope you have a good time wherever you decide to go during your holiday.

You ought to see my bedroom. More confusion and blooming mess with papers than even *Monthly* office when Reade was in it. By the way, is he still in the Party?

Friday, August 28th, 1925.

A short note with *The Miner*. Received September *Labour Monthly* today and haven't read August No. Some game, advising chaps to read papers and magazines which one hasn't read. No. 4 of "The Spark" is only half completed. Will send on copy at weekend. You will have noticed the bad spelling. It takes some doing watching the chap who does the typing to see that he doesn't make some worse bloomers. We are on the track of a typewriter and I have to do the typing — Group decision. Some people shout from the housetops what *they* have done for the movement but by heavens if I am in it for a few years more I will have been initiated into a few stunts which I wouldn't have been had I not been in the Party: SOAP BOX SPEAKER, EDITOR (I write this without blushing), NEWSBOY, and GENERAL MOOCHER. Now — TYPIST. We *SELL* "The SPARK" at 1d. and are getting away without any trouble almost 600 every fortnight and a demand for it every week. Managed 18 dozen 3 *Weekly* and 15 *Labour Monthly* at the Wellesley today, but no recruits to the Party.

Saklatvala was unable to get here last Saturday and we had the place for a radius of 4 miles splattered with advertisements. We didn't receive notice about changing of time of meeting until Friday night and most of us were on foreshift Saturday. The result was that we couldn't get all the advertisements altered, and a crowd of about 400 waited in the rain on Saturday night. The meeting was held at 11 a.m. Sunday and a crowd of between 3 and 400 stood till 2 p.m. listening to Saklatvala. But although they were all pleased with his exposition of the Party Policy we had no offers to join up. I understand that 50 joined up at the end of his meeting in Bowhill. An ardent ex-S.D.F.er, ex-I.L.P.er challenged Saklatvala to debate "Can Britain feed herself?" but has not up to the present stated with whom. We accepted the challenge and I hope Tom Kennedy will be Saklatvala's opponent. If the Political Bureau agrees and we can get it fixed up it will take place in Methil. I think the Organisation Bureau have gone to sleep as they ought to have had Fife kept going all summer with National speakers. When Dick, Fife District Party Committee Secretary, writes for them they can't be got and yet Dundee has one or more regularly and they HAVE TO PASS THROUGH FIFE to get from London to Dundee.

We are going to try and get the District Party Committee to agree to a new move in the Union Dispute — Both Unions to appoint 3 rank and file members to draw up a Constitution, with a Trade Union leader outside the Miners to act as Chairman. The main points of the Constitution to be submitted for ballot vote by the whole coalfield.

A meeting is to take place on Sunday 1st at West Wemyss with representatives from East, West and Coaltown of Wemyss and Methil Trades Council to consider methods of strengthening Trade Unions and deciding on a more militant policy. The following Sunday Methil Trades and Labour Council meet Leven Trades Council for the purpose of discussing Unemployment, etc., in this district and how to meet the various things arising here at present. I have been appointed to represent Methil Trades and Labour Council at both meetings. We are getting a move on although slowly. Hope you have a good time.

September 1st, 1925.
Enclosed No. 4 "The Spark". Had some trouble with this issue due to dud stencils. Have sent on copies of "The Signal", issued by Methil N.U.R., and

"Sawdust", Aberdeen Communist Party and Y.C.L., to Page.[130] Expect you will not receive this note until you return from holiday so will be brief as present news will be stale when you return. Hope you have a good time. P.S. What do you think of the cartoon?

September 13th, 1925.
    Enclosed No. 5 of "The Spark". Expect you are on holiday at time of writing this. Have given Page latest developments of Union dispute. Will write you in a fortnight's time.

September 24th, 1925.
    Received your letter of 16th inst, also postcard from Pourville.[131] Glad you had a good holiday.

The T.U.C. made some good decisions and in my opinion would have made more, especially "More Power to the General Council", had the Lefts been more courageous, or should I say better organised, prior to and at the beginning of the Congress.[132] As it appears to me, per Press, "Big Man Bevin" is out to figure as THE LEADER of the Industrial Section of the Movement and at present is winning.[133]

I expect you will have seen Page by this time and got from him the report I sent re the Party in Fife and the Union Dispute, also the result and decision of the meeting held in Kirkcaldy last Sunday. Other moves are on for Unity. Committees of both Unions at Kelty (West Fife — no Party contacts) took a ballot on Periodical Elections: 1,282 for, 45 against; and Financial Vote,[134] 1,032 for, 143 against. They have also decided to circularise branches of both Unions asking support for a resolution re above which they are putting on the Agenda of both Unions. Good moral gesture but no definite method of organisation behind it to get the ballot taken. On the other hand our proposition should be more successful and decisive, compelling the Scottish Executive to convene a meeting and at the same time getting both organisations pledged to meet for discussion on a definite proposition. We raised the matter at the Trades Council meeting tonight.

Another development has taken place. According to Press reports it was announced at the Old Union Executive meeting last Saturday that it was possible that One Union for Mineworkers would be an accomplished fact by the end of the year. The annual Congress meets on 5th and 6th October, when something more definite will be known. We require Unity in Fife before that happens so that we can, along with the Minority Sections throughout Scotland, get a move on to meet the reactionary officials who will be "building themselves in like a grate", to use a local expression. Methil Reform Union branch officials and collectors are taking some holding to keep them from throwing in and going to the Old Union. Some of them have decided that in the event of Unity not being obtained in 3 months they then are joining the Old Union. It was agreed last Sunday to invite P. Hodge and T. Smith (the latter I understand has got Kirker's job, is a Communist Party member but would not accept the Party decision at Bowhill) to speak at Methil on Sunday, October

11th. Meeting to be widely advertised and need for Unity to be pressed home. Hodge and Smith have accepted.

You will notice we have advertised the *Monthly* in No. 6 issue of "The Spark". It was not exactly forgetfulness on my part, or thinking we had a big enough sale (never be big enough to suit me until almost every house in Methil has an order), but because the others haven't been distributed so widely. I am still the sole contributor to "The Spark", can't get the others to contribute, and have to sell almost 50%, only 3 others selling. 1 does 150, 1 50, and another 50-75. 2 of the comrades have been threatened with the sack for what has appeared in "The Spark" and were told to stop selling them on the pit head. I told them not to sell them openly but to try and organise distribution on an underground basis. "Parliamentary Expressions" was my effort but was more or lessed messed up by our typist, who left out 1st Coal Jock's question. You would notice we had to write "2nd to". The District Party Committee secretary has been "muffing things" by not sending in copies to Headquarters. We will send them ourselves in future. The Kirkcaldy group has now got a duplicator and our cartoonist is to supply design and cartoons for "The Underworld". Thornton branch, Associated Society of Locomotive Engineers and Firemen, intend running a Depot paper and are asking our assistance. Have you seen "The Signal", organ of Methil N.U.R.? Have sent 2 copies to Page. I am also contributing to it.

Am attending a meeting of Minority Executive[135] at Glasgow on Saturday, September 26th, re campaign for Unity in Fife.

The Y.C.L.ers have some face. Wanting the profits from the *Sunday Worker* and not 1 of them prepared to distribute a copy. According to them Rust suggested this.[136] We informed them that they would get ALL PROFITS if they took it over but that WAS a "dug wi' anither name".

We made no extra efforts for Red Week as it was humanly impossible. 4 of us sold £27.6/- of literature (papers, pamphlets and books) for August. 2 of the 4 produced (printed, etc.) 3 issues of "The Spark". 2 of us are involved in Trades Council work and are usually appointed on deputations. At times I feel absolutely fed up and feel like chucking it. We are assured we have tons of sympathy ("Come to us when you are handing out the guns", "We'll be ready when the time comes", etc.) but not a bloody one of them will join the Party. It is quite possible we may be using wrong methods but if so I can't devise others which may be right. Have written King Street for Saklatvala for a meeting in Methil. Like you I don't go much on mass influxes at a meeting but as Communists are not born but made we must get them in before the grain can be separated from the chaff. So far as reading the Party literature is concerned I think we have a good number in Methil who should have more than a nodding acquaintance with the Party's policy, aim, etc., and national speakers will certainly make more impression on those chaps than we locally have appeared to do.

What do you think of the suggestion mooted at last Executive Board meeting of the Reform Union — "Expel all those who are preaching Unity different to the Reform Union official stuff"? I understand it was received favourably but "the time was not opportune as, if some persons in Methil Branch were expelled it would mean expelling the Branch". And it used to be said the Reform Union was financed from MOSCOW.

Did you meet J. Stewart and McArthur at the Minority Conference?

Have just received reply to our request for Saklatvala. Can't get him for our date owing to Executive meeting during same weekend.

Enclosed 2 pamphlets issued by National Seamen and Firemen's Union.[137]

Pit is "idle" today. Met the S.D.F.er who challenged Saklatvala to debate "Can England feed herself?", but couldn't get from him who was to be Saklatvala's opponent. Looks like being a wash-out.

Tuesday night: Was at Glasgow on Saturday. According to reports, Lanarkshire have put the resolution passed at Bowhill to 7 or 8 branches for delegates to raise Fife split at the Congress. Stirlingshire likely to support. Mid and East Lothian support, Ayrshire oppose. No report from West Lothian. After discussion it was agreed to add to original resolution scrapping of present rules of Old Union.

We have disposed of over £23 of literature for September and have gained 1 new member. We are doing things. What do you think of a group who can't hold a meeting unless I am present? I was selling *Sunday Worker* from 11 to 1.30 and had to hurry to get 2 stencils cut (no dinner), assisted printing from 4.30 to 6.30, and arrived at hall for group meeting at 7 (group meets at 6.30), to find nobody there. Met 2 of Group about 7.30 and was informed that 6 of them had been present but because the Group Leader (ME) wasn't present they decided to disperse. Make the bloody Saints weep.

You will notice we are challenging Tom Kennedy, M.P., to discuss his position re support of Dawes Plan. A resolution has been put in front of the Trades and Labour Council calling for the sacking of Comrade O'Neil from the Chair for "Political Unreliability" — criticising Tom Kennedy at Kennedy's meetings — so we have decided to raise the whole matter by trying to get his nibs here.

The October *Labour Monthly* will be advertised in next issue of "The Signal", with special stress on Dobbie's article.[138]

We appear to be in for a slack spell again — 3 days per week. "Idle" tomorrow, Wednesday.

What do you think of the first day at Liverpool? The Press here have only reported defeat of affiliation and are jubilant about it, but are predicting a serious "split" before the end of the week, which certainly does not fulfil their boastings of the "Red" rout.[139]

Wednesday night: Finished No. 6 issue of "The Spark". 2 of us to do the lot — over 600 copies. Enclosed find 2 copies, 1 for Page, also copy of "The Signal" for Page, copy of 1st issue of Blantyre Ferme (Lanarkshire) Pit Group's Paper, and copy of suggested leaflet to be distributed in Fife.

Haven't seen tonight's paper and won't until tomorrow as I am almost "played out". Great placards this morning — "Reds' Black Tuesday", "Ex Premier slaps the Reds", etc. But I think they have over-reached themselves, especially the Glasgow *Record*, because some chaps who take very little interest in politics were remarking this morning, "Bloody queer that rag taking MacDonald's pairt if he's a right Labour man".

You will notice we are getting good results from our machine now, in fact getting experts at the game. The black ink certainly shows the cartoons up better than purple. What do you think of "Billy Goat or She Monkey" in "The Signal"? Marked my lot with a cross.

Headquarters have sent instructions to extend recruiting for other 2 weeks and insist on extra efforts being put forth by the locals. I wish to Christ some of the strategists would come here and have a go at putting some movement into some of our branch. What in Hell's name induced some of them to come into the Party beats me. Can't even give a word of information re happenings at the Pit to go in "The Spark" — "No gaffers come near us", "All Bolshies in our Section" — but admit that everything isn't O.K. but can't or won't give a damned thing. I am out of it myself in the weigh box and have to resort to "talking shop" to all and sundry to get the few items which appear. It is the same when asking some of the old as well as the new members to do anything, sell papers, write reports, etc. — "Am no' cut oot for that", or "Ah hivna time". 5 out of 25 (10 Communist Party and 15 Y.C.L.) active. Y.C.L.ers 100% inactive. However, George, they will have to sit up and take notice in a short time, if not by pressure from us then from the Boss.

October 9th, 1925.

Short note with *The Miner*. The Union dispute is still unsolved but we are getting a slight move on. The Kelty resolution re combined local ballots was on the Reform Union agenda and was adopted at the Executive Meeting on Wednesday,[140] in spite of the fact that practically every branch reported that the local officials of the Old Union refuse to consider combined action. An amendment from Methil pointing out the futility of the Kelty resolution and suggesting the card vote received support from 1 delegate, not because his branch was in favour of Unity but because they consider that the Reform Union should be a permanent organisation and had instructed him to vote against the Kelty resolution. We have P. Hodge and T. Smith at Methil on Sunday and should have a good turn-out of members when we can get a start made on the lines agreed on at Bowhill a few weeks ago. I may state that only 4 or 5 of the Party members in Fife will be active on those lines — the others, if not actively smothering it, are taking no action.

What in hell's name are the methods and who is responsible for the business side of the *Weekly* and Bookshop? We have had an account sent to us for £13 odd for *Weekly* and the Literature Secretary has all receipts. After paying August account and they had sent on receipt they had the bloody cheek to send us 3 letters demanding payment of account. This game if continued means the finish of our Group. We are sending them notice that in the event of our not getting satisfaction that they CANCEL our supply of *Weekly* — 38 Dozen. We have had more than enough of this game. The Bookshop is as bad. Accounts for which we have paid and received receipts being sent to us again.

We have no hesitation in accepting the policy of the Party and making endeavours to apply it, but by Christ we cannot understand and cannot accept the financial stunts of the mandarins in the BUSINESS ? Departments.

Getting a typewriter tomorrow — Oliver, £11.10/-; terms £1.10/- down and £1 per month. Had hard lines by being a little late to secure a Roneo Duplicator, self-feeding, for £3. Haven't received copy of "The Underworld" yet. P.S. J. Bird is to run a pit paper in Bowhill. Printed. Won't pay its way but he "has had PROMISES" from sympathisers of subscriptions varying from 1/- to £1 per week. We'll wait and see.

Tuesday night, October 13th, 1925.

Thanks for your letter of 11th October with October issue of *Trade Union Unity*. Am commencing this one on receipt of yours as "The Spark" is behind this week owing to part of our machine breaking and destroying a stencil, which means a last minute rush for the other Comrade and myself who produce it.

Sorry that Comrade Mrs Hutt is ill. Hope she is well by time you receive this note.

We didn't paint all the copies, only a few specials. The comrade who draws the cartoons does a bit with the brush and touched a few up. I thought I mentioned that in my last letter but due to the fed-up feeling I had at the time of writing I must have omitted it.

As you mention in your letter mine is not a peculiar position in the Party but heavens it does get one's goat at times. No, it isn't entirely a case of trying to get them to sell papers that is the cause of the inactivity. We have given them various jobs — group trainer, industrial, etc., changed them when no results were being obtained, or at any rate saw that no endeavour was being made to get results, and it makes no difference. Aitken Ferguson[141] was speaking here on Saturday night and I had to be laid up with dingy on Saturday afternoon, 5 or 6 of the group attended the meeting and only 2 would sell (or try) it and "take the collection". I think we will lose some of them after the "stuff" appearing in the Press of what the Government is going to do to the "Reds".

You will notice 2 signed paragraphs in "The Spark" this week. The idea you mention struck me last week and I am giving it a show this issue to see what results come from it. I almost forgot to mention that we have got a typewriter —Oliver, £11.10/-, and I have become a typist? We have got it on fairly easy terms: £1.10/- deposit and £1 per month. I can't report breaking records — 1 hour per stencil.

Enclosed copy of "The Signal", poster for meeting of Hearse Society, and report of Reform Union lawyer for Page. I tried before but was unsuccessful in getting a copy of the rules of the Hearse Society but might manage now. You might have heard of this society from Page — MEN CONTRIBUTING FOR A LIFETIME to get buried from a Hearse free of charge. The Society owns the Hearse. Those Societies are common to the fishing villages around here.

We had one Railwayman in the Group but he resigned a few months ago — couldn't accept obligations of the Party, being the excuse. He is Secretary of the local Trades and Labour Council and works with us. I think it was due to those at home which caused him to resign, as they are mostly Kennedyites.

The Kelty "stunt" has become has become the official policy of the Reform Union for Unity. Both P. Hodge and T. Smith belaboured it for all they were worth on Sunday. I had a fairly good innings and after a discussion on the merits of the Kelty stunt and the Minority Movement proposition which lasted over 1 hour, Hodge lost his rag and told me to crawl back to the Old Union. Both admitted that the combined local ballot WOULD NOT be taken in every district; that in the event of the Old Union officials refusing to recognise the results that Unity would not be achieved, and in that event the position was problematical as to whether a big influx of Old Union members to the Reform Union would take place. In fact they openly stated that the Reform Union members should "Wait and See" as Unity might be obtained in a matter of months or maybe a year and if a crisis did arise during that time the United Front would come as the men would then override all the official mandates against the course.

Only about 70 attended the meeting, which had been widely advertised for the past fortnight, and which certainly demonstrates that neither Hodge nor Smith have a big following in this district. The meeting did not show much feeling and I certainly made a bloomer by not moving a resolution calling on the Scottish Trades Union Congress to bring pressure on the Scottish Miners' Executive to convene a Unity Conference between the Reform Union and the Old Union, the Basis to be discussion of the Card Vote. It would certainly have shown what effect the discussion had. However, judging by the results of the last meeting addressed by Hodge in Methil, when I was put in the pillory for advocating Unity, we have nothing to fear from this one. Smith has certainly given good grounds for expulsion from the Party, and I think the District Party Committee should tackle the question as quickly as possible. J. Stewart "agrees with the Minority Movement suggestion" but thinks "the Kelty idea should get a chance".

You will notice by the Paragraph in "The Spark" that we will have the question of the Party and the Labour Party arising at our next meeting of the Trades and Labour Council. Comrade O'Neil, chairman of the Council, immediately after the adoption of candidates requested the Council to submit his nomination to the Branches. He did this "off his own bat" and after I taxed him for an explanation he said he had got information (too late to discuss with us) that the question was to be raised and he decided to make the move first to take the wind out of the other fellows' sails. As if any change had been made since last year, and he was elected Chairman of the Council in March and known as a Party member.

I understand from my "butty" that he has had a questionnaire from the Labour Research Department re rates, etc., in this Burgh. He feels rather flattered and will get the necessary information.

Wednesday night: Will meet a German comrade tomorrow. His ship is in Methil every 5 or 6 weeks. He is to get stuff across but I don't think he will have any this trip as since leaving Methil he has been to Denmark and some British ports.

Notice by tonight's paper that the Fascisti have been at the highly dangerous game of removing the Bookshop sign. Have heard rumours of a branch being formed here but can't get definite information. Some of the names connected with it are likely starters. 2 or 3 were at school with me and right snivellers they are. Bright lads with small 2½d. businesses and have as much idea of their social position as a pig has of a starched shirt.

Good luck to Harry Pollitt. Have thought about that line but stopped at that, and have reached the stage when I compliment myself when I hear "His mother bred a jibber".

Thursday night: So "Jix" has got started.[142] Notice in this morning's and tonight's Press reports of the arrests.[143] Tom Wintringham is described in tonight's *Edinburgh Evening News* as "a young intellectual looking man who seemed rather bored at the proceedings in Court". The usual bloody gush, how the prisoners appeared, dress, demeanour, etc. Nothing about the case other than headlines — Raid on Reds. I expect this will have caused a dislocation at King Street for a short time. Will see the others of the Local Party Committee at the weekend and see about running a special of "The Spark". By the way we have received this week's issue of the *Weekly*. Expect you will have more work.

Enclosed 2 copies of No. 7 "The Spark", one for Page. This typewriter is an improvement on the other. You will notice we have given the *Labour Monthly* prominence this issue.

Will send on receipt Nos., dates, etc., of accounts from *Weekly* and Bookshop at weekend.

October 16th, 1925.

Enclosed 6 copies *Workers' Weekly*. Should you require more let me know and if we have any unsolds will send them on.

4 Policemen were at the Wellesley today — 3 P.C.s and 1 Sergeant — and remained for ½ an hour. They seemed surprised at the *Weekly* being on sale. Sold 29/6d. [worth] of literature, despite their presence — *Workers' Weekly*, "The Spark" and pamphlets.

Notice by Press that bail has been granted.[144] This should shake up some of the supposed Left Wingers who have any guts.

October 18th, 1925.

Excuse brevity of note as I haven't time to write more at present. Hope you received copies of *Weekly* all right. If you can manage you might insert the following in this week's *Workers' Weekly*:

> Methil Branch, Reform Union, calls on the General Council, T.U.C., to rally all the Working Class forces in Great Britain to demand the immediate discharge of the Communists arrested for "sedition", i.e., carrying out a working class policy.

We also call on the Parliamentary Labour Party to carry on an intensive and if necessary obstructive policy in the House of Commons until those old anti-working class Acts are repealed.

We contend that if the Working Class movement in Britain allows the present prosecutions to go unchallenged that no working class leader will be immune from arrest in the future.

The above resolution was passed unanimously at Methil Reform Union branch meeting, and the Secretary instructed to send a copy to the T.U.C. and the Labour Party. It is also to be raised at the Trades and Labour Council meeting on Thursday.

The police here are paying 3 of us some extra attention this past week. 2 Comrades report that an almost continuous watch is being kept on their houses.

Sorry am unable to send on receipts, accounts, etc., re *Workers' Weekly* and Bookshop as the Comrade responsible had an addition to his family yesterday (Saturday), making No. 6. He is to try and get them ready during the week.

October 24th, 1925.

Short Note with *The Miner*. Notice they have made other arrests, Page amongst them. It certainly shows that although we haven't as yet got a Mass Party that the policy advocated has more than riled our "superiors".

The resolution passed by Methil Reform Union was also endorsed by the Trades and Labour Council on Thursday night. We hold a protest meeting tonight in Leven.

A curious position arose at the Trades and Labour Council meeting. By 33 votes to 30 Comrade O'Neil was deposed from the chair, but by 40 votes to 2 the 3 Comrades were endorsed as official Labour candidates for the Parish Council.[145] 4 branches did not vote on the 2nd issue but intended to run candidates in opposition to the official bunch. They after considerable discussion agreed to hold special meetings on Sunday to try and induce their branches to fall in line with the Trades and Labour Council decisions. They are 3 branches of the Old Union and Buckhaven Labour Association — a most reactionary bunch who in discussions object to the word "Socialism' being used.

Tom Kennedy is anticipating the extinction of the S.D.F. as a move is on the boards to get him adopted as candidate of the Divisional Labour Party at the next election. S.D.F. unable to meet all of last election expenses.

You will notice by *The Miner* that P. Hodge refuses to publish the Party's position on the Fife split. He is some tit-bit.

Kirker has got 6 months, and in giving evidence Hodge made some holy bloomers which will be used with some effect against himself by the Old Union.

Will have to close as we are on No. 8 of "The Spark" today. Give Page and the others my best wishes and assurances of getting a move on here. Hope Comrade Mrs Hutt is now all right.

October 29th, 1925.

Thanks very much for copy of *Economic Position of Coal Industry* and letter of 26th.

As you remark this case should be a good medium for propaganda if the Press doesn't muzzle it. Already some of the papers here are only giving a short general report of the proceedings, omitting the cross-examination of police witnesses by Comrades Pollitt, Bell and Campbell.

Another Comrade and one U know held a fairly successful protest meeting last Saturday. 4 policemen present and unable to get names of speakers (although advertised) from any of the crowd. The resolution passed at Methil Reform Union branch and the Trades and Labour Council meetings was carried. I expect the District Party Committee will have sent in a report to Headquarters for the *Weekly*.

I have had a great week, working from 6 a.m. to 10 p.m. for 3 days due to my butty being away on a deputation to Manchester re vertical retorts for the local Gas Works (Municipal).

We are making some headway with subscriptions to Defence Fund.

Enclosed No. 8 "The Spark" (2 copies), "The Signal", and 2 half-yearly Co-operative Balance sheets for Page. I still have the baby to hold. No endeavour on the part of the others to get a move on. What do you think of the cartoons in this issue?

See by today's Press that case "comes up" again on Tuesday. T. Bell seemed to get in a good one yesterday (Wednesday).

You sized up the Lanarkshire comrade's attitude re Unity in Fife. If anything the Reform Union diehard position has been strengthened by Smith's appointment and the District Party Committee is too damned timid. Seem afraid to make a move in the direction indicated by the Bowhill decision. Of course they probably realise that outside 6 at most the decision was only a pious resolution.

According to press reports one Union for Scottish mineworkers will soon be an accomplished fact and the Reform Union will have to face a situation they at present consider BALLS, viz., instead of Adamson and Company being the opposition it will be the Scottish.

A district meeting held in Buckhaven last Sunday of the Reform Union East Fife local Committee addressed by Hodge decided to continue poaching Old Union members to increase the Reform Union "bargaining powers", and despite protests from Methil (who by the way are now known as the Reform Union REACTIONARIES) entirely ignored the non-unionists.

Hope Comrade Mrs Hutt is now A.1.

November 7th, 1925.

A hurried note with *The Miner*. Notice that the case is to go to the High Court. More interest is being focussed on it due to the release of the 3 Fascists for the *Daily Herald* stunt.[146] You ought to hear some of the expressions anent the 2 cases, and what is very hopeful to us is the amount of abuse directed against Tom Kennedy for his statements — "that we should ignore the Fascists".

We had an aggregate meeting last Sunday at Bowhill, Mrs Crawfurd being there. I was the only member from Methil and reported to the Group when I got home. They are a curious lot. Wouldn't have anything to do with protest meetings under the group auspices at present. Decided to try the Trades and Labour Council first. As only 2 of us would be on the box they considered it would be foolish to take risks until we had tried the Trades and Labour Council. We are doing fairly well with the Defence Fund.

The local elections here resulted in No Change in the Town Council, 2 official Labour being returned, 1 renegade Labour, and 1 Independent (4 wards). The Trades and Labour Council ran 9 candidates in the Parish for 9 seats, 3 Party members amongst them. We managed 7 seats, 2 comrades — McArthur and O'Neil — being successful. Let Page know that Jamie Stewart was returned to Lochgelly Town Council under the auspices of Lochgelly Trades and Labour Council, which was only recently formed. If J. Dick[147] hasn't reported those results you might get them inserted in the *Weekly*.

We are still keeping up our sales, almost £27 last month.

Other reductions threatened at the Wellesley. 1 without notice from 4/1¾d. to 2/9 per quantity. Another from 10/- per yard to 5/-, and 3/- to 2/- per yard. Notices of dismissal and no reason given. Manager refuses to discuss, and no response from the men at present.

November 11th, 1925.

Am commencing this note tonight to try and give you some idea how things are going here, as I have only been able to write you a few short notes recently. So far as the group is concerned it is "as you were", with the exception that I have resigned the leadership because I was unable to get into personal touch with every member and the group meetings were becoming a farce. A comrade whose work (credit draper) brings him into contact with practically every one of them is now group leader, although I have still the same amount of work to carry. We have managed to get one more comrade to distribute the *Workers' Weekly*. He does about 4 dozen in a district we organised 7 months ago. This will allow us to get a move on towards organising another district.

I mentioned in my last note about the reductions which had taken place at the Wellesley. You will get the points of it in No. 9 of "The Spark". The manager is playing a bold game and has refused to meet P. Hodge, who was down on Tuesday. It was a case that can be brought to and won in the Courts but it would be a damned lot better if we could get the Wellesley men to stand together and win it by themselves, but they are cowering at present. You can imagine what some of them who are involved in another reduction are like — yardages for cutting from 10/- to 5/- and back brushing from 3/- to 2/- ("Cutting" is paid by the yard and means payment for progress of headings and levels. Back brushing is taking part of the roof down to allow tubs to "run".); and although I pleaded with them to appoint a deputation to interview the manager they refused. Reason fairly obvious — afraid. Others received notice of dismissal and he refused to tell them why they were sacked. Can you beat it?

You will possibly think when you see No. 9 of "The Spark" that we are devoting too much space to Brown[148] and that it looks more like a vendetta between him and us than Communist Party propaganda, but the main thing we have to try at the Wellesley is to point out that Brown is only a puppet (and a damned cowardly one at that) and by those means to get a little more militancy in the Wellesley workers. We have been on steady time for the past 6 weeks and the idea has got abroad that everything is O.K.

We managed to get 2 Comrades elected to the Parish Council (Wemyss), O'Neil and McArthur. The latter is he "who cannot take any active Party work until the Union split is healed". He was with J. Stewart representing the Reform Union at the Minority Conference, and is rather doubtful as to accepting the Party policy re the Split. O'Neil is Group leader.

From information I have got this week it appears the local elections have to some extent helped to pave the way to an understanding between the 2 branches of the Unions in Buckhaven. Previously they were bitter enemies but I understand the Old Union are now agreeable to a joint meeting to discuss the Kelty proposition.

It is also widely rumoured that the Old Union have decided to insert Periodical Elections of full-time officials in their rules and Constitution, exact period to be arranged by the sub-executive. If it is a fact I expect Adamson and Company will refuse to negotiate on the grounds that there is no difference between the 2 Constitutions and that the Reform Union members can come into the Old Union when they so desire. On the other hand it may be a ruse on Adamson's part to appease a few of the branches who have been supporting "Periodical Elections" until the Scottish Union is formed, when in all probability "Periodical Elections" will not be part of the Constitution.

I was at a meeting arranged by the Scottish T.U.C. at Kirkcaldy about a fortnight ago and W. Elger, Secretary, and Duncan, Chairman of the Scottish T.U.C. were present.[149] It was dealing with the need for setting up Trade Union Committees. Naturally the Fife split was mentioned and Elger stated that if it wasn't healed by December 9th (date of meeting to consider 1 Miners' Union for Scotland) pressure would be brought to bear which would compel a remedy.

I also attended a meeting of Fife District Party Committee that night and they are certainly timid about trying to put into operation the Bowhill decision re the split. Their attitude, which I attacked, is "Assist by all means the Kelty proposition but point out that it will not be successful". They call this spineless attitude BOLSHEVIK TACTICS and try to justify it by comparing it with the Party's policy to Parliament. If they had tried to get the Bowhill decision applied and been defeated there would have in my opinion been some justification in assisting to demonstrate the futility of the Kelty proposition but at the same time pointing out the need to come to the Bowhill decision to get Unity. However, I was once more in the glorious ? minority. How in hell's name we in Methil are to carry out the above decision (District Party Committee's) beats me as the Old Union crowd here will not reply to any invitation sent them by the Reform Union. It appears we have unlimited time at our disposal to monkey about with propositions which we consider "tripe".

The Reform Union have resolutions to discuss this month re the arrests. I understand there are 3 proposals, 1 for £50, 1 for £20, and 1 for £5 for the Party Defence Fund.

I notice in the *Sunday Worker* that Comrades R. P. Dutt and Moorhouse have been arrested in Brussels.[150] And it has repeatedly been asserted that the Communist Party of Great Britain is of no consequence! We here have no inside information and have to base our opinions re the likely development of the "case" on the meagre Press reports, and have come to the conclusion that a year at least will be the dose dished out. Get 'em out of the way for May. How are they all sticking it?

Have got another cartoonist. Might have some of his work in No. 10 of "The Spark". Not a Party member. The old firm are still carrying the load. Received No. 20 of Nine Elms "Spark"[151] and No. 8 of "Sawdust". We have them on the run for cartoons. Enclosed No. 8 of "Sawdust" and No. 6 of "The Signal" for Page.

I expect Dutt's arrest will cause more work to be piled on you if it is possible to manage it.

One of the annual circuses would take place today in London: Cenotaph, Unknown Warrior, artificial Poppies, and 2 minutes' silence. Only a few of the unco' respectable and a few other weak minds take any notice of it here, or at least parade their bloody hypocrisy.

I have managed to get another comrade to take my order of *Inprecorr*. If he hadn't taken it on I would have cancelled the order, as the Bookshop were playing a rotten game — sending my accounts along with others to another comrade and at other times sending me those accounts with others due to be paid by the literature secretary, and ignoring our requests to send separate receipts.

Thursday night: See by tonight's paper that the trial commences on Monday.

Enclosed 2 copies of No. 9 "The Spark", 1 for Page. What do you think of the latest development in the Wellesley reduction? Brown[152] has taken the coal-cutting machine out today and issued notices re reduction, thus giving his hand away for his last week's action. And the real tit-bit is the section affected WILL BE FINISHED BEFORE THE NOTICES EXPIRE.

November 20th, 1925.

Short note with *The Miner*. Notice by tonight's paper case adjourned till Monday. Cross-Examination by Pollitt, Campbell and Gallacher getting well home. Pity more of it isn't published. Good idea to get it in pamphlet form. Expect you will be up to the ears at present.

What do you think of the cartoons in No. 9 of "The Spark"? It caused some stir at the Wellesley. Had demands for it up till today. We are printing 700 copies of No. 10. Nearly involved in libel action re paragraph on "Palace", Methil. The manager sent for me on Tuesday night and threatened an action. He hadn't seen the certificate until I showed it him. I got the mother of the girl to meet him and she admitted he hadn't seen it, although she previously told me that he had. I agreed to withdraw that sentence and the manager said it was immaterial, he would proceed with the case. I then made for the door, asking him if he would pay the wages due. He refused to answer and I informed him that the statement he objected to as being untrue in No. 9 would be truthful in No. 10. He immediately "gave in", offered his hand and called me a "sport". Oh, Christ. However, you will notice the correction in No. 10.[153]

We have A. Geddes in Fife for an organising campaign. He was in West Fife for this past week.[154]

You might ask Comrade Beauchamp to let me know if I should return the 31 extra copies sent a few days after order of the November *Labour Monthly*. I am afraid it will be impossible to get them sold. Instead of 91 copies I received 134 copies.

November 24th, 1925.

Received your letter of 22nd November today and having a few minutes tonight am commencing reply. J. R. Campbell, according to the *Herald* report, has certainly been slipping the stuff across. Opinions re the result of case are changing here. Due possibly to the case for the defence, but as you remark it is rather premature to voice an opinion. Sorry that Page isn't too well.

Enclosed No. 7 of "The Signal" and a pamphlet written by my butty for Page.

We have Comrade A. Geddes with us this week. So far our meetings have met with little success, due mainly to insufficient time to get halls, therefore badly advertised, and the rotten damp foggy weather. However, literature sales are still good, and a fairly good response to contribute to the Defence Fund. I have collected almost £3.10/- and still making headway. Some of the others are doing A.1. In addition I have sold over 150 P.C. and the other comrades are getting them away fairly easy. Comrade Geddes like others is puzzled at this locality — good literature sales, ready response with financial assistance, but no inclination to join up. He attributes it to the comparatively better position of the East Fife miners to the majority outside — little unemployment, fairly steady work, and due to the nature of the coal seams, slightly above the average wage.

Thanks very much for the tip re side box head for "The Spark". You are correct about having too much stuff on and also across the page but I sometimes have to rush it and across is not only easier but quicker. I haven't had any criticism here. When I bring the matter up at the group meetings and ask for criticisms, all that is said is "It's great; carry on". Enough to make one have a burst scalp. Some are *kind* enough to think and say that I am asking for compliments when I raise the matter, but don't seem to be inclined to follow up by writing or even giving any information to write about. We are doing 700 of No. 10, which I had just finished cutting when I received your letter. The front page cartoon is by our 2nd cartoonist. Not as neat a job as No. 1 does, but the idea is clear enough.

"The Underworld" is at present out owing to the comrade who managed it leaving the district, and "The Torch" is unable to appear because of lack of premises for printing. Nothing more has been heard of the Bowhill 16 printed pager. Jock Bird appears to have forgotten it.

Enclosed 7 of the pamphlets issued by the Wemyss Coal Company to officials only. I have a collection of the others but think you will have enough when you read the enclosed.

From what I can gather the Old Union have decided on periodical elections every 5 years, and ADAMSON IS TO RESIGN IN JANUARY. NOMINATIONS TO BE SENT IN. Wullie[155] will not have any OPPOSITION and will therefore be SECURE for 5 YEARS. You would notice a rehash of the 1921-22 events which caused the split, in the last issue of *The Miner*. THAT is Smith and Hodge's platform stuff — living in 1922. "No compromise, only one Union in Fife but it MUST BE the REFORM UNION", is their SLOGAN, with some support in the Executive. On the other hand they are antagonising a few who took a stand against us. One of those chaps is now off at the deep end — "LIQUIDATE the Reform Union" — and the Party in Fife is as much confused as the others. No co-ordinated policy — each for himself. J. Stewart is chairman and 2 other Party members on the Sub Executive. Great life this.

Friday morning: The sentences have caused a flutter here and the 7 refusing to be "bound over" by leaving the Party has made a great impression.[156] I haven't time to write much more at present as I shall have to get along to the Wellesley with the *Workers' Weekly* and "The Spark". Expect record sales today. Will send on copy of "The Spark" and any other matter for Labour Research Department c/o you. P.S. Saw G. Allison for a few minutes yesterday.[157] Enclosed statement re Bookshop and *Workers' Weekly* from our Literature Secretary. The article on Thomas[158] and the Workers' Alliance in "The Signal" has caused some commotion in N.U.R. circles here. I sent it and the curious part is THAT NONE OF Methil N.U.R. members ARE IN THE MINORITY MOVEMENT.

November 30th, 1925.
Owing to the hellish weather we are having up here at present I am having a night indoors, drafting a scheme of organisation for the local Trades and Labour Council. Enclosed copy of same. What do you think of it?

Sorry I hadn't time to reply to some of the points in your letter, but the brutal facts are I am tackling more than I am capable of performing successfully. General complaint of Party members at present, I suppose.

The sentences have roused the Labour Movement as nothing else has done for some time, if it has ever been equalled. The Party SHOULD make something out of this case. We had a special meeting of the Methil Trades and

Labour Council last night, dealing with some of the "ratters" at the recent local elections. From the bourgeois standpoint it was a very unedifying spectacle, but it was a striving by those who, although not belonging to the Party, were actually trying to instill the Communist Party discipline into an organisation composed of umpteen different political viewpoints and leanings. After the business for which the meeting had been called, was disposed of, we introduced the Communist Party case and the need for protests, demonstrations, and organisation to meet this attack on the working class movement. It was moved by an S.D.F.er to hold a protest meeting on SUNDAY, December 13th, but when it came to getting speakers, I was the only one who could be got. I was also moved to act as chairman. It isn't as what would appear at first sight — cowardice — but a lack of confidence to speak in public. However, George, the meeting will take place.

Was at the District Party Committee meeting on Saturday and according to instructions am appearing at the Reform Union Executive meeting on Wednesday to raise the position of the Reform Union re the need for Unity, IMMEDIATE UNITY AT ANY PRICE, due to the recent development in the Old Union — periodical elections, and financial vote, and the formation of One Union for Scotland. Comrade Geddes was there and suggested that he and I should have an interview with the Political Bureau re the Fife Split, and a definite lead given which would bring the split to a close and so give the Party a chance to be built up in Fife.

The position as I see it has only one solution — Liquidation of the Reform Union. Adamson has queered their pitch, assisted by themselves, due to their advocacy of the Kelty stunt, which has in my opinion compelled Adamson to accept Periodical elections to appease a few of his big branches; but the actual acceptance and putting into operation of same has reduced the Reform Union bargaining strength and increased Adamson's. "No need to negotiate no difference in Constitutions", "Come inside, we are not keeping you out". Will try and make most of this point. Moral — Can do more inside.[159]

Tuesday night: That is the position as it affects the Reform Union points. There is also the move to form one Union for Scotland. The Conference is due on December 19th and no Reform Union representatives will be there, and as far as I can gather Fife Old Union is keen on the proposal. You will have noticed the Scottish section Executive Miners' Minority Movement suggestion in last issue of *The Worker*. I expect Hodge will play on that tomorrow. Comrade Geddes has formed the same opinion as me — the District Party Committee has been too timid and confused the Party members in Fife. If the Political Bureau agrees to meet us, I will give you a "look up".

We had rotten luck with the last issue of "The Spark", stencils tearing and other misfortunes. Re the picture of the young lady reading "The Spark", it was put in for a fill up. The Wemyss Coal Company are getting annoyed at what is appearing, but so far no attempt has been made to stop its sale at the Wellesley.

Had, as I expected, record sale last Friday. £2.4.3d. for *Workers' Weekly* and "Spark". It is impossible to imagine ALL that and the rest making no impression even if it was the same individuals who are reading it, which is certainly not the case. If it was confined to the same lot we should have some well informed chaps in this man's town.

Today's leader in the *Daily Herald* appears rather hopeful regarding the release of the 12. They must have good information or are merely playing the usual game of the pure Parliamentarian, Parliament will right all wrongs, and by so doing taking all the sting out of the agitation going on at present.

Hope you managed to get some satisfaction out of the list of accounts we sent you.

You are quite correct to keep the contacts made. Who is going to challenge that they are responsible for a good deal of the support the Party is getting at present, without considering their value in the near future.

I expect you will have seen Comrade Allison this week, and will be in possession of more details re the Party and some of its immediate tasks in Fife.

SCHEME OF ORGANISATION

Owing to the decline of Capitalism, with its accompanying deterioration of the workers' standard of life; political intrigues of opposing groups of Imperialists for markets and sources of raw materials, which make for wars; increasing unemployment, and other social evils — bad housing, high rents, heavy infantile mortality, etc., we consider it is absolutely essential that the workers and their wives should be made cognisant of the policy of the LABOUR MOVEMENT in regard to those affairs and their significance to the workers' every day life.

In the past it has been considered sufficient to hold a few meetings at election periods, Parliamentary and Local, at which the policy of the movement, however brilliant or otherwise it has been stated had only a PASSING INFLUENCE on the mind of the average worker. Another phase arising from that was and is — A committee large or small was organised for the purpose of distributing election literature and canvassing votes. After the election those committees were either disbanded or kept intact until the next election by means of socials and whist drives.

We agree with the need for keeping intact those committees but are of the opinion that their services should be utilised for more purposes than that of election committees. We therefore submit the following as a basis of organisation which will be the most effective for enlightening the workers and thereby rallying them to the Labour standard.

(1) As Ward Committees are the Unit of residential representation, being composed of ALL Trade Unionists and/or members of affiliated political organisations to the Trades and Labour Council resident in the ward, we therefore recommend that the present ACTIVE MEMBERS of the

Ward Committees make a thorough canvass of their respective Wards for the purpose of augmenting their numbers.

(2) Ward meetings (well advertised) should then be held, at which ALL members capable of speaking from a platform should be enrolled as speakers for back court meetings to deal with current political and economic questions, from the viewpoint of the LABOUR MOVEMENT. As illustrations we submit the following — Locarno Pact, Unemployment, Suppression of Free Speech, 100% Trade Unionism, International Trade Union Unity, Workers' Defence Corps (need for), Fascist Menace, Rent Restrictions Act, Co-operatives, Support of Labour Candidates at ALL elections, etc. Speakers should be allocated specific subjects and so be able to give a lucid statement. 15 minute speeches and time allowed for questions. All speakers to be GIVEN GENERAL DIRECTION BY THE TRADES AND LABOUR COUNCIL. Speakers could be exchanged amongst the Wards.

As the importance to the Working Class Movement of the Wives, Mothers, and Sisters of the workers is becoming more manifest not only as potential voters for Labour at elections, but actively participating in the big struggles which are impending in the industrial field, and as they are unable, due to domestic and other causes, to attend Labour meetings held in halls, we consider the back court meetings absolutely necessary to reach them with the Labour policy.

Ward Committees could also carry on their social activities, i.e., socials, whist drives, and where it is possible organise choirs, adult and juvenile, to popularise Labour songs. Occasional rallies in Methil, Buckhaven, and Denbeath alternately. Business meetings of the Ward Committees under the auspices of the Trades and Labour Council to exchange methods of work and results therefrom.

We consider the brief outline of our scheme to be sufficient to convey to the affiliated branches the results of such activities, viz., increased interest in the Labour Movement, MORE ACTIVE WORKERS as a result of that increased interest, both of which would stimulate the Movement locally and nationally, and would also "cut out" the need for so much canvassing at election periods.

THE HISTORIC MISSION OF THE WORKING CLASS IS TO OVERTHROW CAPITALISM. TO DO SO EFFECTIVELY REQUIRES AN INTELLIGENT, INFORMED, AND ACTIVE SECTION OF THE WORKING CLASS. MAKE THAT SECTION AS LARGE AS POSSIBLE BY ORGANISED EFFORT, ADOPT AND PUT INTO OPERATION THE ABOVE SCHEME!!!

December 8th, 1925.

Thanks for yours of 4th December. Am commencing the reply tonight so as to give you some idea how things are getting along here.

Re the local group: we haven't held a group meeting since I resigned [as] Group Leader, but the work is proceeding as usual. Some of the local comrades are not playing the game and are in my opinion trying to get an easy way out of the Party. However, if they go it won't damage the Party, as those referred to have only amounted to dead weight. The sentences *might* have something to do with their shyness. But whatever they have or have not been there is no denying the fairly obvious fact that the Party counts here and is looking like counting EVERYTHING. Although our meetings are sparsely attended and no rush is being made to join, one can notice that the Communist Party is a BIG Factor here, and to give Johnny Brown and the Wemyss Coal Company their dues, they are assisting greatly with their recent attacks.

Was at the Reform Union Executive Meeting last Wednesday and had what I considered a field day. The Sub Executive had forward a recommendation: 3 rank and file members from each Union under a neutral chairman to draw up a constitution. The method to be adopted to get it into operation is by BIG DEMONSTRATIONS at which it is expected the Old Union members will get enthusiastic and go to their branch meetings and compel their officials to agree. I had almost ¾ hour explaining Methil Reform Union position in regard to the recent developments. Periodical Elections in Old Union would stiffen more rather than draw Old Union local officials to Reform Union proposals. Reform Union in cold re One Union for Scotland, and when formed Reform Union would have to parley with Scottish and not Adamson and Company, and Reform Union could not hold out against them. All Reform Union propaganda which was successful in Old Union was further weakening Reform Union position as it strengthened Old Union, and the fact that Reform Union could influence Old Union outside presupposed that inside Old Union were those who were favourable to Reform Union policy. Why not join hands INSIDE and PUSH ALL Reform Union Policy? Impending crisis demanded UNITY even at PRICE (which wasn't much) of existence of Reform Union. Time short and no indications of Old Union or Scottish being prepared to parley. Indications otherwise and recent events justified assumption that no Conference would take place. Conditions at Pits becoming worse. Managers doing as they liked and in the majority of cases both Reform Union and Old Union committees manoeuvring from Union standpoints with the results men beaten. Union's strength and prestige lay in maintaining conditions at Pit and not in paper constitutions. Other points, and finished with moving Reform Union liquidation. It was received without any noise and very weak opposition from Hodge and Smith, who both made personal attacks on me. Smith is the best living example of the rapid evolution from a supposed rank and file revolutionary to something worse (you might think it impossible) than J. H. Thomas. Positively stinks. And was (perhaps is still) a Party member. Tried to draw a parallel between the Communist Party and Reform Union with of course the Query, "Did David Proudfoot advocate the liquidation of the

Communist Party?" Liquidation received 4 votes, 2 Branch and 2 Delegate. The proposals will be discussed at the Branches this month and the BRANCH DECISIONS will NOT BE ACTED ON THIS YEAR as the next Board meeting takes place on December 30th. So much for the Reform Union's desire for Unity as expressed by its high heid yins. 1 month wasted.

My candid opinion, George, is that a campaign in favour of liquidation would be successful. The difference of the reception I received when advocating liquidation last week and 21 months ago when advocating the all-in ballot was very marked. In the latter case I was howled at but in the former was given a quiet hearing. Unity is desired NOW and it is necessary to drive home a definite scheme which shows in theory some measure of attaining success. Reform Union granted £50 to Defence Fund, 100 *Circulars* from Labour Research Department monthly.

Enclosed No. 8 of "The Signal" and Jock Bird's election address. Bird was successful in both the County and Parish Council Elections. At least 4 Parish Councils in Fife are now dominated by Labour. We have a good number of Party members on various Parish Councils in Fife.

Noticed Frankie Hodges's attitude at Amsterdam. Give me a worse term than "BASTARD" and I'll dub him with it.[160]

Wednesday forenoon: Enclosed 2 Copies of No. 11 of "The Spark".

The police have been unusually active recently re the printing of "The Spark". They visited a printing place recently opened by a Wellesley night shift gaffer but admitted they couldn't discover "a machine like the one that prints 'The Spark' ". Poor dears, as if we would allow a pit gaffer to print it.

A special meeting of District Party Committee to discuss the Party position re the split on Saturday first.

We have received an account from the *Weekly* for November. 88 Quires @ 1/6d. per Quire = £3.12/-, which will give you some idea re their bookkeeping. Actually we only received 85 Quires and have repeatedly instructed them to send only 17 Quires per week as we cannot get across any more. (I tackle 30 dozen but can't always manage the lot, and find it impossible to try new ground.) We are therefore charged for unsolds which wouldn't happen if they would PAY ATTENTION to OUR ORDER.

Glad to know the 12 are keeping well. If you should visit them let them know I was "asking for them" and that things are beginning to hum here.

December 13th, 1925.[161]

Dear Comrade,

Enclosed £1.18/6d for 7 dozen *Labour Monthly* of November issue. Sorry at delay in payment but owing to extra copies, I gave some to 2 comrades who have returned cash and unsolds today. Their efforts have not resulted in the need for increasing our order, but they are now prepared to try a few copies per month. Send 7 dozen of January issue.

P.S. You might let Comrade Hutt know our protest meeting came off tonight. About 300 of an audience. I was the only speaker on the platform at the commencement of the meeting, but after I finished other 2 speakers, 1 a Party member and another N.U.R. branch Secretary, spoke from the platform.

December 18th, 1925.

A brief note with *The Miner*. The District Party Committee turned down Reform Union liquidation meantime and agreed to press for Unity Conference (as suggested by Smillie[162] to W. Elger, Secretary, Scottish General Council Trades Union Congress, almost two weeks ago) and agree to conditions if they were no more humiliating than previously offered by Scottish. One of our local comrades, who is a member of Reform Union Sub Executive and does NO PARTY WORK had the bloody cheek to move that the meeting instruct me to take over Methil Reform Union delegateship and so add to the Party strength on the Reform Union Executive Board. I agreed if he would relieve me of "The Spark" or some of my present work, but he wasn't prepared to do anything. Others tried to press the meeting but I absolutely refused unless and until some of the Methil local were prepared to take over some of my present work. The idea behind this move is for me to make ALL the running and accept ALL the abuse while some of the Party members on the Board lie back and are able to kow-tow with P. Hodge. (Comrade Joss represented Executive at District Party Committee, and stated the Executive had decided Unity must be obtained even if it meant Reform Union liquidation.) Methil being a residential branch also means that as before I would have to deal with disputes in which Methil members were involved at 13 Pits and Mines, some of them over 5 miles away and no conveyance to them. I am prepared to tackle it but only on condition that some of the others "take over". If I left some of the present work (as I would have to if I took over the delegateship) it would be lost and possibly not be built up again.

We held the protest meeting. Almost 300 attended. A Concert with Pictures 60 yards along the street spoiled our show as far as numbers were concerned but we had a fairly successful meeting. The S.D.F., to show they were with us, held a meeting of their own at the same time as ours, although it was one of their number who moved the Protest meeting be held. Valiant champions of "Democracy". I spoke for almost an hour and had a great reception. It was suggested from the body of the hall that other members of the Trades and Labour Council should also air their views. Comrade McArthur (the comrade above referred to) spoke from the platform for 15 minutes as also did the N.U.R. Secretary — non-Party. 2 others had a go in the body of the hall and vomited SEDITION. It was great, with 5 plain clothes policemen sitting with their ears flapping. A resolution calling for a Joint Conference of General Council T.U.C., Labour Party and Co-operative to call a general strike if release of 12 and Ammanford Miners wasn't granted.[163] A good sprinkling of women were there, which is a good sign.

S.D.F. had resolution for expulsion of Communist Party members from Trades and Labour Council last night. Referred to branches.

Signs of a breakaway from Trades and Labour Council by Old Union branches and Buckhaven Labour Association, which is composed of Buckhaven Old Union officials and some members and wives. See No. 12 "Spark". Won't affect Trades and Labour Council in Methil.

Agreed to run meeting under Council auspices with Y.C.L. speaker.

Tried a new stunt at Wellesley last Friday and today. Collecting Box hung round my neck for Defence Fund — 17/3d last Friday and 12/- today. Weather hellish, soaked to skin with rain last week and snow and sleet today. Collected almost £6 altogether. No lull in Class War due to rotten weather.

An attempt is being made to run another Pit Paper in Kirkcaldy, "The Hutch".[164] I have had to assist with No. 1, which is expected to be out this weekend. Will send on a copy.

The Secretary of the Trades and Labour Council, Albert Duncan, N.U.R. and ex-Party member, is to attend Central Labour College for 18 months, arriving in London January 6th.[165] Will give him address of *Monthly*, where he can "look you up". Good worker and should be kept in sight.

Hope you are getting along all right in your new billet. P.S. Pit Committee idea catching on at Wellesley due to manager's actions. No payment for deficiencies, etc. Will hold a meeting early in New Year and get Committee set up.

December 24th, 1925.

Enclosed 2 copies of "Spark", 1 copy of "The Signal" and 1 copy (No. 1) of "The Hutch", the latter being the "Underworld's" successor, Kirkcaldy group — 150 copies printed.

Received a note from R. Stewart today asking me to report at 16 King Street on January 9th and 10th. Will arrive on Saturday morning, January 9th. As I haven't a timetable handy I can't state exact time. Expect to see you. Will let you know time of train's arrival in note with *The Miner*.

Have got Fife District Party Committee departmentalised and put some comrades who have been "dodging the column" into some of the posts. Comrade Geddes was responsible for organisation.

Wednesday Reform Union Executive meeting should decide how latest Party decision re Split has been taken by Party members. I haven't got any fresh information since I last wrote you.

What do you think of "The Hutch"? The tit-bit about its production is that although there are a few miners in the group a non-miner comrade is responsible for it. I cut the stencils in No. 1 and in No. 2 but I understand they will now manage themselves. "The Spark" is more clear now, we having discovered what was wrong — Inking sheet getting clogged, and we now change it every stencil. Your tip has greatly improved it also. "The Signal" is now on the cartoon hunch as you will see. I will let Albert Duncan (the N.U.R. chap who is to be at the Central Labour College for 18 months) know I am coming to London and arrange to meet him and let you know one another. Can be useful.

You will notice our challenge to Methil S.D.F. in this issue. They are demanding our expulsion again despite the recent decision of the Council.

Matter referred to affiliated branches. Their delegate couldn't answer one question as to the reason for the motion. There is more in it than appears on the surface. As you will also notice in "The Spark", Buckhaven Old Union have withdrawn from Council and behind them is Buckhaven Labour Association, which is controlled by them, being composed mainly of their active membership and wives, although no intimation has as yet been given of the Association's withdrawal. As they are the bunch who are usually pulling wires with the Divisional ex-secretary (an S.D.F.er) and a dirty little scut even for such a body, I anticipate an attempt being made to form a new Trades and Labour Council with the 3 Old Union branches, Labour Association and S.D.F. branch as its basis. Another peculiar point in this situation is the leading S.D.F.ers are members of Denbeath Reform Union branch, but their Union antagonisms are submerged when it is a case of "having a go at the Communists". The real and only solution to this problem, George, is One Union in Fife, when we will be able to control the 3 branches in this district and so prevent this mess recurring at the Trades and Labour Council. Comrade O'Neil, who was put out of the chair 2 months ago, has again been re-elected. Great world this.

Branches have under consideration formation of Workers' Defence Corps. Will be decided at next monthly meeting. I don't expect much from it at present.

Put scheme of organisation to last meeting but it was referred back for discussion at next meeting. "Nero fiddled while Rome was burning."

Met a German comrade on Sunday who was one of leaders during Sailors' Strike in 1924. Poor English (but better than my German), so couldn't get much from him.

December 31st, 1925.

Thanks for yours of 25th and 27th. Have "knocked off" for 3 days and intend having a rest as I am full up with a dose of cold. Will leave Edinburgh 7.45 p.m., Friday 8th, arrive King's Cross 5.55 a.m., Saturday 9th.

Weekly's not here in time for sale at Wellesley today. Sales will be down at least 50% this week due to above and some comrades away on holiday.

You will notice a reference to J. Brown, Wellesley manager, in *The Miner*. It appears a mass onslaught is to be made on the Wellesley by the Reform Union sub executive to compel recognition. Good luck to them. No assistance refused. Best wishes to Comrade Mrs Hutt and expect to see you both in the pink next Saturday. P.S. Thanks very much for your invitation, which I accept. Don't worry about BED. Will it be required?

1926

January 16th, 1926.[166]

Arrived home on Monday morning at 9.45 and at work at 2 p.m. We are making good headway with the Petition forms for the release of the 12 and Welsh miners. It is certainly a good method to bring the average worker's attention to the fact that the prisoners are not yet released but it requires more. The average worker's memory is the shortest thing in the world and to keep the need for release in the forefront will require some doing. But an attempt *must* be made, not only by the Petition but by meetings, collections, etc., and through those organisations.

Have you heard any comments on the Conference of last weekend?

Our bright lads should have but did not hold a group meeting last Sunday, so I have called one for Sunday 1st (tomorrow), to discover how many members we have and how they are prepared to move.

The S.D.F. branch here are it. I believe I told you about their resolution of last month re "the Trades and Labour Council putting into operation the Liverpool decisions". The delegate only spoke of the Communist Party at that meeting and on Thursday night when the branch decisions were given he stated "that the S.D.F. meant the Council to be put on a constitutional basis by expelling the Reform Union branches". Did Liverpool decide anything re the Reform Union? This is the latest move to get at us, as the S.D.F.'s chief wirepuller here as far as I can gather was responsible for this resolution. However, it was more than sat on — it was squashed.

Am sending on to the Labour Research Department 2 ledgers containing last year's output of coal for the Wellesley. Will also try and get all minutes of Reform Union Executive and Sub Executive for year 1925-26 and send on.

The weather is against us, as for the past 6 Fridays we have had rain or snow. It rained continuously yesterday and affected the sales of the *Workers' Weekly* at the Wellesley — 12 dozen. I haven't seen our Literature Secretary yet but will meet him either tonight or tomorrow when the question of the *Weekly* will be settled. I will not be surprised if the group agrees to drop it altogether. Should our present literature secretary drop it none of the others are prepared to take the job on, which will mean no sales here. Rotten, but cannot be avoided.

The affairs of the Wellesley Checkweighmen's Fund are not in a prosperous condition. Taking us tight to get our wages. A special meeting is to be held next Sunday to meet the situation. The Committee threaten to resign.

258

They have been an ineffective bunch and are now reaping the results of their stupidity.

January 21st, 1926.

Enclosed 2 copies of No. 14 of "The Spark" and 1 copy No. 11 of "The Signal".

I understand Albert Duncan, the N.U.R. chap who was to have 18 months at the Central Labour College, is home. I haven't met him so can't state reason for him leaving the College.

What do you think of the cartoon on front page of "The Signal"? Not one member of Minority Movement in Methil Branch, N.U.R., but they are prepared to boost Minority Movement. Rather typifies general position here to the Party — "Communist Party is all right, but don't ask me to join up".

John Brown is again on the warpath: notices issued to ALL brushing contractors to reduce ALL men in their employ to 11/- — 6.6% = 10/3d. Many of these men have 13/- per shift, and most of them 12/-, because of the heavy nature of the work — "setting" heavy girders and "bars" and working amongst redd. Brushing is a job that requires skill and strength. In addition it is mostly night shift, which in itself demands extra payment. I don't know at present how many men will be affected but I was informed today by the chap who reported it to me that many oncost (wheelers, drawers, etc.) men are also being attacked to the tune of 1/- to 1/6d. per shift. I am calling a meeting for Sunday afternoon of ALL those who have received notices of reduction, to determine how they are going to act. I intend trying to get them to cease work at the expiration of the notices (if Brown has not withdrawn them by then), as by doing so the others would be compelled to fall in line in a day or two whether they were willing or not. It would mean the pit standing and the Wellesley "idle" for one day means over £50 for pumping without considering the expense caused by side and roof pressure underground — pavement "heaved up" and sides of roads "squeezed in", so that tubs cannot be moved. The management are aware of that and are not prepared to risk it. From what I can gather Brown has received instructions from the Central Office that he must reduce his staff by 10% with a corresponding or even more reduction in costs. So that this is only a commencement on his part to carry out those instructions. ALL oncost men — wheelers, repairers, drawers, clippers, hangers on, and roadsmen will get the next dose, with an attack on pieceworkers following. A cute move was made by the management in one section to enforce cuts. They gave a few "face" men notice of dismissal and when the notices were almost expired asked them if they had secured another job, and offered them jobs on oncost at 8/- to 8/6d per shift. The chap who informed me couldn't state whether any had accepted.

Nearly a big disaster at Kinglassie (near Bowhill) yesterday. Power plant at pithead broke down causing pumps to stop and 120 to 150 men underground. The men were called to the pit bottom but couldn't get up due to winding gear not having power. They were got out this morning at 2 o'clock, having to sit on top of tubs as the water was rising so quick. Only a small paragraph was given to it in the Press this morning and entirely omitted in tonight's. The pit is expected to be "idle" for 2 or 3 days due to the amount of water. Rescue parties were called on from East Fife, so that meant the Fife Coal Company anticipated something of a serious nature. The silence of tonight's Press gives one the suspicion that the Company has something to hide. J. Bird will probably send something to *Workers' Weekly* or *Worker* if there is anything of a sensational nature to report.

No new development in Union Dispute. I might attend Reform Union Executive meeting next week as our branch delegate (Party member) has received an accident to his eye.

We are going to try and get a local Committee of International Class War Prisoners' Aid formed on Sunday at a special meeting of the Trades and Labour Council which is being held to discuss organisation.

Tom Kennedy was at Buckhaven on Sunday last, addressing a meeting under the auspices of the bunch who have broken away from the Trades and Labour Council. His audience was barely 50, mostly women — a bad slap in the face to Thomas, who used to have packed houses. According to the Press reports of his meeting he dealt with the Locarno Pact and claimed credit for it to the Labah Party.[167] It was rather significant that Methil branch, S.D.F., held their regular branch meeting in Methil when Tom's meeting was on in Buckhaven.

January 29th, 1926.[168]

Enclosed newspaper cuttings which will give you some idea of what is happening here. Have managed to get Wellesley to move at last. On strike since Tuesday night. Only 3 SCABS, out of 1,800 men underground. Firemen and Pumpsmen allowed to work. Pit Committee formed and now biggest point in dispute — men determined that it be recognised by management. W. Adamson and J. Potter[169] howled down and made [to] accept Pit Committee as only body men recognise. Union dispute taboo and Union officials to be allowed in only under direction of Pit Committee. Management withdrawn all notices of reduction except those affecting some 17 men. They agreed to suspend the latter for a week to meet the men individually but mass meetings turned that down, demanding unconditional withdrawal before work resumed. Preparations made for today to call ALL Wemyss Coal Company pits "out". Feeling very good in other Pits. I have had a strenuous time, getting to bed at 11.30 and at Pit at 4 a.m. to picket. Pickets hardly required as men are SOLID and becoming more determined. Am writing this hurried note to mail with *The Miner* and will let you know of fuller details later. Can't manage time to get a special strike sheet of "The Spark" because of meetings, etc. None of other comrades ready to tackle job. P.S. Thanks very much for telegram. Voice almost gone, but croaking along.

February 2nd, 1926.

Thanks very much for yours of January 31st. You will have received prepaid answer to your telegram.[170] As I am in a hurry to get No. 4 page of this issue ready am sending on "Diary of Strike" which will give you some idea of how things went last week. Will give you more at end of week. Enclosed No. 12 of "The Signal" and Nos. 3 and 4 of "The Hutch".

We had the game in our hands and would have had ALL notices withdrawn had the Old Union crowd played the game. As it was we managed to get over 200 notices withdrawn by the deputation. Only 4 remain. P.S. Sorry to report sales of *Labour Monthly* down for January. One comrade lost 12 out of 12.

February 4th, 1926.

Thanks very much for yours of 2nd February. As you correctly point out we have nothing to fear from the results of the strike. Rather the opposite. A certain amount of reaction is bound to manifest itself tomorrow, payday, but I think we can manage to overcome that. Enclosed 2 copies of No. 15 of "The Spark" and a copy of "The Torch" (Cowdenbeath and Lumphinnans local) — 1 man show printing, etc. Hope you are not bored with epistle of last night. P.S. You will notice I have made no mention of "Release the Prisoners" due to having so much local stuff. Could have filled another issue.

February 12th, 1926.

Just a brief note with *The Miner*. Notice report of Wellesley strike in this week's *Weekly*. Expect it is yours and it gives a true report of what occurred and, more important, points the right lessons which have been driven home.

From what I can gather Johnnie Brown, manager, and D. Beveridge, agent, are getting it in the neck from their "superiors", not so much for issuing the notices but being unsuccessful in applying them. NO REDUCTIONS HAVE TAKEN PLACE but Brown and Beveridge are carrying out their petty games, usual after a kick up — sending men home, facemen and brushers. The result is that, 1st, the men are feeling sore and are more and more realising the value of militant action, directed by a Pit Committee composed of men employed in the Colliery, and a growing feeling of hostility to the Colliery management; 2nd, Brown and Beveridge, due to their STUPID actions, are "cutting their own throats" as output is going down (although they at present can show a reduced oncost bill), and in 2 weeks' time at the game they are playing it will be reduced by 25% and an exceptionally heavy oncost charge for brushing, etc., to face for a few weeks before they can reach the pre-strike output. However, George, that's their business and in carrying out their present policy they are building a fairly good platoon for the workers' forces for May.

Last night we attempted to get a local committee of the International Class War Prisoners' Aid formed by the Trades and Labour Council. The S.D.F.ers raised a smell (a corpse can do no other) and the result was a special meeting to be held on February 25th for a general discussion, "ARE THERE ANY SOCIAL DEMOCRATS IN PRISON IN RUSSIA FOR THEIR WORKING CLASS ACTIVITIES?". 'Sawful but it can't be avoided.

The split in the local Trades and Labour Council will come to a climax on Sunday. A special meeting of the Divisional Labour Party is being held and the indications at present are that the existing Council will be expelled for, 1st, repudiating the Liverpool decisions; 2nd, affiliating the Reform Union; 3rd, refusing to alter the rules at the dictates of Ben Shaw and E. Wake.[171]

P.S. Will let you know results of Divisional Labour Party next week. Sold over 16 dozen *Workers' Weekly* today and 6 *Labour Monthly*.

February 13th, 1926.

Am commencing this letter Saturday night. Enclosed is a letter of introduction (in German) from a Commissar in Archangel to Party Headquarters for a German comrade. I am sending it to you to give to the Political Bureau, as by sending it direct it would run the risk of being tampered with in transit.

Am feeling stale, can get down to nothing at all, which will be reflected in No. 16 of "The Spark". Feel in one of those moods — to hell with everything, nothing worth troubling about.

I believe I mentioned the Divisional Labour Party meeting to be held on Sunday in the latter part of the note I sent with *The Miner*, but forgot to mention that I got the Trades and Labour Council to agree to instruct their delegates to move "No Action" until the Unity Conference of the 2 Unions had taken place, which would be in a week or two. Tom Kennedy is to be present as it is also a Selection Committee. He is the only nominee, Reform Union branches having NO VOTE.

Sunday night: I understand from a comrade who was at the Divisional Labour Party meeting today that it agreed to "No Action" pending the result of the Unity Conference.

Our Group is something to write home about. 2 of us waited over 1 hour on the others turning up for the group meeting. None arrived during that time so we shunted. The meeting was due to commence at 6.30 and I met 3 of them on their way AT 8. Some enthusiasm? We had a bit of a row but of course as usual patched it up. Yet we have the bloody cheek to challenge ALL and everything NOT inside the Party.

The Reform Union Sub Executive meet the Sub Committee of the Scottish in Glasgow tomorrow. The Reform Union does not know if the Old Union is to be there. I expect if it was to be a joint meeting that it would take place in Dunfermline. However, whether joint or not it is another move towards Unity.

I notice when reading over the few lines that I haven't explained the position re the German Comrade. I met him 2 years ago. He was on the strike committee at Methil during the German sailors' strike. About 1 month before the New Year I again met him when he informed me that he had left the letter of introduction with a girl in London to forward to Party Headquarters. I wrote Headquarters about it to see if they had received it, but they replied that nobody there knew anything about it. He has since written to the girl who has returned it to him. (He is in Methil at present.) If there are any communications necessary you might tell the Political Bureau to write me.

Enclosed No. 13 of "The Signal". Haven't seen A. Duncan yet but his leaving the Labour College appears rather mysterious as his most intimate friend is not prepared to say anything.

February 16th, 1926.

Enclosed No. 16 of "The Spark" (2 copies) and No. 5 of "The Hutch" (1 copy) and Reports and Synopsis of Committee minutes of Methil and Buckhaven Co-operative Societies.

The front page cartoons were drawn and printed before I saw them or they would have been differently titled. The title is not one to encourage Unity — rather the reverse. Had it been "WHEN WE OBTAIN UNITY OFFICIALS OF THIS TYPE *WILL* BE GOT RID OF" or "UNITY *WILL* PREVENT OFFICIALS DOING THIS" it in my opinion would have been better. But as it was passed by 3 of the group there it is.

Annual elections of Old Union officials are on at present. Changes were made in Denbeath but the delegate is still on the job. A Conference for ALL TRADE UNION Branches and Trades and Labour Councils called by Lochgelly Trades and Labour Council (behind which is the Reform Union) will take place at Lochgelly on Saturday to discuss formation of Workers' Industrial Alliance, Workers' Defence Corps, etc.[172] As the Conference does not commence until 4 p.m. I don't anticipate a thumping success, but it will at least cause considerable discussion, which should bear fruit if not on Saturday at least in the near future. I am one of 2 delegates from Methil Reform Union.

P.S. Had stuff for one page in this issue of "The Spark" intending to have no cartoon on the front page. A comrade gave 2 articles (his first contribution to "The Spark"), and as they haven't appeared due to the cartoon which he, along with 2 others, allowed to pass I expect some more trouble for yours truly — "No more stuff from Me", "You won't print it when you get it", etc. However, there it is. Like me he will have to accept it.

February 18th, 1926.

Enclosed paragraph (in German) from German Comrade I wrote you about. He wishes it to be translated and inserted in the *Workers' Weekly*. As his English is not up to scratch but he was very desirous of getting some stuff in the *Weekly* I suggested that he write it in German and that some of you in London would do the translating. He intends sending on more, so you might do your best to get it published, that is, providing the stuff is all right.

I notice in the local press that ADAMSON HAS BEEN UNANIMOUSLY APPOINTED GENERAL SECRETARY OF THE OLD UNION (they having some time ago agreed on PERIODICAL ELECTION OF OFFICIALS — 5 years' term). Wullie has therefore managed to a certain extent to baulk his opponents in the Reform Union, but it is a significant move re the Unity Campaign which is on at present and in my opinion augurs well as it means that the Old Union bunch realise it has got to come and are safe-guarding their pet in the event of it coming off this time.

J. Brown and Company are lying low at the Wellesley but I understand from a fairly reliable source that they are marking time on me — I have got to go. Forewarned is forearmed. Before they get their desire things will happen that will make little or no difference whether I am on the spot or not. The Wellesley men are showing a more courageous front now than they have done since 1921.

February 26th, 1926.

A few lines with *The Miner*. As you remark in your letter of 17th February you have a tough job in front of you to get the National Union of Journalists on the move. More tough than we in the coalfields. However, it is only part of the Communist Party job and as you will agree must be tackled. I hope you have managed to see Page by this time. If not, let him know we will give him plenty of vocal exercise (if he feels like it) when he next pays us a visit, which I hope won't be long after his release.

I have only managed to read the "Notes of the Month" in the February *Labour Monthly* and I think Dutt is getting better every month, which of course may be, and very likely is, due to myself understanding things more as I go along. Managed to get 6 new readers last Sunday at the Scottish Labour College class.

This class looks like being a good nursery for us. After the tutor has given his lecture we have a class for Public Speaking. We run it this way: one of the Group states a case against the workers (last Sunday I took the Coalowners' case) and it would have done you good to see the attitude some of them took up. At times 3 and 4 wanting to speak at once, and what was best of all — the aggressive attitude they adopted. My cousin's boy (15 years old) gave a short speech on Bonus Shares and their effect on the workers, with the solution — a united militant workers' organisation to smash the Boss, to prevent him smashing *US*.

We could have sold twice as many of last issue of "The Spark" had we printed them. Sold out on Saturday — 670 copies. The centre has brought us up with a jerk re the cartoon: "overstepping the mark", and "likely to cause offence to many workers".[173] I have written R. Stewart re the offence part. It did the entire opposite. We also received an all round criticism on the paper — make up and contents, and had our attention drawn to the fact that we had omitted the International Class War Prisoners' Aid and the Minority Movement Conference in the last issue. The I.C.W.P.A. would have been in had the misunderstanding re the cartoon (which I have already written you about) not arisen. However, we in Methil have done more than write about it, we have managed to get ALL the Reform Union branches affiliated to the I.C.W.P.A. and are well on the way towards getting the local Trades and Labour Council affiliated.

The "discussion" re Social Democrats and Russian Prisons took place last night. What a bloody mess they made of what they had the cheek to call "a case". They had written their Headquarters for ammunition and received plenty — Pamphlets by Jordania and Company[174] in Paris, typewritten sheets galore from London, and not one original thought from themselves. They read parts of the pamphlets and recited with evident relish MURRRDERRS OF

SOCIAL DEMOCRATS' CHILDREN, reading over names and ages. Reminded me of the wooden theatres with the hair-raisers which came periodically to Methil when I was a kid — "The Demon Barber of Fleet Street, or the string of pearls", etc. As the most of the parts of the pamphlets they quoted were parts taken out of the Trade Union Delegation Report[175] and I had my copy with me it was an easy matter to show the audience (30 to 40) that the S.D.F.ers would stoop to any dirty method to smash the working class. An S.D.F.er was stupid enough to say that the delegation were in the pay of the British Capitalists, Trotsky also was a Real Estate Agent, and the Russian workers hadn't enough training and education to run a State on their own behalf. To cut it short, George, we were all over them and left them without a kick. One of them today told me that I had bullied the meeting into accepting our position. I asked him if he had accepted our position and he said, "No". When I asked him if that was so why then didn't he expose our (what he termed) "weak case" and so rouse the weak-minded audience against the bully, he sent me to hell and cleared out. They are a bunch.

I was unable to get to Lochgelly for the Left Wing Conference last Saturday, but you will get a report in *The Miner*.

We have a special meeting of an enlarged District Party Committee tomorrow. Expect the business to be mainly on the Industrial Situation and the Minority Movement Conference.

Have a few factory papers from Dundee. Will send them on to you after I have scanned them. Page wanted as many of those printed in Scotland as he could get. Thornton branch A.S.L.E.&F. have got one, "The Spur", weekly.[176] I have got in touch with them and will forward a copy every week. P.S. We are now getting advertisements to insert in "The Spark".

March 3rd, 1926.

Enclosed No. 17 of "The Spark" (2 copies), 1 copy No. 6 "The Hutch", 1 copy No. 14 "The Signal", 1 copy of "The Spur" (Thornton A.S.E.L.&F.) and a few copies of Dundee factory papers. You will notice that factory papers are becoming quite fashionable up here.

A strike lasting a week took place at Low Valleyfield, West Fife — 700 men, Fife Coal Company. Adamson and Potter played their Wellesley game, also a separate ballot, but it didn't come off as successfully as at the Wellesley. An ALL IN Ballot was taken afterwards and the men voted to stay out. The Company then met the Pit Committee and according to the Press "an amicable settlement was arrived at" and the men resumed work.

I don't know the particulars that led up to the strike, as Valleyfield is at the extreme west of Fife. They had a big advantage, practically all the men employed at the pit being resident in Valleyfield.

The Wellesley management have made another move, but owing to lack of information am unable at present to state extent. According to the many rumours going around a considerable number of men in the Chemiss Dook Splint Sections have received 14 days' notice of dismissal. The same move that has been played in other portions of the coalfield, South Wales, etc., when the management could not enforce reductions by a frontal attack — knock a few sections idle, sometimes a Pit, and after a short period re-engage men at reduced rates. I expect we will get notice from the majority of the men affected when their notices have almost expired, that being the usual procedure.

You will notice we have given the Minority Movement Conference some prominence this issue, but local matter is at a minimum. I might be at the Conference. The verse on the front page is by a Cowdenbeath Comrade.

Methil Reform Union have now decided to deal with Literature. They ordered 4 dozen of the *Coal Crisis*, Labour Research Department, last week.[177] I had 2 dozen at the Wellesley and was sold out in less than 20 minutes. They have ordered another 50. I am to tackle 3 dozen of them. Some of the branch collectors are prepared to try a few, but as they usually meet the womenfolks sales are not easy.

Hope you have seen Page by this time and that he and the others are keeping A.1.

I was at the enlarged District Party Committee meeting Saturday but would have been better in bed as I had a rotten dose of "dingy" and wasn't in a proper state to take part in or follow the discussion.

The palavers re the Union dispute are not very fruitful. The Scottish hasn't as yet brought the 2 parties together, and according to the last meeting of them and the Reform Union Sub Executive they are trying to force the Reform Union to concede more points.

March 12th, 1926.

Thanks for yours of the 7th. Tell Comrade Mrs Hutt that she is "on the wrang side of the dyke" in supporting the viewpoint of the centre re the cartoon. Judging the cartoon from the generally accepted standards of "decency" (when no crisis is on) one would have no hesitation in condemning it along the lines done by the centre, but when one is submerged to the neck against mud, quoting the old saw, "Cleanliness is next to Godliness", does not by any means remove the mud. It requires a bath and the cartoon was the soap used in this bath. Of course it was impossible for anyone outside this district to realise the amount of hostility directed against the Old Union officials. There was a bigger demand for the following issue of "The Spark" than ever before and today a considerable number at the Wellesley were after a copy of last week's issue; but there is no rush to join the Party.

The Wemyss Coal Company have no case for an injunction other than what occurred during the strike.

Notice Valleyfield report in this week's *Workers' Weekly*.

Methil Reform Union have ordered another 50 of the *Coal Crisis*, making 150 altogether. It is good value.

I am not sure if I will be at the Battersea Conference.[178] Last Sunday I raised the question at Methil Reform Union branch meeting and they agreed to send a delegate. I was nominated but declined and persuaded the branch secretary to accept. We are collecting the necessary to send him — £5. My reasons for refusing nomination are, 1st, that it is imperative that others *must* be drawn into *more* active work and to do so they must get a clearer understanding of the movement, nationally, that is, and they cannot get that by confining them to Methil; 2nd, the branch secretary requires some rough corners knocked off and he will get that done at a Conference of the nature that Battersea promises; 3rd, I am making an attempt on Sunday to get the Wellesley to send a delegate and might be elected, although again I would prefer a youngster who shows good promise to be sent; 4th, The local group are considering sending a delegate. The N.U.R. local branch are also sending a delegate, so that if everything materialises no complaint should be lodged against Methil when one knows that it requires at least £5 to cover 1 delegate's expenses.

Remember me to Page and any of the others you happen to see and let Page know that if he feels like letting off steam we can accommodate him when he next visits Fife.

Sorry to hear about *Trade Union Unity*. You will get a few shocks, George, like the one you have had re Purcell and Company. Most of those chaps are good only for fire-work displays, not for the grinding work of wearing down the opposition.

Like you I look at the I.L.P. proposition cautiously, but there is certainly good grounds for the Party getting Fenner Brockway and others who are going out for this move to further declare themselves (if it is possible) as by so doing it will compel MacDonald and his crush to show their hand more, and they will not only be "slating" the Communist Party but Brockway and the others who are really sincere in this move.[179] The result would be that MacDonald and Company will further create more opposition to themselves within the I.L.P. and the Party should and will gain more support if not members.

Glad to know your group is getting along so well. Ours is as usual.

There are no indications that we are going to have Unity in Fife at an early date. From what I can gather the only matter the Reform Union Sub Executive is getting out of the recent happenings is Anti-Adamson Pro-Reform Union propaganda. I have been considering the following line of action and expect your opposition, but here it is. Due to the stalemate position at present if the Party by the end of March does not accept and go out for the Liquidation of the Reform Union to obtain Unity, I intend LEAVING THE PARTY and getting Methil Reform Union Branch to go over to the Old Union and then tackling other districts even if I have to do it myself. The Party can then be exonerated and not get any mud that would be thrown — and there is no dubiety that plenty will be thrown. It will mean that practically no literature will be sold here but that in my opinion will be part of the price to obtain Unity.

Have called a meeting of Wellesley workers for Sunday to ascertain number of notices of dismissal (rumoured 250) and also to try and get a delegate sent to Minority Conference. Almost all the Wemyss Coal Company pits are "idle" tomorrow. Part of the preparations for May.

Did you ever see so much "tripe" ladled out as the amount by the Commission Report.[180] "No Reduction in Wages and No Increase in Hours",

"Pit Baths, and Holidays with Pay WHEN THE INDUSTRY BECOMES PROSPEROUS". Those whom I have talked it over with are amazed at what they term "the bloody cheek to try and slip *that* across us". But Jesus Christ's earthly counterpart — James Cook, Financial Secretary of the Old Union — is convinced that "it is a good report had the suggested reduction of wages not been made", "as what are at present controversial points would have been acceptable", and "Reforms which we have fought and striven for for a number of years are recommended". Some of his kidney will require careful watching as pit head baths, Joint Committees, etc., will be the smoke screen they will chuck up to cloak District Percentage reductions and increase of hours (i.e., the 5 day policy of 42 hours winding). P.S. Will write you on Sunday night if I am appointed to attend Conference. Had a visit today from Comrade Dick's[181] wife for your address. I don't know if he will be at the Conference.

12th March, 1926.[182]

Dear Davy,

I don't know how you will feel about it, but I should be very delighted if you could do a short article on the Coal Situation and the Commission's Report as it strikes you, for *Trade Union Unity*. About four or five pages of your usual writing would be just the length (longer if you like). I am hoping to land one of the M.F.G.B. executive for an article, but he may very likely fall through and in any case we ought to have the rank-and-file corrective. If you feel like doing this, send a little covering note addressed to the Editorial Board, saying that you enclose the article and hope, etc., and also describe yourself as Checkweighman at the Wellesley Colliery, Fife; this little wangle will enable me to swing it round Purcell and Hicks safely.[183] You know the sort of thing we want — not as plain-speaking as in a Party publication, but emphasising the need for unity *concretely* from the point of view of the ordinary worker. Let me have the article by Friday the 19th, if you feel disposed to do it — but don't bother yourself: for *Trade Union Unity* isn't really very important, as you know. Will be writing soon.

March 14th, 1926.

Am writing you as promised. We held the meeting of Wellesley men today and they agreed to send a delegate. As I informed you in my last letter I was "banking" on a young chap being appointed. He was appointed and also a committee to take up the collection to defray the expenses. The meeting also agreed to form a local branch of the National Unemployed Workers' Committee Movement,[184] and as I cannot find the Headquarters' address am enclosing the secretary's name and address for you to forward to them. Only 7 of those receiving notice attended the meeting, but another has been called for next Sunday when they will be on the street, which will ensure a bigger attendance. I will not be at the Conference as I don't feel in the pink at present. The local group wanted me to go but I feel more like a weekend in bed than any Conference.

The group looks like going to pieces and it won't matter very much, as the comradely spirit is sadly lacking due to too much being thrown on 3 or 4 of us and the differences existing as to the solution of the Union Split.

You might give the Industrial Department a quiet tip to occasionally acknowledge reports from Fife Industrial Organiser[185] as he is rather put out at receiving no acknowledgements to his reports.

March 17th, 1926.

Enclosed 2 copies of "The Spark" No. 18, 1 copy of "The Signal" and 1 copy of "The Spur". What do you think of the new title? Stands out better than the last.

You will have received the paragraph for *Trade Union Unity* by this time. I wrote it hurriedly last night. I haven't as yet got or seen a copy of the Report and had to depend on a fairly long report in the *Glasgow Herald*. After sending it away I came to the conclusion that it possibly won't suit and also that there is too much repetition of "smashing the M.F.G.B.". However, it's up to you, George.

The Union dispute still drags on without any signs of a meeting between the 2 Executives. The Reform Union speakers are out every weekend in West Fife but religiously keep away from East Fife.

A circular from the centre re the Minority Movement Conference has set some members of the group going on the need for the group to send a delegate. There might be one sent yet. P.S. Sales of *Sunday Worker* now 26 dozen.

March 26th, 1926.

Enclosed copy of *The Miner*, No. 5 of "The Torch", and No. 7 of "The Hutch".

As I indicated in my last note we called a meeting under auspices of Pit Committee of Wellesley Workers for Sunday last. 5 turned up, and as far as I can gather more notices have been issued this week. Almost all the "face men" who received notices previously were "put up" in other sections and this has in my opinion kept those who are on "notice" away from the meetings: "Ah'll get put up if ah keep ma mooth shut, but nae job if ah gaun tae the meeting". Good luck to them. How many oncost men have been paid off I don't know as they also appear to have been carried away with the above bright idea. However, this game is working just as smoothly and by the present indications as successfully — pressure on oncost especially — as if they were all on the scrap heap, according to output, although a few sections are "idle" and await John Brown and Company's instructions to be re-opened AT REDUCED RATES.

The Wellesley wasn't represented at the Minority Conference, due to those who volunteered to collect NOT TURNING UP. We sent a delegate from the group and he made inquiries at King Street for you but was unable to get in touch with you. Methil Reform Union had a delegate, as did Methil N.U.R. Our group delegate wasn't much impressed with the Conference — too much hot air and splurge, in his opinion.

The Reform Union Sub Executive met the Scottish Sub-Committee on

Wednesday but no meeting has as yet been arranged between the Reform Union and the Old Union. From what I can gather the Scottish have again shown a loving hand to the Reform Union, and agree that resignation of local officials and the financial or card vote isn't asking too much "but they can't decide this issue as a Committee". It appears this method of fighting by proxy is to go on indefinitely. According to McArthur (Industrial organiser) Bird has at an open meeting in Bowhill advocated liquidation of the Reform Union and as a consequence raised the ire of the Reform Union element in West Fife against the Communist Party, so much so that Dunfermline and District Area Committee of the Reform Union have sent in a resolution moving a vote of censure on McArthur, and that he be recalled as a member of the negotiating Committee, that no member of the Communist Party be allowed to speak from a Reform Union platform, and that no more donations be sent to Communist organisations. McArthur is up in arms against Bird and threatens to resign from the Party. If Bird has done this he certainly is not acting according to the Party Policy and should be dealt with. I certainly agree with what he has alleged to have advocated, but not as a Party member at present. Of course McArthur has always maintained that the Reform Union is more important to him than the Party and it is certainly more popular to trounce Adamson from a Reform Union platform to a Reform Union audience than to "get down" to a definite line of action to obtain Unity. He and I have bouts every time we meet and he has suggested that it is not impossible that I am the obstacle to the building up of a big Party group in this district. That will be proven, as I told you in my last letter. The next issue of "The Spark" will in all probability be my last issue and the group can then go on increasing, I hope. If this split is allowed to carry on as at present the whole Labour movement in Fife will be rent and torn. Methil and District Trades and Labour Council is split by it and if it was liquidated we would soon get a proper alignment of forces. In addition to the Union split we have of course the S.D.F. crush who have called a meeting for Sunday to form a NEW Trades and Labour Council. The prominent S.D.F.ers are members of the Reform Union but their anti-Communist feelings have overcome the Union split to the extent that they have only invited the Old Union branches and Buckhaven Labour Association (an organisation composed of Buckhaven Old Union Committee, their wives, and some Kennedyites who are not employed in the Pits) to form the NEW Council. This move is to get at the Communist Party and due to the Union split we are at a disadvantage: (1) The Reform Union although affiliated to the local Trades and Labour Council is not affiliated to the Divisional Council; (2) The present local officials of the Old Union, who are about as reactionary a bunch as one can get, would not be in those positions if one Union was in operation; (3) Branches other than miners who are sympathetic towards us as Communist Party members are at times hostile because of the 2 Unions and the complications arising. You can see by those few points without taking in the effects at the Pits that something of a drastic nature is required.

The Left Wing Conference takes place at Lochgelly tomorrow and the Union split will also be felt there.

270

Page and the other 6 will be out in a fortnight's time. Hope you have a bumper demonstration on the Sunday.

Have you had a visit from a German comrade, Paul Hathe? I had a note from him and he asked me to send his letters to your address. As I hadn't your permission I haven't done so. He was one month in Methil, a fortnight in Dundee and has got to London. I haven't got his address.

38 Powis Square,
London, W.11.
30th March 1926.[186]

Dear Davy,

At last I sit down to reply to your letters of the 12th, 14th, 17th, and 26th. It is very wrong of me to have let so long go by without replying, more especially in view of the extremely serious nature of some of your remarks, but the pressure of work has been unusually hot, and in addition, as you know, I have had the job of looking after our friend P. ———[187] trying to get him a job and so forth.Now to get straight down to business — your suggestion that you should leave the Party in order to secure unity by liquidating the Reform Union. Of course there can be *no question* of your leaving the Party in this way, Dave, without any consultation and entirely off your own bat. That is perfectly clear and straightforward, and I don't think there is any need for me to labour the point. (Mind you, Davy, I'm fully conscious in writing to you like this that I'm an insolent youngster without anything approaching your experience, or other than a second-hand knowledge of the heart-breaking difficulties you have been up against.)

Have you discussed it with your Group — bad as they are? Have you discussed it on the District Party Committee? Have you consulted the Polbureau? *Don't* forget that a step of the kind you are contemplating, involving the severing from the Party of one of its outstanding rank-and-file proletarian members — and one who has an unrivalled position as a Communist leader of the workers in his locality — is one of such a nature that, failing local and district consultation and discussion, it MUST go to the highest authority in the Party — the Political Bureau or the Central Executive Committee.

The matter, from your letters, seems to be urgent, and I am not waiting for your permission to place all the facts of your case before the Polbureau: that, I think, is my simple duty as a Party member.

Davy, you and I realise the need for discipline: and we realise also the need for building our strong, iron Bolshevik Party — we know that without such a Party, getting its roots down into the mass of the workers, really becoming a Mass Party, then there is no hope for the working class of Britain. Now I put it to you: will your action, even though it might achieve trade union unity (and that is by no means clear — what can one man do without any organisation behind him?), assist in any way towards realising this aim?

For, however you explain the matter away, if you leave the Party in order to attempt the liquidation of the Reform Union on your own, you will be giving the Party in Fife such a blow that it will be long before it recovers. It will mean, as you say, dropping the Pit paper (the finest COMMUNIST factory paper in the country — as you will have seen from last week's *Workers' Weekly*), dropping the sales of the *Workers' Weekly*, etc. It will mean the end of your Group, mouldy though that is. It will mean that your influence in the Trades Council and the local movement generally, and your influence among the workers, will be the influence of a good militant worker — BUT NOT OF A COMMUNIST. It will mean, if you act as you seem to be intending, quite on your own, that the Party — supposing that it maintains its present position on the Union question — will have to oppose you. What a spectacle for the Adamsons and their bumsuckers! What a shameful sight for all revolutionary workers!

As for McArthur saying that your attitude is the obstacle to the building of a big Party group in Methil, I should like to tell this comrade, with all fraternal respect, that if he thinks it is Bolshevik to put a "dissident" Union — however justifiable the initial split was — before the Party, then he is singularly unacquainted with the methods and policy which have made the successful revolution in Russia. For merciful Christ's sake, Davy, don't let yourself be galled by the gibes of well-meaning but misguided comrades of this kind: but I don't suppose you will.

The whole thing comes back to simple first principles. You and I know that outside the Party there are no Communists — i.e., no consistent logical revolutionaries. We know that without organised collective work — the work of a Party — individuals on their own can do nothing, NOTHING WHATEVER. We know that, at all costs, once the Party has come to a decision, we must abide by it and loyally carry it out, however mistaken or disastrous we may personally think it. Or if, as in the present case, the Party has *not* taken a certain decision, then we must raise the question through the appropriate channels, NOT HESITATING TO TAKE THE MATTER TO THE CENTRAL PARTY LEADERSHIP, and go on raising it until a decision has been taken, one way or the other. But to break away — however laudable the motive, or however pressing the need, in our INDIVIDUAL, PERSONAL opinion — in order to attempt by one's own individual efforts to carry out a certain task that one thinks the Party should carry out — surely that is a thing that NO COMMUNIST CAN POSSIBLY, UNDER ANY CIRCUMSTANCES WHATEVER, DO.

You can just imagine how Lenin would have dealt with such a suggestion.

Consider: if you do as you say, you will simply be running your head against a brick wall. You won't achieve unity, and you will make confusion worse confounded by making what is in effect a split in the Party. Also you will hopelessly antagonise those good — though muddle-headed — workers who are still in the Reform Union, and will stick to the Reform Union, especially against what they will consider is the most insidious and treacherous attack on it.

Please, Dave, don't take any step in the direction you indicate — a step which I for one do not merely oppose, but think absolutely mistaken, fatal, and in the worst interests of the Party and the working class — until you have consulted all the Party authorities. Bob Stewart is a good fellow, and he will give the best possible advice, I'm sure.

I can't write more, though I know I've put the case rottenly: but I've such a liking and a respect for you, Davy, as the finest Communist worker — an instinctive proletarian Bolshevik of the best type, as I always tell comrades — I've ever met.

April 4th, 1926.

Received yours of 30th March. Enclosed 2 copies of No. 19 of "The Spark", 1 copy No. 8 "The Hutch", and 1 copy of No. 16 of "The Signal".

In reply to your letter I must commence my answer to one of your latter statements, viz., "that you have put a rotten case". I entirely disagree but as your case is built on the premise that WE HAVE AN ORGANISATION in Fife (where the vital issues of the Union split have to be thrashed out and OPERATED), it does not have the effect that it would otherwise have. I agree with the procedure you suggest, also with the need for discipline, and it is due to the latter point that I made up my mind to go on the lines I suggested. Although being the only member who criticised the Political Bureau's recommendations at the various aggregate meetings held during the past year, I was the only Party member to try to operate them, and in trying had the opposition of every Party member on the Reform Union Executive. Hence my opinion of NO ORGANISATION in Fife and my intention to cause a break by, 1st, leaving the Party and, 2nd, getting Methil Reform Union to rejoin the Old Union and trying other branches. I realised the difficulties I would be up against but as they would not be much greater (only more open) than at present I was prepared to tackle it.

However, George, I am at least going to claim that my suggested attitude has (with other factors) brought some of our Party members to some realisation of the position they have been occupying for some time. At an enlarged District Party Committee meeting last night attended by Comrade Joss we had the matter fairly well thrashed out and some of the grievances ventilated, and the Party policy emphasised so that no confusion or deviations either "Right" or "Left" should occur. I have had a few talks with Comrade McArthur since he made the statement re big group and myself and have got him convinced, by drawing his attention to recent happenings, that Hodge has been using him for his (Hodge's) own ends. He is now agreed that although no more "concessions" are granted by the Old Union that we must advocate acceptance of the agreed on points by the Reform Union and thereby effect unity. I therefore withdraw from my suggested position.

I attended the Left Wing Conference at Lochgelly last Saturday as a visitor and the Union Split in my opinion was responsible (along with one or two factors shown at the Conference) for its failure. The Reform Union branches predominated, only a few other bodies being represented. Over 80 delegates. Hodge and Clunie,[188] ex-S.L.P.er and Scottish Labour College, were all out for the creation of another organisation, with local, Area, and

Central Committees for Fife, and were successful in getting the Conference to accept, although with a small majority. It was agreed to make the membership on an individual basis, but Trade Union branches could affiliate. Without going into any further detail, the meeting lasted for 3½ hours — ½ hour devoted for tea and 10 minutes to policy, the remainder to a Constitution for an organisation which is not required. 5 Conveners were elected, and there at present the matter lies. ABORTIVE from 2 aspects: 1st, the desire of Hodge and Clunie for a "place in the sun", and, 2nd, a definite Policy to meet the immediate situation.

We have a nice bloody mess locally, the S.D.F. and Old Union branches trying to create another Trades and Labour Council. They held a meeting last Sunday and a report appeared in the local Press to the effect that they intended to circularise all the affiliated branches re expulsion of Communists and Reform Union. As there are 4 Party members on the Trades and Labour Council and 3 of us represent 2 Reform Union branches, you can realise to what extent our hands are tied due to the Split.Should the affiliated branches decide on Reform Union expulsion 3 of us have to go, but had one Union been in existence only, we could have fought Communist Party expulsions. However, George, the impending scrap will clear things up a great deal. NONE of our opponents WILL SHOW themselves or give a LEAD dealing with the present situation, and we therefore HAVE to GIVE a LEAD.

We have got another machine, Nos. 1 and 4 Pages of No. 19 of "The Spark" being done with it. £25 — to be paid as we can. You will notice I have had to insert "Wage Reductions" and "Misery" in the cartoon due to the cartoonist not carrying out the suggestions I gave him. He had a considerable number printed before I saw it and I had to write over 500 copies, which has caused delay in writing you. We had a good splash in the *Workers' Weekly,* although they made one mistake — *NO* National Agreements. We printed 200 for the centre for distribution to other locals. It certainly made for more interest by local comrades, although nothing other than agreeing to purchase a new machine has come out of it.

Page and the other 6 will be out on Saturday. Hope they are all in the pink for what appear to be strenuous times ahead. Next Sunday's demonstration should be a huge success, at least from numbers attending. I intend trying to get the group to hold a mass meeting next Sunday to deal with the Coal Commission's Report and the Owners' proposals. It takes some doing to get a crowd to turn out here at present, but it has got to be done somehow.

Hope you have had a good time for your holidays. Enclosed short note for P. How did he manage to get your whereabouts? He is some lad.

April 9th, 1926.
Brief note with *The Miner.* Received yours of 7th inst. and will reply later. Am in bed with touch of "dingy", being unable to go to work today, of all days, which means drop of more than 60% of group's *Workers' Weekly* sales. Another comrade is in Edinburgh Infirmary with an eye accident received in the Pit.

April 15th, 1926.

I now have time to reply to your letters of April 7th and 12th. Haven't you received my letter of April 4th in reply to yours of March 30th, enclosed with 2 copies of No. 19 of "The Spark", 1 copy of "The Hutch", 1 copy of "The Signal", and a short note for P.? In it I entirely agreed with the case you put, but pointed out that your case was built on the idea that a Party organisation existed in Fife, and due to the fact that NO ORGANISATION (with a common policy) existed that your case did not have the effect it would otherwise have had. You will possibly have received it by the time you receive this and will know that I have withdrawn from my suggested line of action.

To demonstrate further how the Party works in Fife you would probably have noticed a series of meetings advertised for Fife in last issue of the *Sunday Worker*. West Fife and Central Fife have the meetings, none allocated to East Fife, and the first of us (although on the District Party Committee) knowing about those meetings was in the *Sunday Worker*. Team work? Heavens, it would make a pig vomit.

If you haven't received my last letter with the factory and pit papers enclosed let me know and I will send on the Nos, George.

As to being offended by the tone of your letters I wasn't in the least bit and accept them in the spirit they were written: to correct a comrade who appears to be getting off the rails. It is required, especially at a critical period such as this.

Locally things aren't looking well. The S.D.F. and Old Union have a meeting on Sunday to try and form a new Trades and Labour Council; another Women's Section has been formed and is being sponsored by 3 "Labour" Town Councillors, one of whom is my butty, and the majority of the Union branches are very half-hearted in the whole business. The average miner isn't showing much interest in anything just now, possibly due to us not stirring him sufficiently, but our time is fully occupied with the hundred and one matters arising mainly from the Union Dispute: Constitutionalism of Trades and Labour Council, Disputes at the Pits, Intrigues of S.D.F.ers and "Labour" Councillors, etc., without considering Literature sales, and getting "The Spark" ready.

What do you think of our special this issue? Two of us still have everything to do, and if no assistance is forthcoming I can see it going under in a short time, as both of us are involved in every other group activity. You will be justified in thinking I am getting fed up, George. It is getting absolute hell, with no promise of any assistance to ever increasing work. Here I am getting off at the deep end with all my grousing when I commenced this letter to reply to yours of the 7th and 12th.

Bob Stewart will have informed you of what happened at the District Party Committee meeting at which W. Joss attended.

Glad that Page and the others are in good spirits and so keen to get doing something. By present indications (according to Press reports) there is plenty to be done.

What do you think of the Trades Union Congress Special Industrial

Committee's attitude, as expressed when meeting Baldwin re owners' attitude to District Agreements? Very shaky.

Have you got P. a job yet? He takes some looking after. Glad you have benefited from your holiday. Let Page know I will be on the look-out for him when he gets up to Fife.

April 23rd, 1926.

Just a short note with *The Miner*. Received yours of 14th inst. Sorry to have given you so much trouble, but it required something to make things move in the Party up here.

Yes, the new machine is a Rotary — Lion.

The S.D.F. and the Buckhaven Old Union branch and of course their subsidiary organisation, Buckhaven Labour Association, decided last Sunday to form another Trades and Labour Council but I don't think they will get far. The Divisional Labour Party A.G.M. is on Sunday 1st and the delegates from the local branches will, I think, manage to spike any recognition from that body. Due not to principle but to personal antagonisms there is a split in the Old Union branches regarding the formation of the new Council. In addition [some of] the larger Trade Union branches, although not supporting us, are determined to remain inside the present Council and demonstrated that last night at a special meeting called to discuss and prepare for the 1st of May. A Council of Action comprising the entire Council was agreed to, pamphlets to be printed appealing for members for the formation of a Defence Corps, Cycle Corps, and the Women's Section to organise Nursing and Cooking Sections. A special meeting of the Council, with Labour Councillors of Parish and Town Councils, Labour members on the School Management Committee and Education Authority to be held on Sunday, May 2nd. Co-operatives also invited.

You have sized P. as I see him. Whatever he has done for the movement in the past does not rule out that he is now out to live on it.

By tonight's Press it appears as if we will "lift the toasters" next Friday. The publication in this morning's papers of 2/1d [reduction] per shift for Scotland has wakened the men up. Wild talk, "hand out the rifles", etc., was common enough, but to get some of those talkers to face the manager to be "made up" to 9/4d. takes some doing but it will require to be done.

I was at Dunfermline on Wednesday, at the Reform Union Executive meeting. The anti-Communist resolutions were well whacked, but what a tame opposition. P.S. Excuse brevity of note but I am up to the neck at present, George, carrying on a Press controversy with S.D.F., getting "Spark" ready, etc.

April 28th, 1926.

Received yours of 26th and 27th April. The same symptoms appear to have again attacked the leaders when they are almost up against it — funk. "Let us show 'public opinion' that we are not out for a scrap but are prepared to explore every avenue and so make a lasting and honourable settlement."

Like you, George, I have made up my mind for a big sell-out, owing to the fact that Thomas and his kidney are in the foreground, with a considerable backing inside the M.F.G.B. itself. At the time of writing I don't know how today's delegate Conference has gone, but realising that the Adamson-Cook (Fife Cook) type are usually found in considerable numbers at those affairs (and they are to be found amongst the Miner M.P.s who appear to prefer MacDonald to the M.F.G.B.), I think any little loophole presenting itself will be made the excuse for dodging a fight. However, to get away from the intrigue, you have sized up the situation fairly well re the M.F.G.B. being stiffened by the owners' notices.

Enclosed you will find the notice posted at the Wellesley on Monday and a copy of a poster I drew up and also posted on the Pit head. It has caused some stir. Up to Saturday the prevailing idea with Coal Jock hereabouts was "There will be no scrap", "The Government will come in at the last minute and we'll just carry on", "Didn't Baldwin manage it last July?". But on Monday different expressions were to be heard. "By Christ, ah'll dae some o' the bastards in before ah wud work for that", "Gaun back tae an 8 hours day? Ah'll see the bloody grass growing ower the whorls (pulley wheels) before that happens". All the long range (to the average mineworker) fighting in London hasn't one/hundredth part the effect of a notice posted at the Pit head. In Scotland, where more than 50% of the production is by coal cutters, the clause re youths is a very important one. No exceptional skill is required, only an aptitude to swing a No. 9 shovel, coupled with a whale bone back, is required, and as the tendency amongst young miners is to "get dug into it" (as far as work is concerned) you can appreciate the move of the owners.

Enclosed 2 copies of No. 21 of "The Spark", 1 copy of "The Signal", 1 copy of *The Justiceman*[189] — Jock Bird's paper which you will notice is not a Party paper — Coalowners' notice and Poster. We have decided that one comrade be "told off" to write "The Spark" leader, have it examined and criticised by the group before publication. As we are on different shifts that means we must have it at the group meeting on Sunday, 5 days before publication — which is certainly a disadvantage; but the idea of the entire group being pulled in is better than leaving it to one comrade, and has certain advantages.

How is Page getting along? Feeling fit and now gathered all the threads together? Is P. still hanging around? You will notice by "The Spark" that we are to have J. R. Campbell Friday week. He will "do" 2 meetings in Fife, both the same day. P.S. Will send on copy of Trades and Labour Council leaflet re Workers' Defence Corps, along with any developments should the lock-out take place.

April 29th, 1926.

Enclosed letter which explains itself. I received it tonight from comrade Pattie. As you will have an opportunity of informing the comrades whom P. is staying with (if still in London) and also the Political Bureau, am sending the letter to you. Will you return it to Y. Pattie, 55 Commercial Street, Methil,

Fife. Sorry to cause you any more trouble, George, but you will see the importance of the letter. He has a membership card of the Communist Party of Great Britain, Methil Group.

Tonight's Press contains practically no news as to the position, which looks as if the T.U.C. meeting today[190] has made some strong decisions, which might compel the Government and coalowners to back down. Am doing a double shift tomorrow, 6 a.m. to 10 p.m., owing to my butty going to a Gas Commission meeting in Perth, so am going to turn in.

Methil, May 7th, 1926, 11.24.[191]

[To] Veltass London. Pits Docks Railways Trains Buses 100%. Council Controls. Spirit Invincible. Luck. Davy.

Methil, May 13th, 1926. 2.8.

[To] Veltass London. Still Solid. No Wavering. Davy.

H.M. Prison, Dundee.
May 15th, 1926.[192]

Dear Father and Mother,

I am getting on A.I., doing nothing and being fed for doing so. So far as my experience goes, this is a quiet life. Hope everything is going well at Methil. I understand Sandy Gillespie engaged the lawyer to defend us: let him know I appreciate his action very much.[193] Hope all at home are now settled down after your unfamiliar experience of yesterday morning. You can let O'Neil and the others know I have had 2 days' rest, which were needed, after the strenuous time just gone. You might let George Hutt know what has transpired; you will get his address from one of his letters to me. Don't trouble to answer this letter. See if Nicol[194] has delivered all his *Labour Monthly* and, if not, to do so. Best wishes to all. Your loving son, Davy.

May 15th, 1926.[195]

Thanks wires. Unexampled solidarity London throughout printers spendid Stop General Council betrayal followed degrading railway agreement etcetera produced greatest bitterness indignation gives us finest opportunity to Stop Everyone here still solidest behind miners best luck. George.

May 18th, 1926.[196]

Just a note to say we received your "wire" on Sunday. Sorry to state Davie was arrested at 2 a.m. on Friday, 14th, for a "so-called seditious speech" delivered at Denbeath, Methil, on May 7th. His trial takes place tomorrow, Wednesday, 19th, at Cupar. I will let you know the result. This is a copy of a letter received from him,[197] which shows his spirit is not broken yet.

Yours in the fight,
James Proudfoot, "his father".

278

May 20th, 1926.[198]

Many thanks for package of papers. You will have received the note from my father re my arrest last Friday morning on a charge of sedition, inciting to riot and violence: Good Christ. I duly appeared in front of the old guiser with the wig last Friday and was refused bail ("This is an exceedingly grave charge and I therefore refuse bail.") and remanded until Wednesday, May 19th (yesterday), when 18 of us were granted bail at £5 per head. I appear again on Friday, May 28th. We were detained in Dundee Prison from Friday to Wednesday, during which time I had a decent and needful rest.

I will later give you a detailed statement of what transpired here, organisation, etc., as I am trying to gather a few loose ends at present. Sufficient at present to state that the Party lead re "All Power to Trades Council", Defence Corps, etc., was carried out and meetings still going on every night at which thousands still attend. So far as General Strike is concerned, Pits, Docks and Railways are still at it here, only trams and buses working. A strong International Class War Prisoners' Aid committee has been formed and as far as I can gather almost £100 has been collected for local use (21 of us being arrested, 4 being sentented to 2 months' hard labour) and a fairly decent number have joined as Associate members. The arrests have fairly roused the workers here and a petition has been signed by over 7,000 demanding the withdrawal of the Police Inspector at Methil. He is one of the Prussian school — Baton first and warning after. The Party stands to gain not only in prestige but in numbers.

The Police have all the reports (Bulletins I collected to send you) at present, but I will send on when I receive them. Enclosed is the scheme of organisation I submitted to the Trades Council, which was adopted and worked A.I. We had 3 motor cars and over 100 motor cycles at our disposal in addition to numerous push bikes. I was appointed Convener of all sub-committees, in addition to doing as many as 6 meetings per day. We had requests for speakers from all over Fife and as far as Perth. The spirit all over was MAGNIFICENT. Send me copies of all the revolutionary songs with music you can lay your hands on. It is going strong at present and our slogan must be "Keep it going when the going's good".

Trades and Labour Council

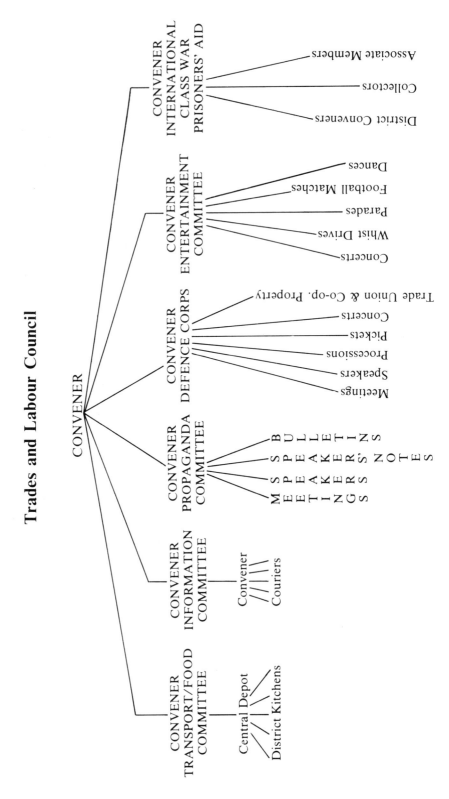

CONVENER

CONVENER TRANSPORT/FOOD COMMITTEE
- Central Depot
- District Kitchens

CONVENER INFORMATION COMMITTEE
- Convener
- Couriers

CONVENER PROPAGANDA COMMITTEE
- MEETINGS
- SPEAKERS
- PAPER SELLING
- BULLETINS

CONVENER DEFENCE CORPS
- Meetings
- Speakers
- Processions
- Pickets
- Concerts
- Trade Union & Co-op. Property

CONVENER ENTERTAINMENT COMMITTEE
- Concerts
- Whist Drives
- Parades
- Football Matches
- Dances

CONVENER INTERNATIONAL CLASS WAR PRISONERS' AID
- District Conveners
- Collectors
- Associate Members

May 23rd, 1926.

Enclosed Strike Bulletings, 2 copies of "The Spark", 1 copy of "The Hutch", 1 copy of "The Spur", 1 copy of "The Signal" and Balance Sheet of Methil Co-operative.

Philip Hodge was speaking at Denbeath today and referred to the money being sent to the M.F.G.B.[199] As the Reform Union is not a section of the M.F.G.B. and is not likely to receive anything through official sources, and as he informed me that arrangements, only partially completed, had been made [with] Miners' Minority Movement to send an allocation to the Reform Union, will you make enquiries about it? As that money will be used by Adamson and Company to make Union capital you will realise the importance of something being done.

Everything is going A.I. here. We had J. R. Campbell here last night and this morning. 14 new members last night. 32 male members, 14 female members and 24 Y.C.L. tonight, and still more to come. 84 for 2 nights. Of course many of them will be shed but it demonstrates how things are moving here. International Class War Prisoners' Aid going strong. I will write you this week as to conduct of strike here. Meetings still being held nightly, opened and closed by singing of *The Red Flag* and *Internationale*. Thousands attending, women very prominent. Arrangements made for Helen Crawfurd to address public meetings and women sympathisers this week. Indications excellent, so much so that Woolley[200] has stated (not at Methil) that Methil is to Fife what Petrograd was to Russia during the Revolution. We must get national speakers sent in to keep things moving, and add freshness to the platform. T.U.C. leaders absolutely discredited, and everywhere heard "By Christ, if ah hear anybody say a bad word aboot the Communists ah'll knock their bloody head aff". Good enough, but the reaction will come in if we don't keep it up. I go up for trial on Friday and judging by Comrade Dick's sentences — 3 months and 14 days — I am likely to get a dose. However, that is only part of the game and will likely do the Party locally some good.

May 24th, 1926.[201]

Am commencing today to write a report of activities carried out during past 3 weeks. A special meeting of Trades and Labour Council was held on Thursday, April 29th, when it was unanimously agreed to form a Council of Action and issue circular for need of Workers' Defence Corps. It was also agreed that another special meeting of Trades and Labour Council, Co-operative Societies, and Labour representatives on Town and Parish Councils, Education and School Management Committees [be held] on Sunday, May 2nd.

A May Day Demonstration was held on May 1st at which ONLY Social Democrats appeared on the platform, our local M.P., Tom Kennedy, being the star, when 500 circulars re Defence Corps were distributed and the crowd was entertained by the Platform to VOTE LABOUR at next election. I got the Executive to agree to hold Public Meetings every night at 6 p.m. to immediately counteract the VOTING DOPE. That was agreed to. At the special meeting called for Sunday, May 2nd, at which the Co-operatives did

NOT attend, it was agreed to augment the Council of Action by Labour representatives on the Public Bodies. At the Public Meeting held at night 8 speakers addressed the meeting, representing Miners, Dockers (N.U.R. and A.S.L.E.&F.), Engineers, and Shop Assistants. 3 Party members and 2 I.L.P.ers were amongst the speakers. I was last, to counter any gush.

Monday, May 3rd, was a day devoted to pressure on Dockers, etc., to come out at night. 6 p.m. meeting was attended by thousands, women being very prominent. 3 Party members out of 5 speakers. Subject: Need for General Strike and local preparations — Defence Corps, Pickets, Couriers, Speakers, pressure on Parish Council, Town Council Child Welfare, and School Management Committee. I was invited by Leven Trades and Labour Council to submit scheme of organisation at 7 p.m. Unanimously agreed to adopt scheme but to call Defence Corps "WORKERS' CONSTABLES". What's in a name?

Meeting of Tramway and Bus workers called for 11 p.m., at which over 1,000 workers attended. Organised a branch of Transport and General Workers (Tramway and Commercial Section) of 65 members where only 10 members previously existed. They unanimously agreed to strike. A rather peculiar item occurred. I addressed the meeting for over an hour, putting the Party Policy forward — All Power to Trades and Labour Council, Defence Corps, etc. — and after I had finished a local Social Democrat asked if he would be permitted to address the meeting. His request was granted and he stated "that he endorsed EVERY WORD I had said, although he and I were poles apart in POLITICS" (Hold your laugh) and that he offered his services to carry out the Policy I had outlined. I accepted his offer and pointed out the moral — "Realisation of the need for Working Class Unity". The meeting broke up at 2.30 a.m. after singing *The Red Flag*.

A rough attempt to put into operation the scheme I have already sent you was made on Tuesday morning when we commandeered the Co-operative Hall, Methil, as our Headquarters. A list of almost 30 speakers was drawn up and in 3s (Railwaymen, Dockers and Miners at each meeting) sent to address meetings all over the district during the day and afternoon. The main meeting being held at 6 p.m. at Denbeath Bridge. Transport Committee immediately took up the Permit granting and I can assure you, George, it was great to see the RESPECTABILITY coming in hat in hand to get permits. Only those possessing a Trade Union card received permits. The result was a fairly decent influx to the Transport and General Workers' Union. The pickets were doing their work in a thorough manner. Everything on wheels was stopped, motor cycles with pillion riders, and if no permit was in the possession of the pillion rider he or she had to get off and walk BACK from whence they came. No attempt was made to run buses or trams. The Party group had by this time taken complete control of the situation so far [as] a lead was concerned. We were at a disadvantage regarding typewriters and Duplicators, as it was agreed to reserve ours till other sources had been tapped.

Wednesday saw us with a courier service second to none in Britain. 3 motor cars and over 100 motor cycles (East Fife Motor Club placed themselves at our disposal). It is the second largest club in Scotland. The result was that we had requests from all over Fife for speakers, etc. We also had requests from Perth and a Party member was sent on Friday. Couriers were on the hop from all the Trades and Labour Councils and Joint Strike Committees in Fife. The Old Union locally were lying low but after a few meetings under the auspices of the Trades and Labour Council a meeting of Buckhaven Old Union instructed their officials to either get to the Trades and Labour Council or get out of their positions. Denbeath and Methil followed, although those representatives only attended 2 or 3 meetings. However, that hasn't been allowed to pass unnoticed and the result, according to present indications, will be a big breakaway from the Old Union.

I along with another Party member addressed two meetings at Perth on Sunday, May 9th. The reception was great. By this time I was tied down mainly to organisation duties — Convener of all Committees — and we were getting great results from the Committees. An S.D.F.er was convener of the Defence Corps and insists it must be kept intact.

Friday, May 7th, saw the first attempt of the police to break us here. A train was being run from Edinburgh to St Andrews and a picket of ours was charged by the police. However, the train (passenger) was side-tracked off the main line. 11 railwaymen were arrested along with me and fined £3 or 20 days. The engine driver was laid out and marines then put on the train. I expect it was my remarks to above incident on which charge is made.

Monday, May 10th, saw another baton charge on another picket of ours at Muiredge Crossing, when 3 were arrested before the picket realised what had happened. They reorganised and the police had to beat it, the Inspector and Sergeant getting their clocks smashed. You will see the petition which was signed by over 7,000 re the Muiredge event. There was no more police interference because the Defence Corps was reorganised and paraded the streets in columns of 4 under commanders — ex-service N.C.O.s. A great sight and not without preparations to "repel boarders". A courier brought information to Muiredge Picket that a motor lorry with beer had burst through Lochgelly, Bowhill and Dysart pickets and was making for Methil. The Muiredge picket did not attempt to stop it but a number got on board and threw the barrels off, bursting them.

On Wednesday, when the N.U.R. received the first telegram declaring the strike off, hell was let loose. The N.U.R. branch met and unanimously decided to abide by any decision of the Trades and Labour Council, also instructing their secretary to get on the phone to Cramp.[202] It was Thursday forenoon that he managed and Cramp had only groans to offer. The Dockers refused to start but the tramway and Bus workers were granted permission. An attempt was made by the Tramway manager to victimise the officials of the newly formed branch which we nipped in the bud.

The Trades and Labour Council held meetings nightly at 9 o'clock at which over 1,000 attended to hear the reports (submitted by me) and the discussions. Those inclined (if any) to take up a splitting or reactionary policy were overawed by the presence of the crowd, who made no attempt to interfere with the proceedings. Impromptu concerts were held after business was disposed of, lasting till 2 and 3 o'clock in the morning. *The Red Flag* opened and terminated all proceedings.

From what I can gather the 18 arrests on Friday morning, May 14th, created a great noise. The International Class War Prisoners' Aid committee formed has done great work, over £120 being collected. It has taken complete hold. 25 arrests were made here. 4 are doing 2 months for being on pickets, 11 fined £3 or 20 days, and the remainder of us are for trial on Friday and Monday next.

As I informed you in last night's note the Party has come out here with flying colours. Hope to be able to report at least 200 members by end of week. The only regrettable part in this locality was the allowing of the central organisation to go to pieces the day after the 18 arrests. However, although being barred from public speaking I have managed to get the Council to realise the importance of keeping the organisation intact and we are again forging ahead, making contacts, applying pressure to the Parish Council, Town Council and School Management Committee and Education Authority. The latter tried to put the onus of feeding school children on the Parish Council and the latter refused to accept the responsibility, supported by Trades and Labour Council, as the Education Authority rates are based on Fife as a county (embracing of course the residential areas) and the Parish Council here covers an industrial area. The Parish Council are only granting 15/- per week to strikers' wives or housekeepers and have decided, with the assistance of the Trades and Labour Council, to commence communal kitchens next week for all adults.

We had the Public Health Committee of the Town Council, augmented with a representative from the 3 districts in the Burgh, granting relief on Friday, May 7th. School Management Committee commenced feeding school children, 3 meals per day 7 days per week, on Monday, May 10th, and the Parish granted relief 2 or 3 days later — over 3,500 applications during the first 2 or 3 days.

As I am writing this from memory I hope you will excuse the jumbled manner in which I am presenting it to you. There is certainly one point which cannot be stretched too far — the magnificent response by the rank and file and the determination of the women. It was a glorious 9 days and so far as this district is concerned is still a great affair. Another 2 or 3 days and it was either complete capitulation of the Government or a bid for Power by the workers. One couldn't move here without hearing "The bloody Communists are right. We'll hae tae tak things into oor ain hands, tae mak a right job o' it."

T. Kennedy was here on Saturday re the arrests and he was politely informed that he had to take ALL cases of arrests into consideration and demand release, not "certain cases . . . that is, rioting and obstruction" only. He is to speak at 2 meetings next weekend and I can assure you that he has his job cut out to get his Parliamentary stuff across. P.S. I forgot to mention 1 important point. I was responsible for issuing notes for ALL speakers and you can bet I did so.

June 1st, 1926.

Received your note of 30th May. Will get necessary information. Enclosed note[203] to Nat Watkins (re matter of telegram) which you might give him. Soup commences tomorrow. Will send copy of local "rag". P.S. Can you read enclosed?

June 2nd, 1926.

Enclosed copy of local paper, which has devoted some space to my case.[204] He has kept out some of the spiciest bits against the police, both during cross-examination by Burke[205] and statements made by me. We had more from Methil at Cupar yesterday — all fined — and a woman today — £12 fine. In all, 23 cases from Methil — 6 doing time: 4 2 months and 2 6 weeks; 12 fined £3, 1 £15, 1 £12 (a woman), 2 discharged, and 1 Not Proven.

I was unable to ascertain the exact numbers you asked for, but according to the Group Leader the following figures do not exaggerate: Party—100, Women—between 40 and 50, Y.C.L.—45, International Class War Prisoners' Aid—106 Associate members. Almost 200, out of which something should be got. I don't know how other groups are doing or what demands they are making on the Centre for organisers and national speakers, but I can't for one moment think Headquarters can afford to overlook us very long, especially in sending a woman organiser.

We are trying to get a Party choir started as we have some promising material to hand.

My cousin[206] thanks Comrade Mrs Hutt for her note and hopes they will meet soon in Methil. So don't forget your promise, George.

The Communal feeding commences tomorrow. Soup will again flow throughout the land. Comrade McArthur is sending the local report to Headquarters via you. You will notice how arrangements locally are going re soup, Parish Councils and School children, in "The Tiger", which by the way is the paper J. K. Neil is employed on.[207] The scheme adopted by Scoonie Parish (Leven) is one I submitted to the Trades and Labour Council, but has not incorporated the main part — Representation and Control by the Trades and Labour Council.

June 8th, 1926.

Sorry at being so late in sending copy of *The Miner*, but have been exceptionally busy during past few days.

We have requests for speakers from Perth, Dundee, and other non-mining areas, but owing to the influx of new members locally have had to refuse those requests meantime as we are all required here to try and get some order created amongst the local Party membership. Was at East Wemyss and Cowdenbeath yesterday, where Gala demonstrations were held. At the former place we had Methil police in attendance. "We take our own, our very own police with us."

A Council of Action for Fife was formed on Saturday, to co-ordinate all activities in the County. The most important news I have to report is one which

I consider should bring Unity in Fife very much nearer. At the Reform Union Executive meeting on Thursday I moved that we should approach the Old Union officials to get a Joint Committee set up to control all monies collected in non-mining areas, control and direct all speakers and collectors in those areas, and distribute the monies so collected to needy areas in Fife. A deputation of 3, consisting of J. Stewart, W. Crooks and myself was sent to interview the Old Union officials, who agreed to the idea. We were to meet on Saturday to discuss the scheme but owing to the Old Union Sub Executive not meeting until 4 p.m. on Saturday the meeting was postponed until tomorrow, Wednesday. Will let you know result of meeting.

Despite attempts at sabotage by Old Union officials the communal feeding is going along fairly well. Denbeath on Sunday morning gave a breakfast of ham and egg, and eggs were issued at the other kitchens. Enclosed wage list issued by the Wemyss Coal Company in this locality. P.S. Many Old Union branches have distributed the M.F.G.B. allocation amongst their members instead of putting it to the Central Pool. The bloody rotters.

June 21st, 1926.

A few lines with *The Miner*. Received your 2 letters of 30th May and 11th June but can't find time to reply to them. Instead of living from day to day we are living from meeting to meeting — Public, Committee, Group, etc. I am about sick looking down from a platform at crowds, but I suppose we have asked for it and are now getting what we asked for.

Yesterday we had a march to the Poorhouse (Workhouse) at Thornton, which meant by road 10 miles each way for the Methil contingent. Absolutely great. A procession in column of 4s of between 3,000 and 3,500, with bands, pipe and brass. A demonstration of over 5,000 at Thornton, composed of those who came on bikes and buses, and the procession. Women's section, Communist Party, with 5 or 6 banners marched back with the column. Tremendous enthusiasm. Arranging for pickets for bings tomorrow morning.

Enclosed 2 copies of circular issued by Methil Trades and Labour Council which explains itself. Don't know how many signatures obtained. Communal feeding still being carried out. Central Council of Action for Fife beginning to be effective.

Re organiser's job, you have stated my position. I don't want it, although up to the present nothing has been said. There are others who are quite capable and who will, due to their activities, require a job when this "do" is terminated.

I have decided to cancel the *Sunday Worker* order, although sales are still going up (20 quires). £2.9.6d. has "gone west", although sent by registered letter, and I have had enough of that game. Snapshots of demonstrations have been sent to the *Weekly* and *Sunday Worker* from this area.

June 29th, 1926.

Am taking this opportunity to reply to yours of 27th inst. Glad to know that Comrade Mrs Hutt has got safely through her ordeal and that both are doing so well. I am instructed to inform you that you are all to come up here when strength allows Comrade Mrs Hutt. You will be in for a new experience, George, but will, I expect, manage to successfully meet it. Here's the best for another little Pioneer.[208]

We are having great times here. On Picket every morning at 4 a.m. at 2 Pits where scabs are filling coal off the bings. The nearest Pit is 2½ miles from Methil and the unfortunate bit is that only Methil has responded so far to the call for Pickets. About 60 Police met us the first morning. They expected a frontal attack on the Pit but were taken aback when they noticed the Picket (80 strong) take up positions at the various entrances to the Pit. We stopped the majority of the scabs before they reached the Pit and caused the Police to come out and patrol the roads in the vicinity. Next morning we changed our tactics by placing decoy pickets in prominent places and had mobile pickets doing the necessary. The Police couldn't tumble to it and only those scabs who slept on the pit premises were at work. We have worn out the most of the Police and they are now very jumpy. They don't seem to be able to anticipate any of our moves and are doing their utmost to create trouble. The Inspector threatened to arrest me "if I spoke to anyone". Nice, affable fellow. However, on Saturday morning they managed to pull off a win, by starting work before 4 a.m. instead of 6 a.m. The Police are now on cycles, push and motor, and go 4 miles to escort the scabs in to work.

I am having a morning off tomorrow as I am feeling a bit off.

13 men are working at pit about 7 miles from here and J. McArthur and myself were there on Saturday at the invitation of the local strike Committee. We arranged a scheme of picketing which if carried out should prove very successful. Up to the present I haven't heard the result.

What do you think of the General Council's latest move in hoodwinking the M.F.G.B. officials? Surely they can't have many supporters amongst the rank and file now.

There are 3 organisers in Fife, ALL in WEST Fife at present: Woolley, Communist Party, Gillies, Y.C.L., and Tapstal, Y.C.L.[209] The 2 former are charged with sedition, etc. I don't know when they are due to appear.

Communal feeding is still proceeding and the kiddies are being well looked after. A move is again afoot to form another Trades and Labour Council here.

I haven't had time to read the June *Monthly*. What do you think of my latest job? Local Party Committee member in charge of the Women's Section. I can get them (jobs, I mean). Enclosed copy of "The Picket", the Lochgelly group's paper.[210] Re "The Spark": due to pressure of work we have been unable to produce it. It is certainly rotten but it can't be helped in the meantime. I am still receiving the *Sunday Worker* and it is going great. 12 Quires before the General strike, this week's order — 24 Quires. The Y.C.L.ers are getting their backs into it, and are building up a decent fund for their group. They have become affiliated to the Trades and Labour Council. One youngster on his first attempt, Sunday past, sold 4 dozen in ¾ hour and asked for 8 dozen of next issue. *Workers' Weekly*, 45 dozen. We are getting some good salesmen and saleswomen amongst the new members. One chap declared he WOULDN'T sell a paper but was amongst the first to volunteer. 3½ dozen first week. Now 7 dozen. One woman comrade "doing" 4 dozen. I can visualise losing my job (with no regrets) at this pace.

Comrade Joss has been up here investigating "trouble" in the Party in Lochgelly — lack of understanding of Party Policy. I don't know what his opinion is but I think J. Stewart will get it in the neck. P.S. Indications that Council of Action for Fife will peter out shortly.

July 7th, 1926.

A few lines with *The Miner*, which I have just discovered hasn't been sent on to you. Sorry I have to report a break in our front here, not by the mineworkers but by the sons of vomits and dregs of Methil, the lowest of a low caste — some of those who load the trawlers at Methil Docks. A Norwegian ship arrived yesterday with coal from Belgium and although we managed to get them to refuse to handle it yesterday and decide at a meeting by 40-2 not to touch it, some of the rotten swine, under police protection, started today. The majority have loyally carried out their decision and at another meeting today reaffirmed their previous decision, although likely to lose their dole. We have promised to feed them at the communal kitchens.

The miners are *standing* solid. Standing is the correct word, as far as *action* is concerned. Christ, it says something when we who go on picket are almost outnumbered by police. However, we have to realise the feeding arrangements are to blame for this. The offer to Scotland amounted to 8 hours shift, immediate reduction of 14.2% on pieceworkers' rates, day wage men to receive April rates, surface workers to work ½ hour more per shift at April rates until September 30th, when ascertainments of industry would determine wages (87 wages, 13 profits) minimum; April 133.1/3% above 1888 basis = 9/4d., to be reduced to 110% = 8/4¾d., surface workers to suffer corresponding reductions in rates and also reductions of subsistence allowances, latter not stated. We are taking the precaution to have pickets posted in case any waverer might make an attempt to crawl back.

I am now Chairman of the local Trades and Labour Council. Only 2 nominations, Comrade McArthur and myself, which indicates to some extent the present influence of the Party here. As I was the Local Party Committee nominee, Comrade McArthur withdrew.

Comrade Mrs Crawfurd has been here for a week and as far as I can gather we have had more increases in membership (23 women in 2 days). I am at present unable to state exact strength (or weakness) of local. Last fortnight 98 males, 56 women, and 45 Y.C.L. had handed in names. P.S. Comrade Mrs Crawfurd will be in London, Monday. She will give you impressions of this district. I am now relieved of duties of looking after women, Comrade Gordon agreeing to accept.[211] Sales of *Sunday Worker* 50½ dozen.

July 23rd, 1926.

I have now managed to secure a few minutes in which to reply to yours of the 7th and 10th. Page will have informed you that I met him last weekend and will also have given you the information re the Fife District meeting of last Sunday in Methil. I am Pit Group convener on the District Party Committee, and as Page suggested or rather wished the sub-District Party Committee is composed of 5 from Methil local and 1 from West Fife. We have now secured premises in Methil for local headquarters, which when furnished will assist in keeping the membership intact. Woolley received 2 months hard yesterday but another comrade is acting for him.

Re the number of members in Methil local, it is rather unfortunate that the comrade responsible for registration can only show slightly over 100 male and almost 90 women, although we should have according to Comrade Gordon 258 male and 138 women, with 58 Y.C.L. However, due to amount of varied work we have had to perform he has done fairly well. We are getting them down to work — Complaints Committees, Parish Council work, Literature Distribution, Trade Union fractions, Co-operative fractions (latter not as yet functioned as no meetings of Co-operatives), and Trades and Labour Council fractions.

You will be aware of the Unity proposals as they are published in this week's *Workers' Weekly*. The Reform Union Executive met on Wednesday and had a full dress debate on the proposals. I was there and received the full force of the attack from the Diehards, but although speaking against Unity they were not prepared to vote against the proposals but voted for no recommendation to the branches. However, "recommendation" was carried by 31-11 and that branch decisions be sent in by Monday, August 2nd. No attack was made on the Party. So far Methil, Buckhaven, Denbeath, Methilhill, East Wemyss and West Wemyss Reform Union branches have *unanimously* accepted the proposals, thereby making East Fife Reform Union branches SOLID for amalgamation. The Old Union have not moved as yet but we are carrying on meetings in all the villages to arouse the Old Union members to bring pressure on their local officials to demand an immediate delegate meeting to discuss the proposals. We have also arranged a Mass Demonstration at Denbeath Bridge for Sunday 1st at which Reform Union officials and Old Union officials, Central and Local, are invited to appear. P. Hodge has agreed to come. Our slogans are "Unity before termination of lock-out" and "Down with everyone opposing Unity".

The *Miners' Supplement* is A.I. and it is a pity that 2 issues of the *Weekly* aren't running every week during the present crisis.[212] Possibly all the worker correspondents won't keep it up after the crisis is over, but attempts should be made to induce them to do so.

Another mix-up has happened at Lochgelly. They are the limit. The Roman Catholics in West Fife, as you will have noticed, have commenced what appears to be an attempt to form a Catholic Union and the Lochgelly Local have actually PRINTED and as far as I can gather ASSISTED to distribute the Catholic miners' appeal to the Hierarchy to intervene on behalf of the miners. It's not organisers they want, it's nursemaids. As you remark, Tapsell is a windbag and receives very little notice in Methil when he makes his appearance. The Y.C.L.ers here stand up to him all right. We have got some good youngsters, both game and intelligent.

You ask "if the relief funds are kept well going, do I think the miners can keep up the struggle for another 2 or 3 months?". Judging by the general attitude here they will keep it up till Doomsday. The only thing not mentioned here is WORK. First class weather and tanned miners receiving fairly decent rations on which to loaf around at their leisure is a new affair that fairly tickles everyone. Everyone is assuring the other that they are more handsome than ever dreamt of and gaining weight also. I don't know whether it is due to my being "too crabbed" but I have refused to put on weight, actually I have lost 12 lbs since May 1st, proving the assertion regularly made by some of the "old gang" here "that I refuse to be like the others". Baldwin and Company in my opinion are going to play a waiting game, relying on the Press attacks on Cook and the reported breakaways, with the Minister of Health cuts in relief causing a stampede back to work on the owners' terms.

What do you think of the *Herald*'s leader of Tuesday, July 20th, re the loan proposals?[213] Christ, they would make a decent cat vomit. But we shouldn't be surprised or riled by anything they put up, especially the loan stunt, as they are only following on the lines laid down by J. R. MacDonald with his Dawes Plan.

We had a first class concert on Tuesday night when Comrade Helen Crawfurd presented International Class War Prisoners' Aid medals to the 6 who "did time". Comrade Crawfurd is fairly "taken" with Methil, despite the fact that we retained her for 1 week. The *Sunday Worker* reported that the presentation took place last Saturday night, which was a "bloomer".

Enclosed copy of *The Miner*, which by the way has not entered into the Unity proposals. We intend making an attempt to run an issue of "The Spark" next week, as it will be the first anniversary of its advent into this area. P.S. Let Page know I had to walk home again from Kirkcaldy on Sunday night (twice in 2 nights), having the luck to see the last bus leave the terminus when 300 yards away. Comrade Gordon and myself have been appointed to represent Methil Trades and Labour Council at the Minority Movement Conference at Battersea on August 28th and 29th.

July 29th, 1926.

As I expect you will be away on holiday for a few days and won't get this until you return, am being very brief. Spirit of men and women here A.I. Local getting down to organised work and, what is a good sign (although looked at by some as unfortunate), some sticking out their jaw. Matter was trivial but it is a start. Y.C.L. meetings are IT. Hell with the lid off. Youngsters of 16 and 17 shaking fists in opponents' faces and stating their case very well. Enclosed 2 copies of No. 26 of "The Spark". We intend running it weekly. P.S. By all accounts Adamson is again at his sabotage re Unity. Hodge is advocating acceptance but in my opinion with his tongue in his cheek, expecting Adamson to win out.

August 18th, 1926.

Thanks for yours of 1st August and postcard of 9th. I expect you will be back at it again after your fortnight's holiday. You are correct re No. 26 of "The Spark". Comrade Gordon was responsible for numbering it. There has not been Nos. 24 and 25.

Enclosed photo of our rooms. Decorations by Comrade Gordon. They cannot be mistaken for a Salvation Army shelter.

We slaughtered the Bishops' Memo in East Fife by a campaign in the villages and were successful in getting 13 OLD UNION branches out of 15 to vote against.[214] An index as to what could be done INSIDE. Scotland must have been AGAINST or Smillie and Company would not have demanded a ballot vote. Cook made a hell of a speech at Buckhaven.[215] Disconnected, full of pessimism, and a rotten apology for the Bishops' Memo. He still has the support of the miners and their wives but a continuation of the Buckhaven stuff will soon undermine him. I see by this morning's paper that the delegate conference have given powers to the Executive to open negotiations. "Unconditional negotiations", according to the *Daily Record*, for the purpose of keeping the Federation intact. It appears that we are in for a 2nd '21, ordered back to work on conditions which the rank and file are against, "to keep the Federation intact". The spirit here is A.I. yet, although the enthusiasm which was manifest during the first 8 weeks has now been displaced by a dogged determination "to see it through".

I expect you will have seen the report of the Balgonie demonstration.[216] You couldn't imagine a more hopeless lot than those scabs. They took the wind out of our sails by asserting themselves "SCABS", "ONCE A SCAB ALWAYS A SCAB", "WE KNOW WHAT WE ARE DOING IN ASSISTING THE BOSS TO REDUCE WAGES AND INCREASE HOURS, BUT WE ARE WILLING TO WORK 9 OR 10 HOURS", *ad nauseam*. Christ, I never felt so much like doing a clog wallop on anyone's face as when talking to those rats. We are keeping a regular campaign on those villages, which is preventing a further drift back.

The Party is getting a fairly good grip here now, although the women are proving the best members. Two meetings — 1 business and 1 Party training — weekly, attended by 80. We have a speakers' class also and 16 to 20 attend. The Y.C.L. is shaping well. 1 of our women members (Mrs Gordon) and 5 Y.C.L.ers held an open air meeting last Friday night and according to reports (I was unable to attend) did very well. A group of the Young Comrades' League is on the way to formation as a result of that meeting.[217] We had a sale of the *Weekly* a week ago of 65 dozen, but as money is scarce we dropped last week to 58 dozen. The *Sunday Worker* sales have increased since May from 12 Quires to 27 Quires. Not bad, considering the scarcity of money. As against that I have to report a decrease of *Labour Monthly*. May order was 78 and I have been compelled to reduce August to 50, due to scarcity of cash. However, George, I think we will make up the leeway when work is resumed.

The Unity campaign is being held up by the Old Union. We have tried to get the Old Union members to compel their officials to move, but only in East

Fife have we had any success. Methil Trades and Labour Council called a delegate conference of all Reform Union and Old Union branches at Lochgelly, but only 23 branches attended — 17 Reform Union and 6 Old Union, 5 of the latter being from East Fife, Bowhill being the only West Fife Old Union branch represented.

The District Party Committee has been departmentalised, Methil Local having 7 out of 12 members. Despite a decision made at last meeting that the District Party Committee members should remain in Fife during the present dispute to consolidate the Party, 2 West Fife members have since gone to Ireland with bands to collect money. This has been the procedure all through with those chaps. Agree to decisions at central meetings and break them immediately they get to their locals. I am in charge of the Pit Group and asked all locals to send in reports with names of Party members, where employed before lock-out, etc., to have at least a skeleton organisation of Pit Groups started immediately work was resumed; but Lochgelly local in their wisdom (?) have decided like the Liberals they are "that the time is not opportune to form Pit Groups". We will possibly have a Bolshevik party in Fife after the Revolution or by drowning some of the supposed leaders. Bird and Lumsden[218] in Bowhill have been too busy collecting money to give the Party any attention and the result is no group in Bowhill.

I was at Aberdeen during the weekend, under Party auspices (arranged 3 weeks ago), and addressed 2 meetings. The Local there has not got down to the new form of organisation as yet, but there are a number of good members.

Black coal is still being unloaded at Methil and those unloading it have broken the dockers' rates for that class of work. 1/6d. per shift "dirt money" is allowed but the crowd here are not receiving it and, with the exception of the dockers' secretary, are making no attempt to get it.

Enclosed copy of *The Miner*. It certainly performs a function = provides some printers with work.

I had a letter from Comrade O'Neil who 2 months ago went to Chatham to open a trade in Kent coalfield, and he informs me that he is due back in Methil on Sunday 1st, owing to being unable to get trade. His assistance to develop the Party here will be welcome.

I hope Comrade Mrs Hutt, Baby and yourself have enjoyed and benefited from your holiday. The youngsters here are saving their pennies for Baby Hutt's visit to Methil.

There is the likelihood of a split here during the November elections. The Town Council Labour Group having refused to recognise the Trades and Labour Council, and as 2 of them retire in November and have stated that they will stand as "Independents", we are going to oppose them.

Will give you a fuller report when Comrade Gordon and myself come to Minority Movement Conference on August 28th and 29th.

August 23rd, 1926.
Received yours of 18th August and Comrade Mrs Hutt's parcel of 20th. The kiddies send their thanks to "Baby Hutt" for the chocolate and hope to see

her soon. I sent the clothes to Comrade Mrs Doig, Secretary of Women's Section of Labour Party here, who is in charge of that work. There have been some very bad cases of hardship. One kiddie was born here last week and no clothes for it, although I understand it was due to ignorance of the existence of Relief Fund on the part of the parents. We have still with us that docile type who are not prepared to even try to do something for themselves or their offspring.

Surely Herb Smith and the other waverers in the M.F.G.B. Executive *NOW* realise that they arc up against something different to what they previously tackled and will go all out as a start for the withdrawal of the "safety men" who are being used all over to produce coal. Scab coal is coming in here in greater quantities and the dockers, instead of showing hostility, are working overtime to get the boats discharged. They struck on Friday last to get what they are entitled [to] (under the National Agreement), 1/6d. per shift "dirty money", but played the dirty on each other. Some of them who were prominent did not get started on Saturday and nothing was said.

Enclosed front page of today's *Daily Record*. They appear to be well up against it when they are put to it to try and raise the "national" feeling. "Scotch miners are stickers, but those bloody Englishmen and Welshmen are letting the Scotsmen down" sort of stuff. It is cutting no ice here at any rate.

Gordon and I will leave Kirkcaldy on Friday night at 8.40 and arrive King's X Saturday at 7.20 a.m. Hope to see you all in the pink.

September 7th, 1926.

Comrade Gordon and myself arrived home all right last Tuesday morning and since then we have all had a fairly busy time with meetings, etc. The Workers' International Relief granted almost £1,000 to Fife and 2/6d. parcels were distributed to youngsters under 5 years. Distribution in Methil area was a debacle due to the women pushing and shoving. Tempers were lost and some statements made that would have been better unsaid.

Attempts have been made by the Fife Coal Company to create a breakaway at Dalbeath Colliery, West Fife. They offered 12/- per shift of 8 hours, with 1/- per shift to assist payment of back rent. It failed. They then offered 15/- per shift of 8 hours with 1/- per shift to assist payment of back rent. It has also failed. Cutting from last night's *Edinburgh Evening News* enclosed to show "activities" of Fife Coal Company. Sir Adam Nimmo is chairman.

Wemyss Coal Company have closed down Earlseat Mines (500 men) for keeps, and a rumour is current that they are also closing down another pit, "Wee Michael", at East Wemyss, which will mean that although work was immediately resumed, 50% of mineworkers in East Fife will not be absorbed this year. I understand from a fairly reliable source that only 250 men at most will be engaged in Wellesley for some time, due to conditions underground, which will mean only 1 shift winding for some time. No attempt has been made by the Wemyss Coal Company to create a stampede. Buckhaven branch of the Old Union has again assisted the Wemyss Coal Company. The manager of the

Rosie applied to them for permission to fill the coal bing "for safety purposes", and the officials called a meeting of their members, who, acting on the lead given by the officials, decided to allow the surface workers employed at Rosie to fill the coal. Reasons: (1) If not granted by Union, management would employ scabs of their own under police protection; (2) Pickets would then be used and would possibly be arrested by Police. "We don't want anyone arrested"; (3) Although other managers of Wemyss Coal Company had violated "safety work" agreement, the Rosie manager hadn't. (So we will give him the opportunity); (4) (The tit-bit) Buckhaven Old Union Committee had laid down conditions to the management which had been accepted, viz., Old Union Committee to be allowed to go to the bing to ascertain if only men allowed by them were employed. In other words, allowed the machinery of the Old Union to be used as a SCAB agency instead of the Police and Wemyss Coal Company. We have held a few protest meetings in Buckhaven urging the Old Union members to call a special meeting to overturn their previous decision, but nothing has resulted so far.

At least 30 more summonses have been issued to pickets (most of them Party and Y.C.L. members) who marched scabs home from Muiredge bing. They appear at Cupar on Thursday and are charged under the Conspiracy against Property Act of 1875. 18 Lochgelly men are also charged and appear at Cupar on September 18th, arising from demonstration to Balgonie a few weeks ago.

Unity appears as far off as ever as we can't get the Old Union membership to move an inch. If Unity is not obtained before the end of the lock-out we will have to consider "going back" to the Old Union without any conditions. The Reform Union is now "broke", I understand. However, we are making another attempt this week in East Fife to get a move on. Invitations have been sent out from Methil Trades Council to both Old Union and Reform Union branch secretaries in East Fife to attend a meeting on Friday to carry on another campaign.

Adamson and Potter are playing their usual game. Safety men have been producing coal in West Fife and although informed by the men in the "affected" areas, those bright lads, Potter especially, ignored the men and phoned Carlow Reid, agent for Fife Coal Company in West Fife,[219] who denied coal was being produced and Potter ACCEPTED HIS STATEMENT rather than men's. If the actions of Adamson and Potter at present do not impress the Party members in Fife for Unity at any price then we in my opinion have collected nothing but dead heads who are going to be of no use to the Party.

I understand that T. Bell is coming to Fife on September 25th and 26th to represent the Political Bureau at the District Party Congress to discuss the Annual Party Congress Agenda. We are having a campaign this week in East Fife, having meetings in every place under Party auspices. 2 speakers at every meeting, 1 of whom is an old and the other a new Party member. Chairman also new Party member. We couldn't get any of the women to "have a go at it". The Y.C.L. are also on the move. Local speakers at every meeting. The Young

Comrades League is making headway. I understand they have at least 80 members. Looks A.I., according to numbers. It would do you good to attend a Young Comrades' meeting, if it was only to hear those youngsters sing *The Red Flag, Internationale,* and other songs. They usually form fours and march away from their meetings singing. Everyone wears their colours, Red ties, and those who haven't red ties have red rosettes, red ribbons, or wool fixed on jackets or jerseys.

Woolley will be released on Saturday and a series of meetings have been arranged for him and local Y.C.L.ers. A young workers' conference has been arranged for Saturday, September 18th, at Lochgelly. 2 Y.C.L.ers have been appointed to represent Methil Trades Council. Trade Union branches in this area will also be represented.

Mrs Sawkill[220] and the kiddies send their thanks to Comrade Mrs Hutt and Baby Hutt for the chocolate and hope to see them both in Methil at an early date.

Pugh, according to this morning's press reports, has been giving a mixture re the General Strike in his Presidential address yesterday.[221] It hasn't been reported to any extent but if it is an index to what is likely to happen this week at Bournemouth the Government and the coalowners will not recede from their present attitude. MacDonald and Company appear to be well in the picture now.

September 11th, 1926.

According to this morning's press the coalowners of Scotland, South Wales and South Yorkshire are against a National Agreement. Notts and Derby owners are reported to have given their delegates a free hand, which is very important, considering the fact that it is in those two districts where the strongest attempt to impose (by breakaways) district settlements have been made. Can it be possible that they have discovered because of those attempts that the rank and file are determined to stick out for a National Agreement, or is it because the Notts and Derby owners are more cute than the others and can see the advantages to them of the acceptance of Churchill's proposals? Nimmo and the other Scottish owners are reported to have been unanimous for "Home Rule". I think their attitude has been determined by the weak attitude of the T.U.C. and from the owners' viewpoint have taken the correct line by depending on MacDonald and the Trade Union leaders further isolating the miners and compelling them to be driven by starvation to accept District Agreements.

The Miner is as good as ever. One would think there was no dispute on other than how were the political funds of the miners spent at last General Election, and Joe Corrie's alleged poetry,[222] and the need to attack the Minority Movement in Lanarkshire.

We have commenced another campaign in East Fife for Unity, but as I mentioned in my last note I am not very hopeful of much success, although we are taking a different line this time due to the amendments to proposals sent in by Old Union and now by Reform Union Executive to Old Union amendment.

We are urging both Reform Union and Old Union to demand the Scottish (by letter direct to Scottish from branches and also via Dunfermline) to call a meeting of Reform Union and Old Union for Saturday, September 25th to discuss amendments and clear away differences. The spirit here is still A.I.

September 18th, 1926.

Received yours of 8th and 12th. It must have been positively agonising to sit and listen to the "tripe" ladled out at Bournemouth with the present struggle going on. It has been demonstrated very forcibly that however much the Minority Movement and Party Policy has got a grip on the rank and file it is a long way from being sufficiently organised to even compel the Trade Union leaders to give it lip service, let alone get put into operation. More and more concentrated activity must be carried out in Union branch meetings and workshop by the Party and the Minority Movement.

As I indicated in my last note we have mapped out a Unity campaign. Again like the General Policy we have had enthusiastic receptions from the rank and file, but when attempting to organise fractions in the Old Union to press the demand on the Old Union and Scottish for a 3 party meeting for September 25th we have failed so far. I addressed 10 meetings in 4 days (mixed meetings of Reform Union and Old Union members) and it was agreed at those meetings to send the resolution to the 3 bodies, but I know of only 3 Old Union branches which have agreed to send on the resolution to "Wullie" and the Scottish. Of course, George, owing to the Reform Union having drawn those with any initiative from the Old Union such a state of affairs was bound to result. The Party fraction on the Reform Union Executive made a big "bloomer" at the last Reform Union Executive meeting when they allowed an amendment re Reform Union office staff, contracts, etc., to be carried unopposed, to an amendment submitted to the Unity proposals by the Old Union. It was either a case of "funking" or being outmanoeuvred. According to some of the Party fraction it was a case of the former on the part of Comrade McArthur, the fraction leader. Possibly you might hear more about it at Headquarters as Comrade E. H. Brown[223] has been investigating when up here during the past few days. Whether funk or not the result has played into the hands of the anti-Unity bunch on each side.

We have had a campaign to withdraw all safety men. It was organised by the Council of Action and good results have been obtained in Lochgelly, Glencraig, Lochore and Bowhill, but we have drawn a blank in East Fife. I had a big meeting at Denbeath on Wednesday where it was unanimously agreed to picket on Friday to withdraw the safety men from the Wellesley, but on Thursday Denbeath Old Union held a branch meeting and turned down the picketing and withdrawal. They agreed to send representatives to inform the officials of the Scottish Underground Firemen's Union[224] what was to happen, and according to the Firemen's local Treasurer stated that "THEY WERE NOT IN FAVOUR OF THE SAFETY MEN BEING WITHDRAWN AS THEY HAD NOT BEEN INSTRUCTED BY THE FEDERATION". The result was that only 7 of us were on picket on Friday morning at the Wellesley.

We were unable to do anything, but we had a picket on for the night shift and one of the electricians I was successful in stopping was sent to his work a few minutes later by an Old Union official. We held a meeting about eleven o'clock last night and appealed for a big picket for this morning at 4.30 a.m. We had a turn-out of about 70 or 80, but the Union split and the craft union problem defeated us, plus of course the "stab in the back" action of the Old Union. Lochgelly and the other West Fife areas were successful because of coal being filled from falls and in some cases being cut, which caused some of the safety men to ask the miners to picket them. In addition the Firemen's Union hasn't a big following there. Those incidents are proving the imperative need for Unity between the Reform Union and Old Union, and also the extermination of the craft unions, who are again being used to defeat us.

We are still plodding along with the new membership, of whom a few are showing good promise of becoming speakers.

By the way, George, the Scotch way is to spell ECK, not as you had in your last letter.

An attempt is to be made on Sunday by Buckhaven Old Union officials to form a new Trades and Labour Council. Ben Shaw, Scottish Organiser of the Labour Party, is to attend the meeting. We are organising a demonstration of protest to give Shaw some idea of the feeling here against such a proposition. This would not occur, or at least would not have any chance of success, were it not for the Union split. However, according to the reports we have received Sunday's meeting will not be successful in forming a new Trades and Labour Council, as some of the bigger Union branches (Methil N.U.R.) have decided not to be represented.

The indications are promising for the formation of new Party Groups in a few villages around here. Sales of *Workers' Weekly* and *Sunday Worker* are good, and the Party Policy re the present dispute is enthusiastically accepted, but should we be successful in forming those groups we are up against the problem of retaining them because of lack of experienced Party members to coach them; but again the Unity of the Reform Union and Old Union assists to partially solve that problem, as we would then be enabled to concentrate more on internal Party business. You will think, and with some justification, that I have allowed this "Unity" business to become an obsession, but every forward move here is handicapped due to the split. Bowhill has now come into line, a new Group having been formed. According to returns submitted (3 locals to report) we have on paper 24 Pit Groups and 6 Pits with 1 Party member, with a total of 202 Party members. A few have no Party members on the Pit head and in one no Party members underground. We will manage to get a real Bolshevik Party in Fife sometime.

Enclosed 16 negatives of photos taken in the Wellesley and 1 photo.[225] Keep the photo, but send back the negatives after getting pictures for *Workers' Weekly* or *Sunday Worker*. Some of them should be useful.

September 25th, 1926.
A few lines enclosed in *The Miner*. Am confined to bed, nothing serious.

Had an exceptionally severe attack of "dingy" on Tuesday and was out speaking on Wednesday afternoon and Thursday. Result — unable to get out yesterday and today. Expect to be out tomorrow.

Had some trouble in Local on Thursday night. Comrade Gordon and Mrs Gordon central figures. Mrs Gordon left meeting and Comrade Gordon refused to go to District Party Congress at Lochgelly on Sunday 1st, although elected last Sunday. Refused to state reason, other than insufficient time to read Theses, etc., issued by Party. I understand he has stated that he has been expelled which is not true, as the Local Party Committee has not yet considered his case. Will give you fuller details later.

No further improvement re Unity.

Had a fairly successful demonstration last Sunday against formation of new Trades and Labour Council, but understand those responsible for new formation intend to carry on. Meeting of Divisional Labour Party Executive tomorrow when matter will be discussed.

Reformed Workers' Defence Corps on Thursday, due to action of police at Glencraig and Lochore. (Expect you will have received report for *Workers' Weekly* of happenings there.)

Formed new group of Party at Methilhill, 14 new members, and have good prospects at Kennoway. Possibly formed yesterday at latter place. Group of 6 formed at Leven also. According to reports from Kirkcaldy and Cowdenbeath good prospects of formation of groups at Burntisland and Inverkeithing. No groups there previously. If successful will bring in workers who are not miners — Railwaymen, Dockers, etc.

No signs of breakaway here. Companies so far have made no attempt to cause stampede. General expression, "Better on dole than at work". F. Hodges' letter to Spencer being denounced by all, I understand.[226] P.S. Hope the negatives were of use to you.

October 4th, 1926.

Just a few lines re the position locally. We have a few questions of importance to deal with at present — Formation of new Trades and Labour Council, trying to stop coal picked from redd bings from being sold, picketing the pits to prevent a breakaway because of terms being again posted at pit head on Saturday, with of course the usual meetings, Party, Trades and Labour Council, etc. It's a hell of a life at present.

Adamson was at Buckhaven yesterday and advocated acceptance of Government proposals. The chairman only allowed 3 questions and closed the meeting. Adamson has not gained any by his attitude. From scraps of conversation I overheard amongst even old men he is looked upon as a "ratter". "By Christ, A. J. Cook wouldn't talk like that", "Have we stuck this bloody lot for 22 weeks to be told a lot of shit like that?", "What the hell does he mean?", "He should get in wi' Baldwin, that's whaur he belongs onywye" and expressions anything but complimentary to the Rt. Hon. Wullie.

Notices were posted on the pit heads on Saturday with the same offer as was posted in July: 8 hours shift, immediate reduction of 14.2% on pieceworkers' rates, same wages as April for shift men. But unlike the July offer this latest one only covers the month of October, after which no suggestion is made as to what the minimum is to be or how wages will be regulated.

It has been widely rumoured that contractors are trying to round up men to start the Wellesley and other pits, so we had pickets out this morning, but nobody but safety men turned out. Pickets will be out again this afternoon and tonight, and will be continued this week as we do not intend leaving anything to chance, as Adamson's Buckhaven speech was the reverse of inspiration. He denounced F. Hodges because he scented that was the popular line, but not because (in my opinion) of what Hodges has said or written but because of the time he has selected to do it. Wullie agreed with me that an embargo and organised levy was necessary to win, but tried to throw cold water on the calling of a special T.U.C. to discuss those, or an approach to the N.U.R. and Transport workers to impose the embargo, because of the rebuffs which he stated the General Council had already given the miners, who had already tried them. When I got on my feet to point out the difference between an approach to the General Council and the calling of a special T.U.C. the chairman closed the meeting, which caused some noise. Wullie was continually being interrupted during his speech. The branches meet to decide on the Government's offer today and if the Old Union members whom I have been in touch with turn out to those branch meetings I think we should have a majority against, but whether we will manage to get them to try and carry the Party's proposals is a different matter, because of them being unable or rather being backward in getting on their feet to move anything.

We cannot get pickets to stop the sale of coal from the redd bings. A spirit of "To hell with this *peaceful* picketing" has now got hold of the handful of reliable men we have and a desire for terrorism has now set in.

I wrote Headquarters last week for a lead as to how we should proceed regarding the formation of the new Trades and Labour Council. It has the blessing of the Divisional Labour Party, who are now determined to disaffiliate the Reform Union. A meeting is to take place Sunday first to form it. We have advised *all* branches to be represented and have some assurance now of opposition to the suggested move but whether the opposition will be maintained at the meeting remains to be seen. We have also written the other Trades Councils in the Division asking them to receive a deputation to hear our case.

In my last note I told you about Comrades Mrs Gordon and A. Gordon's attitude towards the Party. Mrs Gordon made statements that the Local Party Committee did not have the confidence of the Local. She had also been creating a clique or fraction and had been told off about it. When the matter was raised at the aggregate meeting the Local passed a unanimous vote of confidence in the Local Party Committee and the Chairman told Mrs Gordon this tittle-tattle must cease or she would be expelled from the Party. Mrs Gordon, without saying anything, left the meeting. Comrade Gordon had been appointed along with 9 other comrades to attend the District Party

Congress at Lochgelly to discuss the Thesis dealing with the General Strike, International situation, and the draft of the new organisation. He received the copies on Friday night, was appointed to go to Kirkcaldy Local on the Sunday to lead the discussion there (he went) and was on the following Thursday asked to give a summary to Methil Local. He refused on the grounds of not having had time to study them, despite the fact that he had been at Kirkcaldy on the same business 4 days before. The Chairman drew his attention to the fact that those who refused to accept Party decisions without a reasonable excuse were liable to be expelled. Comrade Gordon refused to supplement his reasons for refusal and took up the attitude "I've said all that I intend, to hell with you, do what you like". Next day he was telling all the Party members he met that he had been expelled.

Mrs Gordon and another woman member who had been appointed to go to Lochgelly did not go and did not inform us that they had no intention of going, with the result that we were 2 delegates short. The excuse offered by the other woman (one who acts on Mrs Gordon's lead) was "I haven't had time to read the Theses", although she had them for 9 days and was told that she wouldn't be expected to speak unless she had the desire. The 3 did not attend the Group training class or Local Party Committee meeting. It was agreed to hold a special Local Party Committee meeting and written invitations sent to the 3 of them. The meeting was held but none of them turned up. Another letter was sent to them for another Local Party Committee meeting last night. Comrades Mrs Gordon and A. Gordon turned up and A. Gordon tried to maintain that he had been expelled, although he could not justify his statement. Mrs Gordon adopted a different attitude and said she still considered herself a Party member. The other woman did not turn up but sent a letter resigning from all her positions in the Party. It was a demonstration of pettiness. Had it been any opposition to Party Policy with a wide discussion it would have been of some use to the Local, but it is apparently done with.

We have decided to send a delegate to the Party Congress. The aggregate meeting will decide who will be sent on Thursday night. The Local Party Committee recommend Comrade Robert Thomson[227] (who is due for trial on the 12th along with almost 30 others for picketing), with your humble as substitute.

Just received Headquarters' reply re suggested new Trades and Labour Council. We have to discuss it with Comrade Gallacher, who will be here on Thursday first.

No further progress to report re Unity. We are holding an enlarged District Party Committee meeting today in Kirkcaldy to discuss the position, out of which we might require to revise our present and past policy. I am of the opinion that we have now got to consider getting back without any palaver, as the Old Union and Scottish are not prepared to move in the matter, and no pressure is being made on either of them inside. P.S. Enclosed copy of 1st issue of Scottish T.U.C. *Monthly Bulletin*,[228] Methil Co-operative Committee Minutes, and a Circular issued by General Council T.U.C. during General

Strike. I found the latter amongst some old papers. I expect the 1st and last will interest you.

October 9th, 1926.

Thanks for yours of October 1st. Am kicking around again after 3 days in bed, although I can't report feeling fit after 6 days picketing at the Wellesley. We had a breakaway Tuesday night, 16 scabs starting. Wednesday morning 41 started but we have reduced it, 6 on Wednesday night and 11 on Thursday morning, 3 Thursday night, 16 Friday morning, only 2 seen Friday night and 7 this morning. Nothing serious out of 2,500 men. It's no joke being at it from 4 a.m. to 11 p.m. We cannot get mass pickets in the morning but we can muster from 2 to 3 thousand afternoon and night. The scabs are drawn mainly from Leven and are almost without exception composed of the religious fraternity. One of them when interviewed said, "God had instructed him to start work, and if any violence was committed on him the person who committed it would have to answer to God on the Day of Judgement". (Lower the blind, for Christ's sake.) If the Inspector of Police seconded that, the scab would be less than mince meat by now. However, we shall see what we shall see.

The breakaway has been engineered by contractors who visited some of the men working with them, but the contractors haven't had the guts to "start" themselves. The safety men refuse to come out unless they are asked to work longer hours themselves, which places them in the scabbery also. The police are provocative and are looking for trouble. On Wednesday morning another chap and I were on picket outside the Wellesley check box and had 30 police along with us. They jeered at me, repeated what I said to some of the scabs, stepped between myself and those I was speaking to, told the scabs to ignore me and go to their work, and generally behaved as we expect them to. There is one good thing happened which is worth relating. One scab I was speaking to TOLD OFF A POLICE SERGEANT. It was GREAT. I was speaking to him when 5 sergeants, 1 Inspector and a few constables surrounded us. A sergeant remarked to another that the scab shouldn't pay any attention to me. The scab immediately turned on him and told him he had no business whom he (the scab) spoke to. The scab was very indignant as he contended this was a free country and that he could speak with whom he liked. He then demanded the sergeant's number and peered close into the sergeant's face and repeated aloud his number, saying that he wouldn't forget it. It's a great world. That scab gives promise of being a disrupter in the scab battalion, uniformed and otherwise.

Yesterday morning the Police must have rounded up all the scabs as they (14 of them) brought 16 scabs in a tramcar. The car is due at Wellesley at 5 a.m. but it didn't arrive until 5.40. I was approaching the scabs when the Inspector of Police made a rush at me and told me I was violating the provisions of the Act by PERSISTENTLY WATCHING, and that this was my last warning. Did I hit him across the clock or shake hands and wish him "Good morning"? I was nearly helpless with laughter at his attitude and what he had said because the thought struck me that we could, according to him, put BLIND MEN on picket duty only, which would probably mean "stretcher bearers at the double" (as I understand blind people are supposed to develop their other senses to a remarkable degree) due to the collapse of the picket because of the odour leaking from the scabs.

Thanks very much for the telegram on Thursday night. I received it at Gallacher's meeting in the Co-operative Hall. Gallacher read it to the meeting, who nearly brought the roof down when they heard its contents. Some were for marching up to the Wellesley there and then to draw the safety men. It appears that the Conference has funked the issue, or is this another game to play up to the Labour Party Conference by the reference back to the districts?[229] The best manner in judging the districts' attitude to that question was by issuing telegrams to withdraw ALL safety men, and this weekend would have shown whether they were in favour or not. This weakness will not bring us any nearer victory as we have nothing to expect from the talking shop at Margate.[230]

Comrade Gordon is acting like a youngster. On Thursday night he was informed at Gallacher's meeting that Gallacher was to meet the Local Party Committee immediately after his meeting, in our rooms. Gordon didn't show himself until the meeting, which lasted about 1¼ hours, had finished and only the chap who was locking up was left. I don't know what his game is but he is doing himself no good with the majority of the Party members here.

A very significant thing happened here last Wednesday. The Old Union local officials sent for Adamson to address a meeting re the breakaway. Wullie gave them his advice: stick to the Federation, and desired a "meeting of the combined committees". After half-an-hour's haggling the Reform Union committees were admitted to a joint meeting with the Old Union committees and addressed by Wullie, who pointed out the need for united action (after we have been doing so for 23 weeks, with the exception of Buckhaven Old Union committee). He was against the withdrawal of the safety men and mass pickets. Visit the scabs at their homes only, and that visit by Union officials. "Don't, for heaven's sake, appeal to the rank and file for assistance" kind of attitude.

Enclosed copy of *The Miner*. You will notice an article on Page 3 which looks very much like Hodge trying to have a go at bursting any further move towards Unity. It is more than stupid at present, calling on the Old Union members to *withhold their contributions* and to join the Reform Union as no contributions are being paid, with the Old Union paying out occasionally a few bob and the Reform Union NIL. However, one finds the clue in the last paragraph of "News, Notes and Notions". Hodge appears to have thought that work will be resumed inside a fortnight and intends that the Reform Union will "carry on". I am writing a paragraph for the *Workers' Weekly* re that article.

Also enclosed 25 negatives of photos taken in the Wellesley. You might find some of them of some use. Return them when you are finished with them. The one in this week's *Weekly* is all right. *Sunday morning:* So also is the one in the *Sunday Worker* this morning. Enclosed No. 2 Scottish T.U.C. *Monthly Bulletin* and No. 9 Bulletin of Methil Trades and Labour Council during General Strike, Minutes of Fife Central Council of Action, and Dunfermline Central Strike Committee circular on Picketing issued during General Strike. I

discovered the latter amongst some old papers I was about to burn. You might
be interested in them.

We have 46 cases from this district for trial at Cupar on Tuesday. A
number of Party members are involved. Some of them have 4 charges. All are
arising from picketing Muiredge bing, and picketing the beach at Buckhaven
where coal is washed up and lifted by carters. Expect a few of them will be
"sent down the line", as I understand the position at Methil and District is
designated "critical" by the police, who have stated that other 50 of us are due
to be "jerked up". Nice intelligent fellows.

The Old Union held an Executive Board meeting yesterday but so far I
haven't got their recommendation re safety men. The Reform Union also held
a Sub Executive meeting results of which I don't know yet. Will possibly know
of both this afternoon.

Isn't the Political Bureau sending a reply to the article you mention
written by Page and Murphy? If it is as you state their line of argument should
be easily smashed.[231]

Sunday evening: The Old Union Executive have decided to meet again on
Monday, thus emulating the National Delegate Conference. We are getting
some leadership these days from the Trade Union officials.

The meeting held today to reconstruct the local Trades and Labour
Council agreed to expel the 3 Reform Union branches and hold another
meeting on Friday 1st to receive nominations for the Municipal Elections next
month. We haven't got sufficient information as to what transpired to decide
our future policy, but will get it during the next few days.

Have sent reply to the article in *The Miner* to the *Weekly.*

Some activities here at present. This is the place to gain experience,
George. Enclosed 2 pamphlets which will give you some idea of the "stuff"
which is being distributed in the coalfields.[232]

October 23rd, 1926.

Enclosed few lines with *The Miner*, which is as useful as ever. Have seen
both comrades Thomson and McArthur since they got back home. Both
pleased with Conference.[233] Rather hard luck on Jock McArthur losing his
promised trip to France.[234] However, he won't be neglected so far as work is
concerned here at present.

We have been unable to draw all the scabs at the Wellesley but altogether
there aren't more than 20, most of them loud-voiced followers of the meek and
lowly carpenter. We have attempted to get the safety men withdrawn but the
underground firemen who are members of the Scottish Underground Firemen
and Shotfirers' Association, and the Winding Enginemen of Shirkie's crush,
refuse to stop work. The safety men at Muiredge Pit came out in a body on
Monday because of 5 scabs starting last Saturday, and despite long range
picketing by the Old Union officials (from 500 to 700 yards from the pit) the
scabs continue.

Communal feeding still going on — 6 sausages per head for Sunday
morning breakfast. Despite that we have some scabbing going on. Coal is

being collected from Redd bings and sold and we are unable to stop it. The weather is very cold and hundreds are at the bings, which makes it very difficult to ascertain who are selling the coal. We control 2 bings with Committees who issue permits but are unable to control the Wellesley bing due to its position.

Gordon has been deprived of his job as agent for the *Weekly*. He was making no attempt to get the paper distributed and kept on ordering 65 dozen, with the result we had 24½ dozen left unsold last week. He rarely attends meetings of the Local now. You would get the position from Comrades Thomson and McArthur.

The new Trades and Labour Council has nominated candidates for the Municipal Elections for the 4 wards and we have 3 candidates. We are meeting them tomorrow to come to an arrangement but I don't expect much good will result from the meeting.

Have read article by Page and Murphy in the *International*. They have certainly overlooked the part the Party has played in the Left Wing and the Leftward movement of the masses, and appear to treat the Party as something isolated and apart from the workers, with little influence and afraid to use that influence towards a more militant policy. I understand they also committed a breach of discipline by not submitting the article to the British Central Committee before publication. That was a bad mistake on their part, especially at a time when we are getting so many recruits to the Party.

Am going to Lochgelly tomorrow to an aggregate meeting for West Fife. P.S. The General Council appear to be still carrying out their defeatist policy judging by Pugh's letter. Coal Commission Report. Heavens.

October 31st, 1926.

Have managed today to get a few minutes to write you a few lines re position here. Comrade McArthur was arrested last Sunday night at our rooms by no less than 7 Police on a charge of making a seditious speech likely to cause disaffection amongst the Fife constabulary. Bail of £5 was granted at Cupar on Monday, on him giving a promise not to make speeches dealing with the coal dispute before his trial on November 22nd, but as the Judge had no desire "to deprive him of his rights as a citizen because of his impending trial" the old hypocrite graciously "allowed McArthur permission to speak for and take an active part during the Municipal Elections". Comrade Stewart, Lochgelly, was fined £10 or 60 days a fortnight ago on the same charge. Comrade Watt, Lumphinnans Y.C.L.,[235] was charged the same day as McArthur on the same charge. Comrade Bird was sent down last Monday for 21 days on one charge and £2 or 20 days on another. How I have escaped this round up beats me as McArthur was very mild.

The new agent for the *Weekly* who replaced Gordon has justified his selection as I understand he has managed to get rid of the 50 dozen order this week, which Gordon had allowed to drop to between 30 and 40 dozen.

The new Trades and Labour Council bunch refused to consider our proposals for a United Front and the result is that we have 3-cornered fights in

3 of the wards. The chances of our candidates look rosy in 2 wards but doubtful in one. However, we have managed to make the "Constitution" bunch look very cheap at all their meetings, and as we are holding back-court meetings every day and have big working committees I think we have scotched their game of splitting. Enclosed copy of manifesto to be issued tomorrow (Monday). We are holding it up to the last minute, which has got the other crowd guessing and incidentally making them very uneasy as to our moves. Only one Party member, Comrade O'Neil, is running and his chances of success are good. The S.D.F. branch is split from top to bottom. They have one candidate running against our candidate in No. 4 Ward, while we have 4 of their active members actively supporting us, 1 canvassing for Comrade O'Neil, 2 speaking from our platform and 1 acting as Ward Convener for our candidate against the S.D.F.er.

There are now almost 40 scabs in the Wellesley, mostly young lads from Leven. We managed to get a few safety men, pumpers, bottomers and Banksmen to stop work on Monday but I understand they intend going back to work this week. The underground firemen so far refuse to move. We have tried to get mass pickets but mainly due to the exceptionally cold weather the response has been very poor. The Old Union officials in Denbeath and Methil are acting with us but Buckhaven Old Union officials refuse to have anything to do with us. To give you an illustration. Yesterday I went to Buckhaven to attend a joint committee meeting of Old Union branches, which is held daily to report on the pits in this area. I was refused admission by Buckhaven Old Union chairman "because it had been decided that only Old Union members were to attend". I am good enough to picket the Wellesley with Denbeath Old Union officials but not good enough to sit in the same meeting as Buckhaven Old Union officials. However, George, that doesn't matter much as we have the rank and file solid behind us in Denbeath and Methil.

It is to be hoped that Cook and the M.F.G.B. Executive do not fall for the move to allow the General Council to negotiate with the Government, as Thomas appears to have been doing some nice wire pulling during the past few weeks. According to a Press statement he "considers that should the parties in the dispute recognise the economic facts, peace would be assured in the mining industry".

We held 2 aggregate meetings, 1 in West Fife and 1 in East Fife last Sunday to deal with Pit Groups. So far we haven't received a full registration from all the Locals but are likely to get a move on in some of them now. Another phase of Party work, Work amongst Women, is now being tackled in a more organised manner, a District Committee being set up on Friday. Sorry to report that the sales of the *Monthly* have now gone down to between 30 and 40. Of course it is not to be wondered at, 6 months without pay and relief being paid in kind — tanners are bound to be scarce. The Communal feeding is still going strong. Today we had ½lb of steak for breakfast and are still continuing 3 meals per day, 7 days per week. Not bad, considering past disputes, and this the 27th week of this one.

We are making some progress re the local International Class War

Prisoners' Aid, with prize drawings, dances, whist drives, raffles, concerts, parades and collections at football matches and cinemas. A move is on foot to form an International Class War Prisoners' Aid concert party.

November 6th, 1926.

Thanks for yours of November 1st. Gordon is still in the sulks and as you remark is likely to be outside the Party very soon.

The Wellesley safety men are the limit — SCABS and SQUEALERS, every mother's son. They refuse to move. By Christ, if I was working underground some of them would lose their firemen's ticket. I have been advocating this line to the Wellesley men, in addition of course the complete smashing of theirs and Shirkie's union. Well received at present, but the difficulty will be to get them to move in that direction when work is resumed. Slight addition to SCABS this week, at least 20, most of whom are lads between 16 and 18 from Leven. Leven, although adjoining Methil, is in another Parish and owing to no pressure being applied the Parish Council has done practically nothing, with the result that starvation is the order of the day. It's a hell of a job doing picket these mornings at 4 a.m., not only the cold but standing by seeing the SCABS scuttle like rats from the tram cars under police protection. The SLOGAN: "IT'S DAMN COLD WEATHER THESE NIGHTS TO HAVE NO WINDOWS", has been carried into effect in a few cases. We are still carrying on meetings, outdoor and indoor, the former due to the cold weather being very sparsely attended.

The result of the polls here was 1 of our 3 candidates successful, Labour losing 1 seat due to the split vote. The weather was hellish, rain teeming all day, which meant that we were the losers due to many of our supporters not having boots and clothes to venture out. None of the new Trades and Labour Council candidates were returned in Nos. 2, 3, and 4 Wards. We polled 1,089 votes against their 737. Comrade O'Neill, although unsuccessful, polled 349 against the new Trades and Labour Council candidate's 192, which has made them do some furious thinking.

My butty, although a Reform Union member, has been supporting the new Trades and Labour Council, coming out openly now as an Anti-Communist has received his reward, being now a City Father = Bailieship. He has been invited to attend various meetings of miners but hasn't yet turned up and hasn't been seen on picket, although he promised "if only one other was with him". The result is that an agitation is now afoot for sacking him when work is resumed. He has already had some idea of the feeling against him, almost shouted down at one of the election meetings in what has always been his stronghold, Denbeath. Serves him right. He has for years sat on the dyke but the dispute has shown him in his true colours — an opportunist.

According to the Press reports this morning it appears that Thomas and Company have again managed to get the M.F.G.B. Executive hoodwinked into their defeatist policy. It is to be hoped the delegate Conference will be alive to those moves and come forward with a positive policy to meet the now (very much, in my opinion) weakened position. Practically no enthusiasm is being shown here now, although there is no talk of work. The Communal feeding is still going strong, ½lb sausages per head for breakfast tomorrow and still 3 meals per day 7 days per week. Have made application for Methil's Books re Kitchens, also minute book of Central Food Committee which I will send on to you for Labour Research Department after I receive them.

Enclosed No. 3 Scottish T.U.C. *Monthly Bulletin*, Methil Co-operative Balance Sheet, and 8 snaps, most of them dealing with march on Thornton Poorhouse.[236] Pity we didn't have a big camera for demonstration at Thornton as the 2 enclosed snaps give only ½ of crowd. Will send on copies of all I can get hold of when work is resumed.

We are holding a demonstration tomorrow in Methil — anniversary of Russian Revolution. It is a pity it clashes with a lantern lecture on Co-operative Russia in Buckhaven.

Have been down in bed for 2 days this week due to soaking on Tuesday — Picketing, and addressing open-air meetings.

Owing to McArthur not being allowed to speak, Bob Thomson having a youngster seriously ill, and Gordon in the sulks for the past 6 weeks things haven't been a cake walk. However, we have managed to get a few good workers from amongst the new members and they have taken the selling of the *Weekly* and *Sunday Worker* off our hands. The new agent for the *Weekly* and *Sunday Worker* is doing great work and by the methods he is showing at present will be of greater value in that line than Gordon. It might be a case of "new brooms sweep clean", but we will take more precautions this journey, George. P.S. No *Miner* this week. I understand from the newsagent that it has wound up.[237] Will make inquiries and let you know later.

November 15th, 1926.

Am commencing this letter tonight after being confined to bed for a week with a fairly severe attack of the 'flu. Am feeling like a wet rag and of as much use as that article. Have been unable to read the papers until today, and judging by the reports we are now into the sell-out prepared by the General Council and assisted by the weak-kneed bunch inside the M.F.G.B. itself. What a decision for the delegate conference to make. I expect it will have the effect intended — to cause a stampede back to work, rather than accept the challenge issued by the Government (to smash the M.F.G.B.) and that could only be done by issuing instructions to operate the South Wales resolution and thereby rally the rank and file.[238] Officials' salaries and jobs are now the main consideration and they, the officials (county, etc.), are in my opinion judging the position along the following lines: This Government offer gives us an opportunity of finishing the present struggle and retaining our County and District Unions, with US having the power to negotiate which WE have been deprived of since national settlements operated. Besides, didn't we have a more harmonious time with the coalowners during the operation of District settlements than we have had since the national settlements? That at any rate is the philosophy (?) of most of the Scottish tribe of so-called leaders, Smillie, Adamson, Doonan,[239] etc., and I don't expect they greatly differ from many in the other districts.

I understand Adamson is addressing meetings in this area today. His presence is of course to influence acceptance, with the usual verbiage: "However much *I* detest the offer, *I* detest its alternative more — fighting on and suffering more starvation — and after careful and deliberate consideration of the whole of the circumstances which is impossible for you, *gentlemen*, to be in full possession of, *I* unhesitatingly recommend acceptance of the Government's offer which at any rate leaves us with a semblance of national organisation from which we can carefully and cautiously again build up to protect *our* interests." Will let you know how far he has succeeded. I understand the Reform Union branches have rejected the offer, but no mass meetings have been held to give the lead to the Old Union branches. Why, I cannot say at present but will demand an explanation whenever I get out in a day or two. I will be unable to address outdoor meetings for at least another week as my throat is like a lump of raw meat, tonsils swollen and neck glands also swollen.

The numbers at the Wellesley scabbery are being gradually added to, mainly by young lads and self-confessed followers of the meek and lowly carpenter. There is every possibility that their numbers will be swollen after Adamson's visit today.

Gordon has been invited to meet the Local Party Committee to explain his position re Party but has failed to attend. I understand that a deputation of 3 were appointed to visit him at his house but he wasn't in when they called. He had been also notified that his books were required for the monthly audit but he has also ignored that, and the deputation were instructed to claim and remove all Party property, books, etc. He has played a rotten game and as far as I can gather is going around making lying statements regarding Party members. We have lost a good cartoonist for "The Spark", but to hell with any and everyone who adopts an attitude like he has done. The Party is better rid of them. Whether it is due to his wife or not I don't know, but the most of this trouble commenced after she joined the Party. Since taking the *Weekly* from him our sales are increasing. We had 60 dozen last week and they are almost sold out, and we are now showing a profit where before we were showing a loss. Better still, the new comrade who is in charge is not above accepting advice from some of us and is getting a decent distribution committee organised, which augurs well for increased sales when work is again resumed. He has also done what Gordon would never do despite our instructions — give pamphlets to *Workers' Weekly* distributors to sell with the *Weekly* — and has had a decent sale during the weekend. In addition he has sold 7 *Communist Review* where Gordon only sold 2. Not bad for a new Party member.

We have another 8 cases at Cupar tomorrow and Comrade McArthur's trial is Monday next. We paid £84 in fines last week and are still drawing money from dances, raffles, prize drawings and periwinkles for the local International Class War Prisoners' Aid fund. A delegate from Methil, James

Scott, treasurer of the local section International Class War Prisoners' Aid, will attend the Conference in London on December 12th.[240]

We have advised the Trade Union branches to form up with the new Trades and Labour Council, but are continuing to keep the old intact as a joint strike committee until the end of the dispute when it will go into oblivion. No use allowing the miners' split to cut across the entire movement and thereby depriving some branches of national contact when we are getting close to Unity in the miners' ranks themselves. Most of the active Party members (who are in the Reform Union) will be "in the wilderness" for a short period, but it will be worth it even at that price.

Another Party member went down the line last week for 40 days — P. Lumsden, Bowhill — for making not only a seditious but in my opinion a damned stupid speech.

Got a copy of the Labour Research Department *Trades Councils in Action*[241] which, after reading and comparing those 9 days with present position, makes one wonder if "the 9 days" were only a dream. However, George, we know that they will come, have to come, again and at no far distant date, but the difference today and May, here in Methil and District, causes one to ask oneself, "Will this same crowd rise to the occasion?". All the small, mean, petty things are now multiplied and exaggerated beyond bounds and assume great degrees of importance to the exclusion of THE important issues of the fight in the minds of the workers and their wives. Possibly part of that is due to our not being sufficiently active to keep those matters in their proper sphere, by continually emphasising THE all-important points, or if we have been sufficiently active then our methods have been at fault because we have not gained the desired results. Whatever way one looks at it we must be at least granted this much, that we have at any rate stuck it from the beginning whatever the circumstances and have demonstrated to the workers that the Party is the only one which is prepared to give them, and also participate with them in, a lead to fight. You might think I am getting moody and might attribute that to a form of after effect of the 'flu, but heavens, George, to see the faint response for pickets is to make one take several days of 'flu in one breath. Methil was bidding fair to earn the reputation of "Red Methil", but now it cannot be described truthfully other than "Red-rusted Methil". The barnacles are well encrusted and impede all action. Our duty is to remove those barnacles, I suppose, so I will pipe down on that aspect of the local position.

Communal feeding still as usual, ½lb stew per head yesterday, 3 meals per day, 7 days per week.

Reform Union had Executive Board meeting on Saturday but as I haven't seen McArthur don't know how far Unity has been reached.

We have a regular attendance twice per week, Thursday and Sunday, of between 60 and 70 Party members, not including Leven and Methilhill groups. A sympathisers' meeting is to take place in Leven on Wednesday. One of the comrades there is sure of almost 20 new members, he reports. Methilhill promises to be a good centre for the Party and we intend nursing it. A few women have already joined up and show interest in the Party. Will dry up until tomorrow when I will have the results of branch meetings of Old Union and also Adamson's visit so far as augmenting scabs [goes].

Tuesday: Have been out for a couple of hours today. Enclosed copy of leaflet issued by District Party Committee.

Results of branch votes which I have received are AGAINST: Methil, Buckhaven, Methilhill; FOR: East Wemyss, Leven. Denbeath hold their meeting tonight and I will be surprised if they do not vote against. According to a Party member from Cowdenbeath, the Old Union branches in West Fife are voting AGAINST despite Potter and William Watson, M.P.,[242] doing their utmost for acceptance. WHAT WILL THOSE BLASTED WHITE RATS, SMILLIE AND COMPANY do to get out of the fight if the vote goes AGAINST?

From what I could gather today very few scabs have been added to the Wellesley bunch during the past few days. More have been signing on but have been told they will be sent for when required. Very few coalgetters are working and when any "sign on" are started immediately. The management would give something to get a few good coalgetters, as those who are working are of the type who couldn't "howk machine-cut coal". I know the latter is true, George, having worked beside most of them and knowing also their output when I was in the weigh box. It is rumoured here that the Wemyss Coal Company is deducting 2/6d per week off the pay of those atavists for POLICE PROTECTION. Why shouldn't they do it? They are escorted practically from home to pit and vice versa, and nobody unless a capitalist should expect something (and that something represented by bulk) for nothing under Capitalism.

Our Young Comrades League members in Denbeath are making themselves felt on direct strike issues. We had a refrain which was bawled on every demonstration, which runs like this:

> There's no scabs here! No! There's no scabs here,
> Hallelujah! There's no scabs here.
> Not a penny off the pay,
> Not a minute on the day,
> Hallelujah! There's no scabs here.

The Young Comrades congregate in the near vicinity of a Scab's house and bawl and howl it as only they can, with the alteration of "There's one scab here", or, if more than one in the house, bawl out the number. You can understand that whether or not it affects the scabs it is a good experience for the youngsters. Our rooms, which can at a pinch accommodate 80 adults are almost too small at times to hold the Young Comrades, and when they let go *The Red Flag*, etc., one almost wishes one was born a deaf mute should they happen to be inside the rooms. One of them does a bit of stumping, emphasising his points by beating his hands in the most approved William Gallacher style. Should we manage to keep them together for a few years, the Wemyss Coal Company will not be blessed with their future slaves.

I understand that Pawky Wullie[243] had hot receptions at both Denbeath and Methil. He was due to arrive at Denbeath at 3.30 but was 1 hour late and the crowd held a concert when waiting on him. Reform Union members were present as well as Old Union members, and also a crowd of women. Wullie gave his usual and when questions were asked did his usual and well known glide. But the crowd weren't having any and pressed him. He put both feet into it in answering a question, "What would Adamson call a scab?". Wullie, trying to be funny, said, "Well, I wouldn't call him a man, why not call him a *woman*?" Hell with the lid off then commenced. A woman Party member jumped up and demanded Wullie to withdraw the insult. Wullie stupidly enough persisted that he had nothing to withdraw, but after almost ¼ hour steady bumping he agreed to withdraw any statement "which might be looked at as an insult". It must have been good. He was well soaked at Methil by a new Party member who, after asking a question and not receiving what he considered a satisfactory answer, got up and reviewed the whole Government's offer and showed it up and challenged Adamson to disprove his statements. Not being an Old Union member he was told to leave the meeting and allow the Old Union members to take a vote. The vote was taken today and resulted in majority AGAINST.

According to tonight's press, Scotland looks like going AGAINST, which should make the issue more clear. A Delegate Conference will be held in Glasgow tomorrow, Wednesday, to review the position. It looks as if the Executive anticipate REJECTION and are going to try and saddle the delegate conference with the responsibility of suggesting a way out of the (to them) difficulty. It looks like a big showdown for those washouts.

Enclosed a small piece of German coal (lignite), a cargo of which came to Methil last week. Some stuff. There are 2 boats in Methil at present with unscreened stuff, and also 3 ships of a local Company "tied up", with other 2 due to be "tied up" also.

I haven't as yet got any definite information re *The Miner*, whether it has gone out for good or only temporary.

I expect Baby [Hutt] will be making her presence known now. Soon be scrambling round the house.

November 20th, 1926.

Thanks for yours of 15th. The result of the District voting on the Government terms was a stunner to not only the Government and coalowners but also to the weak-kneed bunch in the M.F.G.B. itself.[244] But the result which should have accrued from such a vote was nullified by the drift back caused by the recommendation of the delegate conference, plus of course the lies broadcast in the Press last weekend. This other recommendation — District agreements — will cause a further stampede, which in turn will strengthen the owners' position, especially in regard to hours. We are going to have a lively time, especially in Fife. The Unions will be helpless and big breakaways from them will be the order of the day and our hands will be tied in Fife with the 2 Unions operating. It isn't a pleasant picture but will have to be met and overcome.

I addressed 2 meetings on Friday and we sent a telegram to the Delegate Conference in the name of Denbeath miners and wives, calling on the Conference to stand by the Slogan and to issue instructions to operate the South Wales resolution. We also agreed to try and get a meeting of those who had broken away at the Wellesley for Sunday (tomorrow). How far the Committees have been successful I cannot at present state as I have been out all day today billposting and selling *Workers' Weekly*. We held 4 meetings in this area yesterday, Comrade O'Neill at Methil, Comrade Thomson, Buckhaven, and your humble at Denbeath and Methilhill. I am due to address 2 meetings tomorrow, 1 at Buckhaven and 1 in Methil. Philip Hodge is to appear on the same platform. I feel completely washed out, but better be washed out in attempting to hold them back then be bowled out for months ahead by standing idly by and allowing the stampede to carry on unchecked. A number of scabs have chucked in, some after their first shift and others when they received their 1st pay.

We haven't been anything too early in appointing a new distribution secretary. A bill of over £1 to pay for *Communist Review*, piled up by Gordon. He *has* played the game during the past year. Makes one feel like vomiting to think of him, after the amount of work we have put in. However, the same game won't go long undetected should it be again tried on, as we now have monthly audits. 60 dozen *Workers' Weekly* now regular. Your idea for workers' correspondents should assist greatly. I was under the impression that Comrade McArthur was acting as workers' correspondent for Methil Local, but that is now put right, as one was appointed on Thursday night. He showed me his report (which you will have by the time you receive this) today. His reports are to be scrutinised by a Press Committee of 3 before being mailed to the *Weekly*, to ensure authentic reports being submitted. He is one of our new members and has shown some activity since joining, especially re sales of *Workers' Weekly* and *Sunday Worker*, in addition to making an attempt to address a public meeting.

Like you I was under the impression that the *Mail* was non-union but I have since learned that the Typographical Association is recognised. Anderson was the successful candidate, defeating the retiring Labour member (a rotter if there ever was one) and another supported by the "Ratepayers' Association", an organisation formed a few months ago by the Wemyss Coal Company and owners of house property.[245] He won't make any fight and is likely to fall in line with others who recognise the "Constitutional" bunch.

According to expressions at different meetings my butty looks like getting butted. The chairman of Denbeath Old Union bunch is continually bumping him — "Not from any personal aspect, because I have no ill-feeling to any white man, but it's very hard to think when on picket at 4 o'clock in the morning that a checkweigher is lying tight up against the wife in bed while we who could be doing the same are getting soaked to the arse one morning and nearly frozen stiff the next, doing work he should be doing". You ought to hear him, George. No poetical effusions, no frills, but straight from the shoulder in Coal Jock's own. He is all out for Unity and his favourite expression when

312

opening out is: "I am the chairman of Denbeath Old Union branch, don't forget. I don't belong to the Reform Union or the Communist Party but I would rather fight the Boss with them, and they have fought, than run away from the fight with Adamson and Potter." He naturally is in the Adamson-Potter blacklist and in every likelihood John Brown's also,[246] although he was a contractor in a small way before the dispute. He had a brother-in-law residing with him, but a few weeks ago when he discovered that the brother-in-law had been engaged selling coal he threw him out of the house. Strange to relate, he is or WAS a member of the S.D.F. The other S.D.F.er who acted as Convener of the Defence Corps has, along with his brother (who was Chairman of the S.D.F.) been expelled from the S.D.F. for POLITICAL UNRELIABILITY during the recent Municipal Elections because the former acted as Happell's[247] agent against the S.D.F. nominee and the other spoke on behalf of the 3 candidates run by us. Every aspect of the struggle has its humorous side — S.D.F. and POLITICAL UNRELIABILITY of members.

I don't think the Company Union danger can be over-emphasised. I expect the coalowners will be doing overtime now with their safety first committees. The Fife Coal Company, I think, are the sponsors for it in Great Britain, having had a full-time man engaged in lecturing and forming those committees since before the war. They haven't shown much activity up to the present, but will likely try to take advantage of the position we are now in. The printing trades are now getting a demonstration of those Unions in operation and your paper should do a lot of good in countering their formation at least in London. 3,000 is something to congratulate yourselves on, considering the short period your paper has been in existence.[248]

Glad to know that Comrade Mrs Hutt is again all right.

Denbeath are preparing for the carrying on of the Communal kitchens for a long period. They are at present getting the food cooked in boilers in houses, but are now having a central kitchen built to meet the position of acute unemployment which will be felt in Denbeath. Those who will be thrown on the dole are to contribute 4/- per week and will receive rations at the kitchen. COMMUNAL FEEDING has now been accepted here as the best method. You can imagine that after 25 or 26 weeks of it the women in the households can say with some truth that it is easier for them. Next time we shall have to improve on present methods, for instance commandeering the local hotels. It will have to be done.

2 or 3 trawlers have been bunkered at Methil this week, with "breakaway coal" from Valleyfield. One of the waggons had chalked on it, "This coal was howked and filled by the biggest bloody scabs in Valleyfield". Good advertisement.

Methil branch of the Dockers meet tomorrow to discuss the recommendation of 6 2/3% reduction. By the mutterings going on there are 2 dangerous tendencies on the boards — Breakaway from the Union and also formation of local union outside the Transport & General Workers. Usual tripe: "We have received no strike pay", and "We had more benefits from our wee union than we have had from the big one, let's get back to our wee union".

313

Never think about fighting their reactionary officials inside the Transport and General Workers. Of course those chaps have never (as dockers) been engaged in any scrap worth talking about and have been exceedingly lucky in getting good conditions practically thrown at them. The result is that they don't appreciate those conditions or realise how they were gained. However, George, in spite of the composition the Labour Movement still struggles along, drifting into trouble, and drifting out again, apparently learning nothing but drift. But leadership counts and indications are not wanting that the old bunch are near the end of their tether. It's up to us to bring it nearer.

Sunday afternoon: Hodge and I had a good meeting at Buckhaven. Owing to the stupidity of Buckhaven Reform Union's Secretary, we had to hold an open-air meeting, and although I spoke less than ½ an hour my throat is like a piece of raw meat. Little or no enthusiasm was shown but the atmosphere was one of "no more drift", "we all came out together so let's go back together". Just finished Methil meeting, which was on a par with Buckhaven. Let Hodge away without asking about *The Miner*. Enclosed copy of minutes of Fife Council of Action which might interest you. The Dockers here have unanimously agreed to accept the 6 2/3% reduction. No opposition put forward. It's a great life. P.S. I notice the *Weekly* is charged by the Durham Chief Constable.[249]

November 25th, 1926.

Am commencing this letter today, being again confined to bed since yesterday afternoon due, I admit, to my pigheadedness in getting out too quick last week. I got hell from the doctor on Monday night for addressing meetings during the weekend and was ordered by him neither to attend nor address any meetings all this week. So much for myself. I am out of it. Jock McArthur will have written you re his case.

As I indicated in my last letter the debacle has set in here, although not sufficient in extent to satisfy the Coal Companies. That applies particularly at the Wellesley, due to skilled brushers and repairers, coal hewers and coal-cutting machinemen not turning out, with the result that the oncost men who have signed on cannot be absorbed. I don't know how it applies at other pits. The worst feature of the "breakaways" here is the number of young chaps who are involved. Whether it is due to having no pocket money or due to them not being alive to the strenuous fight to secure the 7 hours shift, or a combination of both of those factors, the fact remains that a hell of a lot of intensive agitation will be required here to ensure a militant spirit being developed amongst the young element. Another feature of disloyalty to themselves and the working class is demonstrated at the docks. Trawlers in large numbers are now arriving daily and are being bunkered night and day. The usual crowd who perform this class of work are unable to cope with it, with the result that miners and coaltrimmers (from the hoists) are also involved in the scramble to ape the Port Said and Alexandria coolies by loading with baskets, and they undoubtedly are "out-coolieing" those "Gippos" at Methil. Why the brokers are not insisting that loin cloths only should be worn, beats me. So far no attempt has been made to break the rates, possibly due to the fact that Hull and Yarmouth trawlers are coming here because they cannot get bunkered at their home ports. Numbers of miners who are working at the trawlers have the bloody cheek to play hell when their rations are "cut off" at the kitchens. If they made such a hell of a noise with the brokers and pit managers the position would be A.I., but they grovel, crawl and fawn when in front of those august individuals. A different spirit is being shown in Central Fife. You will have probably received news of the set to at Glencraig and Bowhill of Monday last. Police and non-uniformed scabs being beat up and damage done at Glencraig Pit. According to a report I received on Tuesday night there are, in the words of the Young Comrades' song, "No scabs there". Yet the feeding arrangements in those places so far as quantity and quality are concerned are not on a par with what we have had here. That brings us up against the problem: SHOULD ELABORATE FEEDING ARRANGEMENTS BE MADE FOR STRIKERS? Judging the results between East and Central Fife on those grounds alone one would be justified in arriving at the conclusion that too much soup has run in this area and settled where MEN usually possess vertebrae. But that alone is not the explanation. Those villages in Central Fife are purely mining, situated inland and have a big population of Scottish-Irish, a mixture which at all times is liable to explode and play hell without any attempt to organise. We here are living in a seaport, with the miners composing almost half the population, foreign coal being dumped and after the breakaways in West Fife, scab coal sent to the docks, breaking down what at no time (other than during the General Strike) could be termed "a militant proletariat". I hope, George, you are not thinking I am trying to find an excuse for East Fife becoming the Notts portion of the Fife coalfield, because I am of the opinion that we here have put in more organised work than those other areas, but local circumstances have beaten us at the critical period not because our methods were entirely at fault, but because so few of us have had to cope with so large and scattered an area.

According to this morning's Press an agreement is likely to be made for Scotland, although there are no indications as to hours and wages. 8 hours will be the result, I'm afraid, as Nimmo is the chief advocate of the owners and Smillie for the men, and because of the big breakaways during the past fortnight, all of whom are on an 8 hours' shift. These breakaways are entirely due to the weak and cowardly decisions of the last 2 Delegate Conferences, which will have a detrimental effect on Trade Union organisation for some time. Smillie and the other "ratters" in the Scottish Executive Committee will now have got where they have played for all the time, but at a cost that they did not anticipate, viz., loss of reputation amongst the rank and file. Are we in position to effectively take advantage of that position and push them out of it for good? I am afraid not. Due to the Union split not being healed, we in Fife, where the strongest organised force against reactionary officialdom exists in Scotland, our hands are tied. In addition, complications have arisen, Old Union members declaring that they intend joining the Reform Union and Reform Union members playing hell about amalgamation — "Let's fight on by yourselves, to hell with that bunch of twisters", "I'll not be in a Union with that bunch", etc. etc. We will have the donkey work in keeping the Unions intact and thereby allowing Smillie and Company a new lease of Trade Union life.

It is rumoured that my butty is to become pit head gaffer at the Wellesley (he left that job to become checkweigher) after work is resumed. If the votes cast for his Bailieship, Convener of Town Council Works Committee and Chairman of local Municipal Gas Board are any criterion, the rumour is not without foundation. However, George, we will "Wait and See". He hasn't shown himself on picket or at any meeting yet.

Notice by today's press that the *Weekly* has been ordered to pay £1,100 at Manchester. See also that Clynes[250] and the I.L.P. [are] emulating their bourgeois masters by slobbering over the death of Krassin.[251] Slight alteration of war-time slogan: "All good Bolsheviks are dead Bolsheviks". The bloody hypocrites. Krassin is reported in tonight's *Edinburgh Evening News* to have left £3,000,000 in European banks.

Saturday morning, *27/11/26:* Have got out of bed. As I thought, the Scottish terms include an 8 hours shift. Smillie is reported in today's Press to have stated that the men in Scotland could all be at work in a few days. The Reform Union are holding an Executive Board meeting today to discuss the terms. My opinion of the terms agreed on by Smillie and Company is that they should be turned down and an agitation raised against the 8 hours, recommending the men to adopt the same tactics which were employed in Fife 55 years ago, when the Fife miners forced the 8 hours shift by finishing work at the end of 7 hours and making tracks for the pit bottom. A "stay-in strike", which would have some chance of success owing to Scotland being an exporting district. Better to have no agreement at all than be tied down by the terms indicated in the Press: 8 hours shift, April rates of wages until March or April and another agreement to be drawn up before the expiration of present terms. Enclosed cutting from *Edinburgh Evening News*, 26/11/26, which should interest you. Looks very much like a "House Union", caused by the local branch refusing to accept instructions from Headquarters. The Typographical Association in Scotland must now be almost defunct.[252]

[London, n.d.][253]

All letters received safely. Sorry you have been ill. Hope getting better. Take things easy. Keep your pecker up. Best luck to you and all. Letter follows.

December 4th, 1926.

Thanks for yours of 28th November, also telegram. Is it at all possible to discover one with a sufficiently vitriolic pen to picture those so-called leaders of the British working class movement, the majority of the miners' leaders included, in their true colours? What a debacle. Here we see the results of the so-called leaders, but it must have been hellish (as you describe it) to see them all grouped together, making the debacle a certainty.

Scotland is well in the soup, 3 years agreement and Smillie "hopes it will bring peace", "hopes no bitterness will be shown", "hopes no men will be vitimised", "hopes", Jesus Christ, "hopes", "hopes", "hopes", after foisting an agreement like he has on the Scottish miners. I was so bloody wild when I got to know the actual terms last Sunday that I addressed a meeting in Methil on Sunday night and was unable to get about on Monday.

The result of the terms was brought home very forcibly to the men on Monday. Policemen ordered the Union officials off the Wellesley pit head (on instructions from Johnny Brown) and Johnny, to show his power, told the men he would send for them when required, but he wouldn't require any more for at least 6 weeks. There were only 217 underground on Wednesday foreshift out of 800 in April, which means that roughly speaking only ¼ of the Wellesley men have been absorbed. The other pits are even worse than that. It is estimated that between 5 and 6 thousand have signed on the "buroo" in this area on Wednesday and Thursday. I am also on the "dole" and likely to be on it for some time. No checkweighers are required at the Wellesley at present (and perhaps the future also), as the Wemyss Coal Company are working "pan runs" (conveyors) where the men are paid by the yard or shift rates. They are introducing them all over the Wellesley and from what I can gather intend working them on the Co-operative principle (by the yard), which means that the Company will dispose of some of their slave drivers as the men themselves will be "their brother's keeper", viz., seeing to it that the fellow next place will do as much as he can. It certainly will, if adopted, do away with the individual contractor, unless the Wemyss Coal Company "set" a few "pan runs" to some of those swine, who in turn "set" each "pan run" to the men. However, George, whether "set" direct by the Company or not, it will mean that when they get a kick all will be kicked simultaneously on the "run". The worst feature likely to arise is the employment of youths. Last January, during the Wellesley strike, Johnny Brown told us that he could get "halflins" of 17 years to work on those "runs" for 8/- and less per shift, and to meet the requirements of the Coal Mines Act a fireman to supervise the safety arrangements — wood, shots, etc., — was all that was necessary. As the "waste" is practically empty on those "pan runs" it means more "weight" or pressure on the roof and that, coupled with the noise of the "pans" at work, also the hard (unskilled) continuous work of feeding the "pans", plus the inexperience of the majority of youths, [means] the doctor and grave-digger will be kept busy. 1 scab killed at a Wemyss Coal Company pit this week.

Gillespie[254] and I made inquiry at the "burroo" re our position and the "dole", because not being employed by the Company, the Exchange would not receive confirmation of us applying for and being unable to get work from the Company. We were informed that our claims would be accepted with the others, but the clerk who informed us, not being too sure, inquired at the manager, who was interviewing a deputation from the local union branches. He (the clerk) mentioned our names and (according to Comrade McArthur, who was on the deputation) the manager stated: "The Proudfoot case. I was informed last week by the Wemyss Coal Company that he would not get

317

started again at the Wellesley." Only me, not Gillespie. However, George, the Wemyss Coal Company will not have the last word in this matter if any men are employed on the ton and desire my services. On the other hand if, as rumoured, "pan runs" only are to be the vogue in the Wellesley I am stumped in this area so far as the pits are concerned and I can assure you no tears will be lost.

Smillie "hopes no men will be victimised", but I will be surprised if any of those who have been active in Fife will get back, unless we can get the National Unemployed Workers' Committee Movement going and make ourselves such a nuisance to the Parish and Employment Exchange authorities that to choose the lesser of 2 evils the Coal Companies, to stultify the N.U.W.C.M., take back to work some of the active men. We have set up a Department on the District Party Committee to deal with the N.U.W.C.M. for Fife.

You might have a visit from J. McArthur this week, Friday?

The Reform Union Sub-Executive has recommended that 10 organisers should be appointed to get it going again. I am one of the 10 recommendations. Rather have been left out as, although the Party instructions are to keep the Reform Union's end up, owing to amalgamation not having been accomplished before the end of the lock-out, I am still of the opinion that giving the Reform Union a new lease of life will not bring Unity any nearer. It will mean to a certain extent raising the spirit which we had almost flattened out in this area, except for a few diehards on either side.

Re the "Fight Like Hell" supplement,[255] the slogan will be more necessary now than before, but I think the "One Mineworkers' Union" should replace it, as it will be the weapon we will have to forge before we can "fight like hell" again. Policy was the main theme running through the supplement during the past 25 weeks. Policy should not now be neglected but Organisation should receive more attention. Weakness of previous structure of M.F.G.B. continually exposed: District and County autonomy, District leaders only concerned (or at any rate posing as being so)' for "their own" districts, to the detriment of the M.F.G.B. and ultimately of "their own" districts, different rules, subscriptions, etc. If it is possible to get the "worker correspondents" to continue I think the 2 pages should be continued because, 1st, the circulation of the *Weekly* is likely to increase in the mining areas, 2nd, due to District Agreements more attention will naturally be focussed on the District Union Executives, to the exclusion of other districts and the M.F.G.B., 3rd, the letters from all the Districts will serve to keep alive the need for a national union, and 4th, by the present attitude of most of the other big unions the likelihood is that they will not fight the wage reductions and increased hours demands coming to them, which leaves the miners to again become the storm troops. Those points I have suggested look as if I can only see or think about coal and coalminers to the exclusion of everything else, but I think you will agree that owing to the "community" nature of the mineworkers a special appeal must be made to them to get them interested in other matters. That appeal must be one dealing with something they are familiar with and that is fairly well met by the supplement, which in turn gets them to interest themselves in the rest of the matter of the *Weekly*.

The I.L.P. *The Miner* does not circulate here, or if it does I have never seen it or heard anyone talk about it, but it might circulate where I.L.P. branches exist in the coalfield; although to my knowledge I.L.P. branches exist (on paper) in Lochgelly and Cowdenbeath, none of the Party members from there mention it.[256]

Almost 200 arrests have taken place for the Central Fife "do" of a fort-night ago. We had to send a Party member there to form branches of the International Class War Prisoners' Aid on Wednesday, but no proper arrangements had been made for the meetings and only 1 meeting was held (at Lochgelly) but it was decided to form a committee at a future meeting. Bob Thomson was the comrade, and owing to the way things were messed up he lost the last bus from Kirkcaldy and had to walk home.

Jock McArthur has surely been writing you about my spleen. He has got it in his nut that it is the cause of all my troubles. It certainly doesn't behave as it ought to, but it was a dose of the 'flu that caught me napping during the past few weeks. People who don't know they possess a spleen are apt to get kicked over by the 'flu. The dose I managed to collect has left me washed out, so after last Sunday's lesson I am taking things quiet, although, George, this is the time, the real testing time, for the Party in the coalfields and all hands are required, more than we can muster in fact.

The *Workers' Weekly* agent showed me the accounts today. Over £60 in debt. No wonder Gordon tried to get out of it. If the account is correct he hasn't been the least bit shy. He has shown some management. I haven't seen him for over a month and don't know if he has got started yet. I understand there will be a "family event" in his household this month, the eighth, 2 being dead.

The attendance at the Party aggregate meetings has dropped (what was to be expected) but we have instructed the Pit Group leaders to visit all those who signed forms to ascertain how they now stand. West Fife reports big influx to the Party during the past 2 weeks, so we are having another census for the district. Comrade Hope reports that there are good prospects of groups being formed in East and West Wemyss. The trouble isn't so much in getting groups formed as getting them organised and retaining them. It is foolish to form them unless attention can be paid to them for some time, as the usual procedure is for those groups to dissolve and a certain bitterness to the Party is the result. We are running a meeting tomorrow night for recruits, aiming to get some of the young elements, as the majority we recruited are over 40 and not likely to prove of much use.

Sunday, 5/12/26: The Young Comrades League is going strong, 6 school groups with over 100 members, boys and girls. We had a very lengthy discussion at the Local Party Committee on Wednesday night re the continuance of communal feeding at 4/- per week for those in receipt of the "dole". Owing to the sharp division of opinion expressed and considering that it was a national question we decided to write Headquarters for a lead whether we should or should not support it. Those who support continuance do so on the grounds that "those on the street" would not then be a menace to those "inside", and by demonstrating to those "inside" that they could be as well off "outside" as "inside" would cause them to make a kick. Those against (I am in this school) are of the opinion that those who are likely to be of any use would be tied up in the kitchens, apathy would creep in and nullify demonstrations which will be necessary to Parish, etc. Parish Council would refuse to do anything because we would be doing it for them, shopkeepers, etc., would support it to keep down demonstrations, etc., unemployed themselves would gradually accept position and become contented because of ease in obtaining rations, which would have reflection on those employed. We have not committed ourselves so far and are waiting on lead from Party Headquarters.

An attempt is being made to expel Comrade O'Neil from the new Trades and Labour Council because he opposed the so-called official Labour candidate at the Municipal Elections. We are gradually building up the opposition inside the Council to the local MacDonaldites. Women's Section of Labour Party and 2 Co-operative Women's Guilds supporting us. We have Party fractions beginning to function in these bodies.

December 21st, 1926.

Thanks for yours of December 6th. Sorry I cannot accept your offer of a week in London, not because of "Scotch Independence", but the fact is I am to join the silent (?) ranks of benedicts on Friday. Jemima and I are to be married on Friday.[257] Seems damn foolish with no prospects of work, but others get along; don't see why I shouldn't.

None of the Party members who have been prominent during the dispute have started work yet and by present indications will not get started in this locality. Fairly common over the coalfields. Looks as if the Party is to lose touch with the M.F.G.B. due to wholesale victimisation.

The Wellesley is in some mess. Barely 700 out of almost 2,300 in April had started last week when the sides of the old shaft (which was used as an airshaft for the Wellesley) caved in, throwing all sections but two on the streets again. Someone will get it in the neck for this. It is freely rumoured that Johnny Brown has got his notice, but I'm afraid it is the "wish being father to the thought". Johnny has been doing it nicely. Refused to meet and discuss complaints with an Old Union agent last week.

We are reorganising the Local by getting the Departments to function better: Changing the leaders and reducing the numbers of Local Party Committee. I am in charge of Y.C.L. and think we can get more out of them than the Party. They are keener and more inclined to discuss and operate decisions than the mass of the local Party. The Young Comrades are over 100 strong and the Y.C.L. are anxious to get a school paper going. Possibly manage it after Xmas and New Year holidays.

We have a District Pit Group meeting at Lochgelly on Sunday 1st when we should get a good idea of the number of Party members at work in Fife. You will possibly know by this time that school strikes have taken place in West

Fife as a protest against the Education Authority stopping the feeding of school children. We were successful in our area last week in getting the School Management Committee to refuse to operate the Education Authority's decision and only a few children have been "cut off". Those on the "dole" are asked to hand to the Education Authority the 2/- per week grant in respect of children, and the Education Authority undertakes to provide food at 5/3d. per week to each child. At present, if the children are being fed at school, which also includes clothes and boots (30/- per 6 months), the Ministry of Labour deducts the 2/- from the allowance as they contend that the child is not wholly dependent and is not being wholly maintained by its parents or guardians. It's a lovely war. Children at school whose parents were in receipt of Parish Relief were also to be "cut off" but our local Parish Council agreed to meet the bill. It is a deliberate attack on the unemployed and also to further reduce the minimum under which children become eligible for being fed at school. The old scale was 7/- per head per week. The suggested new scale is the "dole", which means a reduction of 9/- per week in a household of 6 — man, wife and 4 children — 42/- to 31/-. We had a good demonstration against it last week. I along with hundreds more "signed on" today for "able-bodied unemployed relief". The suggested scale is 23/- for man and wife, 15/- for single man, 7/6d. for youths between 14 and 17 and a sum for children under school age. 5/- per week is to be deducted from each (10/- man and wife) and to be given to the communal kitchens, which will leave a few bob in the hands of each recipient — 10/- single man, 13/- man and wife. The money expended to be recoverable by the Parish WHEN our claim for the "dole" is granted. "A bird in the hand is worth three in the frying pan."

The Parish Council were to meet tonight to discuss the scheme. At present I don't know the result of their meeting but I expect you will receive it from our Worker Correspondent at the end of the week. Communal feeding is still in vogue here, 3 meals per day, 7 days per week. ½ lb. steak per head last Sunday morning.

We have given the rates a push here, so much so that the Wemyss Coal Company, who are the biggest ratepayers (14/9d. out of every £1 paid in rates), are getting more than anxious. The rule here (I'm not sure whether it is general) is that in all houses let yearly under £12.10/- the landlord is responsible for collecting and paying to the local authority the occupiers' rates. As the tenure of a Coal Company house is not on a yearly but a fortnightly basis the Company is responsible to the local authorities for the collection of the rates. They of course deduct them every fortnight at the pit from the men's pay (excuse the term), along with rent. As the Wemyss Coal Company own Denbeath, 1 or 2 streets in Methil, Methilhill, almost ½ of Buckhaven, a considerable bit of East Wemyss, Muiredge, West Wemyss and Coaltown of Wemyss they are feeling a draught at present since they received their little bill, so much so that they have asked the local authorities to send the assessment notices to each of their tenants. The Town Council, I understand, intend fighting their demand, realising (apart from the legal aspect) the impossibility of getting anything out of men who are still on the streets after almost 8 months lock-out.

I hope you received the small present for Baby Hutt all right. Nicol[258] made the cradle, Jemima the quilt and my mother the ball. Cradles and dolls are what the average proletarian women consider the most appropriate toys for baby girls.

Enclosed copy of skit on a few scab coaltrimmers at Methil who unloaded the German coal. Can you get it in the *Weekly* or the *Sunday Worker* as the author is very keen to see it published? The "Glue Pot" is a pub and the other terms, "Cuddy Lugs", etc., are the pet names of some of the scabs.

Jock McArthur arrived home last Tuesday. He will probably have written you by this time.

[London,] December 22nd, 1926.
Thanks beautiful cradle safely received Virginia will love it stop Suspect Nicol Jemima had hand in making cradle please thank them and all very much for really lovely present stop are you coming here stay with us for short holiday as suggested my last letter stop come New Year if Christmas impossible George Norma Virginia.[259]

December 28th, 1926.
Thanks for yours of 24th December. Received telegrams all right, also present to myself for which accept my thanks. The kiddies send you, Comrade Mrs Hutt and Virginia their thanks for the *Bobby Bear Annual* and hope to see Virginia in Methil soon. We are living in my mother's room until I get a job and following that — a house, so that the address remains unaltered.

Re the Reform Union organising job: it has gone by the board because of the meeting in Glasgow. As far as I can gather the results will be A.I. from this last meeting. A time limit was set, 13th January, which should prevent the sabotage done on the last occasion by the Old Union officials. In addition some Old Union branches had already informed Adamson that in the event of no move being made for Unity they would create village unions. This threat was made at an Old Union Standing Committee meeting on December 4th and the joint meeting was held in Glasgow on December 13th. I haven't seen the proposals but I understand that they are the July 10th proposals with a few details as to election of local officials, etc.

Johnny Brown still reigns at the Wellesley. Headquarters gave us a ruling on the communal feeding — to carry on. They also came down heavy on those of us who were opposed, by suggesting that our attitude was "low wages and rotten conditions for the workers will only make them fight, so let them get it in the neck". These weren't the exact words, but that was their meaning. However, George, up to the present we accepted their ruling and as I reported in my last letter the Parish Council had a scheme in front of them. They agreed to it all right but owing to the "dole" being paid out last Friday to the Wemyss Coal Company unemployed the scheme is "up in the air" again. Last night the Parish Council again met and agreed to terminate the communal kitchens on Thursday first, December 30th. There is a likelihood of them being continued in Denbeath and Methilhill (where centralised kitchens have been established),

322

but owing to the impossibility of centralised kitchens in Methil and Buckhaven, due to scattered nature of those places, I am afraid the kitchens will cease. We require at least 4 in Methil to allow the food to be in a fit condition when those who carry it reach home, which would mean an increase per head (at least 1/- per week) over the centralised kitchen. You can visualise the continuous bickering that would ensure. "How the hell is it that we in Methil who are paying 1/- more per week than those in Denbeath can only get the same as them?", "Some bloody swicking gaun on here", "The b——s in the kitchens are hae'in their share", etc. etc. (To get an idea of the pettiness of some of them one requires to be involved in SOUP.) This has been going on during the past 7 months when they have not been PAYING, but it would be intensified when they commenced PAYING the cash direct. If we can judge the future to any extent by the present we should have some criticism when none possesses economic power over their fellows. If the same truculent, domineering attitude (adopted by many to those in the kitchens) was adopted to the pit managers we would be in a strong position.

We are trying to get the Local into ship-shape order but it takes some doing. Ours is the wrong type of recruit, too old to get much activity out of them. The sales of the *Workers' Weekly* and *Sunday Worker* are dropping not because the demand is not here but because those who are on the Distribution will not get a move on, despite the lines we suggest. Some of them who have started work "haven't time to do anything" ("Strike Communists") but they will either do something or get out. No room for passengers as they cause a "rot" to set in. Enclosed copy of chart re local organisation we have in our rooms to acquaint them with their duties and Party organisation.

It is rumoured tonight that the Wellesley is to be closed down for 3 months, to allow the air shaft to be cleared. Owing to "bad air" many of the back shift were unable to work today not only in the Wellesley but also Rosie and Muiredge.

I informed Jemima about your desire re a present, but she hasn't cleared the matter up — "doesn't know".

J. McArthur, Bob Thomson and J. O'Neill are still idle and likely to remain so for some time. At least 2,000 are still on the streets here.

A Scottish Congress of the Party is to be held in Glasgow on January 8th and 9th to form Scotland into a District, Fife to become a Sub District. They have hurried this Congress, as the Agenda is not likely to be in the possession of the Locals until next week, which will not give some of the new locals much time to digest it.

LOCAL AGGREGATE MEETING

LOCAL ORGANISER

LOCAL PARTY COMMITTEE

INDUSTRIAL DEPT.	PIT & FACTORY GROUPS DEPT.	DISTRIBUTION DEPT.	AGIT-PROP DEPT.	YOUTH DEPT.	I.C.W.P.A. DEPT.	CO-OP. DEPT.	WOMEN'S DEPT.	FINANCE DEPT.
T.U. Branch Fractions	Pit & Factory Groups	Party Lit.	Party Training	Y.C.L.	Defence	Co-op. Fractions	Co-op. Guild Fractions	Members' Subs.
P.&L.C.	Members' Subs.	Manifestoes	Group Trainers	Children's Section	Maintenance	Recruiting	Women's Labour Section Fractions	Monthly Reports
Party Lit.	Party Lit.	Recruiting	Propaganda	Recruiting	Registration	Regular Reports	Recruiting	Entertainment Org.
Minority Movement	Pit & Factory Papers	Regular Reports	Meetings	Regular Reports	Recruiting		Regular Reports	Recruiting
N.U.W.C.M.	Party Training		Speakers		Regular Reports			
Recruiting	Gen. Agitation		Manifestoes					
Regular Reports	Recruiting		Recruiting					
	Regular Reports		Regular Reports					

NOTES
THE LETTERS OF DAVID PROUDFOOT

1　See Chap. 15, Note 2.
2　*Labour Monthly*, Jul. 1921 to date, "a magazine of international labour", its founder and first editor was R. Palme Dutt (see Chap. 27, Note 4).
3　Jimmy Hope: see Chap. 12, Note 1.
4　John Dick, blacksmith, secretary of the Communist Party in Fife.
5　George Lansbury, 1859-1940, editor of *The Herald*, 1919-22 and its general manager, 1922-25; founded *Lansbury's Labour Weekly*, 1925-27; M.P. for Bow and Bromley, 1910-13 and 1922-40; leader of the Labour Party, 1931-35. His amendment in the House of Commons on 3 Apr. 1924 to the Army Bill was intended to allow recruits to the army to opt out of taking duty in aid of the civil power during a trade dispute. The amendment was rejected by 236 votes to 67, and those who voted against it included such leading figures in the Labour Government as J. H. Thomas, J. R. Clynes, Arthur Henderson, Frank Hodges, and William Adamson. See *Daily Herald*, 16 Apr. 1924.
6　Arthur Henderson, 1863-1935, Home Secretary in the Labour Government, 1924, Foreign Secretary 1929-31. No trace of this case has been found in *Hansard* or the press.
7　*Workers' Weekly*, Feb. 1923-Jan. 1927, was the official organ of the Communist Party of Great Britain.
8　I.e., Mineworkers' Reform Union of Fife, Kinross and Clackmannan.
9　I.e., the Fife, Kinross and Clackmannan Miners' Association.
10　Rt. Hon. William Adamson: see Chap. 4, Note 1.
11　Robin Page Arnot, 1890-, a leading member of the Communist Party, Secretary, Labour Research Department, historian of mining trade unionism.
12　The Ruhr miners had been locked out the previous month for refusing to work more than seven hours underground and eight above ground. A settlement was reached at the beginning of Jun. by which the longer hours were accepted by the men until Sep., along with a wage increase. The Communists opposed the settlement. *The Times*, 3 Jun. 1924.
13　A strike by coal trimmers at Leith threatened to become a national strike in protest at the retention of a score of blacklegs taken on by the employers there during the dispute. The dispute was referred by the Ministry of Labour to a Court of Inquiry, which settled the issue by persuading the employers to pay compensation to the blacklegs instead of retaining them. *Scotsman*, 13, 15, 20 and 30 May, and 13 and 21 Jun. 1924.
14　This is probably *The Fife Miners' Union Split. Rank and File v. Officialdom. The struggle for control.* n.p. n.d. (1924). 16 pp. There is a copy in the Proudfoot Papers at Methil Public Library, and another at the T.U.C. Library.

15 Harry Pollitt: see Chap. 17, Note 1. Nat Watkins, see Chap. 25, Note 1. Steve Lawther was a leader of the Durham Miners' Association, and a brother of Will Lawther.

16 The Labour Research Department, originally formed in 1914 as the Fabian Research Department, developed into a federal body after breaking away in 1918, and was supported by many trade unions and other working-class organisations. It still flourishes.

17 John Bird and William Kirker — see Chap. 5, Note 10. For the National Minority Movement, see Chap. 8, Note 6.

18 Willie Joss, see Chap. 19, Note 13.

19 Bob Stewart, see Chap. 19, Note 13.

20 "Henry" was Henry Dubb, i.e. the ordinary worker.

21 H. P. Rathbone, 1895-1969; his article, titled "Whose Budget?", appeared in *Labour Monthly*, Jun. 1924. For R. Palme Dutt, see Chap. 27, Note 4.

22 Tom Kennedy: see Chap. 5, Note 24.

23 Olive Budden, 1892-, wife of R. Page Arnot. Kosa has not been identified, but was presumably some form of medicine.

24 I.e., Executive of the National Union of Scottish Mine Workers.

25 *Bunk*, by the American author W. E. Woodward, 1874-1950, was published in New York and London in 1923.

26 Bert Williams, *Record of the Labour Government*, a pamphlet published by the Communist Party (London, 1924).

27 Albert Inkpin, 1884-1944, General Secretary, Communist Party of Great Britain, 1920-29.

28 John McArthur, see above, pp. 1-167.

29 I.e., a clergyman.

30 Tom Bell: see Chap. 5, Note 21. J. R. Campbell: see Chap. 5, Note 17. For the Campbell Case, see Chap. 16, Note 1.

31 John Turner Walton Newbold, 1888-1943, Communist M.P. for Motherwell, 1922-23, resigned from the Communist Party on 23 Aug. 1924 because "he disapproved of the Communist Party's attitude towards the Labour Party and the Labour Government". Newbold joined the "National" Labour Party in 1931 and supported Winston Churchill in the 1935 parliamentary election. The resignation of Ellen Wilkinson from the Communist Party was announced at the same time as Newbold's but had taken place "several months" before his. *Daily Herald*, 5 and 6 Sep. 1924.

32 Morgan Philips Price, 1885-1973, journalist and author, wrote four articles titled "The Labour Party and Power", in the *Labour Monthly* of Feb., Apr., May and Jul. 1924. *Plebs*, 1909-69, organ of the Plebs League until 1921 and thereafter of the National Council of Labour Colleges.

33 Jack London, *The Iron Heel* (New York, 1907), 354 pp.

34 Reference uncertain but probably either Jack Jones, 1884-1970, Welshman, trade union official, 1923-28, author of *Unfinished Journey*, etc., or Jack Jones, 1873-1941, Irishman, Labour M.P. for Silvertown, 1918-40.

35 See Chap. 8, Note 1. Cook substituted for William Adamson as General Secretary, Fife miners' union, while Adamson was Secretary of State for Scotland in the 1924 Labour Government.

36 I.e., J. R. Campbell.

37 John O'Neil (O'Neill): see Chap. 3, Note 6.

38 See Chap. 16, Note 1.

39 The proposal by the Labour Government to make a loan to Soviet Russia as part of the normalisation of relations between it and Britain was strongly criticised by the Tory and Liberal Parties, and was one of the main reasons for the fall of the Government in October. See, e.g., C. L. Mowat, *Britain between the Wars, 1918-1940* (London, 1955), 182-3.

40 An international commission headed by the American General Charles G. Dawes produced in 1924 a Report or Plan directed to regulating reparations payable by Germany under the Treaty of Versailles. The Labour Government accepted the Plan but it was strongly criticised by the Left.

41 J. Murray, Liberal candidate, Kirkcaldy Burghs, in the 1924 General Election.

42 See Chap. 16, Note 1.

43 The Labour Party's annual conference in Oct. 1924 had passed resolutions that rejected application for affiliation by the Communist Party and precluded members of the latter from standing as Labour candidates for Parliament or local authorities and from being eligible for membership of the Labour Party. *Report of the 24th Annual Conference of the Labour Party, 1924*, 131.

44 Alexander Gillespie, checkweigher with Proudfoot at Wellesley Colliery.

45 Philip Hodge: see Chap. 14, Note 1 and Chap. 16, Note 2.

46 A general election had been held on 29 Oct.

47 See above, p. 66.

48 See Chap. 5, Note 5.

49 A. Bogdanoff, *A Short Course of Economic Science*, first published in Russia in 1897; rev. ed. (1919) published in 1924 by Communist Party of Great Britain, and translated by J. Fineberg.

50 *Manual of Party Training. Principles of Organisation.* (Communist Party, London, 1924), 80 pp; *Party Training Charts: Historical Synopsis* (Communist Party, London, 1924).

51 Edo Fimmen, *Labour's Alternative: the United States of Europe or Europe Limited.* Trans. by Eden and Cedar Paul (London, 1924), 128 pp. Fimmen, a Dutchman, was a Secretary of the International Federation of Trade Unions (the Amsterdam International) and a leader of the Transport Workers' International.

52 *Coquecigrues* was French for twaddle or balderdash.

53 G. Allen Hutt worked at the *Daily Herald* from 1923 until 1925.

54 R. Page Arnot, *The Politics of Oil* (Labour Research Dept., London, 1924), a pamphlet.

55 See above, Note 43.

56 I.e., National Union of Scottish Mine Workers.

57 This is Proudfoot's suggested letter to *The Miner*, mentioned above.

58 See above, Note 14.

59 When men on back shift at Valleyfield Colliery were kept underground thirty-five minutes beyond their hours, all the men held a meeting, protested vigorously and agreed to stop work until the manager restored the original hours. This was agreed pending negotiations. Local officials of the rival Fife unions had worked together in opposing the management.

60 See Chap. 5, Note 14.

61 See Chap. 21, Note 5.

62 G. Zinoviev, *Towards Trade Union Unity. Speech at Fifth Communist International Congress* (Communist Party of Great Britain, London, 1924); R. Page Arnot, *Fight the Slave Plan: The Dawes Report Exposed* (Communist Party

of Great Britain, London, 1924); *Young Worker*, 1923-? 1930s, organ of the Young Communist League; *The Mineworker*, 1924-26, organ of the Miners' Minority Movement.

63 See Chap. 21, Note 1.

64 Guy A. Aldred, 1886-1963, anti-parliamentarian, journalist, pamphleteer, a Londoner who lived most of his life in Glasgow.

65 William Paul, *The Path to Power* (Communist Party, London, 1924).

66 Reservists had been called up by the Government before Black Friday, 1921.

67 Leon Trotsky, 1879-1940, a leader of the Bolshevik Revolution in Russia and founder of the Red Army. The cutting is of the *Glasgow Herald* leader of 21 Jan. 1925, commenting on Trotsky's resignation a week earlier as President of the Revolutionary Military Council, in the course of his struggle with the "Triumvirate" of Zinoviev, Kamenev and Stalin.

68 Sir Adam Nimmo, 1867-1939, President of the Mining Association of Great Britain, Chairman of the Fife Coal Company, 1923-39.

69 Arthur E. E. Reade had moved an unsuccessful amendment at a London aggregate meeting of the Communist Party on 17 Jan. 1925, regretting the "hasty vote" at an earlier Party meeting approving the attitude of the Soviet Communist Party and Communist International toward Trotsky. Reade was later suspended from the London District Party Committee. J. Klugmann, *History of the Communist Party of Great Britain* (London, 1969), Vol. 2, 327.

70 Methil coaltrimmers had struck work in Feb. and Mar. 1924.

71 Joseph Houghton, died 1949, General Secretary, Scottish Union of Dock Labourers until its amalgamation in 1923 into the Transport and General Workers' Union, when he became Scottish Docks Group Secretary.

72 I.e., National Union of Scottish Mine Workers.

73 G. Allen Hutt moved at this time from the *Daily Herald* to *Trade Union Unity*, a left-wing monthly "magazine of international trade unionism", whose editorial board was A. A. Purcell, George Hicks and Edo Fimmen.

74 A. J. Cook spoke at Lochgelly on Sunday, 15 Mar. 1925, under the auspices of the Fife Committee of the Scottish Labour College.

75 *Sunday Worker*, 1925-29, organ of the left wing of the labour movement.

76 *Communist International*, 1919-39, a monthly review, ed. for some time by G. Zinoviev and K. Radek, published in Moscow until 1924, and thereafter in London by the Communist Party of Great Britain.

77 Albert Duncan.

78 James Stewart of Lochgelly — see Chap. 18, Note 1.

79 *Edinburgh Evening News*, 2 Apr. 1925, contained a report, with photograph, of women Fascists opening their headquarters in Edinburgh.

80 *Russia. Official Report of the British Trade Union Delegation to Russia in November and December 1924* (London, 1925), 249 pp.

81 John Wheatley, 1869-1930, I.L.P. leader, M.P. for Glasgow Shettleston, 1922-30, Minister of Health in the 1924 Labour Government. For Maxton, see Chap. 5, Note 16. Albert Arthur Purcell, 1872-1935, Furnishing Trades leader, member of General Council T.U.C., 1919-27 and President, 1924; President of International Federation of Trade Unions; Labour M.P. for Coventry, 1923, and Forest of Dean, 1925-29; founder and member of editorial board of *Trade Union Unity*.

82 For MacDonald, see Chap. 23, Note 1; for Thomas, see Chap. 11, Note 3.

83 Bill Crooks.

84 The Emergency Powers Act, 1920, gave the Government wide powers to maintain public services during a strike.

85 In 1922 the R.A.F. had suppressed a revolt in Iraq by bombing native villages.
86 Philip Snowden, 1864-1937, an I.L.P. leader, Chancellor of the Exchequer in the Labour Governments, 1924 and 1929-31, joined the "National" Labour Party in 1931, became a viscount, 1932.
87 Kelly was Labour candidate for Greenock in 1924. See *Scotsman*, 25 Oct. 1924.
88 William Norman Ewer, 1885-1977, journalist and author, wrote about "Red Plots" and also "Trotsky and his 'friends'", in *Labour Monthly*, Jun. 1925. The *Review* was the *Communist Review*, 1921-35 and 1946-53, which between Feb. 1927 and Dec. 1928 was retitled *The Communist*.
89 I.e., proposals by the National Union of Scottish Mine Workers.
90 Mrs Helen Crawfurd: see Chap. 19, Note 15. Tom Mann, 1856-1941, a leader of the London Dock Strike, 1889, General Secretary, Amalgamated Society of Engineers, 1918-21, Chairman, Red International of Labour Unions, British Bureau, and a leader of the Communist Party. For Shapurji Saklatvala, who was Indian, see Chap. 19, Note 12.
91 Tom Smith, Lumphinnans, President of the Reform Union.
92 A *Labour Monthly* pamphlet (1924), by P. Braun.
93 See above, Note 69.
94 For Selkirk, see Chap. 19, Note 9.
95 I.e., *Communist Review*.
96 Will Thorne, 1857-1946, General Secretary, National Union of Gas Workers and General Labourers, Labour M.P. for West Ham, 1906-45.
97 The Wellesley Colliery weight slip enclosed was stamped "Form a Pit Committee", "No Wage Reductions", "No Increase in Hours" and "Read the *Workers' Weekly*".
98 The growth of nationalism in China resulted in demands in 1925 that the Treaty Ports there should be placed under the sovereignty of China and that concessions wrung from China in the past by foreign powers should be terminated.
99 James Potter: see Chap. 25, Note 5.
100 Kay Beauchamp, 1899-, of the Communist Bookshop in London.
101 Selkirk's letter concerned the National Unemployed Workers' Committee Movement and the class struggle and his denial that he was himself an anarchist-communist. See *The Miner*, 4 Jul. 1925.
102 *Monthly Circular* was, and remains, the organ of the Labour Research Department.
103 John Marchbank, Assistant Secretary, 1925-33, and General Secretary, 1933-42, of the National Union of Railwaymen.
104 No copy of this paper is known to survive.
105 Herbert Smith: see Chap. 6, Note 4.
106 Above, Note 51.
107 A. A. Purcell won the Forest of Dean by-election on 15 Jul. 1925 with an increased majority over his Conservative opponent. The quotation comes from the *Glasgow Herald* leader of 16 Jul.
108 Beth Turner was Communist Party Women's Organiser in 1925 and a member of the Executive Committee.
109 I.e., of "The Spark".
111 See Chap. 16, Note 4.
111 Proudfoot had put this sentence before the preceding one.
112 See Chap. 27, Note 3, though it is possible that the paper referred to was the "Old Torch", of which two undated issues survive in the Hutt Collection at Methil

Public Library.
113 See above, pp. 26-8.
114 See Chap. 6, Note 4.
115 Rev. Welldon has not been further identified, nor the paper in which his letter appeared.
116 The national conference of trade union executive committees at Central Hall, Westminster, called by the T.U.C.
117 Some 30,000 anthracite miners at Ammanford in Carmarthenshire had struck work at the end of Jun. 1925 in defence of long-established customs, including a "seniority rule" under which the most recently employed were to be the first to be made redundant. At the end of Jul. and beginning of Aug. the employment of blacklegs led to violent collisions between strikers and police. The strikers substantially won their case and there was a return to work on 24 Aug. But almost 200 miners were prosecuted and fifty-eight of them were imprisoned from between one and eighteen months. See Hywel Francis, "The Anthracite Strike and Disturbances of 1925", in *Llafur, Journal of the Society for the Study of Welsh History*, Vol. 1, No. 2, May 1973, 15-28.
118 Robert Shirkie, Secretary, Scottish Colliery Engine and Boilermen's Association, and also a leader of the National Federation of Colliery Enginemen, Boilermen and Mechanics. Shirkie died in 1954.
119 *Lansbury's Labour Weekly*, Feb. 1925-Jul. 1927, organ of the left wing of the Labour Party and edited by George Lansbury.
120 Published by the Miners' Federation of Great Britain, May 1925.
121 I.e., Red Friday, as it became known.
122 The Industrial Alliance of 1925 was an attempt to revive the Triple Alliance of 1919-21 in a new form, and consisted of the Miners' Federation of Great Britain, the three railway unions, the Transport and General Workers' Union, the Engineers, and several other unions in heavy industry.
123 See Chap. 17, Note 3.
124 I.e., Rt. Hon. William Adamson.
125 The Mining Association was the coalowners' organisation.
126 I.e., the war in Morocco between the tribesmen on one hand and Spain and France on the other that ended in 1925-26 with the defeat of the tribesmen.
127 *Inprecorr* (International Press Correspondence), 1921-38, organ until 1943 of the Communist International, was published in London, Berlin and Vienna; retitled 1938-53 *World News and Views*, and 1954-62, *World News*.
128 The Communist Bookshop in London.
129 I.e., No. 16 King Street, London, Communist Party headquarters, and address of the Bookshop.
130 "The Signal" ran from c. Aug. 1925 to May 1926, and Nos. 3-19 are preserved in the Hutt Papers in Marx Memorial Library, London. No copies of "Sawdust" are known to survive.
131 On the French Channel coast, about three miles west of Dieppe.
132 The T.U.C. annual congress was held from 7-12 Sep. at Scarborough.
133 Ernest Bevin, 1881-1951, General Secretary, Transport and General Workers' Union, 1921-40, member of the General Council, T.U.C., 1925-40, Minister of Labour 1940-45, Foreign Secretary 1945-51.
134 See above, pp. 19-20.
135 Executive of the Minority Movement.
136 William Rust, 1903-49, Secretary, Young Communist League, and editor of *Young Worker*, 1924; imprisoned for twelve months, 1925, for incitement to

mutiny; editor, *Daily Worker*, 1930-49.

137 One is a reprint from the *Daily Telegraph*, 3 Sep. 1925, of an article headed "The True Analysis of the Red Plot Against the British Empire and Shipping. The Seamen's Strike"; the second is a leaflet headed "Seamen—Think Twice before acting rashly on the advice of Reds, Roughnecks and Troublemakers" and is signed by V. Olander, Secretary-Treasurer, International Seamen's Union of America.

138 William Dobbie, 1878-1950, President, National Union of Railwaymen, 1925-28 and 1930-33, Labour M.P. for Rotherham, 1933-50; Dobbie's article in *Labour Monthly*, Oct. 1925, was titled "Problems of Trade Unionism".

139 The Labour Party annual conference took place at Liverpool from 29 Sep. to 2 Oct. 1925, and resolved by large majorities that no member of the Communist Party was eligible for membership of any individual section of the Labour Party, or to remain a member of it, and also that affiliated trade unions should not elect Communists as delegates to national or local Labour Party conferences. See also above, Note 43, for 1924 Annual Conference decisions.

140 See above p. 236.

141 See Chap. 19, Note 12.

142 Sir William Joynson-Hicks, 1865-1932, Conservative M.P., 1908-29, Home Secretary, 1924-29.

143 Of twelve leaders of the Communist Party: Harry Pollitt, Albert Inkpin, Wal Hannington, William Rust, William Gallacher, and others.

144 To the arrested Communist Party leaders.

145 See Chap. 18, Note 2.

146 Four men — not three, as Proudfoot states — appeared on remand at the Mansion House, London, on 3 Nov., charged with stealing a motor van and about 8,000 copies of the *Daily Herald*. They were bound over to keep the peace in the sum of £100 each, or six months' imprisonment in default. The magistrate said he thought great leniency had been shown by the prosecutor in withdrawing the charge of larceny, and added: "Might I suggest that you, as able-bodied men, join the Police Reserve? They want good men." One of the men was fined £20 for having a pistol without a certificate. *Scotsman*, 4 Nov. 1925.

147 See above, Note 4.

148 J. Brown, manager of the Wellesley Colliery, Methil.

149 William Elger, 1891-1946, born in London of an Austrian father and Scots mother; General Secretary, Scottish T.U.C., 1922-46. Joseph F. Duncan, 1879-1965, General Secretary, Scottish Farm Servants' Union, 1914-45.

150 Dutt and Mary Moorhouse were "suspected by the police of propagandist activities". *The Times*, 7 Nov. 1925.

151 Paper published by the Nine Elms Communist Railwaymen, London.

152 John Brown, manager of Wellesley Colliery.

153 "The Spark", No. 9, 13 Nov. 1925, had reported that the girl, who had been employed at the Palace cinema as a cleaner and assistant, had produced a doctor's certificate ordering "complete rest" but the manager had refused to pay her wages for the days worked until she had worked her notice. "The Spark" had proposed the cinema be boycotted until the wages were paid. Issue No. 10 "unreservedly" withdrew the statement that the manager had seen the doctor's certificate before 17 Nov., when he had paid the wages due and offered the girl a light job in the cinema.

154 Alex Geddes, a leader of the Communist Party, parliamentary candidate at Greenock, 1922, 1923, 1924 and 1929.

155 I.e., Adamson.

156 Upon their conviction seven of the Communist leaders were told by the judge they could go free if they left the Party: their refusal to do so was followed by sentences upon them of six months' imprisonment each. The other five leaders were sentenced to twelve months each.

157 George Allison, 1895-1951, was a Communist Party and Minority Movement leader.

158 J. H. Thomas: see Chap. 11, Note 3.

159 These two last sentences are manuscript insertions that Proudfoot arrowed upward to refer to the words "due to their advocacy of Kelty stunt" above. The rest of this letter is typed.

160 Hodges seconded a compromise resolution at the International Federation of Trade Unions meeting at Amsterdam on 5 Dec. 1925 concerning relations with Soviet trade unions. See *The Times*, 7 Dec. 1925.

161 This letter is not to Hutt but is presumably to the Communist Bookshop in London.

162 See Chap. 6, Note 4.

163 See above, Note 117.

164 See Chap. 27, Note 3.

165 Formed in 1909, originally at Oxford, by students on strike against the regime at Ruskin College, the Central Labour College was supported by trade unions, particularly the South Wales Miners' Federation and National Union of Railwaymen. The College closed in 1929.

166 A two-page typed letter of 6 Jan. 1926 has been omitted here. It was to Hutt from Lawrence Welsh, a London local government employee who in his spare time voluntarily managed the accounts of the Communist Bookshop. The letter indicates that whatever confusion had arisen (e.g., see above, p. 239) over the Bookshop's accounts was due to misunderstanding at Methil, where Alex Gordon ran two accounts with the Bookshop — one for Methil Local Communist Party and the other for the East Fife Book Club.

167 The Locarno Pact, Oct. 1925, guaranteed the French-German and Belgian-German frontiers of 1919, provided for the peaceful settlement of all disputes between these three states failing which Britain and Italy, the two other signatories, would assist the state attacked. In effect, Germany accepted the 1919 settlement in the west but not in the east, where France undertook by Locarno to aid Poland and Czechoslovakia if they were attacked.

168 Before the date here Proudfoot had written "Friday morning" but had inserted above it "6.30 p.m.".

169 See Chap. 25, Note 5.

170 Proudfoot's telegrammed reply is preserved with this letter and reads: Old Union breakaway Saturday Work Sunday night 4 notices remain.

171 Ben Shaw, Secretary, Scottish Advisory Council of the Labour Party, 1914-32, died 1942. Egerton Percival Wake, 1871-1929, National Agent of the Labour Party, 1919-28.

172 The attempt to form an alliance of unions in heavy industry, including the Miners' Federation of Great Britain, and in transport, had been continued after 'Red Friday (see above, Note 122, and p. 249) but because of delays and opposition from J. H. Thomas of the Railwaymen petered out by the spring of 1926. See R. P. Arnot, *The Miners: Years of Struggle* (London, 1953), 400-1. The organisation of Workers' Defence Corps against Fascists and the government-sponsored Organisation for the Maintenance of Services, was strongly

advocated by the Communist Party and Minority Movement. J. Klugmann, op. cit., Vol. 2, 210.

173 The centre was the headquarters of the Minority Movement in London. Part of the cartoon in No. 16 of "The Spark", Feb. 1926, showed a colliery manager, in plus fours, having his boots licked by a small dog with a human head and labelled "O.U.O." (Old Union Official); a second dog, also with human head, stood on its hind legs licking the manager's posterior: this dog was labelled "Denbeath Old Union official".

174 Not further identified.

175 See above, Note 80.

176 Three issues for 1926 are preserved in Marx Memorial Library, London.

177 *The Coal Crisis: Facts from the Samuel Commission, 1925-26* (Labour Research Department, London, 1926), 79 pp.

178 A special national conference of the Minority Movement was held at Battersea Town Hall on 21 Mar. 1926.

179 A. Fenner Brockway, 1888-, pacifist in 1914-18 war, Organising Secretary, I.L.P., 1922, and General Secretary, 1928 and 1933-39, Labour M.P. for East Leyton, 1929-31, and Eton and Slough, 1950-64, created Lord Brockway, 1964.

180 *Report of the Royal Commission on the Coal Industry, 1925-26* (Samuel Commission).

181 John Dick, Fife District Secretary of the Communist Party.

182 This is a typed carbon copy of Hutt's letter to Proudfoot.

183 George Ernest Hicks, 1879-1954, General Secretary, Amalgamated Union of Building Trade Workers, 1921-40, member of General Council of T.U.C. and its Chairman in 1926-27, Labour M.P. for East Woolwich, 1931-50.

184 See Chap. 18, Note 3.

185 Not identified. Despite Proudfoot's reference above (p. 270) John McArthur says he was not the Industrial Organiser.

186 This is a typed carbon copy of a letter from Hutt to Proudfoot.

187 Presumably Paul Hathe.

188 See Chap. 5, Note 21.

189 See Chap. 27, Note 3.

190 I.e., the conference of national executives of trade unions, called by the T.U.C. at Farringdon Hall, London, from 29 Apr. to 1 May 1926.

191 This and the following telegram were from Proudfoot to Hutt.

192 This is a copy by Proudfoot's father of the letter written by Proudfoot to his parents.

193 Gillespie was Proudfoot's fellow checkweigher at Wellesley Colliery.

194 Nicol was the son by her first marriage of Mrs Jemima Sawkill, Proudfoot's future wife.

195 This is a draft of a telegram from Hutt to Proudfoot, and no address is given.

196 This letter is to Hutt from Proudfoot's father at 21 Durie Street, Methil.

197 I.e., letter of 15 May above.

198 This letter, to Hutt, begins "Dear Comrade".

199 I.e., relief funds for distribution to the miners.

200 Ernie Woolley, Minority Movement and Communist Party organiser. See also Chap. 27, Note 1.

201 This letter begins "Dear Comrade", not "Dear George".

202 C. T. Cramp: see Chap. 11, Note 3.

203 This note is not preserved with these letters.

204 *Leven Advertiser and Wemyss Gazette*, 1 Jun. 1926.

205   A. Fordyce Burke, Dundee solicitor.

206   Not further identified.

207   Neither "The Tiger" nor J. K. Neil has been identified, though possibly the first is a reference to the *Leven Advertiser*, and the second to J. O'Neil or O'Neill.

208   The Pioneers were the Communist children's organisation.

209   Gillies has not been further identified. Walter Tapsell (not Tapstal) later became Commissar in the British Battalion, International Brigade, in the Spanish Civil War, and was killed in Spain in Mar. 1938. Hugh Thomas, *The Spanish Civil War* (London, 1961), 519 n.3.

210   See Chap. 27, Note 3.

211   Alex Gordon.

212   Allen Hutt in his spare time worked on *Miners' Supplement* to the *Workers' Weekly* in 1926.

213   The *Daily Herald* leader approved proposals for a loan being made to the coal industry "to enable it to tide over the period during which the recommendations of the Royal Commission are put into force, *as Mr Baldwin promised they should be*". It added that the coal royalties could be used to guarantee the interest on such a loan.

214   Proposals for mediation to end the lock-out, on the basis of an immediate resumption of work on conditions existing before 30 Apr. 1926, temporary assistance by the Government, etc., were put to the M.F.G.B. Executive by representatives of the Churches, headed by the Archbishop of Canterbury, and were recommended by the Executive. A District vote by the miners, however, rejected the proposals by almost 35,000 votes. See R. P. Arnot, op. cit. 470-1.

215   A. J. Cook, General Secretary, M.F.G.B., addressed mass meetings on 6 Aug. 1926 in Fife at Buckhaven, Balgonie and Cowdenbeath, and in Clackmannanshire at Sauchie. At Buckhaven, where he was accompanied by William Adamson, General Secretary, and Charles Tonner, President, of the Fife miners' county union, he had an audience of between 8,000 and 10,000. *Scotsman*, 7 Aug. 1926.

216   See above, pp. 109, 287.

217   The various Communist children's groups were brought together in 1925, under the auspices of the Young Communist League, into the Young Comrades League, the first national conference of which was held in Manchester in Feb. 1926. Klugmann, op. cit., Vol. 2, 356.

218   Peter Lumsden, died c. 1930s.

219   See Chap. 28, Note 5.

220   Mrs Jemima Sawkill was Proudfoot's future wife, see above, p. 320.

221   Arthur Pugh, 1870-1955, General Secretary, Iron and Steel Trades Confederation, 1917-36, Chairman, General Council, T.U.C., 1925-26, knighted 1935. The T.U.C. annual congress met at Bournemouth from 6 to 11 Sep. 1926.

222   See Chap. 15, Note 4.

223   See Chap. 19, Note 16.

224   Scottish Colliery Firemen and Shot-Firers' Association.

225   See also above, p. 302. Fifteen photographs of miners at work underground are preserved in the Proudfoot-Hutt Collection at Methil Public Library.

226   Frank Hodges, Secretary, Miners' International, had written Thomas Spencer of Alfreton, who had been dismissed as a trustee of the Derbyshire Miners' Association because of his criticism of the leaders of the M.F.G.B., sympathising with Spencer and criticising A. J. Cook and Herbert Smith of the M.F.G.B., as

well as the Derbyshire miners. *The Times,* 24 Sep. 1926.

227 See Chap. 11, Note 4.

228 The *Scottish Congress Bulletin* (later titled *Scottish T.U.C. Bulletin*), No. 1, Sep. 1926.

229 The M.F.G.B. delegate conference on 7 Oct. 1926 carried by a large majority a resolution from South Wales pressing for a more militant policy in the lock-out, including withdrawal of all safety men, etc., but the Chairman ruled that the resolution must be referred first to the Districts for their vote. R. P. Arnot, op. cit., 492-4.

230 I.e., Labour Party Annual Conference at Margate, 11-15 Oct. 1926.

231 J. T. Murphy, 1888-1966, an engineer, leader of the Sheffield Workers' Committee in the 1914-18 war, and a leading national figure in the shop stewards' movement; member of the Socialist Labour Party and founder member of the Communist Party of which he remained a leader until his resignation in 1932. The article appears to be that by Murphy and R. Page Arnot on "The British Trades Union Congress at Bournemouth" in the *Communist International*, Vol. III, No. 1, 15 Oct. 1926, to which a reply was made by the Executive Committee of the Communist Party in the next issue of the journal on 30 Oct. Murphy and Arnot argued that after the General Strike there had been "vacillations to the right in the ranks of the British Communist Party or rather in its leadership". See Klugmann, op. cit., Vol. 2, 287-8.

232 These pamphlets are not in the Proudfoot-Hutt Collection at Methil Public Library.

233 I.e., Communist Party, Eighth Congress, at Battersea Town Hall, London, 16-17 Oct. 1926.

234 This reference is not clear. See above, p. 112, where John McArthur recollects that he did go to France and Germany at that period.

235 See Chap. 24, Note 2.

236 These photographs are preserved in the Proudfoot-Hutt Collection at Methil.

237 See Chap. 15, Note 2. The last issue on the file in the National Library of Scotland is No. 106, of 23 Oct. 1926.

238 See above, Note 229. On 12 Nov. the Government proposed terms of settlement for the miners' lock-out which, as they included for instance no guarantee against victimisation, were criticised at the M.F.G.B. Special Conference. The Conference, however, by a majority decided to recommend to the Districts that the terms be accepted. But the Districts rejected the proposals by 460,806 to 313,200. The M.F.G.B. Conference then recommended all Districts to open negotiations with the coalowners. R. P. Arnot, op. cit., 504-5.

239 James Doonan, 1868-1932, agent, West Lothian Miners from c. 1888, President, 1929-32, National Union of Scottish Mine Workers, Provost of Bathgate, 1923-26.

240 The first national conference of the British Section, I.C.W.P.A., held at Nine Elms Baths, Battersea.

241 *The General Strike May 1926: Trades Councils in Action.* Prepared by Emile Burns (London, 1926), 191 pp. There is a report about Methil during the strike on p. 143.

242 See Chap. 7, Note 2.

243 I.e., Rt. Hon. William Adamson, General Secretary, Fife miners' county union.

244 See above, Note 238.

245 James Anderson (Labour) won by 446 votes to 247 for the retiring member.

246 Brown, manager of Wellesley Colliery.

247 Sam Happell (or Happle) was N.U.R. Branch Secretary at Methil.

248 It is uncertain which paper is referred to.

249 Application for a summons against the owners and editors of the *Workers'
Weekly* was granted to the Chief Constable at Chester-le-Street on 17 Nov., on
the grounds of publication two days earlier in the paper of a defamatory libel on
the county police. It appears to have been this case that led to the change of title
in Jan. 1927 from *Workers' Weekly* to *Workers' Life. Scotsman*, 18 Nov. 1926.

250 John Robert Clynes, 1869-1949, President, National Union of General and
Municipal Workers, 1924-37, Labour M.P., 1906-31 and 1935-45, Chairman,
Parliamentary Labour Party, 1921-22.

251 Leonid Borisovich Krasin, 1870-1926, Revolutionary from 1890, Bolshevik
from 1903, Soviet Plenipotentiary in Britain, 1921 and 1926, a member of the
Central Committee of the Soviet Communist Party.

252 The cutting reported refusal by compositors on the *Northern Chronicle* at
Inverness to obey a Scottish Typographical Association instruction to strike
against a non-unionist in the office, and instead the men reached an agreement
with the management for "better benefits" than the Association had provided.
The Scottish Typographical Association lost a tenth of its total membership as a
result of the 1926 General Strike. *Annual Report*, 1926, 110, 120-3.

253 Telegram from Hutt to Proudfoot.

254 Alexander Gillespie, Proudfoot's fellow checkweigher.

255 Of the *Workers' Weekly*. See above, Note 212.

256 *The Miner*, Jun. 1926-Nov. 1930, was published weekly first by the I.L.P. New
Leader Ltd. and later by the M.F.G.B. Its editor in 1926 was John Strachey.

257 See above, Note 220.

258 See above, Note 194.

259 A telegram from Hutt to Proudfoot; Virginia was Hutt's infant daughter.

INDEX

Aberdeen, 67, 175, 236, 292

Acts and Bills: Army Bill, 1924, 182 and n.; Coal Mines Act, 128,317; Conspiracy and Protection of Property Act, 1875, 294, 301; Emergency Powers Act, 1920, 218 and n.; Incitement to Mutiny Act, 1797, 243; Rent Restriction Act, 252; Trades Disputes Act, 1927, 123

Adamson, William, M.P., General Secretary, Fife miners' union, i, iii, 15 and n., 20, 22, 26, 33, 39, 40, 41, 55, 61, 62, 68 and n., 69, 72, 73, 83, 84, 86, 118-35 passim, 146, 147, 148, 182, 183, 190 and n., 192, 193, 198, 202, 207-15 passim, 227, 231, 232, 244-53 passim, 260, 263, 265, 270, 272, 277, 281, 290, 293, 296-302 passim, 308-13 passim, 322, 334

Africa: North, 103; see also Morocco; South — see Ladysmith

Aitchison, Mr, marcher, 104 and n., 105

Aldred, Guy A., anarchist-communist, 201 and n.

Alexander, A. V., Co-operative leader, 149 and n., 150

Alexandria, Egypt, 314

Alfreton, Derbyshire, 298

algebra, 34, 35, 37

Allan, William, Lanarkshire miners, 35 and n., 36, 37, 121, 133, 134

Allan, Mrs, mother of William, 36

Allison, George, Communist Party, 249 and n., 251

Alloway, Ayrshire, 66

America: International Seamen's Union of, 331; United States of, 17, 21, 43, 100, 137, 168, 169, 170, 175; see also Chicago; Indiana; New Jersey; West Virginia

Ammanford, Carmarthen, 229 and n., 255, 258

Amsterdam International—see International Federation of Trade Unions

anarchists, 85, 113, 329

Anderson, James, Labour candidate, 312 and n.

Anglo-Soviet Treaties, 1924, 174

Angus, 175

anti-parliamentarism, 17, 21, 22, 23, 46, 70, 137, 138, 328

Archangel, Russia, 158 and n., 262

arithmetic, 34, 35, 37

armed forces, 44, 53, 54, 69, 89, 158 and n., 170, 171, 177, 178, 179, 182 and n., 187, 201 and n., 283, 329

Arniston, Midlothian, 175

Arnot, R. Page, Communist leader, iii, 183 and n., 186, 188, 191-7 passim, 202, 206, 210, 215-18 passim, 220, 231, 234-48 passim, 264-7 passim, 271-90 passim, 303 and n., 304

Ascot, Berkshire, 227

Australia, 21, 31, 81, 177

Austria-Hungary, 176

Ayrshire, 19, 31, 35, 60, 66, 121 and n., 133, 136, 146, 173, 177, 180, 238

Baird, Dugald, manager, Wemyss Coal Company, 165, 166, 234

Baird, Mr, oversman, 234

Baird, Mr, education official, 185

Baldwin, Stanley, Conservative Party leader, 74 and n., 227, 231, 233, 276, 277, 290, 298, 334

Balgonie, Fife—see Coaltown of Balgonie

Balkans, 220

Ballingry, Fife, 85, 145

bankers, 218

Bank of England, 74

Barriers of the Bureaucrats: Fife Breaks Through, ii

Bathgate, West Lothian, 335

Beattie, Bob, militant tradesman, 25 and n.

Beauchamp, Kay, Communist Bookshop, 224 and n., 233, 248

Belfast, 173

Belgium, 288, 332; see also Brussels

Belhaven, Lord, 153 and n.

Bell, Tom, Socialist Labour Party, 21 and n., 187, 244, 293

Benarty Hill, Fife, 86

benevolent societies, 219, 227, 240

Berlin, 330

Berwickshire, 35

Beveridge, Robert, Communist, 193

Beveridge, Mr, colliery agent, 234, 261

Bevin, Ernest, General Secretary, Transport & General Workers' Union, 236 and n.

Bird, George, brother of John, 38

Bird, John, militant miner, 19 and n., 20, 32-45 passim, 53, 55, 56, 61, 66, 76, 83, 120, 121, 122, 184, 193, 195, 223, 231, 240, 249, 254, 260, 270, 277, 292, 304

Bird, Mrs, wife of John, 33

Bird, Mrs, mother of John, 38

Birrell, Jimmy, Marxist lecturer, 23 and n., 31, 86, 114, 117

Black-and-Tans, 44 and n., 110

Black Friday, 1921, 52, 55, 61, 88, 145, 328

blacklegs: Adamson, W., and, 311; coaltrimmers and, 288, 325; fatal accident to, 317; in Jan., 1926, strike at Wellesley, 260; in lock-out, 1926, 105, 108, 109, 114, 287-325 passim; in South Wales anthracite pits, 330; see also lock-outs, 1921; Organisation for the Maintenance of Supplies

Black Sea, 46

Blacksmiths' union, 76, 177

Blantyre, Lanarkshire, 21, 35, 36, 121

Blatchford, Robert, author, 12

Bobby Bear Annual, 322

Bogdanoff, A., author, 193

Bonthrone, David, Fife county councillor, 158 and n., 159, 160

book: clubs, 115, 332; -keeping, 34, 37; -making, 82

Boreland, Fife, 104, 156

Bournemouth, 295, 296, 335

Bowhill, Fife, 25, 38, 40, 149, 224, 235, 292; Catholics at, 148; Communists at, 148, 207, 215, 225, 236, 245, 292, 297; and Fife miners' unity, 238, 239, 244, 246, 270; lock-out, 1921, at, 51, 52, 53, 1926, 283, 296, 315; Maclean, John, and, 37, 40; militants at, 19 and n., 20, 39, 40, 41,

13, 188, 190, 288, 293, 311, 313; industry: crisis in, 1925-6, 233, 239, 241, 247, nationalisation of, 6, 26, 27, 185, 191, 229, pit ponies in, 50, welfare levy, 27, women in, 203, machine production in, 6, 7, 58, 59, 166, 167, 259, 277; mines: accidents, injuries and safety in, 1, 8, 45, 49, 50, 65, 79, 80, 128, 166, 167, 170, 171, 175, 191, 224, 274, 317, 320, 323; see also miners, safety men; workmen's inspectors; binging, 9; closures of pits in, 130, 197, 204; contractors in, 6, 7, 14, 301, 317; decontrol by government of, 50; height of roofs in, 7, 8; "in-gaunees", 109, 226; lighting and ventilation in, 8, 13; methods of work in, 5, 6, 7, 8, 14, 15; pithead baths in, 3, 13, 165, 175, 211, 268; in Russia, 179; tradesmen in, 5, 31, 50, 166; in U.S.A., 175; owners, 26, 50, 203, 204, 233; and General Strike and lock-out, 1926, 96, 264, 274, 275, 277, 278, 288, 295, 307 and n.; and rival unions, 68, 128, 131, 132, 136; terms offered, 1925, by, 223, 225, 227, 228, 229, 233; see also coal companies; Mining Association of Great Britain; prices, 28, 105, 106, 108, 226; see also collieries; miners
Coaltown of Balgonie, Fife, 19, 76, 81, 109, 291, 294, 334
Coaltown of Wemyss, 98, 104, 114, 173, 235, 321
coaltrimmers, 197, 202 and n., 203, 204, 288, 292, 314, 322, 325
collieries: Auchinleck, Ayrshire, 177; Balgonie, Fife, 287; Blantyre Ferme, Lanarkshire, 238; Bowhill, Fife, 39, 169, 213; at Buckhaven, 2; Cambois, Northumberland, 172; Cadzow, Lanarkshire, 172; Cameron, Fife, 108, 109, 287; Craighead, Lanarkshire, 172; Dalbeath, Fife, 293; Dundonald, Fife, 179; Earlseat, Fife, 117, 293; Frances, Fife, 156, 176, 178; Glencraig, Fife, 110, 131, 213; Greenfield, Lanarkshire, 172; Kinglassie, Fife, 84, 132, 133, 259; Kirkford, Fife, 1; Klondyke, Fife, 197, 203, 221; Lady Victoria, Midlothian, 113, 114; Leven, Fife, 50; Lindsay, Fife, 170; Loanend, Lanarkshire, 172; Lochhead, Fife, 114, 128, 166, 167, 175; Lumphinnans No. XI (Peeweep), 171, 175, 178; Mary, Fife, 83, 86, 132; Michael, Fife, 56, 78, 79, 128, 131, 165, 166, 175, 177, 215, 293 ("Wee Michael"); Muiredge, Fife, 1, 5, 6, 7, 8, 9, 15, 16, 58, 117, 143, 294, 303, 323; Pannie, Fife, 176; Polton, Midlothian, 177; Rosie, Fife, 8, 224, 294, 323; Tannochside, Lanarkshire, 172; Valleyfield, 147, 198 and n., 265, 266, 313; Wellesley, Fife, iii, 49, 70, 88, 117, 175, 195, 203, 212, 216, 239, 254, 268, 316, 327, after lock-out, 1926, at, 293, 312, 314, 317, 320, Benefit Fund, 225, blacklegs at, 305, 308, 310, Checkweighmen's Fund, 258, 258, collapse of shaft at, 320, 323, Communist Defence Fund and, 256, Communist pit group at, 203, 219, conveyors increased at, 317, dismissal of miners at 213, 245, 246, 259, 265, 267, 269, dispute at 212-13, 219, "idle" days at, 204, 218, 221, 225, 238, labour force at, 213, management of, 230, 233, 234, 264, manager at—see Brown, John; militancy at, 246, 264, militant literature and propaganda at, 203, 210, 218, 221 and n., 233, 235, 242, 266, and Minority Movement conference, 267, 268, 269, numbers employed at, 260, output at, 258, 261, photographs of work in, 297, 302, picketing in lock-out, 1926, at, 296, 297, 299, 301, 303, 304, 305, 306, pit committee at, 256, places of residence of miners of, 213, police at, 242, 301, 317, Proudfoot, D., blacklisted at, 317, Red Friday, 1925, and, 228, 229, Reform Union recognition at, 257, safety men at, 296, 302, 306, sales of Workers' Weekly at, 211, 213, 219, 220, 222, 223, 224, 229, 233, 235, 242, 249, 257, 258, Saturday work at, 223, sections in, 213, 265, shifts at, 130, 186, "The Spark" at, 140, 174, 224, 230, 233, 242, 248, 249, 250, 266, strike, Jan. 1926, at, 259, 260, 261, 265, 266, 317, tare of hutches at, 205, 210, Unemployed Workers' Movement formed at, 268, wages at, 216, 226, wages reductions at, 211, 215, 217, 219, 245, 247, 259, 277,

workmen's inspectors at, 128, 129, youths at, 317; Wellsgreen, Fife, 6, 7, 9, 32, 79, 197, 203
Colliery Enginemen—see National Federation of Colliery Enginemen; Scottish Colliery Enginemen
Colonial Office, 120
Communist Book Club—see London, places in
Communist International, 24 and n., 46, 47, 64, 138, 142, 144, 170, 174, 328
Communist Labour Party, 46, 137, 171
Communist League, Fife—see Fife Communist League
Communist Party: anti-war campaign by, 227, 233; arrest and imprisonment of leaders of, 242 and n., 243, 244, 247 and n., 248, 249 and n., 250, 251, 254, 255, 256, 258, 261, 264, 266, 267, 271, 274, 275, 330; branches or local groups: Aberdeen, 236 and n., 247, 292, Bowhill, 297, Burntisland, 298, Crossgates, 223, Cowdenbeath, 178, 209, 220, 222, 226, 230, 231, 261, East Wemyss, 56, 187, 319, Inverkeithing, 298, Kennoway, 298, Kirkcaldy, 81, 82, 140, 182, 225, 231, 237, 256, 300, Lochgelly, 218, 231, 287, 288, 289, 292, Lumphinnans, 178, 261, Leven, 187, 188, 298, 309, Methilhill, 298, 309, Valleyfield, 142, West Wemyss, 223, 319; see also Fife; Central Committee, 172, 304; congresses of, 111, 112, 182, 214, 216, 217, 218, 219, 294, 300, 303 and n., Scottish, 323; and Co-operative Movement, 139, 142, 148, 149, 150, 324; discipline, 143, 146, 271, 272, 273, 300, 304; Executive Committee, 189, 238, 255, 271; financial support for, 82, 188, 189, 194; formation of, 46, 47, 137; and General Strike, 1926, 140, 141, 145, 279, 281, 282, 283, 284, 300, 304, 335; German, 325; Glasgow District Committee, 226, 230; headquarters, 237, 256, 262, 269, 300, 319, 320, 322; Historical Synopsis, 193 and n.; and Independent Labour Party, 217, 218; Industrial Department, 269; and International Class War Prisoners' Aid, 319, 324; Kennedy, T., M.P., and, 197, 201; and Labour Government, 1924, 185, 187, 189, 191, 214; and Labour Party, 77, 138, 139, 188, 189, 191, 192, 195, 200, 208, 214, 238 and n., 241, 243, 245, 258, 267, 327; Lenin week, 203; Manual of Party Training, 193 and n.; and Miners' Federation of Great Britain, 320; and miners' lock-outs, 1921, 140, 1926, 140, 142, 294, 297, 303, 309, 319; and Minority Movement, 70, 73, 145, 324; Organisation Bureau, 187, 235; Pioneers, 287 and n.; pit and factory groups, 142, 178, 190, 203, 210, 211, 215, 219, 221 and n., 231, 238, 292, 297, 305, 319, 320, 324; police and, 155, 156-7, 243, 244, 255; Political Bureau, 210, 214, 223, 235, 250, 262, 271, 273, 277, 294, 303 and n.; and railwaymen, 194, 201, 203, 217; recruitment of, 190, 200, 239, 304; Red Week, 237; and Reform Union, 88, 138, 140, 193, 195, 201, 207, 209, 220, 222, 223, 235, 238, 239, 244, 246, 249, 253, 255, 256, 257, 267, 270, 272, 273, 274, 276, 296, 297, 309, 311, 318; reorganisation, 1920s, of, 142, 323; resignations and expulsions from, iii, 144, 188, 189, 222, 267, 270, 271-3, 275, 276, 326; sales of literature of, 70, 218, 220, 221, 237, 242, 248; school groups, 319, 320; Scottish District Committee, 146; sectarianism in, 138, 141, 142; and split in Fife miners' union, 64, 70, 118, 120, 122, 142, 190, 209, 217, 246, 256, 273, 297; and unemployed, 144, 145, 322; and Unemployed Workers' Committee Movement, 324; and United Mineworkers of Scotland, 128, 135, 136; "vacillations" of leadership of, 304, 335; and Workers' Weekly, 220, 325; see also Fife; London; Methil; newspapers and periodicals; pit, factory and depot papers; victimisation; women; Young Communist League; Young Comrades League
company union, 313, 316 and n.
Connelly, Jim, militant miner, 86 and n.
Connelly, Pat, militant miner, 67 and n., 85, 86, 120
Connolly, James, Irish socialist, 18

workers' control, 190, 217, 227

Workers': Defence Corps, 108, 109, 113, 252, 257, 263 and n., 276, 277, 279, 280, 281, 282, 283, 298, 313, 332; Educational Association, 171; Industrial Alliance, 1925, 231 and n., 249, 1926, 263 and n.; International Relief, 87 and n., 100, 112, 293

workmen's inspectors, 128-9, 129, 131, 133, 135, 164, 165, 172, 175

Wright, Mr, Communist, Kirkcaldy, 182

Yarmouth, Norfolk, 2, 315

Yorkshire: 172; Miners' Association, 170, 171, 295

Young Communist League, 76, 85, 111, 178, 221, 224, 226, 234, 237, 287, 294, 324, 328, 330, 334; Aberdeen, 236; Cowdenbeath, 86; Lumphinnans, 304; Methil, 89, 239, 256, 281, 285, 287, 288, 289, 290, 291, 294, 295, 320

Young Comrades League, 291 and n., 295, 310, 315, 319, 320, 324, 334

Zinoviev, G., Bolshevik leader, 68 and n., 328